THE **SELL** SOLUTION

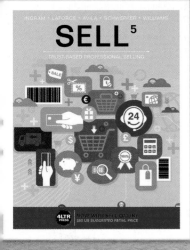

Print + Online

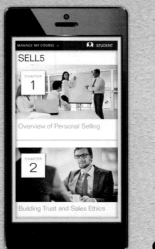

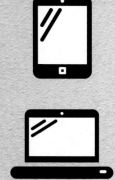

SELL⁵ delivers all the key terms and core concepts for the **Trust-Based Professional Selling** course.

SELL Online provides the complete narrative from the printed text with additional interactive media and the unique functionality of **StudyBits**—all available on nearly any device!

What is a StudyBit™? Created through a deep investigation of students' challenges and workflows, the StudyBit™ functionality of **SELL Online** enables students of different generations and learning styles to study more effectively by allowing them to learn their way. Here's how they work:

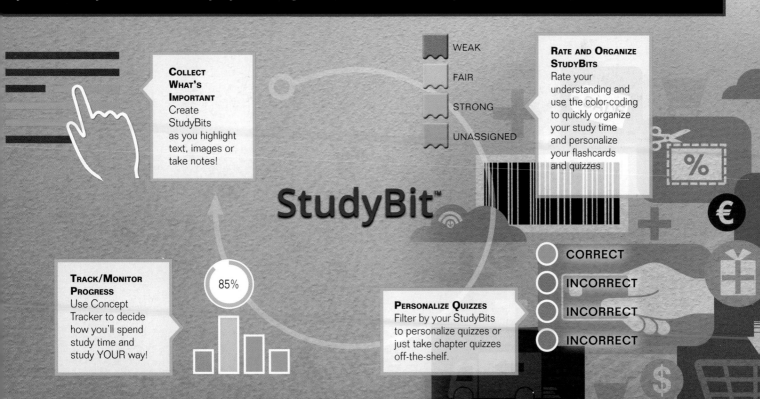

COLLECT WHAT'S IMPORTANT
Create StudyBits as you highlight text, images or take notes!

WEAK
FAIR
STRONG
UNASSIGNED

RATE AND ORGANIZE STUDYBITS
Rate your understanding and use the color-coding to quickly organize your study time and personalize your flashcards and quizzes.

StudyBit™

TRACK/MONITOR PROGRESS
Use Concept Tracker to decide how you'll spend study time and study YOUR way!

85%

PERSONALIZE QUIZZES
Filter by your StudyBits to personalize quizzes or just take chapter quizzes off-the-shelf.

CORRECT
INCORRECT
INCORRECT
INCORRECT

CENGAGE
Learning·

SELL5
Thomas N. Ingram, Raymond W. LaForge, Ramon A. Avila, Charles H. Schwepker, Michael R. Williams

Vice President, General Manager, 4LTR Press: Neil Marquardt

Product Director, 4LTR Press: Steven E. Joos

Product Manager: Laura Redden

Content/Media Developer: Daniel Celenza

Product Assistant: Lauren Dame

Marketing Manager: Jeff Tousignant

Marketing Coordinator: Casey Binder

Content Project Manager: Darrell E. Frye

Manufacturing Planner: Ron Montgomery

Production Service: Prashant Das, MPS Limited

Sr. Art Director: Bethany Casey

Internal Design: Lou Ann Thesing/ Thesing Design

Cover Design: Lisa Kuhn/Curio Press, LLC

Cover Image: Sigal Suhler Moran/ DigitalVision Vectors/Getty Images

Title Page Images: Sigal Suhler Moran/ DigitalVision Vectors/Getty Images

Intellectual Property Analyst: Diane Garrity

Intellectual Property Project Manager: Betsy Hathaway

Computer and tablet illustration: ©iStockphoto.com/furtaev

Smart Phone illustration: ©iStockphoto .com/dashadima

Last ad: Shutterstock.com/Rawpixel.com

For product information and technology assistance, contact us at
Cengage Learning Customer & Sales Support, 1-800-354-9706
For permission to use material from this text or product,
submit all requests online at **www.cengage.com/permissions**
Further permissions questions can be emailed to
permissionrequest@cengage.com

Library of Congress Control Number: 2015959492

Student Edition ISBN: 978-1-305-66208-7

Student Edition with Online ISBN: 978-1-305-66209-4

Cengage Learning
20 Channel Center Street
Boston, MA 02210
USA

Cengage Learning is a leading provider of customized learning solutions with employees residing in nearly 40 different countries and sales in more than 125 countries around the world. Find your local representative at **www.cengage.com**

Cengage Learning products are represented in Canada by Nelson Education, Ltd.

To learn more about Cengage Learning Solutions, visit **www.cengage.com**

Purchase any of our products at your local college store or at our preferred online store **www.cengagebrain.com**

Printed in the United States of America
Print Number: 01   Print Year: 2016

INGRAM / LAFORGE / AVILA / SCHWEPKER / WILLIAMS

SELL⁵

BRIEF CONTENTS

Sigal Suhler Moran/DigitalVision Vectors/Getty Images

CONTENTS

Part 1
The World of Marketing

Charlotte Observer/Tribune News Service/Getty Images

Part 2
Analyzing marketing opportunities

Gustavo Frazao/Shutterstock.com

Part 3
Product decisions

John Keith/Shutterstock.com

Part 4
Distribution Decisions

Jirsak/Shutterstock.com

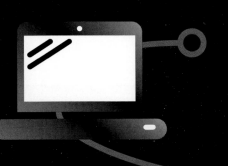

1 | Overview of Personal Selling

LEARNING OBJECTIVES

After completing this chapter, you should be able to:

1-1 Define personal selling and describe its unique characteristics as a marketing communications tool.

1-2 Distinguish between transaction-focused traditional selling and trust-based relationship selling, with the latter focusing on customer value and sales dialogue.

1-3 Understand sales professionalism as a key driver in the continued evolution of personal selling.

1-4 Explain the contributions of personal selling to society, business firms, and customers.

1-5 Discuss five alternative approaches to personal selling.

1-6 Understand the sales process as a series of interrelated steps.

1-7 Describe several aspects of sales careers, types of selling jobs, and the key qualifications needed for sales success.

After finishing this chapter go to
PAGE 23 for **STUDY TOOLS.**

Santiago Cornejo/Shutterstock.com

In the current business environment, buyers are under intense pressure to solve problems, realize opportunities, and cut costs. They are cautious, risk-averse, and have an abundant amount of information about potential suppliers for the products they purchase. Further, they hate to waste time in unproductive meetings with salespeople. This means that successful salespeople must discard high-pressure sales "pitches" in favor of a customer-oriented sales approach. Salespeople must be capable of establishing dialogue with customers to focus on the customer's needs and situation before making a purchase recommendation. According to Hampus Jakobsson, CEO of Brisk, a customer relationship management (CRM) software company, today's buyers value education on the products and services they are looking for more than they do a traditional sales pitch. He recommends

working with customers to make sure they understand the value provided by your offering, rather than employing an aggressive push to influence them to make an immediate purchase. Mr. Jakobsson notes that sales organizations will accomplish more by allowing customers to make their own assessments, with salespeople furnishing timely, relevant information to assist customer decision making.[1]

A productive sales approach first defines customer needs, then illustrates how the sales organization can deliver the value the customer is seeking, and ultimately leads to customer acknowledgment of the value to be gained. This results in a mutually beneficial joint decision between the buyer and seller. With this approach, the sales process is much more about "selling with" customers rather than "selling to" customers. Jamie Anderson, senior vice-president of marketing for SAP, a German multinational software company, says: "Business-to-business buyers are so time-challenged, they don't want the dog and pony show. They don't want the dance. They just want the vendor to be informed and to understand where they are and what they need at that point."

1-1 PERSONAL SELLING DEFINED

The successful professional salesperson of today and the future is likely a better listener than a talker; is more oriented toward developing long-term relationships with customers than placing an emphasis on high-pressure, short-term sales techniques; and has the skills and patience to endure lengthy, complex sales processes. As portrayed in the chapter introduction, today's salesperson strives to deliver relevant presentations based on unique customer needs, and meeting those customer needs requires teamwork between salespeople and others in the organization. For more on teamwork, see "Professional Selling in the 21st Century: The Importance of Teamwork in Sales."

Personal selling, an important part of marketing, relies heavily on interpersonal interactions between buyers and sellers to initiate, develop, and enhance customer relationships. The interpersonal communications dimension sets personal selling apart from other marketing communications such as advertising and sales promotion, which are directed at mass markets. Personal selling is also distinguished from direct marketing and electronic marketing in that salespeople are talking with buyers before, during, and after the sale. This allows a high degree of immediate customer feedback, which becomes a strong advantage of personal selling over most other forms of marketing communications.

Although advertising is a far more visible activity, personal selling is the most important part of marketing communications for most businesses. This is particularly true in business-to-business marketing, where more is spent on personal selling than advertising, sales promotion, publicity, or public relations. In this book, we typically describe personal selling in this business-to-business context, in which a salesperson or sales team interacts with one or more individuals from another organization.

personal selling An important part of marketing that relies heavily on interpersonal interactions between buyers and sellers to initiate, develop, and enhance customer relationships.

trust-based relationship selling A form of personal selling requiring that salespeople earn customer trust and that their selling strategy meets customer needs and contributes to the creation, communication, and delivery of customer value.

customer value The customer's perception of what they get for what they have to give up, for example, benefits from buying a product in exchange for money paid.

1-2 TRUST-BASED RELATIONSHIP SELLING

Trust-based relationship selling (a form of personal selling) requires that salespeople earn customer trust and that their selling strategy meets customer needs and contributes to the creation, communication, and delivery of customer value. As illustrated in Exhibit 1.1, trust-based relationship selling is quite different from traditional selling. Rather than trying to maximize sales in the short run (also called a transaction focus), trust-based relationship selling focuses on solving customer problems, providing opportunities, and adding value to the customer's business over an extended period. Chapter 2 will provide detailed coverage of how salespeople can earn buyers' trust.

1-2a Importance of Customer Value

As personal selling continues to evolve, it is more important than ever that salespeople focus on delivering customer value while initiating, developing, and enhancing customer relationships. What constitutes value will likely vary from one customer to the next depending on the customer's situation, needs, and priorities, but **customer value** will always be determined by customers' perception of what they get in exchange for what they have to give up. In the simplest situations, customers buy a product in exchange for money. In most situations, however, customers define value in a more complex manner, by addressing questions such as:

- Does the salesperson do a good job in helping me make or save money?
- Is this salesperson dependable?
- Does this salesperson help me achieve my strategic priorities?
- Is the salesperson's company easy to work with, i.e., hassle-free?
- Does the salesperson enlist others in his or her organization when needed to create value for me?
- Does the sales representative understand my business and my industry?

Personal selling also recognizes that customers would like to be heard when expressing what they want suppliers and salespeople to provide for them. In days gone by, personal selling often consisted of delivering a message or making a pitch. That approach was typically associated with a "product push" strategy

Exhibit 1.1

Comparison of Transaction-Focused Traditional Selling with Trust-Based Relationship Selling

	Transaction-Focused Traditional Selling	Trust-Based Relationship Selling
Typical skills required	Selling skills, e.g., finding prospects, making sales presentations	Selling skills Information gathering Listening and questioning Strategic problem solving Creating and demonstrating unique, value-added solutions Teambuilding and teamwork
Primary focus	The salesperson and the selling firm	The customer and the customer's customers
Desired outcomes	Closed sales, order volume	Trust, joint planning, mutual benefits, enhance profits
Role of salesperson	Make calls and close sales	Business consultant and long-term ally Key player in the customer's business
Nature of communications with customers	One-way, from salesperson to customer Pushing products	Two-way and collaborative Strive for dialogue with the customer
Degree of salesperson's involvement in customer's decision-making process	Isolated from customer's decision-making process	Actively involved in customer's decision-making process
Knowledge required	Product knowledge Competitive knowledge Identifying opportunities Account strategies	Product knowledge Selling company resources Competitive knowledge Account strategies Costs Identifying opportunities General business and industry knowledge and insight Customer's products, competition, and customers
Postsale follow-up	Little or none: move on to conquer next customer	Continued follow-through to: • Ensure customer satisfaction • Keep customer informed • Add customer value • Manage opportunities

in which customers were pressured to buy without much appreciation for their real needs. Today, sales organizations are far more interested in establishing a productive dialogue with customers than in simply pitching products that customers may or may not want or need. In our highly competitive world, professional buyers have little tolerance for aggressive, pushy salespeople.

1-2b Importance of Sales Dialogue

Sales dialogue refers to the series of conversations between buyers and sellers that take place over time in an attempt to

sales dialogue Business conversations between buyers and sellers that occur as salespeople attempt to initiate, develop, and enhance customer relationships. Sales dialogue should be customer-focused and have a clear purpose.

Goodluz/Shutterstock.com

Selling in Action

The Importance of Teamwork in Sales

Christine Corelli, a corporate trainer whose clients include Honda, Century 21, Pepsi, and Caterpillar, addresses the importance of teamwork in sales:

Today's customers are more service-savvy than ever. Sales and customer service must perform together as a highly effective team working toward the same goal—increasing sales and developing a reputation for superior customer service. Anything less can quickly send customers to your competitors. Working toward a common goal requires open communication, a sense of camaraderie, and trust that everyone will do their part to please the customer. To achieve effective teamwork, it is important to discuss the obstacles to teamwork, including, territorialism, fear of conflict, an "us versus them mentality," competitiveness, egos, finger-pointing, and "it's not my job" attitudes. To build team consensus, it is important to involve sales and service personnel in the decision-making process. By doing so, all team members will recognize their ownership in the final decision, solution, or idea. Individual ownership in team decisions leads to a stronger commitment to the decided line of action. Ms. Corelli stresses that maintaining effective teamwork between service and sales personnel is an ongoing process that constantly seeks improvement. Service flaws must be identified and eliminated. She believes that salespeople should share what they hear in the field, and likewise, that customer service needs to keep salespeople well informed. Perhaps most importantly, both sales and service personnel must be fully dedicated to excellent customer experiences.

Source: "Aligning Your Sales and Service Team for Results Through Teamwork," from www .christinespeaks.com, (May 5, 2015).

build relationships. The purposes of these conversations are to:

- Determine if a prospective customer should be targeted for further sales attention.
- Clarify the prospective customer's situation and buying processes.
- Discover the prospective customer's unique needs and requirements.
- Determine the prospective customer's strategic priorities.
- Communicate how the sales organization can create and deliver customer value.
- Negotiate a business deal and earn a commitment from the customer.
- Make the customer aware of additional opportunities to increase the value received.
- Assess sales organization and salesperson performance so that customer value is continuously improved.

As you can see, sales dialogue is far more than idle chit-chat. The business conversations that constitute the dialogue are customer-focused and have a clear purpose; otherwise, there would be a high probability of wasting both the customer's and the salesperson's time, which no one can afford in today's business environment. Whether the sales dialogue features a question-and-answer format, a conversation dominated by the buyer conveying information and requirements, or a formal sales presentation in which the salesperson responds to buyer feedback throughout, the key idea is that both parties participate in and benefit from the process.

Throughout this course, you will learn about new technologies and techniques that have contributed to the evolution of the practice of personal selling. This chapter provides an overview of personal selling, affording insight into the operating rationale of today's salespeople and sales managers. It also describes different approaches to personal selling and presents the sales process as a series of

Successful salespeople must be able to make sales calls and build relationships at the same time.

Customers want to be heard loud and clear when expressing what they want from suppliers and salespeople.

interrelated steps. The chapter concludes with a discussion of several important aspects of sales careers, including types of selling jobs and characteristics and skills needed for sales success. In the highly competitive, complex international business community, personal selling and sales management have never played more critical roles.

 ## EVOLUTION OF PROFESSIONAL SELLING

For the past several decades, there has been a steady increase in the complexity of the business world, the level of competitive activity, and buyer expectations. These developments have driven an increased focus on **sales professionalism** by the most progressive sales organizations. Sales professionalism requires a customer-oriented sales approach that uses truthful, nonmanipulative tactics to satisfy the long-term needs of both the customer and the selling firm.

In examining the status of sales as a true profession, one study found that sales meets four of the six criteria that define professions, and that progress is still needed on the other two dimensions.[2] This study concluded that sales meets the criterion of operating from a substantial knowledge base that has been developed by academics, corporate trainers and executives, and professional organizations. Second, sales meets the criterion of making a significant contribution to society, which is discussed in the next section of this chapter. Third, through professional organizations such as the Strategic Account Management Association (SAMA) and through a common sales vocabulary such as that found in textbooks and training materials, sales meets the professional criteria of having a defined culture and organization of colleagues. Fourth, sales does have a unique set of professional skills, although these skills vary depending on the specific nature of a given sales position.

Two areas in the study indicated that sales needs additional progress to be viewed as a profession on a par with law, medicine, and other long-recognized professions. The first area has to do with how much autonomy salespeople have to make decisions and the amount of public trust granted to salespeople. Whereas many business-to-business salespeople have considerable decision-making autonomy, others have very little. Public trust could be improved by a widely accepted certification program such as the Certified Public Accountant (CPA) designation for accountants. At present, however, very few salespeople have professional certification credentials. Although many salespeople do have considerable autonomy, public trust in certification programs is modest; thus, the results are mixed as to whether the sales profession meets this professional criterion.

The final area where sales needs to improve is adherence to a uniform ethical code. Many companies have employee codes of conduct and some professional organizations have ethical codes for salespeople, but there is no universal code of ethics with a mechanism for dealing with violators. Until such a code is developed and widely accepted in business, some members of society will not view sales as a true profession.

Whether or not sales is viewed as a true profession comparable to law and medicine, salespeople can benefit tremendously by embracing high ethical standards, participating in professional organizations, and working from a continually evolving knowledge base. In so doing, they will not only be more effective but also they will help advance sales as a true profession.

Future evolution is inevitable as tomorrow's professional salesperson responds to a more complex, dynamic environment. Also, increased sophistication of buyers and of new technologies will demand more from the next generation of salespeople. Exhibit 1.2 summarizes some of the likely events of the future.[3]

sales professionalism A customer-oriented approach that uses truthful, nonmanipulative tactics to satisfy the long-term needs of both the customer and the selling firm.

Sales is becoming more professional, as indicated by a growing number of publications and a market for web-sites with professional development materials and reviews.

Sales Momentum

As noted in Exhibit 1.2, salespeople are using more technological tools and processes to improve sales productivity. For a discussion on how salespeople are using LinkedIn in selling, see "Technology in Sales: Using LinkedIn to Improve Sales Productivity."

economic stimuli Something that stimulates or incites activity in the economy.

Technology in Sales
Using LinkedIn to Improve Sales Productivity

Anna Bratton is a Strategic Accounts Business Development Executive with Salesforce.com, a leading sales technology company. She offers her advice on how to use LinkedIn, a social networking site used primarily in the business sector, in the sales process.

Salespeople are increasingly using LinkedIn to find prospective customers and stay current on new developments with existing

CONTRIBUTIONS OF PERSONAL SELLING

As mentioned earlier in this chapter, more money is spent on personal selling than on any other form of marketing communications. Salespeople are usually well compensated, and salesforces of major companies often number in the thousands. For example, Xerox has 15,000 salespeople, Johnson & Johnson has 8,500, and Coca-Cola has 9,130.[4]

We now take a look at how this investment is justified by reviewing the contributions of personal selling to society in general, to the employing firm, and to customers.

1-4a Salespeople and Society

Salespeople contribute to their nations' economic growth in two basic ways. They stimulate economic transactions and further the diffusion of innovation.

SALESPEOPLE AS ECONOMIC STIMULI Salespeople are expected to stimulate action in the business world—hence the term **economic stimuli**. In a fluctuating economy, salespeople make invaluable

accounts. I spend about three hours a day on LinkedIn to develop new business. I recommend that salespeople constantly assess their contacts on LinkedIn and cultivate contacts in your specific business sector. As you develop your connections, LinkedIn is a great way to organize individuals within specific companies. I deal with some large multinational companies, so there can be numerous people involved in making purchase decisions. I can learn a lot about these people and how they fit into the purchase decision process. When I make initial contact with these people, my familiarity with them and their information needs shows that I have done my homework and that I care about their specific requirements. I integrate information from LinkedIn with our customer relationship management software so I can easily see work experience, education, and shared contacts I have with prospective and current customers. Finally, it is critical that you keep your LinkedIn profile up to date, and establish links to Twitter and Facebook. You know that customers will be looking at you on social media, and making a good first impression is critical in today's complex business world.

Source: Anna Bratton, "Ten Tips for Using LinkedIn for Sales Prospecting," posted on the Salesforce .com website at http://www.salesforce.com/uk/socialsuccess/social-sales/10-tips-for-using-linked -in-sales-prospecting/, accessed May 26, 2015.

Exhibit 1.2

Continued Evolution of Personal Selling

Change	Salesforce Response
Intensified competition	More emphasis on developing and maintaining trust-based, long-term customer relationships
	More focus on creating and delivering customer value
More emphasis on improving sales productivity	Increased use of technology (e.g., mobile devices such as tablets and smartphones connected to the company's sales support content; customer relationship management software)
	Increased use of lower-cost-per-contact methods (e.g., social media such as LinkedIn and Twitter to generate leads and maintain contact with customers; telemarketing and email for some customers)
	More emphasis on profitability (e.g., gross margin) objectives
Fragmentation of traditional customer bases	Sales specialists for specific customer types
	Multiple sales channels (e.g., major accounts programs, telemarketing, electronic networks)
	Globalization of sales efforts
Customers dictating quality standards and inventory/shipping procedures to be met by vendors	Team selling
	Salesforce compensation sometimes based on customer satisfaction and team performance
	More emphasis on sales dialogues rather than sales pitches
Demand for in-depth, specialized knowledge as an input to purchase decisions	Team selling
	More emphasis on customer-oriented sales training

contributions by assisting in recovery cycles and by helping to sustain periods of relative prosperity. As the world economic system deals with issues such as increased globalization of business, more emphasis on customer satisfaction, and building competitiveness through quality improvement programs, it is expected that salespeople will be recognized as a key force in executing the appropriate strategies and tactics necessary for survival and growth.

SALESPEOPLE AND DIFFUSION OF INNOVATION
Salespeople play a critical role in the **diffusion of innovation**, the process whereby new products, services, and ideas are distributed to the members of society. Consumers who are likely to be early adopters of an innovation often rely on salespeople as a primary source of information. Frequently, well-informed, specialized salespeople provide useful information to potential customers. Sometimes those customers ultimately purchase the new product from a lower-cost outlet; nonetheless, the information provided by the original well-informed salesperson contributes critically to the adoption of the innovation and more widespread popularity of the new product. The role of salespeople in the diffusion of industrial products and services is particularly crucial. Imagine trying to purchase a companywide computer system without the assistance of a competent salesperson or sales team!

While acting as an agent of innovation, the salesperson invariably encounters a strong resistance to change in the latter stages of the diffusion process. The status quo seems to be extremely satisfactory to many parties, even though, in the long run, change is necessary for continued

diffusion of innovation The process whereby new products, services, and ideas are distributed to the members of society.

progress or survival. By encouraging the adoption of innovative products and services, salespeople may indeed be making a positive contribution to society.

1-4b Salespeople and The Employing Firm

Because salespeople are in direct contact with the all-important customer, they can make valuable contributions to their employers. Salespeople contribute to their firms as revenue producers, as sources of market research and feedback, and as candidates for management positions.

SALESPEOPLE AS REVENUE PRODUCERS Salespeople occupy the somewhat unique role of **revenue producers** in their firms. Consequently, they usually feel the brunt of that pressure along with the management of the firm. Although accountants and financial staff are concerned with profitability in bottom-line terms, salespeople are constantly reminded of their responsibility to achieve a healthy "top line" on the profit and loss statement. This should not suggest that salespeople are concerned only with sales revenue and not with overall profitability. Indeed, salespeople are increasingly responsible for improving profitability, not only by producing sales revenues but also by improving the productivity of their actions.

MARKET RESEARCH AND FEEDBACK Because salespeople spend so much time in direct contact with their customers, it is only logical that they would play an important role in market research and in providing feedback to their firms. For example, Xerox uses a system called SCOOP to store customer information gathered by the salesforce. This information fully describes each sales territory in terms of Xerox and competitive products currently in use, machine types, age, and potential replacement dates. Marketing executives use this information to develop market forecasts and to help develop marketing and sales strategies for various customer segments.[5]

The emergence of communications technologies gives salespeople and their organizations more opportunities to

360b/Shutterstock.com

gather customer feedback. For example, retailers and service providers routinely use Facebook to solicit customer feedback. In the business-to-business sector, buyers are increasingly sharing their opinions, identifying problems, and asking for vendor recommendations via Twitter and LinkedIn. Customer relationship management programs such as Chatter by Salesforce.com are incorporating social media to improve collaboration between customers and the sales organization.

Some would argue that salespeople are not trained as market researchers, or that salespeople's time could be better used than in research and feedback activities. Many firms, however, refute this argument by finding numerous ways to capitalize on the salesforce as a reservoir of ideas. It is not an exaggeration to say that many firms have concluded that they cannot afford to operate in the absence of salesforce feedback and research.

SALESPEOPLE AS FUTURE MANAGERS In recent years, marketing and sales personnel have been in strong demand for upper management positions. Recognizing the need for a top management trained in sales, many firms use the sales job as an entry-level position that provides a foundation for future assignments. As progressive firms continue to emphasize customer orientation as a basic operating concept, it is only natural that salespeople who have learned how to meet customer needs will be good candidates for management jobs.

1-4c Salespeople and The Customer

Given the increasing importance of building trust with customers and an emphasis on establishing and maintaining long-term relationships, it is imperative that salespeople are honest and candid with customers. Salespeople must also be able to demonstrate knowledge of their products and services, especially as they compare competitive offerings. Customers also expect salespeople to be knowledgeable about market opportunities and relevant business trends that may affect a customer's business. There has been a long-standing expectation that salespeople need to be the key contact for the buyer, who expects that they will

> Along with the management of a firm, salespeople occupy the somewhat unique role of revenue producers in their firms.

revenue producers A role fulfilled by salespeople that brings in revenue or income to a firm or company.

coordinate activities within the selling firm to deliver maximum value to the customer.

> As salespeople serve their customers, they simultaneously serve their employers and society.

The overall conclusion is that buyers expect salespeople to contribute to the success of the buyer's firm. Buyers value the information furnished by salespeople, and they expect salespeople to act in a highly professional manner. See "An Ethical Dilemma" for a scenario in which the salesperson must think about where to draw the line in sharing information with customers.

As salespeople serve their customers, they simultaneously serve their employers and society. When these parties' interests conflict, the salesperson can be caught in the middle. By learning to resolve these conflicts as a routine part of their jobs, salespeople further contribute to developing a business system based on progress through problem solving. Sales ethics will be discussed in detail in Chapter 2.

 ## 1-5 ALTERNATIVE PERSONAL SELLING APPROACHES

In this section, we take a closer look at alternative approaches to personal selling that professionals may choose from to best interact with their customers. Some of these approaches are simple. Other approaches are more sophisticated and require that the salesperson play a strategic role to use them successfully. Five basic approaches to personal selling have been in use for decades: stimulus response, mental states, need satisfaction, problem solving, and consultative selling.[6] All five approaches to selling are practiced today. Furthermore, many salespeople use elements of more than one approach in their own hybrids of personal selling.

Recall from earlier in the chapter that personal selling differs from other forms of marketing communications because it is a personal communication delivered by employees or agents of the sales organization. Because the personal element is present, salespeople have the opportunity to alter their sales messages and behaviors during a sales presentation or as they

Individuals that figure out that all customers are different and can adapt, will be the most successful.

encounter unique sales situations and customers. This is referred to as **adaptive selling**. Because salespeople often encounter buyers with different personalities, communications styles, needs, and goals, adaptive selling is an important concept. Adaptive selling is prevalent with the need satisfaction, problem-solving, and consultative approaches. It is less prevalent with mental states selling and essentially nonexistent with stimulus-response selling.

1-5a Stimulus Response Selling

Of the five views of personal selling, **stimulus response selling** is the simplest. The theoretical background for this approach originated in early experiments with animal behavior. The key idea is that various stimuli can elicit predictable responses. Salespeople furnish the stimuli from a repertoire of words and actions designed to produce the desired response. This approach to selling is illustrated in Figure 1.1.

An example of the stimulus response view of selling would be **continued affirmation**,

adaptive selling The ability of salespeople to alter their sales messages and behaviors during a sales presentation or as they encounter different sales situations and different customers.

stimulus response selling An approach to selling where the key idea is that various stimuli can elicit predictable responses from customers. Salespeople furnish the stimuli from a repertoire of words and actions designed to produce the desired response.

continued affirmation An example of stimulus response selling in which a series of questions or statements furnished by the salesperson is designed to condition the prospective buyer to answering "yes" time after time, until, it is hoped, he or she will be inclined to say "yes" to the entire sales proposition.

FIG. 1.1 STIMULUS RESPONSE APPROACH TO SELLING

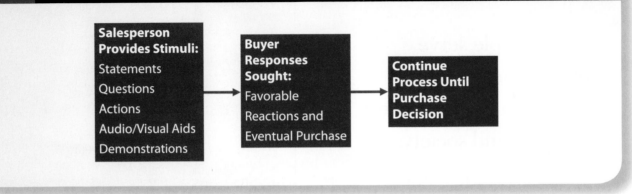

Salesperson Provides Stimuli:
Statements
Questions
Actions
Audio/Visual Aids
Demonstrations

Buyer Responses Sought:
Favorable Reactions and Eventual Purchase

Continue Process Until Purchase Decision

The salesperson attempts to gain favorable responses from the customer by providing stimuli, or cues, to influence the buyer. After the customer has been properly conditioned, the salesperson tries to secure a positive purchase decision.

Telemarketing sales representatives use stimulus response selling, relying on comprehensive scripts that are read or delivered from memory.

a method in which a series of questions or statements furnished by the salesperson is designed to condition the prospective buyer to answering "yes" time after time, until, it is hoped, he or she will be inclined to say "yes" to the entire sales proposition. This method is often used by telemarketing personnel, who rely on comprehensive sales scripts read or delivered from memory.

Stimulus response sales strategies, particularly when implemented with a canned sales presentation, have some advantages for the seller. The sales message can be structured in a logical order. Questions and objections from the buyer can usually be anticipated and addressed before they are magnified during buyer–seller interaction. Inexperienced salespeople can rely on stimulus response sales methods in some settings, and this may eventually contribute to sales expertise.

The limitations of stimulus response methods, however, can be severe, especially if the salesperson is dealing with a professional buyer. Most buyers like to take an active role in sales dialogue, and the stimulus response approach calls for the salesperson to dominate the flow of conversation. The lack of flexibility in this approach is also a disadvantage, as buyer responses and unforeseen interruptions may neutralize or damage the effectiveness of the stimuli.

Considering the net effects of this method's advantages and disadvantages, it appears most suitable for relatively unimportant purchase decisions, when time is severely constrained and when professional buyers are not the prospects. As consumers in general become more sophisticated, this approach will become more problematic.

1-5b Mental States Selling

Mental states selling, or the *formula approach* to personal selling, assumes that the buying process for most buyers is essentially identical and that buyers can be led through certain mental states, or steps, in the buying process. These mental states are typically referred to as **AIDA** (attention, interest, desire, and action). Appropriate sales messages provide a transition from one mental state to the next. The mental states method is illustrated in Exhibit 1.3. Note that this version includes "conviction" as an intermediate stage

mental states selling An approach to personal selling that assumes that the buying process for most buyers is essentially identical and that buyers can be led through certain mental states, or steps, in the buying process; also called the formula approach.

AIDA An acronym for the various mental states the salesperson must lead customers through when using mental states selling: attention, interest, desire, and action.

Exhibit 1.3

Mental States View of Selling

Buyer's Mental State	Common Sales Tactics
Attention	Build rapport with the prospect, ask questions to generate excitement for the sales offering
Interest	Discover buyer needs; uncover purchase decision process; gain precommitment to consider purchase of seller's product
Desire	Build a sense of urgency; demonstrate the product; persuade the buyer to try the product, e.g. a test drive or hands-on involvement with the product
Action	Overcome buyer resistance and make the sale; multiple attempts to close the sale are sometimes used

between interest and desire. Such minor variations are commonplace in different renditions of this approach to selling.

As with stimulus response selling, the mental states approach relies on a highly structured sales presentation. The salesperson does most of the talking, as feedback from the prospect could be disruptive to the flow of the presentation.

A positive feature of this method is that it forces the salesperson to plan the sales presentation prior to calling on the customer. It also helps the salesperson recognize that timing is an important element in the purchase decision process and that careful listening is necessary to determine which stage the buyer is in at any given point.

A problem with the mental states method is that it is difficult to determine which state a prospect is in. Sometimes a prospect is spanning two mental states or moving back and forth between two states during the sales presentation. Consequently, the heavy guidance structure the salesperson implements may be inappropriate,

confusing, and even counterproductive to sales effectiveness. We should also note that this method is not customer oriented. Although the salesperson tailors the presentation to each customer somewhat, this is done by noting customer mental states rather than needs. See "An Ethical Dilemma" for a situation in which the salesperson is contemplating the movement of the prospect into the "action" stage.

1-5c Need Satisfaction Selling

Need satisfaction selling is based on the notion that the customer is buying to satisfy a particular need or set of needs. This approach is shown in Figure 1.2. It is the salesperson's task to identify the need to be met, then to help the buyer meet the need. Unlike the mental states and stimulus response methods,

need satisfaction selling An approach to selling based on the notion that the customer is buying to satisfy a particular need or set of needs.

FIG. 1.2 NEED SATISFACTION APPROACH TO SELLING

Uncover and Confirm Buyer Needs → Present Offering to Satisfy Buyer Needs → Continue Selling Until Purchase Decision

The salesperson attempts to uncover customer needs that are related to the product or service offering. This may require extensive questioning in the early stages of the sales process. After confirming the buyer's needs, the salesperson proceeds with a presentation based on how the offering can meet those needs.

An Ethical Dilemma

Courtney Jacobs sells corporate sponsorship packages for the Bellview Blasters, a minor league hockey team in New England. The packages include advertising in game programs throughout the season, signage in the arena, and a block of season tickets. The packages range in price from $5,000 to $10,000, depending on the size of the ads and signs, and how many season tickets are included. Courtney's sales manager is pushing the salesforce to sell as many $10,000 packages as possible. Courtney tries to match the sponsorship package to the budget and needs of each potential customer rather than pushing the $10,000 packages. Her sales manager is not happy and told Courtney, "You need to get with the program and max your sales of the $10,000 packages. This is a good deal for sponsors. What's the matter—don't you believe in your product?"

What should Courtney do?

a) Be a loyal employee and follow her manager's directive.

b) Try to convince her manager that a customer-oriented approach will be best over the long run.

c) Tell her manager that she will try to sell more $10,000 packages, but continue her current sales approach.

this method focuses on the customer rather than on the salesperson. The salesperson uses a questioning, probing tactic to uncover important buyer needs. Customer responses dominate the early portion of the sales interaction, and only after relevant needs have been established does the salesperson begin to relate how his or her offering can satisfy these needs.

Customers seem to appreciate this selling method and are often willing to spend considerable time in preliminary meetings to define needs prior to a sales presentation or written sales proposal. Also, this method avoids the defensiveness that arises in some prospects when a salesperson rushes to the persuasive part of the sales message without adequate attention to the buyer's needs.

> **problem-solving selling** An extension of need satisfaction selling that goes beyond identifying needs to developing alternative solutions for satisfying these needs.

1-5d Problem-Solving Selling

Problem-solving selling is an extension of need satisfaction selling. It goes beyond identifying needs to developing alternative solutions for satisfying these needs. The problem-solving approach to selling is depicted in Figure 1.3. Sometimes even competitors' offerings are included as alternatives in the purchase decision.

The problem-solving approach typically requires educating the customer about the full impact of the existing problem and clearly communicating how the solution delivers significant customer value. This is true in cases where the customer does not perceive a problem

FIG. 1.3 PROBLEM-SOLVING APPROACH TO SELLING

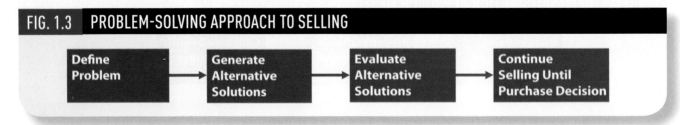

Define Problem → Generate Alternative Solutions → Evaluate Alternative Solutions → Continue Selling Until Purchase Decision

The salesperson defines a customer problem that may be solved by various alternatives. Then an offering is made that represents at least one of these alternatives. All alternatives are carefully evaluated before a purchase decision is made.

14

or even when the solution seems to be an obviously beneficial course of action for the buyer. According to The Brooks Group, a leading sales training firm, problem-solving selling is not so much about convincing someone to buy, but rather it is about offering a logical solution to a problem faced by the client. Of course, the salesperson is trying to make the sale as soon as possible, but first they must learn exactly what the problem is and determine the best solution from the customer's perspective.[7] To be successful in problem-solution selling, salespeople must be able to get the buyer to agree that a problem exists and that solving it is worth the time and effort required.

The problem-solving approach to selling can take a lot of time. In some cases, the selling company cannot afford this much time with each prospective customer. In other cases, the customers may be unwilling to spend the time. Insurance salespeople, for example, report this customer response. The problem-solving approach appears to be most successful in technical industrial sales situations, in which the parties involved are usually oriented toward scientific reasoning and processes and thus find this approach to sales amenable.

1-5e Consultative Selling

Consultative selling is the process of helping customers reach their strategic goals by using the products, services, and expertise of the sales organization.[8] Notice that this method focuses on achieving strategic goals of customers, not just meeting needs or solving problems. Salespeople confirm their customers' strategic goals, and then work collaboratively with customers to achieve those goals.

In consultative selling, salespeople fulfill three primary roles: strategic orchestrator, business consultant, and long-term ally. As a **strategic orchestrator**, the salesperson arranges the use of the sales organization's resources in an effort to satisfy the customer. This usually calls for involving other individuals in the sales organization. For example, the salesperson may need expert advice from production or logistics personnel to address a customer problem or opportunity fully. In the **business consultant** role, the salesperson uses internal and external (outside the sales organization) sources to become an expert on the customer's business. This role also includes an educational element—that is, salespeople educate their customers on products they offer and how these products compare with competitive offerings. As a **long-term ally**, the salesperson supports the customer, even when an immediate sale is not expected.

Terrence Hockenbull, an accomplished sales consultant in the Philippines, has observed the increased usage of consultative selling in recent years. He says that consultative selling requires knowledge of the customer's strategic priorities and how the customer can pursue those priorities as they make major purchase decisions. Salespeople must determine exact customer needs and the varying information needs of multiple individuals on the buying side. For example, a company that is considering a fleet purchase of company automobiles may want to focus on maintaining a given quality level while simultaneously working toward a corporate priority of reducing travel costs. The consultative salesperson in this scenario must be able to address the needs of all of the individuals who influence the purchase decision, while clearly addressing the corporate cost-cutting priority.[9]

1-6 THE TRUST-BASED SALES PROCESS

The nonselling activities on which most salespeople spend a majority of their time are essential for the successful execution of the most important part of the salesperson's job: the **sales process**. The sales process has traditionally been described as a series of interrelated steps beginning with locating qualified prospective customers. From there, the salesperson plans the sales presentation, makes an appointment to see the customer, completes the sale, and performs postsale activities.

As you should recall from the earlier discussion of the continued evolution of personal selling (refer to Exhibit 1.1), the sales process is increasingly being viewed as a relationship management process, as depicted in Figure 1.4.

consultative selling The process of helping customers reach their strategic goals by using the products, services, and expertise of the sales organization.

strategic orchestrator A role the salesperson plays in consultative selling where he or she arranges the use of the sales organization's resources in an effort to satisfy the customer.

business consultant A role the salesperson plays in consultative selling where he or she uses internal and external (outside the sales organization) sources to become an expert on the customer's business. This role also involves educating customers on the sales firm's products and how these products compare with competitive offerings.

long-term ally A role the salesperson plays in consultative selling where he or she supports the customer, even when an immediate sale is not expected.

sales process A series of interrelated steps beginning with locating qualified prospective customers. From there, the salesperson plans the sales presentation, makes an appointment to see the customer, completes the sale, and performs postsale activities.

FIG. 1.4   TRUST-BASED SALES PROCESS

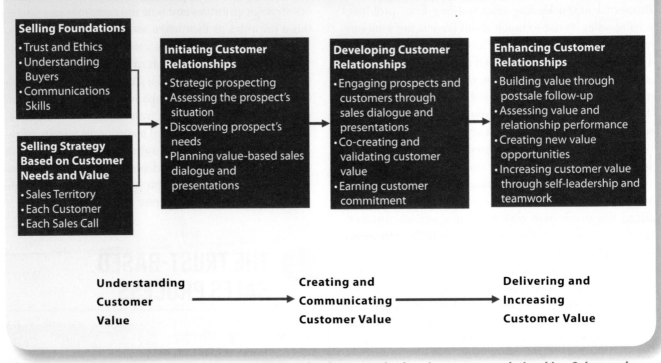

Selling Foundations
- Trust and Ethics
- Understanding Buyers
- Communications Skills

Selling Strategy Based on Customer Needs and Value
- Sales Territory
- Each Customer
- Each Sales Call

Initiating Customer Relationships
- Strategic prospecting
- Assessing the prospect's situation
- Discovering prospect's needs
- Planning value-based sales dialogue and presentations

Developing Customer Relationships
- Engaging prospects and customers through sales dialogue and presentations
- Co-creating and validating customer value
- Earning customer commitment

Enhancing Customer Relationships
- Building value through postsale follow-up
- Assessing value and relationship performance
- Creating new value opportunities
- Increasing customer value through self-leadership and teamwork

Understanding Customer Value → **Creating and Communicating Customer Value** → **Delivering and Increasing Customer Value**

The three major phases of the sales process are initiating, developing, and enhancing customer relationships. Salespeople must possess certain attributes to earn the trust of their customers and be able to adapt their selling strategies to different situations. Throughout the sales process, salespeople should focus on customer value, first by understanding what it is, then by working with customers to create value, communicate value, and continually increase customer value.

In this conceptualization of the sales process, salespeople strive to attain lasting relationships with their customers. The basis for such relationships may vary, but the element of trust between the customer and the salesperson is an essential part of enduring relationships. To earn the trust of customers, salespeople should be customer oriented,

In consultative selling, the salesperson is a lot like an orchestra conductor. The salesperson must involve all parts of the selling firm.

honest, and dependable. They must also be competent and able to display an appropriate level of expertise to their customers. Finally, the trust-building process is facilitated if salespeople are compatible with their customers; that is, if they get along and work well with each other.[10] These attributes are reflected by Jordan Lynch, a Workforce Management Consultant with ADP in Denver, Colorado:

> *The key to having productive relationships with your customers is genuine trust. From day one, I work to earn the customer's trust by consistently doing what I say I will do. This means that I must be realistic and not overpromise in terms of what we can do for our customers. It is important to show the customer that you truly care about their success, and of course, basic honesty is essential. Customers expect me to be an expert in our field, and to get answers quickly if I need to call in other experts to suit the customer's needs. I want to do business with trustworthy people, and I firmly believe that my customers feel the same way.*[11]

Another important element of achieving sound relationships with customers is to recognize that individual customers and their particular needs must be addressed with appropriate selling strategies and tactics. In selling, we discuss strategy at four levels: corporate, business unit, marketing department, and the overall sales function. An individual salesperson is strongly guided by strategy at these higher levels in the organization but must also develop selling strategies and tactics to fit the sales territory, each customer, and, ultimately, each sales call. Our coverage in this text focuses on developing sales strategies for individual customers and specific sales calls.

When studying the sales process, note that there are countless versions of the process in terms of number of and names of steps. If, however, you were to examine popular trade books on selling and training manuals used by corporations, you would find that the various depictions of the sales process are actually more alike than different. The sales process shown in Figure 1.4 is comparable to most versions of the sales process, with the exception of those versions that advocate high-pressure methods centering on how to get the customer to "say yes" rather than focusing on meeting the customer's true needs. Our version of the sales process suggests that salespeople must have certain attributes to inspire trust in their customers and that salespeople should adapt their selling strategy to fit the situation.

Another point that should be stressed is that the sales process is broken into steps to facilitate discussion and sales training, not to suggest discrete lines between the steps. The steps are actually highly interrelated and, in some instances, may overlap. Further, the stepwise flow of Figure 1.4 does not imply a strict sequence of events. Salespeople may move back and forth in the process with a given customer, sometimes shifting from step to step several times in the same sales encounter. Finally, claiming a new customer typically will require multiple sales calls.

1-7 SALES CAREERS

In this section, we first discuss various aspects of sales careers, and then describe several different types of personal selling jobs. The chapter concludes with a discussion of the skills and qualifications necessary for success in sales careers. For some advice on how to achieve success in a sales career, see "From the Classroom to the Field: Building a Successful Career in Sales."

From the Classroom to the Field

Building a Successful Career in Sales

Mallory Wilbourn, sales manager with Insight Global, a major staffing services company, is a 2009 graduate of Colorado State University. She shares these thoughts with new college graduates about getting a sales career off to a good start:

You need a good foundation that includes understanding your services and how you and your company can benefit your clients. To get this understanding, you will study like you did in college, but it's also important to think like your customer and understand how they think. Ultimately, your success depends on your ability to build great relationships with your clients. To build relationships, you need to be genuine—just be yourself. You need to find common ground with your clients. Some of that might

be personal, but being on the same page in terms of helping the customer is the key. Good customer relationships are based on mutual trust. If you and your clients trust each other, business is more efficient and also more enjoyable. New salespeople must learn to be fully accountable for their actions. Rather than placing blame when things go wrong, look to yourself first to solve the problem. When you first start out, don't hesitate to ask a lot of questions to those in your own company. More experienced people have walked in your shoes, so benefit from their experience. Finally, have a positive attitude. Things don't always go perfectly, and it is important to stay positive as you work through any bumps in the road. Sales is a great career because you largely control your own destiny—make the most of it!

1-7a Characteristics of Sales Careers

An important element in career success is the match between the individual's capabilities and career goals with the chosen profession. As you read the following sections on the characteristics of sales careers, you might think about what you expect from a career and whether your expectations could be met by working in sales. The characteristics to be discussed are:

- Occupational outlook
- Advancement opportunities
- Immediate feedback
- Job variety
- Independence
- Compensation

OCCUPATIONAL OUTLOOK As shown in Exhibit 1.4, the U.S. government projects stable demand for salespeople through 2022.[12] Compared to overall labor force growth rates, sales and sales management occupations are expected to increase at average rates.

Salespeople are revenue producers and thus enjoy relatively good job security compared with other occupational groups. Certainly, individual job security depends on individual and company performance, but in general, salespeople are usually the last group to be negatively affected by personnel cutbacks. Competent salespeople also have some degree of job security based on the universality of their basic sales skills. In many cases, salespeople are able to move successfully to another employer, maybe even change industries, because sales skills are largely transferable. For salespeople working in declining or stagnant industries, this is heartening news.

ADVANCEMENT OPPORTUNITIES As the business world continues to become more competitive, the advancement opportunities for college-educated salespeople remains an attractive dimension of sales careers. One reason that many successful salespeople ultimately find their way into top management is that they display some of the key attributes required for success in executive positions. Top executives must have highly developed personal skills, be able to communicate clearly and persuasively, and have high levels of self-confidence, motivation, business judgment, and determination.

IMMEDIATE FEEDBACK Salespeople receive constant, immediate feedback on their job performance. Usually, the results of their efforts can be plainly observed by both salespeople and their sales managers—a source of motivation and job satisfaction. On a daily basis, salespeople receive direct feedback from their customers, and this can be stimulating, challenging,

---

Exhibit 1.4

Occupational Outlook for Salespeople

Job Type	2012 Employment	Projected Growth 2012–2022 Percentage
Manufacturers and wholesalers (nontechnical)	1,813,000	9
Manufacturers and wholesalers (technical)	154,900	−1
Advertising sales representatives	422,000	
Real estate agents	443,000	11
Insurance agents	443,400	10
Securities, commodities, and financial services	354,600	11
Retail	4,668,000	10
Sales engineers	66,000	9
Sales managers	359,000	8

and productive. The opportunity to react immediately to customer feedback during sales presentations is a strong benefit of adaptive selling, and it distinguishes selling from other forms of marketing communications such as advertising and public relations. The spontaneity and creativity involved in reacting to immediate feedback is one dimension of selling that makes it such an interesting job.

JOB VARIETY Salespeople rarely vegetate due to boredom. Their jobs are multifaceted and dynamic. Multicultural diversity is increasing in most customer segments, and selling into global markets is on the rise. For a person seeking the comfort of a well-established routine, sales might not be a good career choice. For those who dislike office jobs, sales can be an especially good fit. In sales, day-to-day variation on the job is the norm. Customers change, new products and services are developed, and competition introduces new elements at a rapid pace. In addition to interacting with customers, many salespeople spend a considerable amount of time on activities such as training, attending trade shows, working with other salespeople at the distributor and retail levels to stimulate demand, and completing administrative tasks.

INDEPENDENCE Independence of action and freedom to make decisions are usually presented as advantages that sales positions have over tightly supervised jobs. This independence is frequently a byproduct of decentralized sales operations in which salespeople live and work away from headquarters, therefore working from their homes and making their own plans for extensive travel.

Despite its appeal, however, independence does present some problems. New recruits working from their homes may find the lack of a company office somewhat disorienting. They may need an office environment to relate to, especially if their past work experience provided regular contact in an office environment.

The independence of action traditionally enjoyed by salespeople is being scrutinized by sales managers more heavily now than in the past. The emphasis on sales productivity, accomplished in part through cost containment, is encouraging sales managers to take a more active role in dictating travel plans and sales call schedules.

Givaga/Shutterstock.com

COMPENSATION Compensation is generally thought to be an advantage of sales careers. Pay is closely tied to performance, especially if commissions and bonuses are part of the pay package. Starting salaries for inexperienced salespeople with a college degree typically average $45,000, with opportunities to earn more through bonuses and commissions. Between the extremes of the highly experienced salesperson and the inexperienced recruit, an average salesperson earns approximately $60,000–$70,000 per year. More experienced salespeople, including those who deal with large customers, often earn in the $85,000–$135,000 range. Top salespeople can earn hundreds of thousands of dollars annually, with some exceeding $1 million in annual earnings.

1-7b Classification of Personal Selling Jobs

Because there are so many unique sales jobs, the term *salesperson* is not by itself very descriptive. A salesperson could be a flower vendor at a busy downtown intersection or the sales executive negotiating the sale of Boeing aircraft to a major airline.

We briefly discuss six types of personal selling jobs:

- Sales support
- New business
- Existing business
- Inside sales (nonretail)
- Direct-to-consumer sales
- Combination sales jobs

1-7c Sales Support

Sales support personnel are not usually involved in the direct solicitation of purchase orders. Rather, their primary responsibility is dissemination of information and performance of other activities designed to stimulate sales. They might concentrate at the end-user level or another level in the channel of distribution to support the overall sales effort. They may report to another salesperson who is responsible for direct handling of purchase orders, or to the sales manager. There are two well-known categories of support salespeople: missionary or detail salespeople and technical support salespeople.

Missionary salespeople usually work for a manufacturer but might also work for brokers and manufacturing representatives, especially in the grocery industry. Sales missionaries, like religious missionaries, are expected to "spread the word" with the purpose of conversion, in this case, to customer status. Once converted, the customer receives reinforcing messages, new information, and the benefit of the missionary's activities to strengthen the relationship between buyer and seller.

In the pharmaceutical industry, the **detailer** is a fixture. Detailers working at the physician level furnish valuable information regarding the capabilities and limitations of medications in an attempt to get the physician to prescribe their product. Another sales representative from the same pharmaceutical company will sell the medication to the wholesaler or pharmacist, but it is the detailer's job to support the direct sales effort by calling on physicians.

Technical specialists are sometimes considered to be sales support personnel. These **technical support salespeople** may assist in design and specification processes, installation of equipment, training of the customer's employees, and follow-up service of a technical

ronstik/Shutterstock.com

nature. They are sometimes part of a sales team that includes another salesperson who specializes in identifying and satisfying customer needs by recommending the appropriate product or service.

1-7d New Business

New business is generated for the selling firm by adding new customers or introducing new products to the marketplace. Two types of new-business salespeople are pioneers and order-getters.

Pioneers, as the term suggests, are constantly involved with new products, new customers, or both. Their task requires creative selling and the ability to counter the resistance to change that will likely be present in prospective customers. Pioneers are well represented in the sale of business franchises, in which the sales representatives travel from city to city seeking new franchisees.

Order-getters, also called *hunters*, are salespeople who actively seek orders, usually in a highly competitive environment. Although all pioneers are also order-getters, the reverse is not true. An order-getter may serve existing customers on an ongoing basis, whereas the pioneer moves on to new customers as soon as possible. Order-getters might seek new business by selling an existing customer additional items from the product line. A well-known tactic is to establish a relationship with a customer by selling a single product from the line, then to follow up with subsequent sales calls for other items from the product line.

Most corporations emphasize sales growth, and salespeople operating as pioneers and order-getters are at the heart of sales growth objectives. The pressure to perform in these roles is fairly intense; the results are highly visible. For these reasons, the new-business salesperson is often among the elite in any company's salesforce.

1-7e Existing Business

In direct contrast to new-business salespeople, other salespeople's primary responsibility is to maintain and further cultivate relationships with existing customers. Salespeople who specialize in this role include **order-takers** or *farmers*. These salespeople frequently work for wholesalers and, as the term order-taker implies, they are not too involved in creative selling. Route salespeople who work an established customer base,

missionary salespeople A category of sales support personnel who are not typically involved in the direct solicitation of purchase orders. Their primary roles are disseminating information, stimulating the sales effort to convert prospects into customers, and reinforcing customer relationships.

detailer A category of sales support personnel in the pharmaceutical industry working at the physician level to furnish information regarding the capabilities and limitations of medications in an attempt to get the physician to prescribe their product.

technical support salespeople Technical specialists who may assist in the design and specification process, installation of equipment, training of customer's employees, and follow-up technical service.

pioneers Salespeople who are constantly involved with either new products, new customers, or both. Their task requires creative selling and the ability to counter the resistance to change that will likely be present in prospective customers.

order-getters Also called hunters, these salespeople actively seek orders, usually in a highly competitive environment.

order-takers Also called farmers, these salespeople specialize in maintaining current business.

taking routine reorders of stock items, are order-takers. They sometimes follow a pioneer salesperson and take over the account after the pioneer has made the initial sale.

These salespeople are no less valuable to their firms than the new-business salespeople, but creative selling skills are less important to this category of sales personnel. Their strengths tend to be reliability and competence in ensuring customer convenience. Customers grow to depend on the services provided by this type of salesperson. As most markets are becoming more competitive, the role of existing-business salespeople is sometimes critical to prevent erosion of the customer base.

Many firms, believing that it is easier to protect and maintain profitable customers than it is to find replacement customers, are reinforcing sales efforts to existing customers. For example, Frito-Lay uses 18,000 route service salespeople to call on retail customers at least three times weekly. Larger customers see their Frito-Lay representative on a daily basis. These salespeople spend a lot of their time educating customers about the profitability of Frito-Lay's snack foods, which leads to increased sales for both the retailer and for Frito-Lay.

1-7f Inside Sales

In this text, **inside sales** refers to nonretail salespeople who remain in their employer's place of business while dealing with customers. The inside-sales operation has received considerable attention in recent years not only as a supplementary sales tactic but also as an alternative to field selling.

Inside sales can be conducted on an active or passive sales basis. Active inside sales includes the solicitation of entire orders, either as part of a telemarketing operation or when customers walk into the seller's facilities. Passive inside sales imply the acceptance, rather than solicitation, of customer orders, although it is common practice for these transactions to include add-on sales attempts. We should note that customer service personnel sometimes function as inside-sales personnel as an ongoing part of their jobs.

1-7g Direct-To-Consumer Sales

Direct-to-consumer salespeople are the most numerous type of salespeople. There are approximately 4.9 million retail salespeople in this country and more than a million selling real estate, insurance, and securities directly to consumers. Add to this figure another several million

selling direct to the consumer for companies such as Tupperware, Mary Kay, and Avon.

This diverse category of salespeople ranges from the part-time, often temporary salesperson in a retail store to the highly educated, professionally trained stockbroker on Wall Street. As a general statement, the more challenging direct-to-consumer sales positions are those involving the sale of intangible services such as insurance and financial services.

1-7h Combination Sales Jobs

Now that we have reviewed some of the basic types of sales jobs, let us consider the salesperson who performs multiple types of sales jobs within the framework of a single position. We use the case of the territory manager's position with GlaxoSmithKline (GSK) Consumer Healthcare to illustrate the **combination sales job** concept. GSK, whose products include Aqua-Fresh toothpaste, markets a wide range of consumer healthcare goods to food, drug, variety, and mass merchandisers. The territory manager's job blends responsibilities for developing new business, maintaining and stimulating existing business, and performing sales support activities.

During a typical day in the field, the GSK territory manager is involved in sales support activities such as merchandising and in-store promotion at the individual retail store level. Maintaining contact and goodwill with store personnel is another routine sales support activity. The territory manager also makes sales calls on chain headquarters personnel to handle existing business and to seek new business. And it is the territory manager who introduces new GSK products in the marketplace.

1-7i Qualifications and Skills Required for Success By Salespeople

Because there are so many different types of jobs in sales, it is rather difficult to generalize about the qualifications and skills needed for success. This list would have to vary according to the details of a given job. Even then, it is reasonable to believe that for any given job, different people with different skills could be successful.

inside sales Nonretail salespeople who remain in their employer's place of business while dealing with customers.

combination sales job A sales job in which the salesperson performs multiple types of sales jobs within the framework of a single position.

An enthusiastic attitude mixed with enthusiasm for sales usually will lead to great results and plenty of recognition.

These conclusions have been reached after decades of research that has tried to correlate sales performance with physical traits, mental abilities, personality characteristics, and the experience and background of the salesperson.

Being careful not to suggest that sales success is solely a function of individual traits, let us consider some of the skills and qualifications that are thought to be especially critical for success in most sales jobs. According to the O*NET Resource Center, a centralized source of occupational information developed by the U.S. Department of Labor/Employment salespeople in a wide variety of industries need these attributes to be successful[13]:

- Active listening—to include asking appropriate questions, and not interrupting at inappropriate times

- Service orientation—actively seeking ways to help customers

- Oral communications skills—including persuasive communications

- Coordination and problem solving—to include bringing others together and reconciling differences

- Written communications skills—including computer and other technologically facilitated communications

- Logical reasoning resulting in rational reasons to take action

- Strategic and organizational skills so work can be planned and executed efficiently

- Dependability and attention to detail

- Motivation and persistence in the face of obstacles

- Integrity—honest and ethical

- Initiative—willing to take on responsibilities and challenges

- Adaptability—open to change and devoted to continual learning

In addition to these attributes, sales recruiters are looking for enthusiastic job candidates. They are usually referring to dual dimensions of enthusiasm—an enthusiastic attitude in a general sense and a special enthusiasm for selling. On-campus recruiters have mentioned that they seek students who are well beyond "interested in sales" to the point of truly being enthusiastic about career opportunities in sales.

Our discussion of factors related to sales success is necessarily brief, as a fully descriptive treatment of the topic must be tied to a given sales position. Veteran sales managers and recruiters can often specify with amazing precision what qualifications and skills are needed to succeed in a given sales job. These assessments are usually based on a mixture of objective and subjective judgments.

Professional selling offers virtually unlimited career opportunities for the right person. Many of the skills and qualifications necessary for success in selling are also important for success as an entrepreneur or as a leader in a corporate setting. For those interested in learning more about sales careers, consult these sources: *Sales & Marketing Management* magazine at http://salesandmarketing.com; *Selling Power* magazine at http://sellingpower.com; the Sales Management Association at http://www.salesmanagement.org; and SalesHQ, an online community for sales professionals at http://www.saleshq.monster.com/.

The remainder of this book explores the sales process shown in Figure 1.4. Part I, composed of Chapters 2–4, is entitled Foundations of Professional Selling. Chapter 2 discusses the important topics of building trust and sales ethics. Chapter 3 provides in-depth coverage of buyer behavior, and Chapter 4 focuses on the communications skills necessary for sales success. Part II, Initiating Customer Relationships, opens with strategic prospecting in Chapter 5. Chapter 6 covers planning value-based sales dialogue and presentations as well as initiating contact with the customer. Developing customer relationships is treated in Part III. Chapter 7 discusses issues that arise during sales dialogues and presentations, and Chapter 8 discusses how salespeople can validate customer value and earn customer commitment. Part IV, Enhancing Customer Relationships, focuses on how salespeople add customer value through follow-up in Chapter 9, and through self-leadership and teamwork in Chapter 10.

STUDY TOOLS 1

LOCATED IN TEXTBOOK

☐ Rip-out and review chapter review card

LOCATED AT WWW.CENGAGEBRAIN.COM

☐ Review key term flashcards and create your own from StudyBits

☐ Organize notes and StudyBits using the StudyBoard feature within 4LTR Press Online

☐ Complete practice and graded quizzes to prepare for tests

☐ Complete interactive content within the narrative portion of 4LTR Press Online

☐ View chapter highlight box content at the beginning of each chapter

SPECIALTY SPORTS INC.

BACKGROUND

Specialty Sports Inc. (SSI) is a California-based supplier of custom-made novelty sports items such as bobble-head figures, caps, sunglasses, and sweatshirts. Most of SSI's sales are to medium-sized businesses that use SSI products in employee motivation programs or as specialty advertising giveaways. SSI has been in business for 40 years, and has an excellent reputation as a reliable, competitive supplier. SSI has built a successful business across the United States. SSI sales representatives are knowledgeable and can advise their customers about how to use specialty advertising to build employee morale, introduce new products, and reinforce brand images.

CURRENT SITUATION

Jeff Weatherby had recently been assigned to the Indianapolis territory. Although this was his first sales job, he felt confident and was eager to begin. Jeff had just completed SSI's training program and had a good understanding of SSI's products and the sales process. For most sales situations, SSI's sales trainers had recommended the use of an organized sales presentation in which the salesperson organizes the key points into a planned sequence that allows for adaptive behavior by the salesperson as the sales call progresses.

Jeff had been in his territory for 60 days, and he was enjoying his job. Days passed quickly, and he was never bored. He had landed some major customers, but was frustrated at how long it took some customers to make a buying decision. Overall, he thought he was doing a good job and the feedback form Felicia Jameson, his sales manager, had been consistently positive. Jeff tried to be honest with himself as a way of improving his performance, and he was not happy as he reviewed today's last sales call.

Jeff had called on H2G, a large manufacturer of garden tools. He intended to sell H2G several specialty advertising items to be used as giveaways at major trade shows in the coming year. After researching H2G on the Internet, he arranged a 4:00 pm meeting with Greg Cox, the director of marketing. Throughout the day, Jeff was running late due to an unexpected snow storm and heavy traffic. He called to let Greg know that he would be late, but the best he could do

was to leave a message. Jeff arrived 15 minutes late, and was relieved to be shown into Greg's office without delay.

Jeff apologized to Greg about running late, and was surprised to learn that Greg had not received his message. Jeff was irritated that his message had not been passed along, but Greg did not seem to mind, indicating that he had plenty of time to meet with Jeff. Given this signal, Jeff decided to give Greg an overview of SSI's capabilities and success stories. Fifteen minutes later, Greg interrupted Jeff and the following dialogue ensued.

Greg: Thanks for the overview, Jeff. I had a pretty good idea what SSI offers, but some of what you told me might be helpful. What have you learned about H2G that makes you think that SSI would be a good fit for our trade show programs?

Jeff: Well, I know that H2G participates in two national shows and several regional shows every year.

Greg: That's right, and we work really hard to stand out at those shows.

Jeff: What works well for you in terms of standing out at the shows?

Greg: Having a terrific, eye-catching product display is key. Doing a lot of pre-show communications to be sure key buyers visit our booths, and being sure we have enough people on hand to sustain a high-energy atmosphere during the show.

Jeff: How about specialty advertising to spice things up, maybe add to the fun element?

Greg: I am not sure what you mean. We have wasted a lot of money on giveaways in the past and I don't believe that it differentiates us from our competitors.

Jeff: That's because you haven't worked with SSI. We're the best and I can fill you in on how we can add sizzle to your trade shows.

Greg: O.K., but I just remembered that I need to pick my daughter up after her piano lesson. With the snow and traffic, that leaves us about 15 minutes.

Jeff proceeded to describe how SSI works with most of their customers to supplement trade show communications. He felt rushed, as there were a lot of alternatives depending on the customer's budget and objectives for each trade show. About 10 minutes into his monologue, Greg told Jeff: "Thanks for coming today. We will talk about this internally and I will get back with you if we decide to do more with specialty advertising this year. I really do have to run now. Sorry."

As Jeff drove home, he realized that he had never asked Greg about H2G's trade show objectives or their budget. With the abrupt end to the meeting, he also failed to try to get another appointment with Greg Cox. Jeff realized that his call with H2G was not his best performance.

QUESTIONS

1. What problems do you see with Jeff's H2G sales call?
2. If you were Jeff's sales manager, what would you recommend he do to improve his chances of succeeding?

ROLE PLAY

Characters: Jeff Weatherby and four other SSI sales representatives; Felicia Jameson, SSI sales manager

Scene:

Location—SSI's Indianapolis office during a weekly sales meeting shortly after his sales call with H2G.

Action—Jeff reviews his H2G sales call with other SSI sales representatives and their sales manager, Felicia Jameson. This is a regular feature of the weekly meetings, with the idea being that all sales representatives can learn from the experiences of others. Jeff has decided to compare his call on H2G to some of the material from his sales training with SSI. This material, which contrasts transaction-focused selling with trust-based relationship selling, is shown in Exhibit 1.1. His review will analyze whether he did or did not practice trust-based relationship selling during his call with Greg Cox at H2G.

Upon completion of the role play, address the following questions:

1. Is Jeff's review of his sales call accurate?
2. What steps should Jeff take to begin to develop a strong relationship with Greg Cox at H2G?

CHAPTER ROLE PLAY
Overview of Personal Selling Sales Stars, Inc.

BACKGROUND

Sales Stars, Inc (SSI) was founded five years ago by Mark Eaton and Sandra Orr as an employment agency specializing in the placement of professional sales representatives and sales trainees in a wide variety of industries. SSI is paid by the hiring companies, and job candidates are never charged fees for SSI's services. SSI represents college-educated individuals with sales experience levels ranging from zero (sales trainees) to several years of experience. For SSI to succeed, the company has to consistently do two things: (1) adapt to the hiring companies' needs and specific job descriptions in the sales area; and (2) save the hiring companies time and money in the hiring process by recommending only prescreened, highly qualified candidates. By focusing on these core competencies, SSI had grown to a company with fifty employees in five regional offices across the United States. SSI's revenues were increasing at an annual rate of 15 percent, which far outpaced revenue growth in the broadly defined employment agency sector.

Mark Eaton and Sandra Orr have a good feel for how SSI can save hiring companies time and money by recommending only prescreened, highly qualified job candidates. Now that SSI was getting to be a larger company, Mark and Sandra needed to spread their knowledge to other SSI staff members who would also be involved in prescreening sales job candidates. In addition to their own experience over the years, Mark and Sandra had conducted research on the qualifications and skills needed for success in professional selling. Interestingly, there is a high correlation between their research findings and the research presented on page 22 of this textbook. Mark and Sandra noted that some skills needed for sales success would be hard to assess until the salesperson had been on the job for a while. For example, being honest and ethical would probably take more time to assess. Even though a complete assessment of all of the attributes needed for sales success might extend past the job placement process, Mark and Sandra decided to identify key indicators for each of the twelve attributes shown on page 22:

1. Active listening—to include asking appropriate questions and not interrupting at inappropriate times.

2. Service orientation—actively seeking ways to help customers.

3. Oral communications skills—including persuasive communications.

4. Coordination and problem solving—to include bringing others together and reconciling differences.

5. Written communications skills—including computer and other technologically facilitated communications.

6. Logical reasoning resulting in rational reasons to take action.

7. Strategic and organizational skills so that work can be planned and executed efficiently.

8. Dependability and attention to detail.

9. Motivation and persistence in the face of obstacles.

10. Integrity—honest and ethical.

11. Initiative—willing to take on responsibilities and challenges.

12. Adaptability—open to change and devoted to continual learning.

In the coming weeks, Mark and Sandra planned to work independently to identify a minimum of two to three indicators for each of the twelve qualifications and skills needed for sales success. They would then meet and select the best three indicators for each of the twelve success attributes and decide how and when each attribute would be assessed as they screened job candidates. For example, what could be assessed in personal interviews with job candidates? Alternatively, could some of these attributes be assessed from candidate resumes? Mark and Sandra were confident that if they could come up with the key indicators for each of the twelve success attributes, they would be able to train other SSI personnel to effectively prescreen job candidates and thus contribute to SSI's future growth.

ROLE PLAY

Situation: Review the above SSI case. Working in teams of two, select at least two success attributes from the list of twelve.

Characters: Mark Eaton and Sandra Orr, cofounders of SSI, Inc.

Scene: After Mark and Sandra have independently developed two to three indicators for two of the twelve success factors, they meet to choose the best three indicators for each success factor and to determine how and when each indicator will be assessed. Both Mark and Sandra should distribute their written lists to each other and to others who will observe the role-play.

Upon completion of the role-play, address the following questions:

1. How would you rate Mark and Sandra in terms of preparedness? Can you identify any overlooked indicators for the chosen sales success attributes?

2. How well did Mark and Sandra work together to find the three best indicators for each success attribute?

Part One

2 | Building Trust and Sales Ethics
Developing Trust and Mutual Respect with Clients

LEARNING OBJECTIVES

After completing this chapter, you should be able to explain and understand:

2-1 What trust is.

2-2 Why trust is important.

2-3 How to earn trust.

2-4 Knowledge bases help build trust and relationships.

2-5 Sales ethics.

After finishing this chapter go to
PAGE 47 for **STUDY TOOLS.**

Self-Worth and the Sales Profession

A "teachable moment." That's how former USC football coach Pete Carroll described the situation at his old school after the NCAA handed down a series of harsh sanctions, the consequences of multiple rule violations that occurred while he and the USC Trojans were racking up multiple championships during the past decade.

Having since moved on to coach the Seattle Seahawks in the NFL, Carroll will not have to face the consequences of the sanctions, but his reputation has been indelibly tarnished, while former star USC running back Reggie Bush—who was at the center of many violations—was forced to return the Heisman trophy.

Carroll didn't elaborate on what the "teachable" lesson was. That it's never OK to break the rules? That coaches need to pay closer attention to what their players are up to? or that if you do break the rules, to make sure that you get out of Dodge before the Sheriff shows up?

For sales leaders, these questions represent more than an academic exercise. As Sean Wheat, a Houston-based regional sales director for Precision Therapeutics, points out, the sales profession's lingering negative image requires that salespeople—and sales managers—maintain the highest level of integrity and professional ethics.

Wheat says most of the teachable moments he's encountered have arisen over relatively minor matters, such as when inexperienced reps on sales calls have made mistakes out of nervousness or fear of losing a sale.

"I've been in meetings with reps who, when they don't know an answer to a question, have said something that they didn't know was 100 percent true instead of saying, 'I don't know,' and telling the customer that they'll find out the answer," he says. "When that's happened, I've pulled the reps aside and let them know they may be misrepresenting themselves and the company by answering a question they don't know the answer to."

Wheat cautions that this sort of intervention is only likely to work if the manager has already established a personal, one-on-one relationship with his or her rep.

"As a manager, you have to open a communication forum with each individual, not just with the team, to the point that you can pick up on any of the little things that he or she says and does, and then probe harder, because my task is no different from what my reps do selling to customers; they have to probe, ask questions, pick up on hot buttons. That's what allows me to get reps off that track and preventatively stop something before it goes too far."

—Malcom Fleschner

The extent of the buyer's confidence in the salesperson's integrity is known as **trust**. But trust can mean different things to different people. According to John Newman,[1] vice president of the Integrated Supply Chains Segment at

> **trust** The extent of the buyer's confidence that he or she can rely on the salesperson's integrity.

FIG. 2.1   TRUST BUILDERS

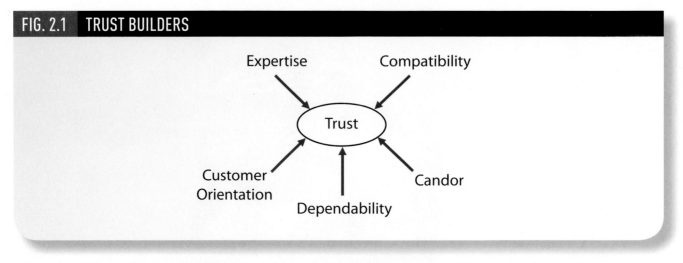

Expertise   Compatibility

Trust

Customer
Orientation

Candor

Dependability

Trust means different things to different people. Trust can be developed by using any of the trust builders. It is the salesperson's job through questioning to determine what trust attributes are critical to relationship building for a specific buyer.

A. T. Kearney, trust is defined in many ways. Buyers define trust with such terms as **openness**, dependability, candor, **honesty**, **confidentiality**, **security**, **reliability**, **fairness**, and predictability.[2] For example, in a Kearney study, one manufacturer related trust to credibility: "What trust boils down to, in a nutshell, is credibility, and when you say you are going to do something, you do it, and the whole organization has to be behind that decision." Another manufacturer related trust to confidentiality in that "they were afraid that the sales guys were going around and telling account B what account A is doing," which was identified as a violation of trust. Another company related trust to openness, claiming "we have to share information that traditionally is not shared." One president told how his engineers were sharing manufacturing secrets with their suppliers that would have cost the engineers their jobs five years earlier.[3]

Research reveals that little is known about what ongoing behaviors (i.e., service behaviors) salespeople can employ to satisfy and build trust with customers.[4] A salesperson has to determine what trust means to each of his or her buyers, as shown in Figure 2.1. If it is confidentiality, then the salesperson must demonstrate how his or her company handles sensitive information. If credibility is the concern, then the salesperson must

demonstrate that all promises will be kept. Therefore, the buyer defines trust; it is the salesperson's job through questioning to determine what trust attributes are critical to relationship building for a specific buyer.

In this chapter, we first discuss the meaning of trust in the sales context. Next, we explore the importance of trust to salespeople. This is followed by a discussion of how to earn trust and what knowledge bases a salesperson can use to build trust in buyer-seller relationships. Finally, we review the importance of sales ethics in building trust.

2-1   WHAT IS TRUST?

Trust is earned when an industrial buyer believes and can rely on a salesperson's claims or promises when the buyer is dependent on the salesperson's honesty and reliability.[5] One of the keys to a long-term relationship with any client is to create a basis of trust between the sales representative and the client organization.[6]

Thus, gaining trust is essential in order to be seen as a reliable salesperson. Long-term sales success in any industry will generally be built on the concept of referral, in which trust plays an important role. Others argue that truthfulness is valuable for its own sake and instrumental to other goals, such as improved long-term relationships.[7] Clients obviously seek a salesperson they can trust. The problem is, depending on the industry and the situation, previous bad experiences might make them wary of future partners. "An Ethical Dilemma" illustrates the challenges a salesperson faces on a daily basis. Consultative salespeople are in a unique position

openness Completely free from concealment: exposed to general view or knowledge.

honesty Fairness and straightforwardness of conduct.

confidentiality The state of being entrusted with information from a buyer that cannot be shared.

security The quality of being free from danger.

reliability Consistency of a salesperson over time to do what is right.

fairness Impartiality and honesty.

From the Classroom to the Field

A short time ago, Kelly Cathcart (2014 grad) was in the classroom at Ball State University learning about trust and ethics in Sales. Today, Kelly is with ADP and here are her thoughts about the importance of trust and ethics in her sales career.

"My professors in college stressed the importance of trust and ethics in my classes, but in a very short period of time I've seen how trust plays a vital role in ADP's success. We must do what we say we are going to do. It's that simple. Too much is at stake with each client if we fail them by not keeping our promises. Payroll is a major function in any organization, and our word to be available with each client when needed is critical."

Automatic Data Processing, Inc.

360b/Shutterstock.com

---

to capitalize on building credibility with customers who place a high value on trust. Customers are looking for trustworthy business partners but may have difficulty trusting most salespeople; the salesperson should recognize this as an opportunity. Kelly Kathcart, a recent college graduate, discusses the importance of trust during her brief sales career. (See From the Classroom to the Field)

The "trust" described here is beyond the typical transaction-oriented trust schema. Many issues—Will the product arrive as promised? Will the right product actually be in stock and be shipped on time? Will the invoice contain the agreed-on price? Can the salesperson be found if something goes wrong?—are only preliminary concerns. In relationship selling, trust is based on a larger set of factors due to the expanded intimacy and long-term nature of the relationship. The intimacy of this relationship will result in both parties sharing information that could be damaging if leaked or used against the other partner.

Trust answers the questions:

1. Do you know what you are talking about?—competence; expertise

2. Will you recommend what is best for me?—customer orientation

3. Are you truthful?—honesty; candor

4. Can you and your company back up your promises?—dependability

> Trust is an integral part of the relationship between customers and suppliers.

5. Will you safeguard confidential information that I share with you?—customer orientation; dependability

Trust is an integral part of the relationship between customers and suppliers and results in increased long-term revenues and profits.[8]

2-2 WHY IS TRUST IMPORTANT?

In today's increasingly competitive marketplace, buyers typically find themselves inundated with choices regarding both products and suppliers. In this virtual buyers' market, traditional selling methods that focused on closing the sale have been found to be inefficient and often counterproductive to the organization's larger, longer-term marketing strategy. In this new competitive environment, buyers are demanding unique solutions to their problems—product solutions that are customized on the basis of their particular problems and needs. Additionally, the adversarial, win-lose characteristics so customary in traditional selling are fading fast. In their place, long-term buyer-seller relationships are evolving as the preferred form of doing business. Although buyers are finding it more effective and efficient to do *more* business with *fewer* suppliers, sellers are finding it more effective to develop a continuing stream of business from the right customers. Such long-term relationships develop mutually beneficial outcomes and are characterized by trust, open communication, common goals, commitment to mutual gain, and organizational support.[9]

This shift toward relationship selling has altered both the roles salespeople play and the activities and skills they exercise in carrying out these roles—the selling process itself. Today's more contemporary selling process is embedded within the relationship marketing paradigm. As such, it emphasizes the initiation and nurturing of long-term buyer-seller relationships based on mutual trust and value-added benefits. As Sean Wheat emphasized in the opening vignette, it is difficult for a salesperson to build a relationship or sustain trust with a prospect or client if they are misrepresenting themselves or their company by answering a question they don't know the answer to. The level of problem-solving activity common to relationship selling requires deliberate and purposeful collaboration between both parties. These joint efforts are directed at creating unique solutions based on an enhanced knowledge and understanding of the customer's needs and the supplier's capabilities so that both parties derive mutual benefits. The nature of this integrative, win-win, and collaborative negotiation relies on augmented communication and interpersonal skills that nurture and sustain the reciprocal trust that allows all parties to share information fully and work together as a strategic problem-solving team.

The skills and activities inherent to relationship selling can be classified according to their purpose as (1) initiation of the relationship (Chapters 5 and 6); (2) development of the relationship (Chapters 7 and 8); and (3) enhancement of the relationship (Chapters 9 and 10). As the activities comprising the selling process have changed, so too have the relative importance and degree of selling effort devoted to each stage of the process.

> A salesperson can build trust by demonstrating dependability when assisting in an order delivery.

expertise The ability, knowledge, and resources to meet customer expectations.

2-3 HOW TO EARN TRUST

Trust is important to any relationship. Several critical variables help salespeople earn a buyer's trust, such as **expertise**, dependability, candor, customer orientation, and compatibility. The importance of each is briefly discussed.

2-3a Expertise

Inexperience is a difficult thing for a young salesperson to overcome. Most recent college graduates will not have the expertise to be immediately successful, especially in industrial sales. Companies spend billions of dollars to train new recruits in the hope of speeding up the expertise variable. Training to gain knowledge on company products and programs, industry, competition, and general market conditions are typical subjects covered in most sales training programs. Young salespeople can shadow more experienced salespeople to learn what it takes to be successful. They must also go the extra mile to prove to their customers their dedication to service. For example, Karl Decker, a sales rep for Stryker Neuro/Spine for five years, has witnessed over four hundred hip replacements. Karl is in the operating room to answer the orthopedic surgeons' questions and to assist in the fitting of the hip. Sizing the titanium rod that goes into the femur and the

A salesperson can build trust by demonstrating dependability when assisting in an order delivery.

polyurethane ball that goes into the socket are critical for success in a hip replacement. Karl must be available for emergency surgeries and several of these have taken place at 3:00 or 4:00 A.M.

Another factor to consider is that many organizations have recently been downsized, thus dramatically cutting the purchasing area in terms of both personnel and support resources. As a result, buyers are having to do more with less and, as such, are thirsty for expertise, be it current insights into their own operations, financial situation, industry trends, or tactical skills in effectively identifying emerging cost-cutting and revenue opportunities in their business. Of course, expertise will be even more critical with certain buyers who are technical, detail-driven, and/or just uninformed in a certain area.

Salespeople should strive to help clients meet their goals. As an example, individuals or business owners can go online and trade stocks for themselves, but if they think a financial planner or securities company is more knowledgeable and brings more expertise to the table, then they will employ him or her.

Today's buyers will respond positively to any attempts to assist them in their efforts to reach bottom-line objectives, be it revenue growth, profitability, or financial or strategic objectives. Thus, "expertise" will take on an even more important role in the customer's assessment of the seller's credibility. For some buyers, especially those with economic or financial responsibilities (e.g., CFO, treasurer, owner-manager), a representative's ability to "contribute" to the bottom line will dominate the perception of a seller's credibility. This is a very important consideration for salespeople, given their pivotal strategy of penetrating accounts at the economic buyer level. Salespeople are seeking to convince clients that they are (1) actively dedicated to the task of positively influencing their bottom-line objectives and (2) capable of providing assistance, counsel, and advice that will positively affect the ability to reach objectives.[10] This is easier said than done because salespeople frequently do not understand the long-term financial objectives of their client.[11]

Buyers today want recommendations and solutions, not just options. Salespeople must be prepared to help their clients meet their goals by adding value.

Buyers are continually asking themselves whether or not the salesperson has the ability, knowledge, and

> Salespeople must be prepared to update their customers on product upgrades or industry trends.

resources to meet his or her prospective customers' expectations. Not only are salespeople selling their knowledge, but also the entire organization and the support that they bring to the buyer. Does the salesperson display a technical command of products and applications (i.e., is he or she accurate, complete, objective)? During one sales call, a buyer asked about a specific new product that the company was promoting in its advertising. The salesperson responded that the product was launched before he was trained on it. This not only casts doubt on the salesperson's ability but also on the company for failing to train the salesperson.

Expertise also deals with the salesperson's skill, knowledge, time, and resources to do what is promised

Salespeople must be prepared to update their customers on product upgrades or industry trends.

Selling in Action

The Importance of Knowing My Limitations

Tom Simpson, senior sales representative for Elite Printing in Muncie, Indiana states, "It is important for me to know my limitations. We provide smart, results-driven business communication solutions. We help clients design and execute statement processing, online billing and payment, print management, and direct mail solutions that increase revenue, reduce overhead and enable long-term success. We call on small mom-and-pop shops all the way up to mega network hospitals. I cannot know all the answers all the time. I ask good questions to gather information about each process. Sometimes, throughout this process, a prospect asks me a question I may not be sure about. At this time my best answer is, 'I don't know, but I will find out and get right back to you'. It is better for me to do this and retain my integrity than to try and fake an answer and potentially lose their trust."

and what the buyer wants. Customers from small accounts must think that they are being treated as well as customers from large accounts and have access to the same resources.

Salespeople must exhibit knowledge generally exceeding that of their customer, not just in terms of the products and services they are selling but in terms of the full scope of the customer's financial and business operations (e.g., products, programs, competitors, customers, vendors). They must bring skills to the table, be it discovery, problem solving, program and systems development, financial management, or planning. These skills must complement those of the customer and offer insight into the best practices in the customer's industry. It is not enough to be an expert. This expertise must translate into observable results and **contributions** for the buyer.

contributions Something given to improve a situation or state for a buyer.

dependability Predictability of a person's actions.

predictability A salesperson's behavior that can be foretold on the basis of observation or experience by a buyer.

candor Honesty of the spoken word.

2-3b Dependability

Dependability centers on the **predictability** of the salesperson's actions. Buyers have been heard to say, "I can always depend on her. She always does what she says she is going to do." Salespeople must remember the promises they make to a customer or prospect. Once a promise is made, the buyer expects that promise to be honored. The buyer should not have to call the salesperson to remind him or her of the promise. The salesperson should take notes during all sales calls for later review. It is harder to forget to do something if it is written down. A salesperson is trying to establish that his or her actions fit a pattern of prior dependable behavior. That is, the salesperson refuses to promise what he or she cannot deliver. The salesperson must also demonstrate an ability to handle confidential information. Buyers and sellers depend on each other to guard secrets carefully and keep confidential information confidential!

2-3c Candor

Candor deals with the honesty of the spoken word. A sales manager was overheard telling his salesforce "whatever it takes to get the order." One of the salespeople replied, "Are you telling us to stretch the truth if it helps us get the order?" The manager replied, "Of course!" The trustworthy salesperson understands doing "anything to get an order" will ultimately damage the buyer-seller relationship.

Salespeople have more than words to win over the support of the buyer; they have other sales aids such as testimonials, third-party endorsements, trade publications, and consumer reports. The salesperson must be just as careful to guarantee that the proof is credible. It takes only one misleading event to lose all credibility. Tom Simpson, vice-president of sales with Elite Printing (See Selling in Action: The Importance of Knowing My Limitations), states, " I won't always have all the answers to questions; sometimes I have to say I don't know but I'll find out and get back right back to you. It is better for me to do this and retain my integrity, than to try and fake an answer and potentially lose a client or prospect's trust."

2-3d Customer Orientation

Customer orientation means placing as much emphasis on the customer's interests as you would on your own. An important facet of customer orientation is that salespeople work to satisfy the long-term needs of their customers rather than their own short-term goals.

A salesperson who has a customer orientation gives fair and balanced presentations. This includes covering both the pros and cons of the recommended product. The pharmaceutical industry has done a good job understanding this principle, as many firms require their salespeople to describe at least one side effect of their drug for each benefit given. This is done not only because of the legal consideration but also to demonstrate expertise and trustworthiness to the physician. Traditional salespeople often ignored negative aspects of a product, which can turn off many buyers. A customer orientation should also include clear statements of benefits and not overpower the buyer with information overload.

Salespeople must truly care about the partnership, and they must be willing to "go to bat" for the client when the need arises. A warehouse fire left one company without any space to store inventory. The salesperson worked out same-day delivery until the warehouse was rebuilt. This left a lasting impression on the buyer. They knew that if they ever needed any help, their salesperson would come through for them.

Salespeople must be fully committed to representing the customer's interests. Although most salespeople are quick to "talk the talk" about their absolute allegiance to their customer's interests, when it comes to "walking the walk" for their customer on such issues as pricing, production flexibility, and design changes, many lack the commitment and/or skills necessary to support the interests of their clients.

To be an effective salesperson and gain access to a customer's business at a partnership level, the client must feel comfortable with the idea that the salesperson is motivated and capable of representing his or her interests. Exhibit 2.1 looks at some of the questions salespeople need to answer satisfactorily to gain the buyer's trust and confidence.

2-3e Compatibility/Likability

Customers generally like to deal with sales representatives they know, they like, and with whom they can feel a bond.

customer orientation
The act of salespeople placing as much emphasis on the customer's interests as their own.

An Ethical Dilemma

As a key account manager for Foster Controls, Chris had developed a strong relationship with Memphis-based Alcorn Manufacturing and the members of the Alcorn team of buyers. In place for several years now, this relationship has propelled Chris into Foster Control's top salesperson and transformed Alcorn into Chris' top customer account for 25 percent of Chris' annual sales. Working to increase his territory sales, Chris has been calling on Minneapolis-based Park Products for the previous seven months. Park manufactures a wide assortment of production equipment in plants spread throughout North and South America and is a direct competitor to Alcorn. Park selected Chris as one of three vendors requested to develop and submit proposals related to a major plant renovation and expansion. While developing the proposal, Chris had access to a great deal of proprietary information regarding Park's new production processes and business plans and had signed the typical confidentiality agreement—obligating him to avoid disclosing any of Park's plans to any other parties. During his visit to Alcorn Manufacturing, Pat Laurence—director of purchasing for Alcorn—began asking Chris about Park. It was apparent that Pat was interested in learning anything he could about Park's plant expansion and business plans. All things considered, if you found yourself in Chris' position, how would you handle this situation?

A) Go ahead and give Pat all the information he asked for, because he is your biggest and best customer.

Paul Vasarhelyi/Shutterstock.com

B) Give Pat some of the minor information you know but not the big info, to stay within your confidentiality agreement.
C) Tell Pat you have a confidentially agreement with Park and you can't help him and risk losing Alcorn's business.

Gary Schliessman of Gary Schliessman and Associates states that his best friends are his clients. He takes an annual trip to walk the Appalachian Trail with one of his clients. Another favorite activity is to take biking trips with his customers that like to ride. He enjoys these activities and learns something new about his clients on each trip. He goes on to state, "Not all of my clients have the same interests that I do, but the ones that do are especially fun to do business with. I believe that compatibility does play a big role in my success."[12]

Some salespeople are too quick to minimize the importance of rapport building in this era of the economic buyer. It may also be true that today's buyers are not as prone to spend time discussing personal issues in sales calls as they might have been 10 or 15 years ago. Salespeople today have to be more creative and resourceful when attempting to build rapport. It is not unusual for a pharmaceutical salesperson to take lunch for the entire staff into a physician's office. These lunches can be for as many as 20 to 40 people. The

> Good salespeople are never in a hurry to earn commitment!

salesperson now has time to discuss his or her products over lunch to a captive audience.

Salespeople have to be aware that their buyers are under considerable time pressure and that some will find it difficult to dedicate time to issues outside of the business. However, remember that buyers are human and do value compatibility, some more, some less.

Compatibility and **likability** are important to establishing a relationship with key gatekeepers (e.g., receptionists and secretaries). First impressions are important, and a salesperson's ability to find commonalities with these individuals can go a long way in building much-needed allies within the buying organization. Likeability is admittedly an emotional factor that is difficult to pin down, yet it is a powerful force in some buyer-seller relationships. "An Ethical Dilemma" on page 36 demonstrates the challenges salespeople might face when trying to build key relationships with potential clients.

If a salesperson has done a good job of demonstrating the other trust-building characteristics, then compatibility can be used to enhance trust building. Buyers do not necessarily trust everyone they like; however, it is difficult for them to trust someone they do not like.

2-4 KNOWLEDGE BASES HELP BUILD TRUST AND RELATIONSHIPS

The more the salesperson knows, the easier it is to build trust and gain the confidence of the buyer. Buyers have certain expectations of the salesperson and the knowledge that he or she brings to the table. As outlined in Figure 2.2, salespeople might draw from several knowledge bases. Most knowledge is gained from the sales training program and on-the-job training.

Sales training will generally concentrate on knowledge of the industry and company history, company policies, products, promotion, prices, market knowledge of customers, **competitor knowledge**, and basic selling techniques. Exhibit 2.2 summarizes topics generally covered during initial sales training programs.

2-4a Industry and Company Knowledge

Salespeople may be asked what they know about their company and industry. Every industry and company has a history.

compatibility/likeability
A salesperson's commonalities with other individuals.

competitor knowledge
Knowledge of a competitor's strengths and weaknesses in the market.

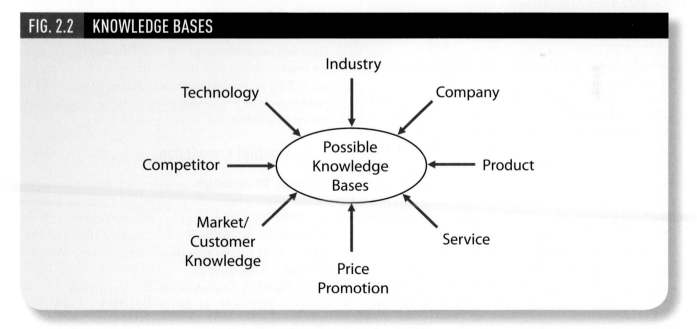

FIG. 2.2   KNOWLEDGE BASES

The more the salesperson knows, the easier it is to build trust and gain the confidence of the buyer. Buyers have certain expectations of the salesperson and the knowledge that he or she brings to the table. Most knowledge is gained from the sales training programs and on-the-job training.

Exhibit 2.2

Topics Generally Covered During Initial Sales Training Programs

- Industry history
- Company history and policies
- Product
  - —promotion
  - —price
- Market
  - —line of business (*know your customer*)
  - —manufacturing
  - —wholesaling
  - —financial
  - —government
  - —medical, etc.
- Competitive knowledge
- Selling techniques
- Initiating customer relationship
  - —prospecting
  - —precall
  - —approaching the customer
- Developing customer relationships
  - —sales presentation delivery
  - —handling sales resistance
- Enhancing customer relationships
  - —follow-up
  - —customer service

The personal computer industry has a short history of 35 years; fax technology, even shorter. Other industries have been around for centuries. Some industries change so quickly, such as the pharmaceutical industry through multiple mergers, that it is critical for the salesperson to know his or her industry to keep physicians informed on new companies, drugs, and procedures. Many buyers are too busy to stay informed and count on their salespeople to help them make sound decisions.

Salespeople should be familiar with their own company's operation and policies. Buyers might ask the salesperson questions such as: How long has your company been in the market? How many people does the company employ? Does the company have a local, regional, national, or international

product knowledge Detailed information on the manufacture of a product and knowing whether the company has up-to-date production methods.

customer base? Who started the company? Who is the president? CEO? What is their market share? What is their market share on this particular product? Salespeople who could not answer such questions would not inspire the trust of the buyer.

Each company initiates policies to ensure consistent decisions are made throughout the organization. An organization implements policies to control factors such as price, guarantees, warranties, and how much to spend per week taking clients out to lunch. Knowing the company's policies prevents a misunderstanding.

> Companies provide extensive training to be sure they send knowledgeable sales representatives into the field.

For example, if a representative says a customer can return goods 60 days after receipt when company policy is 30 days, the shipping department might refuse to accept the returned merchandise. The salesperson looks incompetent to both sales management and the customer. If the customer is not allowed to return the goods to the factory, the angry customer probably will never buy from the salesperson again.

Salespeople must understand their company policies. This includes being familiar with the company's formal structure and key personnel. It is important to work as a team with all company personnel. This helps build team spirit and a willingness to cooperate when a salesperson needs help in meeting a customer's need. It is difficult to provide outstanding service when the sales department is not on good terms with shipping and delivery.

2-4b Product Knowledge

Product knowledge includes detailed information on the manufacturer of a product and knowing whether or not the company has up-to-date production methods. What materials are used when making the products? What quality control procedures are involved? Who are the design engineers?

Salespeople representing their company are expected to be experts on the products they sell. The fastest way to win the respect of a buyer is to be perceived as being an expert. If the buyer truly feels the salesperson knows what he or she is talking about, then the buyer will be more willing to discuss the salesperson's solution to the buyer's problems or opportunities.

Exhibit 2.3

Service Superiority

Dimension	Potential Superiority
1. Delivery	Can our company demonstrate speed? Deliver more often?
2. Inventory	Can we meet the demands of our customers at all times?
3. Training	Do we offer training? At our site? At our customer's?
4. Field maintenance	Do we go to the field to fix our products? Do our customers have to bring their equipment to us to fix?
5. Credit and financial consideration	Do we grant credit? Do we help finance?
6. Installation	Do we send a team to your site for start-up?
7. Guarantees and warranties	What are our guarantees? How long? What do we cover?
8. Others	Do we offer anything unique that our competition does not?

The salesperson must know what his or her product can and cannot do. Just knowing product features is insufficient.

2-4c Service

The effective salesperson must be ready to address **service issues** such as:

- Does the company service its products or does the company send them to a third party?
- Does the company service its products locally or send them off to another state for service?
- Does the price include service or will there be a service charge when service is needed?
- What does the service agreement include? Shipping? Labor? Or neither of these?
- How long does the service generally take? Same day? Within a week? Will a loaner be provided until the product is fixed?
- Are there any conditions that make service not available? After five years? Damage from flood? From fire?

Buyers need to be comfortable answering these questions, and a good salesperson will make sure they are answered appropriately.

Darrell Beaty from Ontario Systems in Muncie, Indiana, spends quite a bit of time discussing service with each of his prospects.[13] His company sells collection software (i.e., receivables) that requires support from his field engineers. Ontario Systems also has a support

group that takes calls 24 hours a day, seven days a week. Why is this important to Beaty? One of his major competitors also has a support group, but only 8 A.M. to 5 P.M., Monday through Friday. Beaty knows that he has service superiority. Salespeople who can offer the better service have an advantage for generating new business and taking away business from the competition. The salesperson's service mission is to provide added value for the customer. It is important for the salesperson to understand what service dimensions concern the buyer.

For instance, delivery, installation, training, field maintenance, and investing are all issues that a salesperson might be prepared to talk about. Buyers, however, might be concerned only with inventory because their current supplier runs out of stock frequently.

Exhibit 2.3 reviews service dimensions in which a salesperson could demonstrate service superiority. Additions can be made depending on specific customer demands.

2-4d Promotion and Price

Promotion knowledge and **price knowledge** are other knowledge tools that the salesperson must understand. The ability

service issues Concerns of the buyer that the salesperson should address.

promotion knowledge Knowledge tools salespeople must possess to explain their firms' promotional programs.

price knowledge Knowledge tools salespeople must have about pricing policies in order to quote prices and offer discounts on products.

Promotional programs must be explained properly so the buyer can place the correct order size during the promotion.

2-4e Market and Customer Knowledge

Market knowledge and **customer knowledge** are critical to the success of today's salesperson. Some companies today, because of their size, send their salesforce out to call on all customer types. Larger companies typically break their customers into distinct markets. Computer manufacturers may break out their customer types by markets (i.e., salespeople sell to a particular line of business). For instance, the salesperson may sell only to manufacturers, wholesalers, financial institutions, government, education, or medical companies. This allows the salesperson to become an expert in a line of business. For a salesperson to be effective, the salesperson must learn what the client needs, what benefits the client is seeking, and how the salesperson's products satisfy the buyer's specific needs. Buyers are not interested in factual knowledge unless it relates to fulfilling their specific needs. Having the salesforce learn one line of business well allows the salesperson to concentrate on the needs of a specific market. The salesperson can become an expert in one line of business more quickly than if he or she had to know how the entire marketplace used the salesperson's products.

Information about customers is gathered over time and from very different sources. A salesperson can use trade associations, credit agencies, trade magazines, trade directories, newspapers, and the World Wide Web as valuable resources. The AT&T Toll-free Internet Directory has directories on people, businesses, and Web sites. Using the Web to do an initial search on a company can tell a salesperson what products a company makes, what markets they serve, and so on. A salesperson must use his or her time wisely when gathering information. Richard Crist, COO, Whitinger & Company, states,: "I have to thoroughly know my industry and my customer's business. I must know where to find this information."

2-4f Competitor Knowledge

Salespeople will probably be asked how their product stands up against the competition. The buyer might ask— Who are your competitors in our marketplace? How big are you compared with your competitors? How do your company's prices compare with others in your industry? How does your product quality compare with the industry norm? These are important questions that every salesperson must be prepared to answer. Salespeople must have knowledge of their competitor's strengths and weaknesses to better understand their own products' position when comparing. A good salesperson must adjust his or her selling strategy depending on the competition.

to use this knowledge often makes the difference between a well-informed buyer who is ready to make a decision and another buyer who is reluctant to move the sales process forward. Hershey Foods Corporation supports its retailers with heavy promotions during Halloween, Christmas, and Easter. The promotional programs must be explained properly so the buyer can place the correct order size during the promotion. How many dollars are to be spent? Is it a national program? Is this a co-op program? What will it cost the buyer? If these questions are answered properly, the buyer will be more at ease and ready to make a purchase.

Price can be another area that makes a buyer hesitant if not properly explained. Knowledge of pricing policies is important because the salesperson is often responsible for quoting prices and offering discounts. As a representative of the selling firm, these quotes legally bind a company to their completion.

Salespeople need complete understanding of their companies' pricing policies. Does the company sell its products for a set price or can the salesperson negotiate? Can the salesperson give additional discounts to get a potential client whom the company has been after for years? Does the company allow trade-ins?

market knowledge
Information salespeople must have if larger companies break their customers into distinct markets; salespeople must be familiar with these markets to tailor their sales presentations.

customer knowledge
Information about customers that is gathered over time and from very different sources that helps the salesperson determine customer needs to better serve them.

Technology in Selling

GPS Tracking Systems

GPS tracking systems are intended for tracking both automobiles and salespeople. Employed as part of a sales fleet's management strategy, GPS systems are able to improve sales force effectiveness and minimize costs. GPS systems allow a company to monitor the salespeople wherever they may be.

The benefits to a company using GPS to track their sales force are numerous: quick recovery of stolen vehicles (keep

insurance costs down), helps salespeople plan their routes effectively, ensures that the sales force is taking the most effective routes, and GPS systems can alert the company and emergency responders if a salesperson's automobile is involved in a road traffic incident.

Modern technologies like GPS have been designed to make a salesperson's driving more efficient and much safer.

Maxx-Studio/Shutterstock.com

Salespeople must be able to deliver complete comparative product information in a sales presentation. Comparisons of competitors' products for a customer's decision are critical, especially when your features and benefits are superior to those of the competition.

It is important that salespeople distinguish their products from the competition. The ultimate question a buyer asks is—Why should I use your product over the one I am currently using? A salesperson must have competitive knowledge to answer this question. What are the competitor's relative strengths and weaknesses? What weaknesses make this competitor vulnerable? Once the salesperson can determine the competitor's limitations, the salesperson

> Salespeople must be well versed in technology tools and how to use them effectively to build a bridge to the buyer.

can demonstrate the superiority of his or her product. A salesperson must answer the questions—How are you different from the competition? How are you better than the competition? A salesperson must be able to determine his or her differential competitive advantage.

2-4g Technology Knowledge

Salespeople must use **technology knowledge** to their advantage. Twenty years ago, salespeople had to know where a reliable pay phone was located in each of the cities they visited. Many opportunities were missed because salespeople could not reach prospects while they were in the field. Today's salesperson has the luxury of smartphones, facsimile technology, the World Wide Web, voice mail, and e-mail. Salespeople should communicate in the manner their prospects and clients prefer. Some clients use e-mail extensively and want to use e-mail over phone conversations. Some buyers like to fax orders in and would rather not meet the salesperson face to face. A good salesperson must recognize these preferences and act accordingly.

technology knowledge
Information salespeople must have about the latest technology.

Exhibit 2.4

Using Technology to Build Bridges to Customers

Technology	Bridge
World Wide Web	Price updates can be placed on the Web for customers to access. New product information can be made available to customers and prospects.
E-mail	Buyer and salesperson can communicate virtually 24 hours a day. Mass communications can be sent out to all customers and prospects.
Facsimile	Non-electronic documents can be transmitted 24 hours a day. Fax on demand.
Cell phones	Buyer and seller have immediate access to each other.
Voice mail	Salesperson and buyer can leave messages for each other and save time and effort.

Each of these can either be a bridge to the customer or an obstacle. Salespeople should be building bridges to all their prospects and customers by using technology appropriately (see Exhibit 2.4). If a buyer likes to e-mail requests to a salesperson, then the salesperson must not use e-mail to block buyers. Likewise, if a facsimile number is given to prospects, then the fax machine must be turned on at all times and working properly.

Probably the most oversold form of technology is voice mail. Many companies have gone to this method of communication hoping to free secretaries and make it easier to leave messages for the salesperson. The difficulty arises when a customer wants to talk to a salesperson and can only get a recording. Sometimes, the voice mailbox is full and it is impossible to leave a message. It is also possible to use voice mail to screen calls, and many buyers and salespeople complain that it is virtually impossible to make contact when their counterpart refuses to return their call. Salespeople can use GPS technology to better serve their clients. Coverage in a territory can be improved with the implementation of a GPS system in each salesperson's car. See Technology in Selling to learn about the benefits of GPS tracking systems.

Technology can be a friend or a foe of a salesperson. If used properly, technology can build bridges to prospects and clients and develop relationships. If technology is not used properly, a salesperson can find himself or herself alienating the customers and turn a potential resource into a reason for a prospect not to do business with the salesperson.

ethics The right and wrong conduct of individuals and institutions of which they are a part.

2-5 Sales Ethics

Ethics refers to right and wrong conduct of individuals and the institutions of which they are a part. Personal ethics and formal codes of conduct provide a basis for deciding what is right or wrong in a given situation. Ethical standards for a profession are based on society's standards, and most industries have developed a code of behaviors that are compatible with society's standards. Professions in this country owe much of their public regard to standards of conduct established by professional organizations. Reflecting this, the American Marketing Association has adopted a code of ethics, which is available on this book's companion Web site.[14]

Salespeople are constantly involved with ethical issues. In fact, salespeople are exposed to greater ethical pressures than individuals in many other occupations.[15] A sales manager might encourage his or her salesforce to pad their expense account in lieu of a raise, or ask a rep to withhold information from a prospect.[16] A salesperson might sell a product or service that the buyer does not need or exaggerate the benefits of a product to get a sale. The list can go on and on.

Recall that sales professionalism requires a truthful, customer-oriented approach. Customers are increasingly intolerant of nonprofessional, unethical practices. Sales ethics is closely related to trust. Deceptive practices, illegal activities, and non-customer-oriented behavior have to be attempted only once for a buyer to lose trust in his or her salesperson. Research has identified some of the sales practices deemed unethical, as shown in Exhibit 2.5.[17]

Exhibit 2.5

What Types of Sales Behaviors Are Unethical?

According to a survey of 327 customers, salespeople are acting unethically if they:

1. Shows concern for their own interest, not the clients'.
2. Pass the blame for something they did wrong.
3. Take advantage of the poor or uneducated.
4. Accept favors from customers so the seller feels obliged to bend policies.
5. Sell products/services that people do not need.
6. Give answers when they do not really know if they are correct or not.
7. Pose as market researcher when doing phone sales.
8. Sell dangerous or hazardous products.
9. Withhold information.
10. Exaggerate benefits of product.
11. Lie about availability to make sale.
12. Lie about competitors.
13. Falsify product testimonials.

2-5a Image of Salespeople and Sales Executives

Sales and Marketing Executives International (SMEI) has been concerned with the image of salespeople and has developed a code of ethics as a set of principles that outline the minimum requirements for professional conduct. SMEI has developed a 20- to 30-hour certification process that declares that a salesperson shall support and preserve the highest standards of professional conduct in all areas of sales and in all relationships in the sales process. Exhibit 2.6[18] is the SMEI Code of Ethics that pledges a salesperson will adhere to these standards.

A sales professional deserves and receives a high level of respect on the job. Buyers who do not interact with professional salespeople on a regular basis might believe in the negative stereotype of the salesperson as pushy, shifty, and untrustworthy. Where does this stereotype come from? Some salespeople are not professional in their approach, and contribute to the negative stereotype. In the past, television programs, movies, and Broadway productions have fostered the negative image of salespeople. During the 1960s and 1970s, the popular press also contributed to this negative image. A study of how salespeople are portrayed in the popular press found that salespeople are often associated with deceptive, illegal, and non-customer-oriented behavior.[19] Dilemmas exist also for sales executives implementing strategic account relationships regarding such issues as information sharing, trust, and hidden incentives for unethical behaviors.[20] Three of the more important areas of unethical behavior, deceptive practices, illegal activities, and non-customer-oriented behavior, are discussed.

2-5b Deceptive Practices

Buyers have been turned off by all salespeople because of experience with only a few unscrupulous salespeople. All salespeople (good and bad) pay the price for this behavior. Unfortunately, some salespeople do use quota pressure as an excuse to be deceptive. The salesperson has the choice to either ignore the trust-building approach and persuade the customer to buy or go to the next sales meeting and catch the wrath of his or her sales manager for being under quota. Salespeople giving unfounded answers, exaggerating product benefits, and withholding information might appear only to shade the truth, but when it causes harm to the buyers, such salespeople have jeopardized future dealings with the buyer.

2-5c Illegal Activities

Misusing company assets has been a long-standing problem for many sales organizations. Using the company car for personal use, charging expenses that did not occur, and selling samples for income are examples of misusing company assets. Some of these violations of company

Exhibit 2.6

SMEI Certified Professional Salesperson Code of Ethics

The SMEI Certified Professional Salesperson (SCPS) Code of Ethics is a set of principles that outline minimum requirements for professional conduct. Those who attain SCPS status should consider these principles as more than just rules to follow. They are guiding standards above which the salesperson should rise.

An SCPS shall support and preserve the highest standards of professional conduct in all areas of sales and in all relationships in the sales process. Toward this end an SCPS pledges and commits to these standards in all activities under this code.

As an SCPS I pledge to the following individuals and parties:

I. With respect to **the customer, I** will:

Maintain honesty and integrity in my relationship with all customers and prospective customers.

Accurately represent my product or service in order to place the customer or prospective customer in a position to make a decision consistent with the principle of mutuality of benefit and profit to the buyer and seller.

Continually keep abreast and increase the knowledge of my product(s), service(s), and industry in which I work. This is necessary to better serve those who place their trust in me.

II. With respect to **the company** and other parties whom I represent, I will:

Use their resources that are at my disposal and will be utilized only for legitimate business purposes.

Respect and protect proprietary and confidential information entrusted to me by my company.

Not engage in any activities that will either jeopardize or conflict with the interests of my company. Activities that might be or appear to be illegal or unethical will be strictly avoided. To this effect I will not participate in activities that are illegal or unethical.

III. With respect to **the competition**, regarding those organizations and individuals that I compete with in the marketplace, I will:

Obtain competitive information only through legal and ethical methods.

Portray my competitors, and their products and services, only in a manner that is honest, truthful, and based on accurate information that can or has been substantiated.

IV. With respect to **the community** and society that provide me with my livelihood, I will:

Engage in business and selling practices that contribute to a positive relationship with the communities in which I and my company have presence.

Support public policy objectives consistent with maintaining and protecting the environment and community.

Participate in community activities and associations that provide for the betterment of the community and society.

I AM COMMITTED to the letter and spirit of this code. The reputation of salespeople depends upon me as well as others who engage in the profession of selling. My adherence to these standards will strengthen the reputation and integrity for which we strive as professional salespeople.

I understand that failure to consistently act according to the above standards and principles could result in the forfeiture of the privilege of using the SCPS designation.

Candidate's Name (Please Print) _____

Signature _____

Date _____

Exhibit 2.7

Areas of Unethical Behavior

Deceptive Practices	Non-Customer-Oriented Behavior	Illegal Activities
Deceive	Pushy	Defraud
Hustle	Hard sell	Con
Scam	Fast talking	Misuse company assets
Exaggerate		
High pressure		
Withhold		
information/bluff		

property also constitute violations of Internal Revenue Service (IRS) regulations and are offenses that could lead to jail or heavy fines.

Bribery is another area that causes some salespeople to run afoul of the law. A competitor might offer bribes; this, in turn, puts pressure on the salesperson's company to respond with bribes of its own. It is difficult for a salesperson to see potential sales going to the competition. Salespeople offering bribes on their own can be punished. Companies that engage in bribery could find themselves being prosecuted and fined. Rockwell International and Lockheed made illegal payments to foreign customers and had to suffer the humiliation of bad publicity and fines.

Another area of legal concern that involves the salesforce is product liability. Salespeople can create product liabilities for a company in three ways: **express warranty**, **misrepresentation**, and **negligence**. A salesperson can create a product warranty or guarantee that obligates the selling organization even if they do not intend to give the warranty. Express warranties are created by any affirmation of fact or promise, any description, or any sample or model that a salesperson uses, which is made part of the basis of the bargain.

Basis of the bargain is taken to mean that the buyer relied on the seller's statements in making the purchase decision. If a salesperson tells a prospect that a machine will turn out 50 units per hour, a legal obligation has been created for the firm to supply a machine that will accomplish this. A salesperson's misrepresentation can also lead to product liability even if the salesperson makes a false claim thinking it is true. The burden of accuracy is on the seller. Salespeople are required by law to exercise "reasonable care" in formulating claims. If a

salesperson asserts that a given drug is safe without exercising reasonable care to see that this claim is accurate, the salesperson has been negligent. Negligence is a basis for product liability on the part of the seller.

Although these tactics might increase sales in the short run, salespeople ruin their trust relationship with their customer and company. Given the legal restrictions that relate to selling practices, a salesperson, as well as the selling organization, should exercise care in developing sales presentations.

2-5d Non-Customer-Oriented Behavior

Most of today's sales organizations emphasize trust-building behaviors and are customer-oriented. Unfortunately, there are a few salespeople and companies today that concentrate on short-term goals and allow outmoded sales tactics to be practiced. Most buyers will not buy from salespeople who are pushy and practice the hard sell. Too much is at stake to fall for the fast-talking, high-pressure salesperson. Buyers have been through their own training, and they understand the importance of developing a long-term relationship with their suppliers. Exhibit 2.7 summarizes these practices.

express warranty A way a salesperson can create product liabilities by giving a product warranty or guarantee that obligates the selling organization even if the salesperson does not intend to give the warranty.

misrepresentation False claim(s) made by a salesperson.

negligence False claim(s) made by a salesperson about the product or service he or she is trying to sell.

basis of the bargain When a buyer relies on the seller's statements in making a purchase decision.

2-5e How are Companies Dealing With Sales Ethics?

Many companies spend time covering ethics in their training programs. These programs should cover topics such as the appropriateness of gift giving, the use of expense accounts, and dealing with a prospect's unethical demands. Each company will have its own policies on gift giving. John Huff of Schering-Plough states, "Just a few years ago, I could spend my expense account on Indiana Pacers tickets or a golf outing with doctors. That is not the case today. There is a lot of gray area concerning gift giving by salespeople to their business clients and prospects. The pharmaceutical industry has policed itself so now gift giving has all but been eliminated. I must know the rules of my company and industry."[21] Some buyers are not allowed to accept gifts from salespeople.

Another important training area is the use of expense accounts. Salespeople should be trained in how to fill out the expense account form and what is acceptable for submission. Some companies allow personal mileage to be included; others do not. If guidelines are established, there is less of a chance for salesperson misunderstanding.

Sometimes unethical behavior is not initiated by the salesperson but by the buyer.[22] Salespeople must be trained in dealing with prospects who make unethical demands. Buyers can be under pressure from their company to stay within budget or to move up the timetable on an order. A buyer might ask a salesperson to move him or her up on the order list in exchange for more business down the road. One pharmacist set up a deal with a salesperson to buy samples illegally. The trust-based salesperson has to shut down any short-term gain for long-term success. A salesperson's career is over if the word circulates that he or she cannot be trusted.

A salesperson must also be concerned with our legal system and those of other countries. It cannot be an excuse for today's well-trained salesperson to say he or she did not know that a law was being broken. When in doubt, the salesperson must check out all state and local laws. In addition, there are industry-specific rules and regulations to be considered. Exhibit 2.8 covers a number of legal reminders.

A salesperson has his or her reputation to tarnish only once. In this age of mass communication (phone, e-mail, Web sites), it is easy for a buyer to get the word out that a salesperson is acting unethically, possibly ending that salesperson's career.

Exhibit 2.8

Legal Reminders

For salespeople:

1. Use factual data rather than general statements of praise during the sales presentation. Avoid misrepresentation.
2. Thoroughly educate customers before the sale on the product's specifications, capabilities, and limitations.
3. Do not overstep authority, as the salesperson's actions can be binding to the selling firm.
4. Avoid discussing these topics with competitors: prices, profit margins, discounts, terms of sale, bids or intent to bid, sales territories or markets to be served, rejection or termination of customers.
5. Do not use one product as bait for selling another product.
6. Do not try to force the customer to buy only from your organization.
7. Offer the same price and support to buyers who purchase under the same set of circumstances.
8. Do not tamper with a competitor's product.
9. Do not disparage a competitor's product without specific evidence of your contentions.
10. Void promises that will be difficult or impossible to honor.

For the sales organization:

1. Review sales presentations and claims for possible legal problems.
2. Make the salesforce aware of potential conflicts with the law.
3. Carefully screen any independent sales agents the organization uses.
4. With technical products and services, make sure the sales presentation fully explains the capabilities and dangers of products and services.

STUDY TOOLS 2

LOCATED IN TEXTBOOK

☐ Rip-out and review chapter review card

LOCATED AT WWW.CENGAGEBRAIN.COM

☐ Review key term flashcards and create your own from StudyBits

☐ Organize notes and StudyBits using the StudyBoard feature within 4LTR Press Online

☐ Complete practice and graded quizzes to prepare for tests

☐ Complete interactive content within the narrative portion of 4LTR Press Online

☐ View chapter highlight box content at the beginning of each chapter

KELLY MEYERS' DILEMMA

BACKGROUND

Kelly Myers has spent the past three months trying to gather all the information she needs to submit a bid on an order that is very important to her company. Bids are due tomorrow and the decision will be made within a week. She has made a great impression on the purchasing agent, Janet Williams, and she has just ended a conversation with her sales manager who believes Kelly needs to make one more call on Williams to see if she can find out any additional information that might help her prepare the bid. Kelly's boss specifically wants to know who the other bidders are.

CURRENT SITUATION

Later that day, Kelly visited with Janet Williams. During the course of the conversation with Williams, Kelly asked who the other bidders were. Williams beat around the bush for a while, but she did not reveal the other bidders. She did mention the other bids were in and pulled the folder out of the filing cabinet where they were kept. Janet opened the file and looked over the bids in front of Kelly.

There was a knock on the door and Janet's boss asked if he could see her for a minute and she walked down the hall with her boss. Kelly realized all the bids were left out in front of her. There was a summary sheet of all of the bids on top and she could easily see all the bids. When Williams returned she returned the folder to the file and the two made some small talk and ended their conversation.

Kelly returned to her office and completed her bid and turned it in to Janet Williams the next morning. Kelly knew her bid would be the lowest by $500.00. One week later Kelly learned she won the bid.

QUESTION

1. What are the ethical issues involved in this situation?

2. If you were Kelly Myers, do you think Janet Williams intended for you to see the competitive bids? What would you have done, given this situation? Why?

BRISBANE UNIFORM COMPANY

CASE BACKGROUND

Brisbane Uniform Company (BUC) specializes in providing uniforms to hotels and restaurants. BUC is a new company from Australia trying to break into the U.S. market. They have had trouble breaking into larger accounts (Marriott, Hilton, Sheraton) because as a new company, they don't have the name recognition in the United States.

As the account exec in the area, you have been working on a new Hilton hotel with over 5,000 rooms and 500 employees. Recently you submitted a proposal, and the buyer, Mark Dunn, has told you he is leaning your way with the order. He also told you that this order must come off without a hitch as his hide is on the line if things go wrong. You know there could be a problem down the road as one of your unions has been negotiating a contract that is about to expire. The last time this contract came up, there was a strike and orders were backlogged for weeks. The hotel has many customized uniforms and has to have these for their grand opening in three months. What is your obligation to the hotel having this information? This order will make your year and probably send you on a trip to Rome for exceeding quota.

ROLE PLAY ACTIVITY

Location: Mark Dunn's office

Action: Role play a sales call with Mark Dunn addressing the issues in the case.

3 | Understanding Buyers

LEARNING OBJECTIVES

After completing this chapter, you should be able to:

3-1 Categorize primary types of buyers.

3-2 Discuss the distinguishing characteristics of business markets.

3-3 List the different steps in the business-to-business buying process.

3-4 Discuss the different types of buyer needs.

3-5 Describe how buyers evaluate suppliers and alternative sales offerings by using the multiattribute model of evaluation.

3-6 Explain the two-factor model that buyers use to evaluate the performance of sales offerings and develop satisfaction.

3-7 Explain the different types of purchasing decisions.

3-8 Describe the four communication styles and how salespeople must adapt and flex their own styles to maximize communication.

3-9 Explain the concept of buying teams and specify the different member roles.

3-10 Understand means for engaging customers.

After finishing this chapter go to
PAGE 79 for **STUDY TOOLS.**

Abc Photo/Shutterstock.com

Philips is one of the world's leading producers of healthcare, consumer lifestyle, and lighting products. As a 120+ year-old company, it knows what it takes to succeed in today's business environment. According to Wim Van Gils, vice-president of Global Commercial Excellence, "To be a successful global brand in the 21st century you need to be agile and locally relevant." Philips has found that one of the best ways to achieve this is to fully understand its customers. To help it achieve this goal, Philips has equipped its sales force with a popular customer relationship management tool called Salesforce.

As a global company, Philips strives to create local solutions while leveraging global scale. According to Van Gils, "Salesforce is helping us develop tools, processes, and new ways of working so we can cater to the needs of customers and consumers in specific markets. It's a collaborative tool that connects the dots." As such, salespeople across the globe are able to access real-time customer insight to ensure that every customer interaction is meaningful. Salespeople are able to get a 360-degree view of customers through their ability to draw

on insight gathered by different departments within Philips around the world. "We want to connect sales, service, marketing, and anyone that's customer-facing with Salesforce so we can share best practices and pockets of excellence. We also want to give our R&D, supply chain, and product groups insight into evolving customer needs and opportunities," says Van Gils.

Salesforce's Chatter collaboration software enables Philips' salespeople, engineers, and service technicians to share information and collaborate across time zones to more fully understand customer needs. Additionally, Philips is using Marketing Cloud by Salesforce to gain a deeper understanding of customers by engaging them on social channels. "To be a customer-centric company, you need to listen to your customers every day, and—since listening alone isn't enough—you need to have a dialogue with them," claims Van Gils. According to Jeroen Tas, CEO of Informatics Solutions and Services, Philips

Healthcare, "Whether it's lighting or healthcare devices, ultimately we want to create a better, healthier world and improve people's lives, by better understanding of our customers and consumers. Salesforce is helping us."[1]

As the opening vignette illustrates, understanding customers is necessary to succeed in today's highly competitive global marketplace. At Philips, understanding the unique needs of each customer allows salespeople to tailor specific solutions for those needs. In doing so, salespeople are able to bring about value for these customers.

This chapter focuses on preparing you to better understand buyers. Following a discussion on different types of buyers, this chapter develops a model of the buying process and the corresponding roles of the salesperson. Buyer activities characteristic to each step of the purchase decision process are explained and related to salesperson activities for effectively interacting with buyers. This is followed by an explanation of different types of purchasing decisions to which salespeople must respond. The influence of individual communication styles on selling effectiveness is also discussed. The growing incidence of multiple buying influences and buying teams is then demonstrated, along with their impact on selling strategy. Finally, means for engaging buyers—such as focusing on the customer experience, making relevant information easily accessible to buyers, and adding value demanded by buyers—are discussed from the perspective of the salesperson.

3-1 TYPES OF BUYERS

Salespeople work and interact with many different types of buyers. These buyer types range from heavy industry and manufacturing operations to consumers making a purchase for their own use. These variants of customer types arise out of the unique buying situations they occupy. As a result, one type of buyer will have needs, motivations, and buying behavior that are very different from another type of buyer. Consider the different buying situations and the resulting needs of a corporate buyer for Foot Locker compared with the athletic equipment buyer for a major university or Joe Smith, attorney at law and weekend warrior in the local YMCA's basketball league. As illustrated in Exhibit 3.1, each of these buyers may be looking for athletic shoes, but their buying needs are very different. To maximize selling effectiveness, salespeople must understand the type of buyer with whom they are working and respond to their specific needs, wants, and expectations.

The most common categorization of buyers splits them into either the (1) **consumer market** or (2) **business market**. Consumers purchase goods and services for their own use or consumption and are highly influenced by peer group behavior, aesthetics, and personal taste. Business markets are composed of firms, institutions, and governments. These members of the business market acquire goods and services to use as inputs into their own manufacturing process (e.g., raw materials, component parts,

consumer market A market in which consumers purchase goods and services for their use or consumption.

business market A market composed of firms, institutions, and governments who acquire goods and services to use as inputs into their own manufacturing process, for use in their day-to-day operations, or for resale to their own customers.

derived demand Demand in business markets that is closely associated with the demand for consumer goods.

and capital equipment), for use in their day-to-day operations (e.g., office supplies, professional services, insurance), or for resale to their own customers. Business customers tend to stress overall value as the cornerstone for purchase decisions.

3-2 DISTINGUISHING CHARACTERISTICS OF BUSINESS MARKETS

Although there are similarities between consumer and business buying behaviors, business markets tend to be much more complex and possess several characteristics that are in sharp contrast to those of the consumer market. These distinguishing characteristics are described in the following sections.

3-2a Concentrated Demand

Business markets typically exhibit high levels of concentration in which a small number of large buyers account for most of the purchases. The fact that business buyers tend to be larger in size but fewer in numbers can greatly impact a salesperson's selling plans and performance. For example, a salesperson selling high-grade industrial silicon for use in manufacturing computer chips will find that his or her fate rests on acquiring and nurturing the business of one or more of the four or five dominant chip makers around the world.

3-2b Derived Demand

Derived demand denotes that the demand in business markets is closely associated with the demand for consumer goods. When the consumer demand for new cars and trucks increases, the demand for rolled steel also goes up. Of course, when the demand for consumer products goes down, so goes the related demand in business markets. The most effective salespeople identify and monitor the consumer markets that are related to their business customers so they can better anticipate shifts in demand and assist their buyers in staying ahead of the demand shifts rather than being caught with too much, too little, or even with the wrong inventory. Republic Gypsum's salespeople accurately forecasted a boom in residential construction and the pressure it would put on the supply of plasterboard. Working closely with their key customers, order quantities and shipping dates were revised to prevent those

Exhibit 3.1

Different Needs of Different Athletic Shoe Buyers

	Buyer for Foot Locker Shoe Stores	University Athletic Equipment Buyer	Joe Smith—YMCA Weekend Warrior
Functional Needs	• Has the features customers want • Well constructed—minimizes returns • Offers point-of-sale displays for store use • Competitive pricing	• Individualized sole texture for different player performance needs • Perfect fit and size for each team member • Custom match with university colors • Size of supplier's payment to coach and school for using their shoes	• Offers the leading edge in shoe features • Prominent brand logo • Highest-priced shoes in the store
Situational Needs	• Can supply stores across North America • Ability to ship to individual stores on a just-in-time basis • Offers 90-day trade credit	• Ability to deliver on time • Provide supplier personnel for team fittings • Make contract payments to university and coach at beginning of season	• Right size in stock, ready to carry out • Takes Visa and MasterCard
Social Needs	• Invitation for buying team to attend trade show and supplier-sponsored reception	• Sponsor and distribute shoes at annual team shoe night to build enthusiasm • Include team and athletes in supplier brand promotions	• Offers user-group newsletter to upscale customers • Periodic mailings for new products and incentives to purchase
Psychological Needs	• Assurance that shoes will sell at retail • Brand name with strong market appeal • Option to return unsold goods for credit	• Brand name consistent with players' self-images • The entire team will accept and be enthusiastic toward product decision • Belief that the overall contract is best for the university, team, and coaches	• Reinforces customer's self-image as an innovator • Product will deliver the promised performance • One of only a few people having purchased this style of shoe
Knowledge Needs	• Level of quality—how the shoe is constructed • How the new features impact performance • What makes the shoe unique and superior to competitive offerings • Product training and materials for sales staff	• What makes the shoe unique and superior to competitive offerings • Supporting information and assurance that the contracted payments to university and coaches are superior to competitive offerings	• What makes the shoe unique and superior to competitive offerings • Assurance that everybody on the court will not be wearing the same shoe

customers from being caught with inadequate inventories to supply the expanded demand. This gave those customers a significant competitive advantage over their competitors, who were surprised and suddenly out of stock.

3-2c Higher Levels of Demand Fluctuation

Closely related to the derived demand characteristic, the demand for goods and services in the business market is more volatile than that of the consumer market. In economics, this is referred to as the **acceleration principle**. As demand increases (or decreases) in the consumer market, the business market reacts by accelerating the buildup (or reduction) of inventories and increasing (or decreasing) plant capacity. A good example would be the rapidly growing demand for smartphones with advanced capabilities such as inductive wireless charging and larger screens. In response to higher consumer demand, wholesalers and retailers are increasing their inventories of these advanced phones while decreasing the number of wired charging small screen devices they carry. In response, manufacturers have shifted their production towards these improved models. Salespeople are the source of valuable information and knowledge, enabling their customers to anticipate these fluctuations and assisting them in developing more effective marketing strategies. As a result, both the buying and selling organizations realize mutual positive benefits.

3-2d Purchasing Professionals

Buyers in the business markets are trained as purchasing agents. The process of identifying suppliers and sourcing goods and services is their job. This results in a more professional and rational approach to purchasing. As a result, salespeople must possess increased levels of knowledge and expertise to provide customers with a richer and more detailed assortment of application, performance, and technical data.

acceleration principle When demand increases (or decreases) in the consumer market, the business market reacts by accelerating the buildup (or reduction) of inventories and increasing (or decreasing) plant capacity.

supply chain management The strategic coordination and integration of purchasing with other functions within the buying organization as well as external organizations.

3-2e Multiple Buying Influences

Reflecting the increased complexity of many business purchases, groups of individuals within the buying firm often work

Salespeople in retail businesses work closely with buyers to satisfy their needs.

together as a buying team or center. As a result, salespeople often work simultaneously with several individuals during a sales call and even different sets of buyers during different sales calls. Buying team members come from different areas of expertise and play different roles in the purchasing process. To be effective, the salesperson must first identify, then understand and respond to, the role and key buying motives of each member.

3-2f Collaborative Buyer-Seller Relationships

The smaller customer base and increased usage of **supply chain management**, characterized by the strategic coordination and integration of purchasing with other functions within the buying organization as well as external organizations, has resulted in buyers and sellers becoming much more interdependent than ever before. This increased interdependence and desire to reduce risk of the unknown has led to an emphasis on developing long-term buyer-seller relationships characterized by increased levels of buyer-seller interaction and higher levels of service expectations by buyers.

Rather than competing to win benefits at the expense of one another, leading organizations are discovering that it is possible for all parties to reduce their risk and increase the level of benefits each receives by sharing information and coordinating activities, resources, and capabilities.[2] For instance, Wal-Mart and Sam's Club stores share information with suppliers on the products they supply. Procter & Gamble synchronizes its product data with Wal-Mart, saving it an estimated $1 million annually.[3] These longer-term buyer-seller relationships are based on the mutual benefits received by and the interdependence between all parties in this value network. In addition to being keenly aware of changing customer needs, collaborative relationships require salespeople to work closely with buyers to foster honest and open two-way communication and develop the mutual understanding required to create the desired solutions. This suggests that salespeople understand the buyer's customers to determine how to help the buyer succeed by better serving their customers. Such understanding provides insights to challenges facing the buyer, enhances the salesperson's credibility, and helps to establish a strong business partnership.[4] Further, salespeople must consistently demonstrate that they are dependable and acting in the buyer's best interests.

 ## 3-3 THE BUYING PROCESS

Although not always the case in the consumer marketplace, buyers in the business marketplace typically undergo a conscious and logical process in making purchase decisions. As depicted in Figure 3.1, the sequential and interrelated phases of the business buyer's purchase process begin with (1) recognition of the problem or need, (2) determination of the characteristics of the item and the quantity needed, (3) description of the characteristics of the item and quantity needed, (4) search for and qualification of potential sources, (5) acquisition and analysis of proposals, (6) evaluation of proposals and selection of suppliers, (7) selection of an order routine, and (8) performance feedback and evaluation.

Depending on the nature of the buying organization and the buying situation, the buying process may be highly formalized or simply a rough approximation of what actually occurs. The decision process General Motors employs for the acquisition of a new organization-wide computer system will be highly formalized and purposefully reflect each of the previously described decision phases. Compared with General Motors, the decision process of Bloomington Bookkeeping, a single office and four-person operation, could be expected to use a less formalized approach in working through their buying decision process for a computer system. In the decision to replenish stock office supplies, both of the organizations are likely to use a much less formalized routine—but still, a routine that reflects the different decision phases.

As Figure 3.1 further illustrates, there is a close correspondence between the phases of the buyer's decision process and the selling activities of the salesperson. It is important that salespeople understand and make use of the interrelationships between the phases of the buying process and selling activities. Effective use of these interrelationships offers salespeople numerous opportunities to interact with buyers in a way that guides the shaping of product specifications and the selection of sources while facilitating the purchase decision.

3-3a Phase One—Recognition of the Problem or Need: The Needs Gap

Needs are the result of a gap between buyers' **desired states** and their **actual states**. Consequently, need recognition results when an individual cognitively and emotionally processes information relevant to his or her actual state of being and compares it to the desired state of being. As illustrated in Figure 3.2, any perceived difference, or **needs gap**, between these two states activates the motivation or drive to fill the gap and reach the desired state. For example, the SnowRunner Company's daily production capacity is limited to 1,000 molded skimobile body housings. Their research indicates that increasing capacity to 1,250 units per day would result in significant reductions in per-unit costs and allow them to enter additional geographic markets—both moves that would have significant and positive impacts on financial performance. The perceived need to expand production activates a corresponding motivation to search for information regarding alternative solutions and acquire the capability to increase production by 250 units.

However, if there is no gap, then there is no need and no active buying motive. It is common for salespeople to find themselves working with buyers who, for one reason or another, do not perceive a needs gap to be present. It is possible that they do not have the right information or lack a full understanding of the situation and the existence of options better than their current state. It is also possible that their understanding of the actual state might be incomplete or mistaken. For example, SnowRunner's buyers might not understand the cost reduction possibilities and increased market potential that could result from increased capacity. As a result, they perceive

desired states A state of being based on what the buyer desires.

actual states A buyer's actual state of being.

needs gap A perceived difference between a buyer's desired and actual state of being.

FIG. 3.1

COMPARISON OF BUYING DECISION PROCESS PHASES AND CORRESPONDING STEPS IN THE SELLING PROCESS

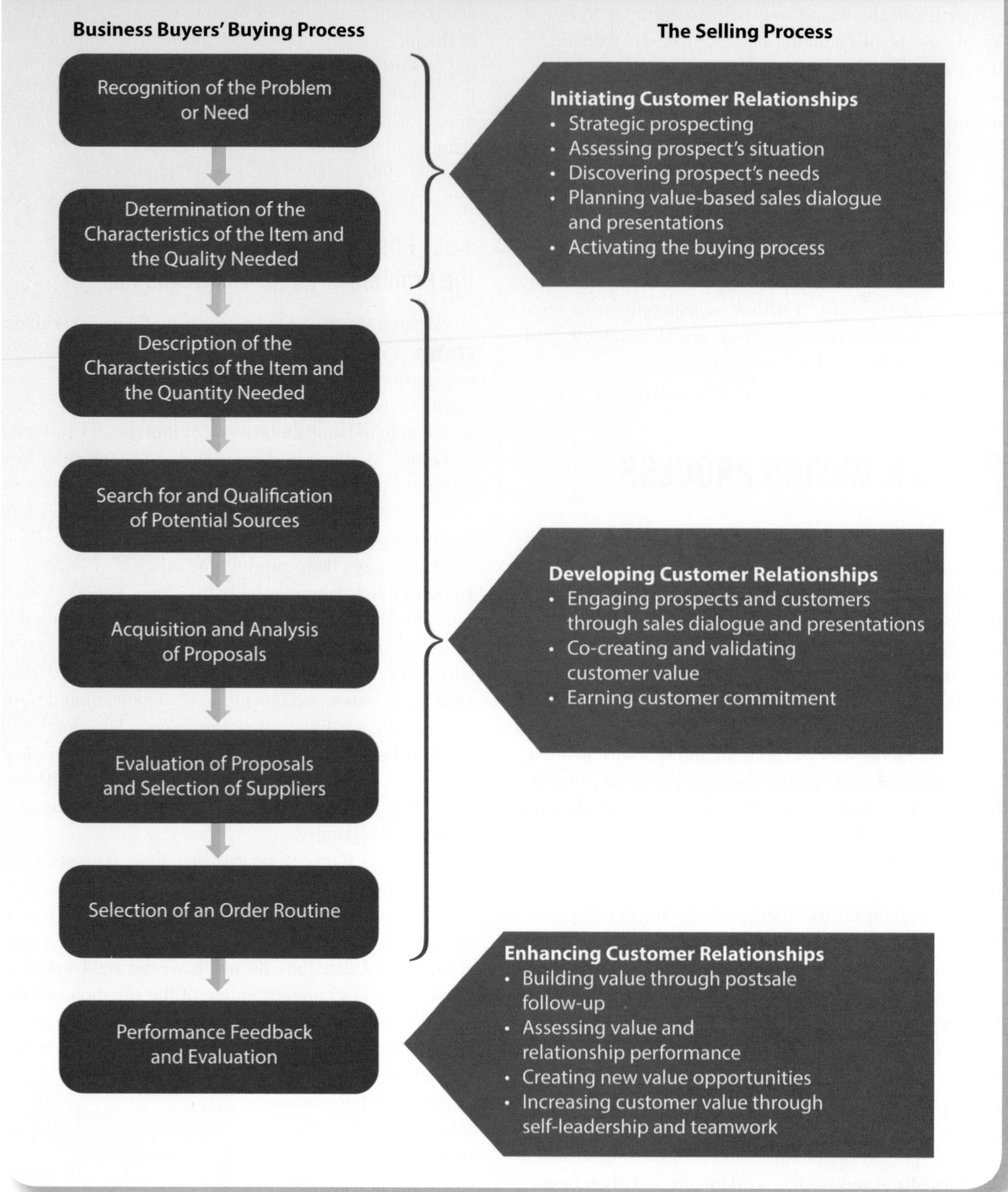

Business Buyers' Buying Process

The Selling Process

Recognition of the Problem or Need

Determination of the Characteristics of the Item and the Quality Needed

Initiating Customer Relationships
- Strategic prospecting
- Assessing prospect's situation
- Discovering prospect's needs
- Planning value-based sales dialogue and presentations
- Activating the buying process

Description of the Characteristics of the Item and the Quantity Needed

Search for and Qualification of Potential Sources

Acquisition and Analysis of Proposals

Developing Customer Relationships
- Engaging prospects and customers through sales dialogue and presentations
- Co-creating and validating customer value
- Earning customer commitment

Evaluation of Proposals and Selection of Suppliers

Selection of an Order Routine

Enhancing Customer Relationships
- Building value through postsale follow-up
- Assessing value and relationship performance
- Creating new value opportunities
- Increasing customer value through self-leadership and teamwork

Performance Feedback and Evaluation

FIG. 3.2   THE NEEDS GAP

Desired State
Produce 1,250 units per day

The Gap or Need
250 units per day

Actual State
Produce 1,000 units per day

The needs gap is the difference between the buyer's perceived desired state and the buyer's perceived actual state.

no need to increase production—the desired state is the same as their actual state. Similarly, the buyers might be functioning with incomplete information regarding the company's actual state of reduced production capacity due to Snow-Runner's existing molding machines requiring increased downtime for maintenance. Properly realized, this lowering of the actual state would result in a needs gap. Successful salespeople position themselves to assist buyers in identifying and understanding needs as a result of their broader expertise and knowledge regarding product use and application. Salespeople can also use sales conversations to present buyers with information and opportunities that effectively raise the desired state, generate a need, and trigger the purchase decision process. Top-performing salespeople understand the importance of assisting their buyers in forming realistic perceptions of the actual state and the desired state. In this manner, the salesperson can continue to serve as a nonmanipulative consultant to the buyer while affecting buying motives that yield mutual benefits to all parties. However, it should be noted that the persuasive power of assisting the buyer in determining and comparing desired and actual states can also be misused and lead to unethical and manipulative selling behaviors such as those exhibited in "An Ethical Dilemma."

> Business buyers typically undergo a conscious and logical process in making purchase decisions.

3-4   TYPES OF BUYER NEEDS

The total number of potential customer needs is infinite and sometimes difficult for salespeople to grasp and understand on a customer-by-customer basis. Consequently, many salespeople find it helpful to group customer needs into one of five basic types or categories that focus on the buying situation and the benefits to be provided by the product or service being chosen.[5] These five general types of buyer needs are described as follows:

- **Situational needs** are the specific needs that are contingent on, and often a result of, conditions related to the specific environment, time, and place (e.g., emergency car repair while traveling out of town, a piece of customized production equipment to fulfill a customer's specific situational requirements, or providing for quick initial shipment to meet a buyer's out-of-stock status).

- **Functional needs** represent the need for a specific core task or function to be performed—the functional purpose of a specific product or service. The need for a sales offering to do what it is supposed to do (e.g., alcohol disinfects, switches open and close to control some flow, the flow control valve is accurate and reliable).

- **Social needs** are the need for acceptance from and association with others—a desire to belong to some reference group. For example, a product or service might be associated with some specific and desired affinity group or segment (e.g., Polo clothing is associated with upper-income, successful people; ISO 9000 Certification is associated with high-quality vendors; leading e-commerce Web sites include discussion groups to build a sense of community).

situational needs The needs that are contingent on, and often a result of, conditions related to the specific environment, time, and place.

functional needs The need for a specific core task or function to be performed.

social needs The need for acceptance from and association with others.

An Ethical Dilemma

Bob Labels is a sales representative for a firm that manufactures and sells various packaging machines. Bob is meeting with a prospect, Andrew Ale, who is a purchaser for a midsized beer manufacturer looking to expand its business. Thus, the company is in need of an additional bottle labeler. The bottle labeler currently used by the company was bought at auction several years ago. Having found Bob's company on the Internet, Andrew contacted Bob and they set up a meeting at Andrew's office. Upon assessing Andrew's needs, Bob determined that Andrew was looking for a roll-fed bottle labeler capable of labeling up to 1,200 bottles per minute. This concerned Bob because the fastest bottler he carried was capable of labeling only up to 1,000 bottles per minute. Currently, Andrew's company was not running at full capacity, but he felt he would need this capability in the near future to meet expected demand. While Bob knew his labeler would work fine for the near future, he also knew that given Andrew's future needs, a faster bottler would actually be the

most beneficial purchase. Bob really wanted to make this sale as it would be instrumental in him achieving a bonus. The bonus would be particularly useful to help Bob pay the hospital bills associated with his wife's cancer. Bob believes that he could work with Andrew to get him to reassess his needs and convince him that the machine he has to offer will be quick enough to meet production needs now and in the future, particularly given that there is no guarantee of an expected growth in sales. Bob surmises that if Andrew's company outgrew this labeler, they could always purchase an additional labeler from him down the road.

What should Bob do?

a) Try to convince Andrew that he does not need a labeler that does 1,200 labels per minute.
b) Suggest an alternate label machine supplier and ask Andrew to keep him in mind for additional packaging machinery needs.
c) Refer to his company's code of conduct and/or contact his sales manager and ask for advice.

- **Psychological needs** reflect the desire for feelings of assurance and risk reduction, as well as positive emotions and feelings such as success, joy, excitement, and stimulation (e.g., a Mont Blanc pen generates a feeling of success; effective training programs create a sense of self-control and determination; selection and use of well-known, high-quality brands provide assurance to buyers and organizations alike).

- **Knowledge needs** represent the desire for personal development, information, and knowledge to increase thought and understanding as to how and why things happen (e.g., product information, newsletters, brochures, and training and user support group meetings/conferences provide current information on products and topics of interest).

Categorizing buyer needs by type can assist the salesperson in bringing order to what could otherwise be a confusing and endless mix of needs and expectations. Organizing the buyer's different needs into their basic types can help salespeople in several ways. First, as Exhibit 3.1 and the example worksheet in Exhibit 3.2 illustrate, the basic types can serve as a checklist or worksheet to ensure that no significant problems or needs have been overlooked in the process of needs discovery. Organizing what at first might appear to be different needs and problems

psychological needs The desire for feelings of assurance and risk reduction, as well as positive emotions and feelings such as success, joy, excitement, and stimulation.

knowledge needs The desire for personal development, information, and knowledge to increase thought and understanding as to how and why things happen.

Exhibit 3.2

Example Worksheet for Organizing Buyer Needs and Benefit-Based Solutions

Primary Buyer: **Bart Waits**
Buying Organization: **SouthWest Metal Stampings**
Primary Industry: **Stamped Metal Parts and Subcomponents**

Basic Type of Need	Buyer's Specific Needs
Buyer's Situational Needs	• Requires an 18 percent increase in production to meet increased sales • On-hand inventory will not meet production/delivery schedule • Tight cash flow pending initial deliveries and receipt of payment
Buyer's Functional Needs	• Equipment to provide effective and efficient increase in production • Expedited delivery and installation in six weeks or less • Equipment financing extending payments beyond initial receipts
Buyer's Social Needs	• Expansion in production transforms them into top 10 in industry • Belonging to user group of companies using this equipment • Feeling that they are an important customer of the supplier
Buyer's Psychological Needs	• Confidence that selected equipment will meet needs and do the job • Assurance that seller can complete installation in six weeks • Saving face—to believe borrowing for equipment is common
Buyer's Knowledge Needs	• Evidence that this is the right choice • Understanding new technology used by the selected equipment • Training program for production employees and maintenance staff

into their common types also helps the salesperson better understand the nature of the buyer's needs along with the interrelationships and commonalities between them. In turn, this enhanced understanding and the framework of basic types combine to serve as a guide for salespeople in generating and then demonstrating value-added solutions in response to the specific needs of the buyer.

As previously discussed, the specific circumstances or types of solution benefits that a buyer is seeking should determine a salesperson's strategy for working with that buyer. Consequently, it should be noted that the needs of business buyers tend to be more complex than consumers' needs. As with consumers, organizational buyers are people and are influenced by the same functional, social, psychological, knowledge, and situational experiences and forces that affect and shape individual needs. However, in addition to those individual needs, organizational buyers must also satisfy the needs and requirements of the organization for which they work. As Figure 3.3 depicts, these organizational needs overlay and interact with the needs of the individual. To maximize selling effectiveness in the organizational or business-to-business market, salespeople must generate solutions addressing both the individual and organizational needs of business buyers. For more on the importance of understanding customer needs see "From the Classroom to the Field: The Importance of Understanding Buyer Needs."

3-4a Phase Two—Determination of the Characteristics of the Item and the Quantity Needed

Coincident to recognizing a need or problem is the motivation and drive to resolve it by undertaking a search for additional information leading to possible solutions. This particular phase of the buying process involves the consideration and study of the overall situation to understand what is required in the form of a preferred solution. This begins to establish the

FIG. 3.3 COMPLEX MIX OF BUSINESS BUYER NEEDS

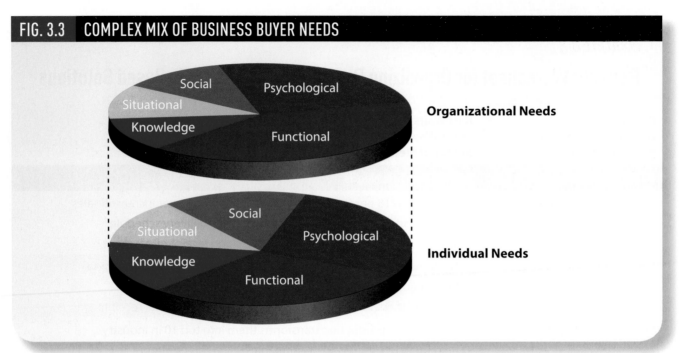

A business buyer's needs are a combination of the buyer's individual needs and the organization's needs.

general characteristics and quantities necessary to resolve the need or problem. Through effective sales dialogue, salespeople use their knowledge and expertise at this point to assist the buyer in analyzing and interpreting the problem situation and needs. Salespeople offer valuable information about problem situations and solution options that buyers typically perceive as beneficial.

From the Classroom to the Field

The Importance of Understanding Buyer Needs

Brett Eiskina graduated from the University of Central Missouri in May 2012 and is a corporate acquisition account executive at Sprint Nextel. Brett discusses the importance of understanding buyer needs.

Throughout my seven years of professional sales, I have sold in both business and consumer markets. At first thought, you might think that the two are completely different sales cycles with different approaches. However, the sales cycle itself is almost the exact same for each buyer in each market. In my college sales classes, we learned how to identify customer needs. In my opinion, the single most important step in understanding the buyer is finding his or her specific needs. This step is what separates the good salespeople from the great salespeople. In the business world, different decision makers have different needs that are usually more specific to their title within the company. For example, what is important to a CFO may not be nearly as important to a COO or a CIO, so it is up to you as a salesperson to be able to accurately determine what is important to the decision maker you are pitching. Most of the time, if you can accurately identify and solve that buyer's most important needs, then you will get the sale.

3-4b Phase Three—Description of the Characteristics of the Item and the Quantity Needed

Using the desired characteristics and quantities developed in the previous phase as a starting point, buyers translate that general information into detailed specifications describing exactly what is expected and required. The determination of detailed specifications serves several purposes. First, detailed specifications guide supplier firms in developing their proposals. Second, these specifications provide the buyer a framework for evaluating, comparing, and choosing among the proposed solutions. Postpurchase specifications serve as a standard for evaluation to ensure that the buying firm receives the required product features and quantities. Trust-based buyer-seller relationships allow salespeople to work closely with buyers and collaboratively assist them in establishing the detailed specifications of the preferred solutions. Such is the case, for instance, with consumer packaged goods company Procter and Gamble, who even located offices near Wal-Mart's headquarters in Bentonville, Arkansas, to work more collaboratively with the world's largest retailer.

3-4c Phase Four—Search for and Qualification of Potential Sources

Next, buyers must locate and qualify potential suppliers capable of providing the preferred solution. Although buyers certainly utilize information provided by salespeople to identify qualified suppliers, there is an abundance of information available from other sources, such as trade associations, product source directories, trade shows, the Internet, advertising, and word of mouth. Once identified, potential suppliers are qualified on their ability to perform and deliver consistently at the level of quality and quantity required. Due to the large number of information sources available to buyers researching potential suppliers, one of the most important tasks in personal selling is to win the position of one of those information sources and keep buyers informed about the salesperson's company, its new products, and solution capabilities.

3-4d Phase Five—Acquisition and Analysis of Proposals

Based on the detailed specifications developed in phase three, **requests for proposals** (known in the trade as an **RFP**) are developed and distributed to the qualified potential suppliers. Based on the RFP, qualified suppliers develop and submit proposals to provide the

Buyers sometimes attend trade shows to find qualified suppliers.

products as specified. Salespeople play a critical and influential role in this stage of the buying process by developing and presenting the proposed solution to the buyers. In this role, the salesperson is responsible for presenting the proposed features and benefits in such a manner that the proposed solution is evaluated as providing higher levels of benefits and value to the buyer than other competing proposals. Consequently, it is imperative that salespeople understand the basic evaluation procedures used by buyers in comparing alternative and competitive proposals so they can be more proficient in demonstrating the superiority of their solution over the competition.

3-5 PROCEDURES FOR EVALUATING SUPPLIERS AND PRODUCTS

Purchase decisions are based on buyers' comparative evaluations of suppliers and the products and services they propose for satisfying buyers' needs. Some buyers might look for the sales offering that receives the highest rating on the one characteristic they perceive as being most important. Others might prefer the sales offering that achieves some acceptable assessment score across every attribute desired by the buyer. However, research into

> **requests for proposal (RFP)** A form developed by firms and distributed to qualified potential suppliers that helps suppliers develop and submit proposals to provide products as specified by the firm.

Exhibit 3.3

Important Product Information

Characteristics	BondIt #302	AdCo #45	StikFast #217
Ease of application	Excellent	Good	Very good
Bonding time	8 minutes	10 minutes	12 minutes
Durability	10 years	12 years	15 years
Reliability	Very good	Excellent	Good
Nontoxic	Very good	Excellent	Very good
Quoted price	$28 per gallon	$22 per gallon	$26 per gallon
Shelf-life in storage	6 months	4 months	4 months
Service factors	Good	Very good	Excellent

how purchase decisions are made suggests that most buyers use a compensatory, **multiattribute model** incorporating weighted averages across desired characteristics.[6] These weighted averages incorporate (1) assessments of how well the product or supplier performs in meeting each of the specified characteristics and (2) the relative importance of each specified characteristic to the buying firm.

3-5a Assessment of Product or Supplier Performance

The first step in applying the multiattribute model is to rate objectively how well each characteristic of the competing products or suppliers meets the buyer's needs. Let us use the example of General Motors (GM) evaluating adhesives for use in manufacturing. The buyers have narrowed the alternatives to products proposed by three suppliers: BondIt #302, AdCo #45, and StikFast #217. As illustrated in Exhibit 3.3, the GM buying team has assessed the competitive products according to how well they perform on certain important attributes. These assessments are converted to scores as depicted in Exhibit 3.4, with scores ranging from 1 (very poor performance) to 10 (excellent performance).

multiattribute model
A procedure for evaluating suppliers and products that incorporates weighted averages across desired characteristics.

As illustrated, no single product is consistently outstanding across each of the eight identified characteristics. Although BondIt #302 is easy to apply and uses the buyer's current equipment, it is also more expensive and has the shortest durability time in the field. StikFast #217 also scores well for ease of application, and it has superior durability. However, it has the longest bonding time and could negatively influence production time.

3-5b Accounting for Relative Importance of Each Characteristic

To compare these performance differences properly, each score must be weighted by the characteristic's perceived importance. In the adhesive example, importance weights are assigned on a scale of 1 (relatively unimportant) to 10 (very important). As illustrated in Exhibit 3.5, multiplying each performance score by the corresponding attribute's importance weight results in a weighted average that can be totaled to calculate an overall rating for each product. Keep in mind that each alternative product generally must meet a minimum specification on each desired product characteristic for it to be considered. The product or supplier having the highest comparative rating is typically the product selected for purchase. In this example, AdCo has the highest overall evaluation, totaling 468 points, compared with BondIt's 430 points and StikFast's 446 points. In some cases, the

Exhibit 3.4

Product Performance Scores

Characteristics	BondIt #302	AdCo #45	StikFast #217
Ease of application	10	5	8
Bonding time	8	6	4
Durability	6	8	9
Reliability	8	10	5
Nontoxic	8	10	8
Quoted price	5	9	7
Shelf-life in storage	9	6	6
Service factors	5	8	10

buyer may be focusing on one characteristic as being the most important and will choose the seller that performs best on that characteristic, assuming that minimum performance specifications are met across all other criteria. In the GM example, if "durability" were the most important characteristic, with a minimum performance specification of "4" for all other criteria, then StikFast #217 would be chosen.

3-5c Employing Buyer Evaluation Procedures to Enhance Selling Strategies

Understanding evaluation procedures and gaining insight as to how a specific buyer or team of buyers evaluates suppliers and proposals is vital for the salesperson to be effective and requires the integration of several bases of knowledge. First, information gathered prior

Exhibit 3.5

Weighted Averages for Performance (P) Times Importance (I) and Overall Evaluation Scores

Characteristics	BondIt #302			AdCo #45			StikFast #217		
	P	I	P × I	P	I	P × I	P	I	P × I
Ease of application	10	8	80	5	8	40	8	8	72
Bonding time	8	6	48	6	6	36	4	6	24
Durability	6	9	54	8	9	72	9	9	81
Reliability	8	7	56	10	7	70	5	7	35
Nontoxic	8	6	48	10	6	60	8	6	48
Quoted price	5	10	50	9	10	90	7	10	70
Shelf-life in storage	9	6	54	6	6	36	6	6	36
Service factors	5	8	40	8	8	64	10	8	80
Overall evaluation score			430			468			446

to the sales call must be combined with an effective needs-discovery dialogue with the buyer(s) to delineate the buyer's needs and the nature of the desired solution. This establishes the most likely criteria for evaluation. Further discussion between the buyer and seller can begin to establish the importance the buyer's place on each of the different performance criteria and often yields information as to what suppliers and products are being considered. Using this information and the salesperson's knowledge of how his or her products compare with competitors' offerings allows the salesperson to complete a likely facsimile of the buyer's evaluation. With this enhanced level of preparation and understanding, the salesperson can plan, create, and deliver a more effective presentation using the five fundamental strategies that are inherent within the evaluation procedures buyers use.

- Modify the Product Offering Being Proposed. Often, in the course of preparing or delivering a presentation, it becomes apparent that the product offering will not maximize the buyer's evaluation score in comparison with a competitor's offering. In this case, the strategy would be to modify or change the product to one that better meets the buyer's overall needs and thus would receive a higher evaluation. For example, by developing a better understanding of the adhesive buyer's perceived importance of certain characteristics, the BondIt salesperson could offer a different adhesive formulation that is not as easy to apply (low perceived importance) but offers improved durability (high perceived importance) and more competitive price (high perceived importance).

- Alter the Buyer's Beliefs about the Proposed Offering. Provide information and support to alter the buyer's beliefs as to where the proposed product stands on certain attributes. This is a recommended strategy for cases in which the buyer underestimates the true qualities of the proposed product. However, if the buyer's perceptions are correct, this strategy would encourage the salesperson to exaggerate and overstate claims and, thus, should be avoided. In the instance of BondIt #302's low evaluation score, the salesperson could offer the buyer information and evidence that the product's durability and service factors actually perform much better than the buyer initially believed. By working with the buyer to develop a more realistic perception of the product's performance, BondIt #302 could become the buyer's preferred choice.

competitive depositioning
Providing information to evidence a more accurate picture of a competitor's attributes or qualities.

- Alter the Buyer's Beliefs about the Competitor's Offering. For a variety of reasons, buyers often mistakenly believe that a competitor's offering has higher level attributes or qualities than it actually does. In such an instance, the salesperson can provide information to evidence a more accurate picture of the competitor's attributes. This has been referred to as **competitive depositioning** and is carried out by openly comparing (not simply degrading) the competing offering's attributes, advantages, and weaknesses. As an illustration, the BondIt salesperson might demonstrate the total cost for each of the three product alternatives, including a quoted price, ease of application, and bonding time. BondIt is much easier to apply and has a faster bonding time. Consequently, less of it needs to be applied for each application, which results in a significantly lower total cost and a much improved evaluation score.

- Alter the Importance Weights. In this strategy, the salesperson uses information to emphasize and thus increase the importance of certain attributes on which the product offering is exceptionally strong. In the case of attributes on which the offering might be short, the strategy would be to deemphasize their importance. Continuing the adhesive purchase decision, BondIt's salesperson might offer information to influence the buyer's importance rating for ease of application and storage shelf-life—two characteristics in which BondIt is much stronger than the two competitors.

- Call Attention to Neglected Attributes. In the case in which it becomes apparent that significant attributes may have been neglected or overlooked by the buyer, the salesperson can increase the buyer's evaluation of the proposed offering by pointing out the attribute that was missed. For instance, the BondIt #302 adhesive dries to an invisible, transparent, and semiflexible adhesive compared with the two competitors, which cure to a light gray color that could detract from the final product in cases in which the adhesive flowed out of the joint. The appearance of the final product is a significant concern, and this neglected attribute could substantially influence the comparative evaluations.

3-5d Phase Six—Evaluation of Proposals and Selection of Suppliers

The buying decision is the outcome of the buyer's evaluation of the various proposals acquired from potential suppliers. Typically, further negotiations will be conducted with the selected supplier(s) for the purpose of establishing the final terms regarding product characteristics, pricing, and delivery. Salespeople play a central role in gaining the buyer's commitment to the purchase decision and in the subsequent negotiations of the final terms.

3-5e Phase Seven—Selection of an Order Routine

Once the supplier(s) has been selected, details associated with the purchase decision must be settled. These details include delivery quantities, locations, and times along with return policies and the routine for reorders associated with the purchase. For cases in which the purchase requires multiple deliveries over a period of time, the routine for placing subsequent orders and making deliveries must be set out and understood. Is the order routine standardized on the basis of a prearranged time schedule, or is the salesperson expected to monitor usage and inventories in order to place orders and schedule shipments? Will orders be placed automatically through the use of electronic data interchange or the Internet? Regardless of the nature of the order routine, the salesperson plays a critical role in facilitating communication, completing ordering procedures, and settling the final details.

3-5f Phase Eight—Performance Feedback and Evaluation

The final phase in the buying process is the evaluation of performance and feedback shared among all parties for the purpose of improving future performance and enhancing buyer-seller relationships. Research supports that salespeople's customer interaction activities and communication at this stage of the buying process become the primary determinants of customer satisfaction and buyer loyalty. Consequently, it is critical that salespeople continue working with buyers after the sale. The salesperson's follow-up activities provide the critical points of contact between the buyer and seller in order to ensure consistent performance, respond to and take care of problems, maximize customer satisfaction, create new value opportunities, and further enhance buyer-seller relationships.

iQoncept/Shutterstock.com

3-6 UNDERSTANDING POSTPURCHASE EVALUATION AND THE FORMATION OF SATISFACTION

Research shows that buyers evaluate their experience with a product purchase on the basis of product characteristics that fall into a **two-factor model of evaluation** as depicted in Figure 3.4.[7] The first category, **functional attributes**, refers to the features and characteristics that are related to what the product actually does or is expected to do—its functional characteristics. These functional characteristics have also been referred to as **must-have attributes**, features of the core product that the customer takes for granted. These are the attributes that must be present for the supplier or product to even be included among those being considered for purchase. Consequently, they tend to be fairly common across the set of suppliers and products being considered for purchase by a buyer. Characteristics such as reliability, durability, conformance to specifications, competitive pricing, and performance are illustrative of functional attributes.

Psychological attributes make up the second general category. This category refers to how things are carried out and done between the buyer and seller. These supplier and market offering characteristics are described as the **delighter attributes**—the augmented features and characteristics included in the total market offering that go beyond buyer expectations and have a significant positive impact on customer satisfaction. The psychological or delighter characteristics are

two-factor model of evaluation A postpurchase evaluation process buyers use that evaluates a product purchase using functional and psychological attributes.

functional attributes The features and characteristics that are related to what the product actually does or is expected to do.

must-have attributes Features of the core product that the customer takes for granted.

psychological attributes A category of product characteristics that refers to how things are carried out and done between the buyer and seller.

delighter attributes The augmented features included in the total market offering that go beyond buyer's expectations and have a significant positive impact on customer satisfaction.

FIG. 3.4 THE TWO-FACTOR MODEL OF BUYER EVALUATION

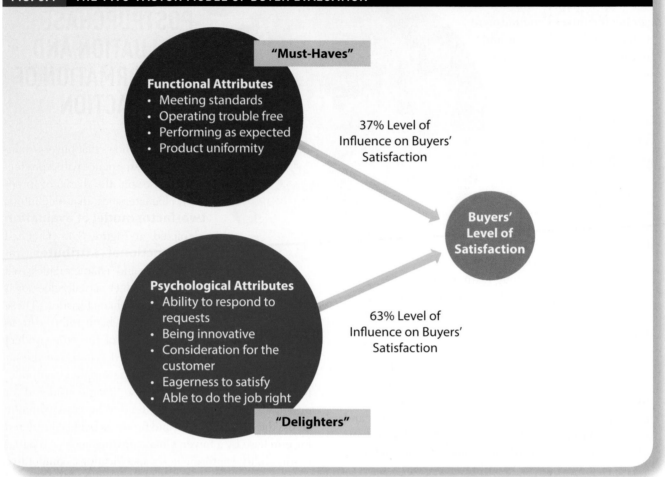

"Must-Haves"

Functional Attributes
- Meeting standards
- Operating trouble free
- Performing as expected
- Product uniformity

37% Level of Influence on Buyers' Satisfaction

Buyers' Level of Satisfaction

Psychological Attributes
- Ability to respond to requests
- Being innovative
- Consideration for the customer
- Eagerness to satisfy
- Able to do the job right

63% Level of Influence on Buyers' Satisfaction

"Delighters"

Buyers evaluate functional attributes and psychological attributes of a sales offering to assess overall performance and satisfaction.

not perceived as being universal features across the evoked set of suppliers and market offerings being considered. Rather, these are the differentiators between the competitors. The competence, attitudes, and behaviors of supplier personnel with whom the buyer has contact, as well as the salesperson's trustworthiness, consideration for the customer, responsiveness, ability to recover when there is a problem, and innovativeness in providing solutions are exemplary psychological attributes.

3-6a The Growing Importance of Salespeople in Buyers' Postpurchase Evaluations

Understanding the differential impact of functional (*must-haves*) and psychological (*delighters*) attributes is important for salespeople. Functional attributes possess a close correspondence to the technical and more tangible product attributes, whereas the psychological attributes are similar to the interpersonal communication and behaviors of salespeople and other personnel having contact with customers. Numerous research studies across a variety of industries evidence psychological attributes as having up to two times more influence on buyer satisfaction and loyalty than functional attributes. This observation underscores special implications for salespeople, as it is their interpersonal communication and behaviors—what they do—that make up the psychological attributes. Although both categories of product characteristics are important and have significant influences on buyer satisfaction, the activities and behaviors of the salesperson as she or he interacts with the buyer have more impact on that buyer's evaluation than the features of the product or service itself.[8]

3-7 TYPES OF PURCHASING DECISIONS

Buyers are learners in that purchase decisions are not isolated behaviors. Buyer behavior and purchase decisions are based on the relevant knowledge that buyers have accumulated from multiple sources to assist them in making the proper choice. Internally, buyers reflect on past experiences as guides for making purchase decisions. When sufficient knowledge from past experiences is not available, buyers access external sources of information: secondary sources of information (e.g., trade journals, product test reports, white papers advertising) and other individuals e.g., salespeople, the buyer perceives as being trustworthy and knowledgeable in a given area.

The level of experience and knowledge a buyer or buying organization possesses relevant to a given purchasing decision is a primary determinant of the time and resources the buyer will allocate to that purchasing decision. The level of a buyer's existing experience and knowledge has been used to categorize buyer behavior into three types of purchasing decisions: straight rebuys, modified rebuys, and new tasks. As summarized in Exhibit 3.6, selling strategies should reflect the differences in buyer behaviors and decision-making characteristic of each type of buying decision.

3-7a Straight Rebuys

If past experiences with a product resulted in high levels of satisfaction, buyers tend to purchase the same product from the same sources. Comparable with a routine repurchase in which nothing has changed, the **straight rebuy decision** is often the result of a long-term purchase agreement. Needs have been predetermined with the corresponding specifications, pricing, and shipping requirements already established by a blanket purchase order or an annual purchase agreement. Ordering is automatic and often computerized by using **electronic data interchange (EDI)** and e-commerce (Internet, intranet, and extranet). Mitsubishi Motor Manufacturing of America uses a large number of straight rebuy decisions in its acquisition of component parts. Beginning as a primary supplier of automotive glass components, Vuteq developed a strong relationship with Mitsubishi Motor Manufacturing of America over a period of several years. As a result, Vuteq's business steadily increased and now includes door trims, fuel tanks, and mirrors in addition to window glass. These components are purchased as straight rebuys by using

> **straight rebuy decision**
> A purchase decision resulting from an ongoing purchasing relationship with a supplier.
>
> **electronic data interchange (EDI)** Transfer of data electronically between two computer systems.

Exhibit 3.6
Three Types of Buying Decisions

	Decision Type		
	Straight Rebuy	Modified Rebuy	New Task
Newness of problem or need	Low	Medium	High
Information requirements	Minimal	Moderate	Maximum
Information search	Minimal	Limited	Extensive
Consideration of new alternatives	None	Limited	Extensive
Multiple buying influences	Very small	Moderate	Large
Financial risk	Low	Moderate	High

FIG. 3.5   CONTINUUM OF TYPES OF BUYING DECISIONS

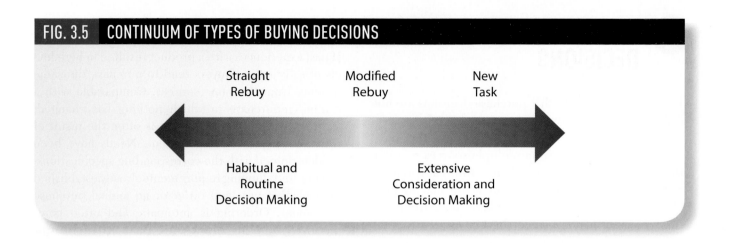

EDI, allowing Vuteq to deliver these components to Mitsubishi on a minute-to-minute basis, matching on-going production.

Although no buying decision begins as a straight re-buy, once established buyers allocate little, if any, time and resources to this form of purchase decision. The primary emphasis is on receipt of the products and their continued satisfactory performance. With most of the purchasing process automated, straight rebuy decisions are little more than record keeping that clerical staff in the purchasing office often handles.

For the in-supplier (a current supplier), straight rebuys offer the advantage of reduced levels of potential competition. Rather than becoming complacent, however, in-salespeople must continually monitor the competitive environment for advances in product capabilities or changes in price structures. They should also follow up on deliveries and interact with users as well as decision makers to make sure that product and performance continue to receive strong and positive evaluations.

Straight rebuy decisions present a major challenge to the out-salesperson. Buyers are satisfied with the products and services from current suppliers and see no need to change. This is a classic case where the buyer perceives no difference or needs gap between the actual and desired state. Consequently, there is no active buying motive to which the out-salesperson can respond. In this case, out-salespeople are typically presented with two strategy choices. First, they can continue to make contact with the buyer so that when there is a change in the buying situation or if the current supplier makes a mistake, they are there to respond. Second, they can provide information and evidence relevant to either the desired or actual states so that the buyer will perceive a needs gap. For example, Vuteq's competitors will find it most difficult to gain this portion of Mitsubishi's business by offering similar or equal products and systems. However, a competitor might adopt future advances in technology that would enable them to offer significant added value over and beyond that which Vuteq offers. Effectively communicating and demonstrating their advanced capabilities holds the potential for raising the desired state and thus producing a needs gap favoring their solution over Vuteq's existing sales offering.

3-7b New Tasks

The purchase decision characterized as a **new task decision** occurs when the buyer is purchasing a product or service for the first time. As illustrated in Figure 3.5, new task purchase decisions are located at the opposite end of the continuum from the straight rebuy and typify situations in which buyers have no experience or knowledge on which to rely. Consequently, they undertake an extensive purchase decision and search for information designed to identify and compare alternative solutions. Reflecting the extensive nature of this type of purchase decision, multiple members of the buying team are usually involved. As a result, the salesperson will be working with several different individuals rather than a single buyer. Mitsubishi buyers and suppliers were presented with new task decisions when the new Mitsubishi four-wheel-drive sport utility vehicle was moving from design to production. Moving from their historical two-wheel-drive to four-wheel-drive power lines and transmissions presented a variety of new needs and problems.

Relevant to a new task purchasing decision, there is no in- or out-supplier. Further, the buyer is aware

new task decision A purchase decision that occurs when a buyer is purchasing a product or service for the first time.

of the existing needs gap. With no prior experience in dealing with this particular need, buyers are often eager for information and expertise that will assist them in effectively resolving the perceived needs gap. Selling strategies for new task decisions should include collaborating with the buyer in a number of ways. First, the salesperson can provide expertise in fully developing and understanding the need. The salesperson's extensive experience and base of knowledge is also valuable to the buyer in terms of specifying and evaluating potential solutions. Finally, top salespeople will assist the buyer in making a purchase decision and provide extensive follow-up to ensure long-term satisfaction. By implementing this type of a consultative strategy, the salesperson establishes a relationship with the buyer and gains considerable competitive advantage.

© Val Dodge

Sea World worked with St. Charles based Craftsmen Industries to develop a pod of six Shamu cruisers to meet its new task decision on a means for conducting a special Shamu promotion.

3-7c Modified Rebuys

Modified rebuy decisions occupy a middle position on the continuum between straight rebuys and new tasks. In these cases, the buyer has experience in purchasing the product in the past but is interested in acquiring additional information regarding alternative products and/or

Mitsubishi uses a mix of company trainers, community colleges and universities to provide education and training to its employees.

Vytautas Kielaitis/Shutterstock.com

suppliers. As there is more familiarity with the decision, there is less uncertainty and perceived risk than for new task decisions. The modified rebuy typically occurs as the result of changing conditions or needs. Perhaps the buyer wishes to consider new suppliers for current purchase needs or new products that existing suppliers offer. Continuing the example of buyer-seller experiences at Mitsubishi, the company's decision to reexamine their methods and sources for training and education corresponds to the characteristics of a modified rebuy decision. Since its beginning, Mitsubishi Motor Manufacturing of America has used a mix of company trainers, community colleges, and universities to provide education and training to employees. Desiring more coordination across its training programs, the company requested proposals for the development and continued management of a corporate university from a variety of suppliers, including several current as well as new sources.

Often a buyer enters into a modified rebuy type of purchase decision simply to check the competitiveness of existing suppliers in terms of the product offering and pricing levels. Consequently, in-salespeople will emphasize how well their product has performed in resolving the needs gap. Out-salespeople will use strategies similar to those undertaken in the straight rebuy. These strategies are designed to alter the relative positions of the desired and actual states in a way that creates a perceived gap and influences buyers to rethink and reevaluate their current buying patterns and suppliers.

3-8 UNDERSTANDING COMMUNICATION STYLES

Verbal and nonverbal messages can also provide salespeople with important cues regarding buyers' personalities and communication styles. Experienced salespeople emphasize the importance of reading and responding to customer communication styles. Effectively sensing and interpreting customers' communication

modified rebuy decision
A purchase decision that occurs when a buyer has experience in purchasing a product in the past but is interested in acquiring additional information regarding alternative products and/or suppliers.

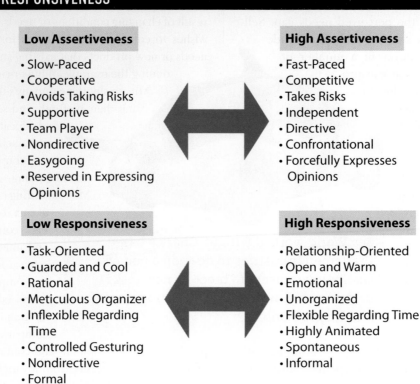

Low Assertiveness
- Slow-Paced
- Cooperative
- Avoids Taking Risks
- Supportive
- Team Player
- Nondirective
- Easygoing
- Reserved in Expressing Opinions

High Assertiveness
- Fast-Paced
- Competitive
- Takes Risks
- Independent
- Directive
- Confrontational
- Forcefully Expresses Opinions

Low Responsiveness
- Task-Oriented
- Guarded and Cool
- Rational
- Meticulous Organizer
- Inflexible Regarding Time
- Controlled Gesturing
- Nondirective
- Formal

High Responsiveness
- Relationship-Oriented
- Open and Warm
- Emotional
- Unorganized
- Flexible Regarding Time
- Highly Animated
- Spontaneous
- Informal

Most sales training programs use a two-by-two matrix as a basis for categorizing communication styles into four primary types. The four styles are based on two dimensions: assertiveness and responsiveness.

styles allows salespeople to adapt their own interaction behaviors in a way that facilitates buyer-seller communication and enhances relationship formation. Most sales training programs use a two-by-two matrix as a basis for categorizing communication styles into four primary types.[9] As Figure 3.6 illustrates, the four styles are based on two determinant dimensions: assertiveness and responsiveness.

Assertiveness—**Assertiveness** refers to the degree to which a person holds opinions about issues and attempts to dominate or control situations by directing the thoughts and actions of others. Highly assertive individuals tend to be fast-paced, opinionated, and quick to speak out and take confrontational positions. Low-assertive individuals tend to exhibit a slower pace. They typically hold back, let others take charge, and are slow and deliberate in their communication and actions.

Responsiveness—**Responsiveness** points to the level of feelings and sociability an individual openly displays. Highly responsive individuals are relationship-oriented and openly emotional. They readily express their feelings and tend to be personable, friendly, and informal. However, low-responsive individuals tend to be task-oriented and very controlled in their display of emotions. They tend to be impersonal in dealing with others, with an emphasis on formality and self-discipline.

> Verbal and nonverbal messages can provide salespeople with important cues regarding buyers' personalities and communication styles.

assertiveness The degree to which a person holds opinions about issues and attempts to dominate or control situations by directing the thoughts and actions of others.

responsiveness The level of feelings and sociability an individual openly displays.

FIG. 3.7 COMMUNICATION STYLES MATRIX

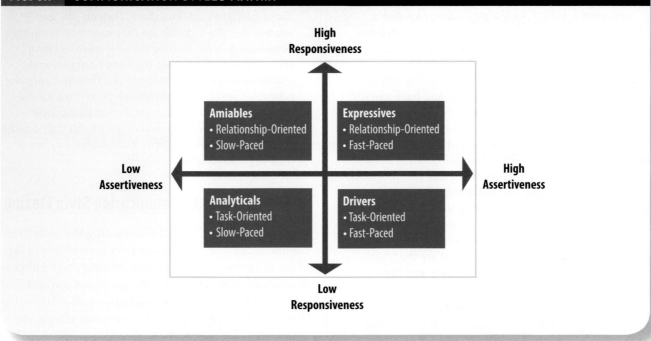

The four quadrants characterize an individual as one of four different communication styles on the basis of his or her demonstrated levels of assertiveness and responsiveness. A salesperson's skill in properly classifying customers can provide valuable cues regarding customer attitudes and behaviors.

The actual levels of assertiveness and responsiveness will vary from one individual to another on a continuum ranging from high to low. An individual may be located anywhere along the particular continuum, and where the individual is located determines the degree to which he or she possesses and demonstrates the particular behaviors associated with that dimension. The following figure illustrates the range of behaviors commonly associated with each dimension.

Overlaying the assertiveness and responsiveness dimensions produces a four-quadrant matrix as illustrated in Figure 3.7. The four quadrants characterize an individual as exhibiting one of four different communication styles on the basis of his or her demonstrated levels of assertiveness and responsiveness. *Amiables* are high on responsiveness but low on assertiveness. *Expressives* are defined as high on both responsiveness and assertiveness. *Drivers* are low on responsiveness but high on assertiveness. *Analyticals* are characterized as being low on assertiveness as well as responsiveness. A salesperson's skill in properly classifying customers can provide valuable cues regarding customer attitudes and behaviors. In turn, these cues allow the salesperson to be more effective by adapting his or her communication and responses to better fit the customer's style.

Amiables—Developing and maintaining close personal relationships are important to **amiables**. Easygoing and cooperative, they are often characterized as friendly back-slappers due to their preference for belonging to groups and their sincere interest in other people—their hobbies, interests, families, and mutual friends. With a natural propensity for talking and socializing, they have little or no desire to control others but rather prefer building consensus. Amiables are not risk takers and need to feel safe in making a decision. Somewhat undisciplined with regard to time, amiables appear to be slow and deliberate in their actions. They avoid conflict and tend to be more concerned with opinions—what others think—than with details and facts. When confronted or attacked, amiables tend to submit. In working with an amiable customer, salespeople should remember that their priority "must-have" is to be liked and their fundamental "want" is for attention.

Expressives—**Expressives** are animated and highly communicative. Although very

amiables Individuals who are high on responsiveness, low on assertiveness, prefer to belong to groups, and are interested in others.

expressives Individuals who are high on both responsiveness and assertiveness, are animated, communicative and value building close relationships with others.

competitive by nature, they also exhibit warm personalities and value building close relationships with others. In fact, they dislike being alone and readily seek out others. Expressives are extroverted and are highly uninhibited in their communication. When confronted or crossed, they will attack. Enthusiastic and stimulating, they seem to talk in terms of people rather than things and have a ready opinion on everything. Yet, they remain open-minded and changeable. Expressives are fast paced in their decision making and behavior and prefer the big picture rather than getting bogged down in details. As a result, they are very spontaneous, unconcerned with time schedules, and not especially organized in their daily lives. They are creative, comfortable operating on intuition, and demonstrate a willingness to take risks. The two keys for expressives that salespeople must keep in mind are the "must-have" of never being hurt emotionally and their underlying "want" is attention.

Drivers—Sometimes referred to as the director or dictator style, **drivers** are hard and detached from their relationships with others. Described as being cool, tough, and competitive in their relationships, drivers are independent and willing to run over others to get their preferred results. As they seek out and openly demonstrate power and control over people and situations, they are difficult to get close to and appear to treat people as things. Drivers are extremely formal, businesslike, and impatient, with a penchant for time and organization. They are highly opinionated, impatient, and quick to share those opinions with those around them. When attacked or confronted, drivers will dictate. Drivers exhibit a low tolerance for taking advice, tend to be risk takers, and favor making their own decisions. Although they are highly task-oriented, drivers prefer to ignore facts and figures and instead rely on their own gut feelings in making decisions—after all, they do know it all. When working with drivers, salespeople should remember that this style's "must-have" is winning, and their fundamental "want" is results.

Analyticals—The descriptive name for this style is derived from their penchant for gathering and analyzing facts and details before making a decision. **Analyticals** are meticulous and disciplined in everything they do. Logical and very controlled, they are systematic problem solvers and thus very deliberate and slower in pace. In stressful situations and confrontations, analyticals tend to withdraw. Many times, they appear to be nit-picky about everything around them. They do not readily express their feelings nor are they spontaneous in their behaviors. As a result, they are often seen as being cool and aloof. Analyticals shy away from personal relationships and avoid taking risks. Time and personal schedules are close to being a religious ritual for the analytical. The two fundamentals that salespeople must keep in mind when working with this style are the "must-have" of being right and the underlying "want" for analytical activities.

3-8a Mastering Communication Style Flexing

In addition to sensing and interpreting the customer's communication style, a salesperson must also be aware of his or her own personal style. Mismatched and possibly clashing styles can be dysfunctional and present significant barriers to communication and relationship building. To minimize possible negative effects stemming from mismatched styles, salespeople can flex their own style to facilitate effective communication. For example, an expressive salesperson calling on an analytical buyer would find considerable differences in both pace and relationship/task-orientation that could hinder the selling process unless adjustments are made. Flexing his or her own style to better match that of the buyer enhances communication. In terms of our example, the salesperson would need to make adjustments by slowing down his or her natural pace, reining in the level of spontaneity and animation, and increasing task orientation by offering more detailed information and analysis.

Adapting to buyers by flexing his or her own communication style has been found to have a positive impact on salespeople's performance and the quality of buyer-seller relationships. Nevertheless, flexing should not be interpreted as meaning an exact match between a salesperson's style and that of a customer. Not only is it not required, exact matches could even be detrimental. For example, a buyer and seller with matching expressive styles could easily discover that the entire sales call regressed to little more than a personal discussion with nothing of substance being accomplished. However, a buyer and seller matched as drivers could find it difficult, if not impossible, to reach a decision that was mutually beneficial. Rather than matching the buyer's style, flexing infers that the salesperson should adjust to the needs and preferences of the buyer to maximize effectiveness. Growmark, an international agricultural product and service organization, teaches

drivers Individuals who are low on responsiveness, high on assertiveness and detached from relationships.

analyticals Individuals who are low on responsiveness and assertiveness, analytical and meticulous, and disciplined in everything they do.

its salespeople to flex throughout their interaction with a buyer by studying different behaviors a salesperson might demonstrate with each style of buyer. (See Appendix 3 online.)[10]

Study and compare the flexing behaviors that Growmark recommends that their salespeople demonstrate when working with each buyer communication style. Note the differences in recommended salesperson behavior and rationalize them in terms of the specific characteristics of each buyer's style. Overlaying and integrating these two sets of information will enhance the understanding of how to flex to different buyers and why that form of flexing is recommended.

It is not always possible to gain much information about a buyer's communication style, especially if the buyer is new. If this is the case, it may be more appropriate to assume that the buyer is an analytical-driver and prepare for this style. If the buyer proves to be close to an amiable-expressive, then the salesperson can easily adapt. It is much more difficult to prepare for the amiable-expressive and then switch to an analytical-driver style.

 ## 3-9 BUYING TEAMS

A single individual typically makes routine purchase decisions such as straight rebuys and simpler modified rebuys. However, the more complex modified rebuy and new task purchase decisions often involve the joint decisions of multiple participants within a buying center or team. **Buying teams** (also referred to as buying centers) incorporate the expertise and multiple buying influences of people from different departments throughout the organization. At Xerox, for example, there are on average four customer employees involved in every Xerox sale.[11] As the object of the purchase decision changes, the makeup of the buying team may also change to maximize the relevant expertise of team members. The organization's size, as well as the nature and volume of the products being purchased, will influence the actual number and makeup of buying teams. The different members of a buying team will often have varied goals reflecting their individual needs and those of their different departments.

Buying team members are described in terms of their roles and responsibilities within the team.[12]

- *Initiators*—**Initiators** are individuals within the organization who identify a need or perhaps realize that the acquisition of a product might solve a need or problem.

- *Influencers*—Individuals who guide the decision process by making recommendations and expressing preferences are referred to as **influencers**. While they could be anyone, they are often technical or engineering personnel.

- *Users*—**Users** are the individuals within the organization who will actually use the product being purchased. They evaluate a product on the basis of how it will affect their own job performance. Users often serve as initiators and influencers.

- *Deciders*—The ultimate responsibility for determining which product or service will be purchased rests with the role of **deciders**. Although buyers might also be deciders, it is not unusual for different people to fill these roles.

- *Purchasers*—**Purchasers** have the responsibility for negotiating final terms of purchase with suppliers and executing the actual purchase or acquisition.

Complex buying decisions incorporate buying influences of people from different departments of an organization.

Dotshock/Shutterstock.com

buying teams Teams of individuals in organizations that incorporate the expertise and multiple buying influences of people from different departments throughout the organization.

initiators Individuals within an organization who identify a need.

influencers Individuals within an organization who guide the decision process by making recommendations and expressing preferences.

users Individuals within an organization who will actually use the product being purchased.

deciders Individuals within an organization who have the ultimate responsibility of determining which product or service will be purchased.

purchasers Organizational members who negotiate final terms of the purchase and execute the actual purchase.

- *Gatekeepers*—Members who are in the position to control the flow of information to and between vendors and other buying center members are referred to as **gatekeepers**. This often includes secretaries and administrative assistants.

Although each of these influencer types will not necessarily be present on all buying teams, the use of buying teams incorporating some or all of these multiple influences has increased in recent years. One example of multiple buying influences is offered in the experience of an Executive Jet International salesperson selling a Gulfstream V corporate jet to a Chicago-based pharmaceutical company. Stretching over a period of six months, the salesperson worked with a variety of individuals serving different roles within the buying organization:

- *Initiator:* The initiator of the purchase process was the chief operating officer of the corporation who found that the recent corporate expansions had outgrown the effective service range of the organization's existing aircraft. Beyond pointing out the need and thus initiating the search, this individual would also be highly involved in the final choice based on her personal experiences and perceived needs of the company.

- *Influencers:* Two different employee groups acted as the primary influencers. First were the corporate pilots who contributed a readily available and extensive background of knowledge and experience with a variety of aircraft types. Also playing a key influencer role were members from the capital budgeting group in the finance department. Although concerned with documented performance capabilities, they also provided inputs and assessments of the different alternatives using their capital investment models.

- *Users:* The users provided some of the most dynamic inputs, as they were anxious to make the transition to a higher performance aircraft to enhance their own efficiency and performance in working at marketing/sales offices and plants that now stretched over the continents of North and South America. Primary players in this group included the vice presidents for marketing and for production/operations in addition to the corporate pilots who would be flying the plane.

- *Deciders:* Based on the contribution and inputs of each member of the buying team, the chief executive officer would make the ultimate decision. Her role as decider was based more on her position within the firm rather than her use of the chosen alternative, given that she traveled

primarily by commercial carriers. As the organization's highest operating officer, she was in a position to move freely among all members of the buying team and make the decision on overall merits rather than personal feelings or desires.

- *Purchaser:* The corporate purchasing department was responsible for making the actual purchase, negotiating the final terms, and completing all the required paperwork, with the director of purchasing actually assuming the immediate contact role. The purchasing office typically handles purchasing contracts and is staffed to draw up, complete, and file the related registrations and legal documents.

- *Gatekeepers:* This purchase decision actually involved two different gatekeepers within the customer organization: the executive assistant to the chief operating officer and an assistant purchasing officer. The positioning of these gatekeepers facilitated the salesperson's exchange of information and ability to keep in contact with the various members of the buying team. The COO's executive assistant moved easily among the various executives influencing the decision and was able to make appointments with the right people at the right times. However, the assistant purchasing officer was directly involved with the coordination of each member and bringing their various inputs into one summary document for the CEO. The salesperson's positive dealings and good relationships with each of the gatekeepers played a significant role in Executive Jet getting the sale.

A classic and all-too-common mistake among salespeople is to make repetitive calls on a purchasing manager over a period of several months only to discover that a buying team actually exists and that someone other than the purchasing manager will make the ultimate decision. Salespeople must gather information to discover who is in the buying team, their individual roles, and which members are the most influential. This information might be collected from account history files, people inside the salesperson's organization who are familiar with the account sources within the client organization, conversations with the initial buyer contact, and even other salespeople. A salesperson should work with all members of the buying team and be careful to address their varied needs and objectives properly. Nevertheless, circumstances sometimes prevent a salesperson from working with all members of the team, and it is important that the salesperson reaches those that are most influential.

It may be difficult, however, to get past the gatekeeper to reach those individuals most influential in the buying process. Brett Eiskina, Corporate Acquisition

gatekeepers Members of an organization who are in the position to control the flow of information to and between vendors and other buying center members.

Account Executive at Sprint Nextel, has found that using social media allows him to bypass the gatekeeper and go directly to decision makers. As Brett explains, "In the past, effective gatekeepers have been a salesperson's worst nightmare. There is nothing worse than repeatedly calling on a client only to learn that they are always "In a meeting" or "Out of the office" EVERY time you call. Well, with the growing number of people using social media, it is becoming increasingly easier for salespeople to skip those gatekeepers and go straight to those decision makers. I have found LinkedIn to be particularly valuable. It gives me information and insight to buyers (e.g., college, field of study, groups they belong to, etc.) that I would never have known before contacting them. I've set many appointments simply by mentioning that I was an alum of the same college as the person I was trying to reach out to. LinkedIn will also show you if you have any mutual connections that you can query for information before reaching out for the appointment. Don't just stick to LinkedIn though; Hoovers, Data.com, Twitter and even Facebook are all very powerful tools that can help you get an edge over the other salespeople reaching out to the same decision maker."

 ## 3-10 ENGAGING CUSTOMERS

Today's business organizations are undergoing profound change in response to ever-increasing competition and rapid changes in the business environment. The worldwide spread of technology has resulted in intense and increasingly global competition that is highly dynamic in nature. Accelerating rates of change have fragmented what were once mass markets into more micro and niche markets composed of more knowledgeable and demanding customers with escalating expectations. In response, traditional purchasing practices are also rapidly changing to ensure that customers are fully engaged.

3-10a Focusing on the Customer Experience

A study of customer experience professionals from large multinational B-to-B organizations representing an array of industries provides insight on what the business customer experience will look like moving forward.[13] According to the study, customers will expect companies to have a clear understanding of their needs and to proactively address their current and future needs with a personalized customer experience. Accessing the internet to get the most current information on products, solutions and best practices, customers will have a more informed base of understanding and will expect an equally informed salesperson. Consequently, salespeople must move beyond providing solutions to current needs and move toward "insight selling" by anticipating and fulfilling customer needs necessary for them to adeptly face the future. Salespeople must have access to customer intelligence and emphasize proactive and personalized customer support. According to the survey, 62% of respondents indicated that they are investing in understanding individual customer characteristics to better meet the changing needs of customers. To keep customers, salespeople will be required to anticipate needs along the stages of the customer lifecycle and proactively respond. This will entail the use of big data to generate customer intelligence that can be used to provide a comprehensive view of the customer. Customers will expect sellers to keep them informed by interacting with them using the buyer's preferred method of communication. Exhibit 3.7 indicates communication channels most likely to be used often by business customers in 2020.[14]

3-10b The Role of Information Technology

Buyers and sellers alike are using technology to enhance the effectiveness and efficiency of the purchasing process. Business-to-business e-commerce is rapidly growing. Although EDI over private networks has been in use for some time, nearly all the current growth has been in Internet-based transactions.

Information technology electronically links buyers and sellers for direct and immediate communication and transmission of information and data. Transactional exchanges such as straight rebuy decisions can now be automated with Internet- and World Wide Web-enabled programs tracking sales at the point of purchase and capturing the data for real-time inventory control and order placing. By cutting order and shipping times, overall cycle times are reduced, mistakes are minimized, and working capital invested in inventories is made available for more productive applications. Further, the automation of these routine transactions allows buyers and salespeople to devote more time to new tasks, complex sales, and postsale service and relationship-building activities.

Customer relationship management (CRM) systems integrated with the Web allow reps to have a more informed conversation with prospects and customers by helping them better understand customers. Sales

Exhibit 3.7

Communication Channels Likely to Be Used Often in 2020

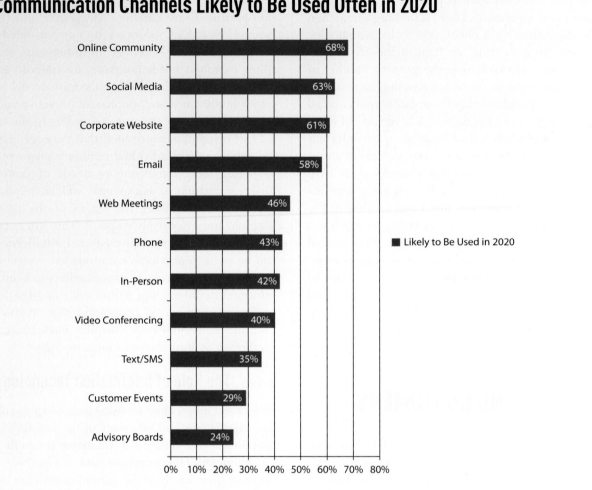

organizations know keywords searched to find the seller's company, pages clicked on the company's Web site, and particular products and services buyers examined prior to asking for more information. Additionally, data collected on customer demographics, sales and customer service histories, and marketing preferences and customer feedback can be easily accumulated through a CRM system and used to better understand customers and provide customized offerings to best serve their needs. Celanese Corporation, a leading chemicals manufacturer, credits its CRM system with allowing sales dialogue to advance based on the premise that the customer has a specific need it can fulfill.[15] Social networking technologies are likely to play an important role in CRM systems, making it more convenient for customers to provide information that goes into product planning and development, as well as provide deeper insights into customer buying motives.

For instance, Microsoft offers its Sales Productivity CRM software that incorporates Outlook, Lync, Skype and Yammer to allow for social collaboration between buyers and sellers. For an example of how Dell goes beyond CRM with predictive analytics, see "Technology in Selling: Deeper Customer Insight at Dell"[16].

In addition to facilitating exchange transactions, applications integrating the Internet are also being used to distribute product and company information along with training courses and materials. Several companies have begun publishing their product catalogs online as a replacement for the reams of product brochures salespeople have traditionally had to carry with them. The online catalogs can be easily updated without the expense of obsolete brochures and can be selectively downloaded by salespeople to create customized presentations and proposals.

Technology in Selling

Deeper Customer Insight at Dell

Although Dell already used CRM technology, in order to better understand customers and improve salesforce productivity, Dell turned to Lattice Engines, a company that specializes in predictive analytics. Lattice software determines purchasing patterns of Dell business customers and then searches Web and customer information for prospects that match those patterns. The Lattice software looks for buying triggers and behaviors and converts them into mathematical algorithms that can predict the likelihood that a potential customer will buy a certain product. If, for instance, companies who sign an office lease typically purchase Dell small-business products, the software could ascertain information about new office leases, LinkedIn announcements, website information, and other public statements or sources of information to identify likely prospects. The application also uses information from social networks such as LinkedIn to provide a more comprehensive customer profile for salespeople, enabling reps to better understand customers and prospects more quickly. Using this software, Dell sales reps are provided with comprehensive intelligence (e.g., past purchases, corporate activity, likely next purchase from Dell) that allows them to participate in relevant and timely discussions with prospects and customers.

3-10c Buyers' Demand for Access to Relevant Information

With ever-expanding information technology, buyers have easier access to information on vendors and are utilizing technology to become more informed buyers. This has shifted some of the power to buyers, who can accompany more bidders, making the landscape even more competitive. As buyers increasingly undertake a larger share of the purchase process on their own, they are demanding that sellers make available to them relevant content to help them justify their buying decisions. In a survey of how customers choose, approximately two-thirds of respondents indicated that they do their own research rather than waiting for salespeople to contact them.[17] As such, buyers are demanding that information be made available to them via their laptops, desktops, iPads, and smartphones as they seek out more and more information prior to connecting with a salesperson. These buyers are looking for personalized dialogue that can help guide them through the decision process. For instance, content aimed at an economic buyer might include a return-on-investment (ROI) calculator. To help the analytical buyer understand the company's novel approach to solving a problem, a case study might prove valuable.[18]

Blogs, white papers, webinars, videos, recorded interviews, product demos, and presentations—providing anything from expert analysis and advice, to product announcements, should be offered to targeted customers through media such as a company Web site, Twitter stream, or LinkedIn discussion group.[19] Logicalis, an integrated information and communication technologies provider, tries to gain attention as a thought leader by helping buyers understand cutting-edge IT topics by posting informative content on its own Web site and having a presence on Facebook and LinkedIn. Citrix Systems, a provider of virtualization and cloud-computing technologies, is using blogs to provide information to those searching for

Vika-Mika/Shutterstock.com

Selling in Action

How to Become Invaluable to Your Customers

Adrian Davis, author, certified speaking professional and expert in strategic selling and account management discusses three steps to collaborative value creation:

"Sales teams are taught that value begins with their product. First, they learn the product, then they learn its critical features, and then they learn the benefits of these features to their customers. Product, features, benefits — in that order. This is completely wrong and it is rooted in an Industrial Age framework. In the Industrial Age, manufacturers used "value-added" processes to add value to raw materials and create finished products. In other words, they defined value. In this post-Industrial Age, vendors do not create value. I'll repeat that in case you read over it. Vendors do not create value!

Value is defined and created by customers. Therefore, your approach to value creation must begin with, and be in partnership with, and end with the customer. Follow these three steps for a sound approach to selling value:

1. Start with the customer
   Rather than start with your product, start with the customer's strategy and processes. In order to create value, you must

understand where the customer is going, how they are trying to get there, and what is getting in their way.

2. Collaborate with the customer
   Work out how your capabilities (product or services) can be applied to their processes in order to address external pressures, internal obstacles and/or emerging opportunities for growth.

3. Work with your customer
   Over the long term, ensure that your customers are actually deriving value from the use of your products and services. As much as possible, aim to quantify this value to be sure that both you and your customer understand the economic impact of your intervention.

By taking this rigorous approach to collaborative value creation, you will separate yourself from the hordes of vendors that are stuck in The Product-Push TrapTM. You will be able to, very quickly, identify those customers with a real need for your product or service. It is these customers that will work with you as a partner because they quickly recognize that partnering with you creates value for them. As you create value for them, you'll create demand for your solutions."

---

trends in cloud computing and virtualization, while Link-Ware, a developer of electronic forms, posts relevant information on community sites that prospective customers visit.[20] The more streamlined and personalized the information, the better, as buyers increasingly face information overload. Overwhelmingly, buyers are looking for information that proves how the seller's product will result in savings, enhance productivity, and positively affect profitability.

3-10d The Need for Adding Value

The increased interdependence between buyer and seller organizations hinges on the salesperson's capabilities to serve as a problem solver in a dynamic and fast-changing business environment. According to a study of 80,000 business customers, buyers expect several things from salespeople.[21] For one, they expect salespeople to personally manage their businesss. In fact, many buying organizations **outsource** to a supplier certain activities that the buying organization previously performed. These activities are necessary for the day-to-day functioning of the buying organization but are not within the organization's core or distinct possibilities. Moreover, buyers depend on the salesperson to provide unique and value-added solutions to their changing problems and needs. To shape such innovative solutions, salespeople must have broad-based and comprehensive knowledge readily available and the ability to use that knowledge in creative ways. This includes knowledge of one's own products and capabilities, as well as the products and capabilities of competitors. More important, the salesperson must possess a thorough understanding of product applications and the needs of the customer to work with the buyer in generating innovative solutions. Finally, buyers expect salespeople to be easily accessible in order to respond to ongoing concerns and solve problems that may arise after the sale. By fulfilling these expectations, salespeople can add value to the customer buying experience and more fully engage the buyer. For more information on how to grow customer relationships through customer value creation, see "Selling in Action: How to Become Invaluable to Your Customers."[22]

> **outsourcing** The process of giving to a supplier certain activities that were previously performed by the buying organization.

STUDY TOOLS 3

LOCATED IN TEXTBOOK

☐ Rip-out and review chapter review card

LOCATED AT WWW.CENGAGEBRAIN.COM

☐ Review key term flashcards and create your own from StudyBits

☐ Organize notes and StudyBits using the StudyBoard feature within 4LTR Press Online

☐ Complete practice and graded quizzes to prepare for tests

☐ Complete interactive content within the narrative portion of 4LTR Press Online

☐ View chapter highlight box content at the beginning of each chapter

SELLING FOR RELATIONSHIPSFIRST, INC.: UNDERSTANDING COMMUNICATION STYLE, BUYING TEAMS, AND BUYING NEEDS

BACKGROUND

RelationshipsFirst, Inc. is a relatively new entrant in the cloud computing business management software industry, having been in existence for a little over four years. It specializes in providing Web-based customizable customer relationship management software solutions that support an entire company, from accounting to Web capabilities. Its software is constructed around an individual customer record so that accounting, sales, support, shipping, and billing all access identical information for each interaction. The company currently serves a variety of businesses across a number of industries. Customer satisfaction is the company's top priority and it acts with integrity to fulfill this mission. Its technology is easy to learn and easy to use, and its information technology staff is extremely knowledgeable and customer friendly.

The company currently employs more than 75 salespeople who call directly on businesses and organizations throughout the United States. Salespeople are trained to be customer-oriented problem solvers who seek to establish long-term relationships with customers. This approach has allowed RelationshipsFirst to experience steady sales gains since its beginning and it hopes to continue its upward growth trajectory.

CURRENT SITUATION

Dawn, a recent college graduate who just completed the sales rep training program at RelationshipsFirst, is excited about her upcoming meeting with Green Meadows Nursery and Landscape, LLC of Kansas City, Missouri. Privately owned, Green Meadows serves the nursery and landscaping needs of its customers through its two large metro retail locations. Each location has a store manager, and several full-and part-time employees to assist with sales and operations. The company's owner serves as president and they also employ a director of marketing and sales, who among other things oversees a staff of five outside salespeople, a director of operations, a director of information technology (whose primary responsibility is to run the Web side of their business), and a director of accounting and finance. The outside sales force solicits both residential and commercial accounts and in large part is responsible for growing the non-retail business for Green Meadows.

A good friend of Dawn's, Taylor Shift, happens to be neighbors with Stewart Strong, Green Meadows director of marketing and sales. In a recent conversation with Stewart, Taylor mentioned Dawn and how she might be able to help him at Green Meadows. Stewart suggested that Taylor have Dawn give him a call and subsequently Dawn was able to secure a meeting with Stewart Strong the following Tuesday morning.

Dawn was delighted that Taylor provided her with this prospect and was confident that this would help her get off to a fast start at RelationshipsFirst. Dawn has been friends with Taylor since grade school. This is not unusual for Dawn, who has many friends and close relationships, likely because she shows such a sincere interest in others, particularly in their hobbies, interests, family, and mutual friends. She enjoys listening to the opinions of others and seems to get along with most everyone, generally avoiding conflict rather than submitting to others. Dawn credits her ability to communicate well orally (she loves to talk and socialize), get along well with others, and build a consensus, in part, for her landing a position in sales at RelationshipsFirst.

Prior to her meeting with Stewart Strong, Dawn asked Taylor if she could meet her for lunch to find out a little more about Stewart and Green Meadows. When Dawn finally arrived for lunch, late as usual, she wasn't able to learn as much about Green Meadows as she would have liked, but she did learn the following about Stewart. Taylor indicated that Stewart was a good neighbor, but he certainly wasn't a friendly, outgoing relationship builder such as Dawn. In fact, he tended to be rather cool, tough, and competitive when it came to relationships. He liked to be in charge of people and situations and was not willing to let others stand in the way of achieving his goals. Stewart manages his time well, is impatient with others, and tends to be very businesslike. He likes extreme sports and appears to have a penchant for taking risks. According to Taylor, at annual home owners' association meetings, Stewart tends to be the most outspoken individual in attendance. While opinionated, Stewart rarely takes advice from others and prefers to make his own decisions.

Although Dawn believed she still had additional work to do before meeting with Stewart, she was at least glad to know a little bit about the person she would be meeting. The more she knew about her buyer, she surmised, the better she could tailor her offering to meet his needs.

QUESTIONS

1. Based on your understanding of both Dawn and Stewart, how would you characterize the communication style of each?
2. What, if any, preparations and style flexing should Dawn make to better relate to and communicate with Stewart Strong?
3. Who all might be involved in the buying decision for Green Meadows with regard to Dawn's offering? For each, explain why and how.
4. Explain at least two needs that might be met by Green Meadows by purchasing the software offered by RelationshipsFirst.

ROLE PLAY

Situation: Read the case.

Characters: Dawn, sales rep for RelationshipsFirst, Inc.; Stewart Strong, director of marketing and sales, Green Meadows Nursery and Landscape, LLC.

Scene:

Location—Stewart Strong's office at Green Meadows.

Action—Dawn meets with Stewart to find out more about Green Meadows operations and needs to see if she can help them. She is also trying to determine who else might be involved in the buying decision and what influence each might have. She has no plans to make a sale on this call.

SHOES UNLIMITED

BACKGROUND

You are a sales representative for Shoes Unlimited, a manufacturer and marketer of an array of styles of men's and women's casual shoes, located in southern Texas. You are responsible for calling on a variety of accounts throughout the midwestern U.S., many of which are independently owned shoe retailers, often in small cities and towns.

CURRENT SITUATION

You recently scheduled a meeting with Joe Jackson, owner of Fantastic Footwear, an independent retail shoe store located in a small rural community in southeast Missouri. Joe contacted you after finding your company on the Internet. He is in the process of evaluating several suppliers for his soon-to-be-opened shoe store.

Before meeting with Joe, you have decided to prepare a series of questions to ask Joe to identify his situational, functional, social, psychological, and knowledge needs. When meeting with Joe you want to ask him several questions so that you can fully understand his needs and then demonstrate to him how you and your company can best satisfy those needs.

ROLE PLAY

Location: Joe Jackson's office at Fantastic Footwear

Characters: You, Shoes Unlimited sales representative; Joe Jackson, owner of Fantastic Footwear

Action: Using the questions you developed, have a conversation with Joe to assess his five general types of needs (ask at least one to two questions to assess each need).

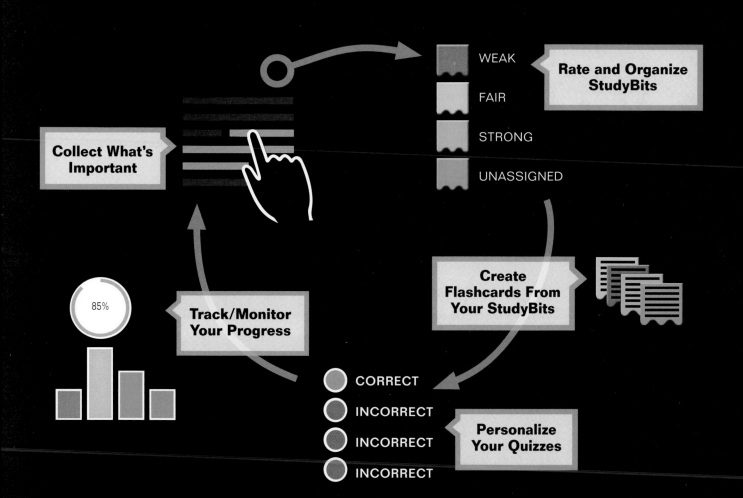

SELL ONLINE

STUDY YOUR WAY WITH STUDYBITS!

WEAK

Rate and Organize StudyBits

FAIR

STRONG

UNASSIGNED

Collect What's Important

Create Flashcards From Your StudyBits

85%

Track/Monitor Your Progress

CORRECT

INCORRECT

INCORRECT

Personalize Your Quizzes

INCORRECT

4LTR PRESS

Access SELL ONLINE at www.cengagebrain.com

4 | Communication Skills

LEARNING OBJECTIVES

After completing this chapter, you should be able to:

4-1 Explain the importance of collaborative, two-way communication in trust-based selling.

4-2 Explain the primary types of questions and how they are applied in selling.

4-3 Illustrate the diverse roles and uses of strategic questioning in trust-based selling.

4-4 Identify and describe the five steps of the ADAPT questioning sequence for effective fact-finding and needs discovery.

4-5 Discuss the four sequential steps for effective active listening.

4-6 Discuss the superiority of pictures over words for explaining concepts and enhancing comprehension.

4-7 Describe and interpret the different forms of nonverbal communication.

After finishing this chapter go to

PAGE 106 for **STUDY TOOLS.**

Pio3/Shutterstock.com

Alex Pirouz, with RIDC Advisory, emphasizes that "rapport in sales is EVERYTHING." Without feeling the respect and trust that comes from rapport between the prospect and salesperson, the rest of the conversation and relationship will have little impact on sales outcome. Yet, Pirouz observes, it is surprising that there are so many salespeople these days trying to sell products without first building the necessary rapport.[1]

Rapport is a special relationship between a prospect and a salesperson that is based on trust and emotional affinity—two individuals being "in sync" or being "on the same wavelength." When this rapport is authentic, it enables the salesperson to connect with the buyer by demonstrating his or her empathy for the buyer's situation, along with an understanding of the buyer's needs.

Pirouz explains that because of the changes the Internet has brought to the buying-selling environment, the days of push and hard-selling are gone. With the widespread availability and use of the Internet, buyers can easily research and compare products and features of competitive offers. Just as the buying-selling environment has changed, so too has the role of the salesperson. The emerging role of the salesperson is

that of a trusted advisor—a role that is fundamentally based on mutual trust, a unique form and high level of trust that only comes about through a sincere and purposeful rapport-building process between the buyer and seller.

At the very heart of the rapport-building process is collaborative conversation: an interactive conversation focused on learning more about the buyer, about the buyer's situation and needs, and demonstrating the salesperson's sincere and empathetic interest in the buyer's well-being. As Pirouz reminds us, "No one likes to be sold—buyers want to feel they have bought" based on the best-value solution and the salesperson should be part of the value proposition. "When talking with prospects and buyers, if all you are thinking about is when you're going to make the next sale, you are guaranteed little success, compared to focusing on serving the client and building rapport. Always

approach your customers with a mind-set of 'what is in it for them', and follow that up by finding out how you can be of service to them, so they feel like they have bought rather than been sold."

The need to build rapport through collaborative communication, illustrated by Alex Pirouz in this chapter's introduction, underscores the critical role of communication for selling success in today's business landscape. On the one hand, selling is basically interpersonal communication. The skill and effectiveness of a salesperson's interpersonal communication are fundamental determinants of selling performance. Nevertheless, effective communication continues to be one of the least understood and understudied skills for successful selling.

This chapter addresses the need to better understand and master the art of collaborative, two-way communication. First, we will examine the basic nature of

From the Classroom to the Field

Employing Technology to Maximize Collaborative Conversations

Upon graduating from Oklahoma City University, Sy Stewart entered the world of professional selling as a distributor for BG Products, with responsibility for selling chemical additives to automobile dealerships across southwest Oklahoma and north Texas. During a recent conversation, Sy explained how he uses technology to better engage buyers in the sales conversation.

"When I started selling, I prepared individualized business planners for each account in the form of a booklet linking my products' features and benefits to clients' needs and ending with a financial analysis detailing their investment, pricing, profits, and even the incentive bonus their mechanics and personnel could receive. Booklets were individualized to the specific dealership, but it was difficult to keep the buyer focused on a specific portion of the booklet. They tended to shuffle through the booklet at their

own pace which limited their engagement and interaction in the sales conversation.

As a solution, I converted the booklets into slide shows using my Microsoft Surface Pro. This allows me to control the sequencing of pages to match the sales conversation. Additionally, I can highlight, circle, and point to specific items to direct the buyer's attention to what is important to them. My spreadsheet-based financial analysis allows me to make changes on the fly as suggested by the buyer. The buyer becomes an active partner in the sales conversation and I can customize the benefits and value to their specific situation. In a competitive industry crowded with channel suppliers vying for each buyer's business, this adaptation of technology sets me apart as a unique provider of added service and value for my customers. As a result it has had a tremendous, positive impact on my sales performance and the loyalty of my customers."

---

trust-based sales communication. Building on this preliminary understanding, the authors have divided the content on trust-based sales communication into its component and subcomponent parts to facilitate study, application, and mastery. The verbal dimension of communication is examined first with an emphasis on three communication subcomponents: (1) developing effective questioning methods for use in uncovering and diagnosing buyers' needs and expectations, (2) using active listening skills to facilitate the interchange of ideas and information, and (3) maximizing the responsive dissemination of information to buyers in a way that fully explains and brings to life the benefits of proposed solutions. Finally, the nonverbal dimension of interpersonal communication is examined with an emphasis on its application and meaningful interpretation.

4-1 SALES COMMUNICATION AS A COLLABORATIVE PROCESS

Neither people nor organizations buy products. Rather, they seek out the satisfaction and benefits that certain product features provide. Although traditional selling has been described as "talking *at* the customer," trust-based

> **trust-based sales communication** Talking *with* rather than *at* the customer. A collaborative and two-way form of communication that allows buyers and sellers to develop a better understanding of the need situation and work together to co-create the best response for resolving the customer's needs.

selling has been referred to as "talking *with* the customer." Trust-based sales communication is a two-way and naturally collaborative interaction that allows buyers and sellers alike to develop a better understanding of the need situation and work together to generate the best response for solving the customer's needs. Although trust-based selling has become the preeminent model for contemporary selling, Sy Stewart's experiences discussed in "From the Classroom to the Field" illustrates that effectively engaging the buyer in collaborative conversations takes some thought and planning.

Trust-based sales communication is the sharing of meaning between buying and selling individuals that results from the interactive process of exchanging information and ideas. It is important to note that the purpose of sales communication is not agreement but rather the maximization of common understanding among participants. With this emphasis on establishing understanding, communication is fundamental throughout each stage of the selling process. Effective communication skills are needed to identify buying needs and to demonstrate to buyers how a salesperson's proposed solution can satisfy those needs better than competitors. The critical capabilities for effective selling include questioning, listening, giving information, nonverbal communication, and written communication skills. Although each of these skills is pervasive in everyday life, they are literally the heart and soul of the interpersonal exchange that characterizes trust-based selling.

4-1a Verbal Communication: Questioning

There are two ways to dominate or control a selling conversation. A salesperson can talk all the time, or the salesperson can maintain a more subtle level of control by asking well-thought-out questions that guide the discussion and engage the customer. Salespeople should think like doctors—they ask relevant questions

Technology in Selling
Business Intelligence Software

Kevin McGirl, President of Sales-I—a leading provider of sales intelligence software, is emphatic that effectively leveraging technology to record, organize, retain, and analyze customer information is a must-have competency for selling success. This access to better information gives a salesperson a clear advantage when it comes to winning new customers and retaining existing ones. Today's second-generation Business Intelligence software and applications for salespeople are highly intuitive and gaining traction in sales and marketing.

Business Intelligence software enables salespeople to have more customer information available when and where they need it. Being able to retrieve all the critical information you could possibly need by typing a name into the search bar enables the salesperson to demonstrate the knowledge and understanding of the client—their situation and needs—so essential in developing and enhancing relationships. The predictive analytics capability of Business Intelligence tools efficiently scours the data from multiple sources to identify correlations leading to the identification of trends and recommendations for specific customers. This level of insight deepens the salesperson's value as a trusted advisor for the customer and outpaces the competition.

Sales-i.com

to methodically diagnose the situation and problems before presenting solutions. To present a cure to a patient before understanding the problem would be malpractice. In a similar fashion, salespeople must be masters at thinking through what they need to know, planning the questions they need to ask, and then asking those diagnostic questions in a sequential manner that builds understanding of the situation for themselves as well as for the customer. They should know exactly what information they require and which type of questions are best suited for eliciting that information from a prospective buyer.

Purposeful, carefully crafted questions can encourage thoughtful responses from a buyer and provide richly detailed information about the buyer's current situation, needs, and expectations. This additional detail and understanding is often as meaningful for the buyer as it is for the salesperson. That is, proper questioning can facilitate both the buyer's and seller's understanding of a problem and its possible solutions. For example, questions can encourage meaningful feedback regarding the buyer's attitude and the logical progression through the purchase decision process. Questioning also shows interest in the buyer and his or her needs and actively involves the buyer in the selling process. Questions can also be used tactically to redirect, regain, or hold the buyer's attention should it begin to wander during the conversation. In a similar fashion, questions can provide a convenient and subtle transition to a different topic of discussion and provide a logical guide promoting sequential thought and decision making.

> Successful salespeople are experts at considering what information they need to know and purposefully planning and asking the questions they need to ask.

Questions are typed by the results they are designed to accomplish. Does the salesperson wish to receive a free flow of thoughts and ideas or a simple yes/no confirmation? Is the salesperson seeking a general description of the overall situation or specific details regarding emergent needs or problematic experiences with current suppliers? To be effective, a salesperson must understand which type of question will best accomplish his or her desired outcome. In this manner, questions can be typed into two basic categories: (1) amount of information and level of specificity desired and (2) strategic purpose or intent.

4-2 TYPES OF QUESTIONS CLASSIFIED BY AMOUNT AND SPECIFICITY OF INFORMATION DESIRED

4-2a Open-End Questions

Open-end questions, also called nondirective questions, are designed to let the customer respond freely. That is, the customer is not limited to one- or two-word answers, but is encouraged to disclose personal and/or business information. Open-end questions encourage buyers' thought processes and deliver richer and more expansive information than closed-end questions. Consequently, these questions are typically used to probe for descriptive information that allows the salesperson to better understand the specific needs and expectations of the customer. The secret to using open-end questions successfully lies in the first word used to form the question. Words often used to begin open-end questions include *what*, *how*, *where*, *when*, *tell*, *describe*, and *why*. Examples of open-end questions include:

- What happens when . . . ?
- How do you feel . . . ?
- "Describe the. . . ."

4-2b Closed-End Questions

Closed-end questions are designed to limit the customers' response to one or two words. This type of question is typically used to confirm or clarify information gleaned from previous responses to open-end questions. Although the most common form is the yes/no question,

open-end questions
Questions designed to let the customer respond freely; the customer is not limited to one- or two-word answers but is encouraged to disclose personal and/or business information.

closed-end questions
Questions designed to limit the customer's responses to one or two words.

closed-end questions come in many forms—provided the response is limited to one or two words. Common closed-end questions include:

- Do you . . . ?
- Are you . . . ?
- How many . . . ?
- How often . . . ?

4-2c Dichotomous/Multiple-Choice Questions

Dichotomous questions and multiple-choice questions are directive forms of questioning. This type of question asks a customer to choose from two or more options and is used in selling to discover customer preferences and move the purchase decision process forward. An example of this form of question would be: "Which do you prefer, the _____ or the _____?"

TYPES OF QUESTIONS CLASSIFIED BY STRATEGIC PURPOSE

4-2d Probing Questions

Probing questions are designed to penetrate below generalized or superficial information to elicit more articulate and precise details for use in needs discovery and solution identification. Rather than interrogating a buyer, probing questions are best used in a conversational style: (1) request clarification ("Can you share with me an example of that?" "How long has this been a problem?"), (2) encourage elaboration ("How are you dealing with that situation now?" "What is your experience with _____?"), and (3) verify information and responses ("That is interesting; could you tell me more?" "So, if I understand correctly, _____. Is that right?").

4-2e Evaluative Questions

Evaluative questions use open- and closed-end questions to confirm and uncover attitudes, opinions, and preferences the prospect holds. These questions are designed to go beyond generalized fact finding and uncover prospects' perceptions and feelings regarding existing and desired circumstances and potential solutions. Exemplary evaluative questions include "How do you feel about _____?" "Do you see the merits of _____?" and "What do you think _____?"

4-2f Tactical Questions

Tactical questions are used to shift or redirect the topic of discussion when the discussion gets off course or when a line of questioning proves to be of little interest or value. For example, the salesperson might be exploring the chances of plant expansion only to find that the prospect cannot provide that type of proprietary information at this early stage of the buyer-seller relationship. To avoid either embarrassing the prospect or himself/herself by proceeding on a forbidden or nonproductive line of questioning, the seller uses a tactical question designed to change topics. An example of such a tactical question might be expressed as "Earlier you mentioned that _____. Could you tell me more about how that might affect _____?"

4-2g Reactive Questions

Reactive questions are questions that refer to or directly result from information the other party previously provided. Reactive questions are used to elicit additional information, explore for further detail, and keep the flow of information going. Illustrative reactive questions are "You mentioned that _____. Can you give me an example of what you mean?" and "That is interesting. Can you tell me how it happened?"

dichotomous questions A directive form of questioning; these questions ask the customer to choose from two or more options.

probing questions Questions designed to penetrate below generalized or superficial information to elicit more articulate and precise details for use in needs discovery and solution identification.

evaluative questions Questions that use the open-and closed-end question formats to gain confirmation and to uncover attitudes, opinions, and preferences the prospect holds.

tactical questions Questions used to shift or redirect the topic of discussion when the discussion gets off course or when a line of questioning proves to be of little interest or value.

reactive questions Questions that refer to or directly result from information the other party previously provided.

Exhibit 4.1

Guidelines for Combining Types of Questions

		Strategic Objective or Purpose of Questioning			
		Explore and Dig for Details	Gain Confirmation and Discover Attitudes/ Opinions	Change Topics or Re-direct Buyer's Attention	Follow-up Previously Elicited Statements
Amount and Specificity of Information Desired	Discussion and Interpretation	*Open-end* questions designed to be *Probing* in nature	*Open-end* questions designed to be *Evaluative* in nature	*Open-end* questions designed to be *Tactical* in nature	*Open-end* questions designed to be *Reactive* in nature
	Confirmation and Agreement	*Closed-end* questions designed to be *Probing* in nature	*Closed-end* questions designed to be *Evaluative* in nature	*Closed-end* questions designed to be *Tactical* in nature	*Closed-end* questions designed to be *Reactive* in nature
	Choosing from Alternatives	*Dichotomous or Multiple-choice* questions designed to be *Probing* in nature	*Dichotomous or Multiple-choice* questions designed to be *Evaluative* in nature	*Dichotomous or Multiple-choice* questions designed to be *Tactical* in nature	*Dichotomous or Multiple-choice* questions designed to be *Reactive* in nature

These different groupings of question types are not mutually exclusive. As depicted in the guidelines for combining question types in Exhibit 4.1, effective questions integrate elements from different question types. For example, "How do you feel about the current trend of sales in the industry?" is open-end (classified by format) and evaluative (classified by purpose) in nature.

Regardless of the types of questions one might combine in a sales dialogue, the natural tendency is to overuse closed-end questions. Monitor the types of questions you ask over the next several hours and see if you share the tendency to use more closed-end than open-end questions. It is not uncommon to find salespeople using an average of ten closed-end questions for every open-end question used in a sales conversation. This overuse of closed-end questions is dangerous in selling. The discovery and exploration of customer needs are fundamental to trust-based selling, and discovery and exploration are best done with open-end questions. As previously discussed, closed-end questions certainly have their place in selling,

but they are best used for clarification and confirmation, not discovery and exploration. An additional issue in overusing closed-end questions is that when they are used in a sequence, the resulting communication takes on the demeanor of interrogation rather than conversation.

4-3 STRATEGIC APPLICATION OF QUESTIONING IN TRUST-BASED SELLING

Effective questioning skills are indispensable in selling and are used to address critical issues throughout all stages of the selling process. In practice, salespeople combine the different types of questions discussed earlier to accomplish multiple and closely related sales objectives:

- *Generate buyer involvement.* Rather than the salesperson dominating the conversation and interaction, purposeful and planned questions are used to encourage prospective buyers to participate actively in a two-way collaborative discussion.

- *Provoke thinking.* Innovative and effective solutions require cognitive efforts and contributions from each participant. Strategic questions stimulate buyers and salespeople to think thoroughly and pragmatically about and consider all aspects of a given situation.

- *Gather information.* Good questions result from advance planning and should be directed toward gathering the information required to fill in the gap between "What do we need to know?" and "What do we already know?"

- *Clarification and emphasis.* Rather than assuming that the salesperson understands what a buyer has said, questions can be used to clarify meaning further and to emphasize the important points within a buyer-seller exchange further.

- *Show interest.* In response to statements from buyers, salespeople ask related questions and paraphrase what the buyer has said to demonstrate their interest in and understanding of what the buyer is saying.

- *Gain confirmation.* The use of simple and direct questions allow salespeople to check back with the prospective buyer to confirm the buyer's understanding or agreement and gain his or her commitment to move forward.

- *Advance the sale.* Effective questions are applied in a fashion that guides and moves the selling process forward in a logical progression from initiation through needs development and through needs resolution and follow-up.

With the aim of simultaneously targeting and achieving each of these objectives, several systems have been developed to guide salespeople in properly developing and using effective questions. Two of the more prominent questioning systems are SPIN and ADAPT. Both of these systems use a logical sequencing—a sort of funneling effect—that begins with broad-based, nonthreatening, general questions. Questioning progressively proceeds through more narrowly focused questions designed to clarify the buyer's needs and to propel the selling process logically toward the presentation and demonstration of solution features and benefits.

4-3a SPIN Questioning System

The **SPIN** system sequences four types of questions designed to uncover a buyer's current situation and inherent problems, enhance the buyer's understanding of the consequences and implications of those problems, and lead to the proposed solution.[2] SPIN is actually an acronym for the four types of questions making up the multiple question sequence: situation questions, problem questions, implication questions, and need-payoff questions.

- *Situation questions.* This type of question solicits data and facts in the form of general background information and descriptions of the buyer's existing situation. **Situation questions** are used early in the sales call and provide salespeople with leads to develop the buyer's needs and expectations fully. Situation questions might include "Who are your current suppliers?" "Do you typically purchase or lease?" and "Who is involved in purchasing decisions?" Situation questions are essential, but they should be used in moderation as too many general fact-finding questions can bore the buyer. Further, their interrogating nature can result in irritated buyers.

- *Problem questions.* **Problem questions** follow the more general situation questions to probe further for specific difficulties, developing problems, and areas of dissatisfaction that might be positively addressed by the salesperson's proposed sales offering. Some examples of problem questions include "How critical is this component for your production?" "What kinds of problems have you encountered with your current suppliers?" and "What types of reliability problems do you experience with your current system?" Problem questions actively involve the buyer and can assist him or her in better understanding his or her own problems and needs. Nevertheless, inexperienced and unsuccessful salespeople generally do not ask enough problem questions.

- *Implication questions.* **Implication questions** follow and relate to the information flowing from problem questions. Their purpose is to assist the buyer in thinking about the potential consequences of the problem and understand the urgency of resolving the problem in a way that motivates him or her to seek a

SPIN A questioning system that sequences four types of questions designed to uncover a buyer's current situation and inherent problems, enhance the buyer's understanding of the consequences and implications of those problems, and lead to the proposed solution.

situation questions One of the four types of questions in the SPIN questioning system used early in the sales call that provides salespeople with leads to develop the buyer's needs and expectations fully.

problem questions One of the four types of questions in the SPIN questioning system that follows the more general situation questions to further probe for specific difficulties, developing problems, and areas of dissatisfaction that might be positively addressed by the salesperson's proposed sales offering.

implication questions One of the four types of questions in the SPIN questioning system that follows and relates to the information flowing from problem questions; they are used to assist the buyer in thinking about the potential consequences of the problem and understanding the urgency of resolving the problem in a way that motivates him or her to seek a solution.

solution. Typical implication questions might include "How does this affect profitability?" "What impact does the slow response of your current supplier have on the productivity of your operation?" "How would a faster piece of equipment improve productivity and profits?" and "What happens when the supplier is late with a shipment?" Although implication questions are closely linked to success in selling, even experienced salespeople rarely use them effectively.

- *Need-payoff questions.* Based on the implications of a problem, salespeople use **need-payoff questions** to propose a solution and develop commitment from the buyer. These questions refocus the buyer's attention to solutions rather than problems

and get the buyer to think about the positive benefits derived from solving the problems. Examples of need-payoff questions are "Would more frequent deliveries allow you to increase productivity?" "If we could provide you with increased reliability, would you be interested?" "If we could improve the quality of your purchased components, how would that help you?" and "Would you be interested in increasing productivity by 15 percent?" Top salespeople effectively incorporate a higher number of need-payoff questions into sales calls than do less successful salespeople.

need-payoff questions One of the four types of questions in the SPIN questioning system that is based on the implications of a problem; they are used to propose a solution and develop commitment from the buyer.

ADAPT A questioning system that uses a logic-based funneling sequence of questions, beginning with broad and generalized inquiries designed to identify and assess the buyer's situation.

4-4 ADAPT QUESTIONING SYSTEM

As Figure 4.1 illustrates, the **ADAPT** questioning system uses a logic-based funneling sequence of questions, beginning with broad and generalized inquiries designed to identify and assess the buyer's situation. Based on information gained in this first phase,

FIG. 4.1 FUNNELING SEQUENCE OF ADAPT TECHNIQUE FOR NEEDS DISCOVERY

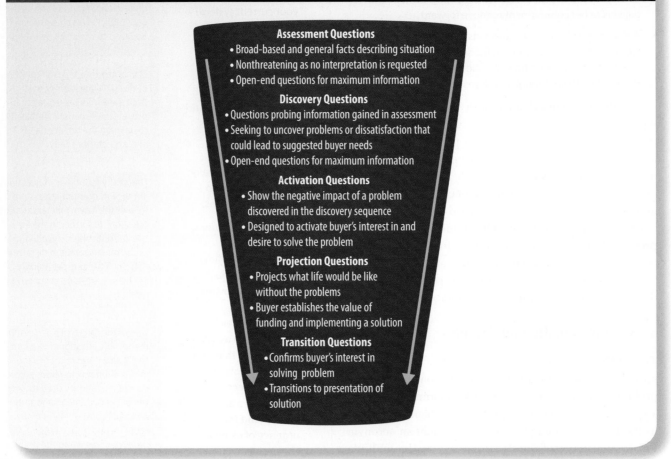

Assessment Questions
- Broad-based and general facts describing situation
- Nonthreatening as no interpretation is requested
- Open-end questions for maximum information

Discovery Questions
- Questions probing information gained in assessment
- Seeking to uncover problems or dissatisfaction that could lead to suggested buyer needs
- Open-end questions for maximum information

Activation Questions
- Show the negative impact of a problem discovered in the discovery sequence
- Designed to activate buyer's interest in and desire to solve the problem

Projection Questions
- Projects what life would be like without the problems
- Buyer establishes the value of funding and implementing a solution

Transition Questions
- Confirms buyer's interest in solving problem
- Transitions to presentation of solution

The ADAPT questioning technique logically sequences questions from broad and general inquiries through increasingly detailed questions for effective needs discovery.

further questions are generated to probe and discover more details regarding the needs and expectations of the buyer. In turn, the resulting information is incorporated in further collaborative discussion in a way that activates the buyer's motivation to implement a solution and further establishes the buyer's perceived value of a possible solution. The last phase of ADAPT questioning transitions to the buyer's commitment to learn about the proposed solution and grants the salesperson permission to move forward into the presentation and demonstration of the sales offering. ADAPT is an acronym for the five stages of strategic questioning and represents what the salesperson should be doing at each stage: assessment questions, discovery questions, activation questions, projection questions, and transition questions.[3]

- *Assessment questions.* This initial phase of questioning is designed to be nonthreatening and to spark conversation that elicits factual information about the customer's current situation that can provide a basis for further exploration and probing. As illustrated in Exhibit 4.2, **assessment questions** do not seek conclusions—rather, at a macro or 40,000-foot level of focus, these questions should address the buyer's company and operation, goals and objectives, market trends and customers, current suppliers, and even the buyer as an individual. The information sought should augment or confirm precall research. Examples would include "What is the current level of your production?" "How long has the current equipment been in place?" "How many suppliers are currently being used?" "What are the growth objectives of the company?" and "What individuals have input into purchase decisions?"

- *Discovery questions.* As portrayed in Exhibit 4.3, these questions follow up on the responses gained from the preceding assessment questions. At a more micro and ground-level focus, **discovery questions** should drill down and probe for further details needed to fully develop, clarify, and understand the nature of the buyer's problems. Facts as well as the buyer's interpretations, perceptions, feelings, and opinions are sought in regard to the buyer's needs, wants, dissatisfactions, and expectations relevant to product, delivery requirements, budget and financing issues, and desired service levels. The goal is to discover needs and dissatisfactions that the salesperson's sales offering can resolve. Examples of discovery questions might include "How often do these equipment failures occur?" "How well are your current suppliers performing?" "What disadvantages do you see in the current process?" "How satisfied are

assessment questions
One of the five stages of questions in the ADAPT questioning system that do not seek conclusions but rather should address the buyer's company and operations, goals and objectives, market trends and customers, current suppliers, and even the buyer as an individual.

discovery questions
One of the five stages of questions in the ADAPT questioning system that follows up on the assessment questions; they should drill down and probe for further details needed to develop, clarify, and understand the nature of the buyer's problems fully.

Exhibit 4.2

Assessment Questions

These questions are designed to elicit factual information about the customer's current situation. These questions do not seek conclusions; rather, they seek information that describes the customer and his or her business environment. The information sought should augment or confirm precall research.

Examples:

1. **Question—"What types of operating arrangements do you have with your suppliers?"**
   Answer—We use a Just-in-Time (JIT) system with our main suppliers.

2. **Question—"Who is involved in the purchase decision-making process?"**
   Answer—I make the decisions regarding supplies. . . .

Assessment questions are generally open end; however, closed-end questions are used when seeking confirmation or basic descriptive information. For example, "So, you currently work with 10 different suppliers?" or "How many years have you been in business?" Assessment questions are necessary for drawing out information early in the sales cycle.

Discovery Questions

Discovery questions are used to uncover problems or dissatisfactions the customer is experiencing that the salesperson's product or company may be able to solve. Basically, these questions are used to "distill" or "boil down" the information gained from the preceding assessment questions and from precall research into suggested needs.

Examples:

1. **Question—I understand you prefer a JIT relationship with your suppliers—how have they been performing?**
   Answer—Pretty well . . . an occasional late delivery . . . but pretty well.

2. **Question—How do you feel about your current supplier occasionally being late with deliveries?**
   Answer—It is a real problem . . . for instance . . .

The *suggested* needs gained from discovery questions are used as a foundation for the rest of the sales call. Yet, a *suggested* need is usually not sufficient to close the sale. Often, a customer will believe that a particular problem does not cause any significant negative consequences. If this is the case, finding a solution to the problem will be a very low priority. The professional salesperson must then help the customer to reevaluate the impact of the *suggested* need by asking activation questions.

---

you with the quality of components you are currently purchasing?" and "How difficult are these for your operators to use?"

- *Activation questions.* The implied or suggested needs gained from discovery questions are not usually sufficient to gain the sale. Often, a buyer will believe that a particular problem does not cause any significant negative consequences; hence, the motivation to solve the problem will carry a low priority. Successful salespeople help the customer realistically evaluate the full impact of the implied need through the use of **activation questions**. As detailed in Exhibit 4.4, the objective is to "activate" the customer's interest in solving discovered problems by helping him or her gain insight into the true ramifications of the problem and to realize that what may initially seem to be of little consequence is, in fact, of significant consequence. Examples include "What effects do these equipment breakdowns have on your business operations?" "To what extent are these increases in overtime expenses affecting profitability?" "How will the supplier's inability to deliver on time affect your planned expansion?" and "When components fail in the field, how does that failure influence customer satisfaction and repurchase?"

- *Projection questions.* As a natural extension of the activation questions, **projection questions** encourage and facilitate the buyer in "projecting" what it would be like without the problems that have been previously "discovered" and "activated." The use of good projection questions accomplishes several positive outcomes. First, the focus is switched from problems and their associated consequences to the upside—the benefits to be derived from solving the problems. What were initially perceived as costs and expenses are now logically structured as benefits to the buyer and his or her organization—the payoff for taking action and investing in a solution. Second—and equally important—the benefit payoff allows the buyer to establish the realistic value of implementing a solution. In this manner, the benefit payoff is perceived as a positive value received and serves as the foundation for demonstrating what the solution is worth—what the buyer would be willing to pay. As illustrated in Exhibit 4.5, projection questions encourage the buyer to think about how and why he or she should go about resolving a problem. In essence, projection questions assist the buyer in

activation questions One of the five stages of questions in the ADAPT questioning system used to "activate" the customer's interest in solving discovered problems by helping him or her gain insight into the true ramifications of the problem and to realize that what might initially seem to be of little consequence is, in fact, of significant consequence.

projection questions One of the five stages of questions in the ADAPT questioning system used to encourage and facilitate the buyer in "projecting" what it would be like without the problems that have been previously "discovered" and "activated."

Activation Questions

Activation questions are used to show the impact of a problem, uncovered through discovery questions, on the customer's entire operation. The objective is to "activate" the customer's interest in solving the problem by helping him or her to gain insight into the true ramifications of the problem and realize that what might seem to be of little consequence is, in fact, of significant consequence.

Examples:

1. **Question—What effect does your supplier's late delivery have on your operation?**
   Answer—It slows production. . . . Operating costs go up.

2. **Question—If production drops off, how are your operating costs affected, and how does that affect your customers?**
   Answer—Customer orders are delayed. . . . Potential to lose customers.

Activation questions show the negative impact of a problem so that finding a solution to that problem is desirable. Now, the salesperson can help the customer to discover the positive impact of solving the problems by using projection questions.

Projection Questions

Projection questions help the customer to "project" what life would be like without the problems or dissatisfactions uncovered through activation questions. This helps the customer to see value in finding solutions to the problems developed earlier in the sales call.

Examples:

1. **Question—If a supplier was never late with a delivery, what effects would that have on your JIT operating structure?**
   Answer—It would run smoother and at a lower cost.

2. **Question—If a supplier helped you meet the expectations of your customers, what impact would that have on your business?**
   Answer—Increased customer satisfaction would mean more business.

These questions are used to let the customer tell the salesperson the benefits of solving the problem. By doing so, the customer is reinforcing in his or her mind the importance of solving the problem and reducing the number of objections that might be raised.

---

selling himself or herself by establishing the worth of the proposed solution. The customer, rather than the salesperson, establishes the benefits of solving the problem. This reinforces the importance of solving the problem and reduces the number of objections that might be raised. Examples of projection questions include "If a supplier was never late with a delivery, what effects would that have on your overall operation?" "What would be the impact on profitability if you did not have problems with limited plant capacity and the resulting overtime expenses?" "How would a system that your operators found easier to use affect your business operations?" and "If component failures were minimized, what impact would the resulting improvement in customer satisfaction have on financial performance?"

- *Transition questions.* **Transition questions** are used to smooth the transition from needs discovery into the presentation and demonstration of the proposed solution's features and benefits. As exemplified in Exhibit 4.6, transition questions are typically closed-end and evaluative in format. These questions confirm the buyer's desire to seek a solution and give their consent to the salesperson to move forward with the selling process. Examples include "So, having suppliers that are consistently on time is important to you—if I could show you how our company ensures on-time delivery, would you be interested?" "It seems that increasing capacity is a key to reducing overtime and increasing profitability—would you be interested in a way to increase capacity by 20 percent through a simple addition to your production process?" and "Would you be interested in a system that is easier for your operators to use?"

4-4a Verbal Communication: Listening

Listening is the other half of effective questioning. Asking the customer for information is of little value if the salesperson does not listen. Effective listening is rated among the most critical skills for successful selling. Yet, most of us share the common problem of being a lot better at sending messages than receiving them. Considerable research identifies effective listening as the number-one weakness of salespeople.[4]

> **transition questions** One of the five stages of questions in the ADAPT questioning system used to smooth the transition from needs discovery into the presentation and demonstration of the proposed solution's features and benefits.

Poor listening skills have been identified as one of the primary causes of salesperson failure.[5] In order to get the information needed to best serve, identify, and respond to needs, and nurture a collaborative buyer-seller relationship, salespeople must be able to listen to and understand what was said *and* what was meant. Nevertheless, situations similar to the one depicted in "An Ethical Dilemma" are all too common. As Figure 4.2 illustrates, effective listening can be broken down into six primary facets:

1. *Pay attention*—Listen to understand, not to reply. Resist the urge to interrupt and receive the full message the buyer is communicating.

2. *Monitor nonverbals*—Make effective eye contact and check to see if the buyer's body language and speech patterns match what is being said.

3. *Paraphrase and repeat*—Confirm your correct understanding of what the buyer is saying by paraphrasing and repeating what you have heard.

4. *Make no assumptions*—Ask questions to clarify the meaning of what the buyer is communicating.

5. *Encourage the buyer to talk*—Encourage the flow of information by giving positive feedback and help the buyer stay on track by asking purposeful, related questions.

6. *Visualize*—Maximize your attention and comprehension by thinking about and visualizing what the buyer is saying.

The practiced listening skills of high performance salespeople enable them to pick up, sort out, and

Selling in Action

Funneling Sequence of Questions Are Key for Understanding Buyer's Needs

Steve O'Connor, district sales representative for Edward Don & Company—the leading distributor of food-service equipment and supplies in the United States, emphasizes the importance of using a funneling sequence of open-ended questions to drill down and fully understand a prospective customer's problems and needs before starting to pitch products.

"At Edward Don, our annual sales plan calls for 20% of our business during the year to come from new accounts. Needless to say, strategic prospecting is very important in reaching that objective. When meeting with a prospect, it is also very important to use a funneling sequence of questions to drill down and develop an in-depth understanding of the prospect's situation, challenges, and needs, which we can address with added-value solutions unique to Edward Don. I consistently use the ADAPT Question Sequence I learned to use as a student in Illinois State University's professional selling classes. Using this sequence of questions allows me to engage the prospect in a comfortable discussion of their business situation, goals, strategic plans, and challenges. This collaborative conversation leads to follow-up questions that begin to identify unmet needs and problems and activate the prospect's interest and desire to resolve the problems in a way that significantly benefits their business. The natural outcome of the funneling questions is the opportunity to present my solutions to their problems and unmet needs, close the sale on an initial order, and establish a solid foundation for a buyer-seller relationship where I am a trusted advisor assisting them in meeting challenges and achieving their business goals. It is just a natural way to work with customers."

Olivier Le Moal/Shutterstock.com

interpret a greater number of buyers' verbal and non-verbal messages than lower-performing salespeople can. In addition to gaining information and understanding critical to the relational selling process, a salesperson's good listening behaviors provide the added benefits of positively influencing the formation and continuation of buyer-seller relationships. A salesperson's effective use and demonstration of good listening skills is positively associated with the customer's trust in the salesperson and the anticipation of having future interactions with

> Effective listening requires more than just hearing what is being said.

the salesperson.[6] Clearly, effective listening is a critical component in trust-based, relational selling, and success requires continuous practice and improvement of our listening skills.

USING DIFFERENT TYPES OF LISTENING

Communications research identifies two primary categories of listening: *social and serious*.[7] **Social listening** is an informal mode of listening that can be associated with day-to-day conversation and entertainment. Social listening is characterized by low levels of cognitive activity and concentration

social listening An informal mode of listening that can be associated with day-to-day conversation and entertainment.

FIG. 4.2   SIX FACETS OF EFFECTIVE LISTENING

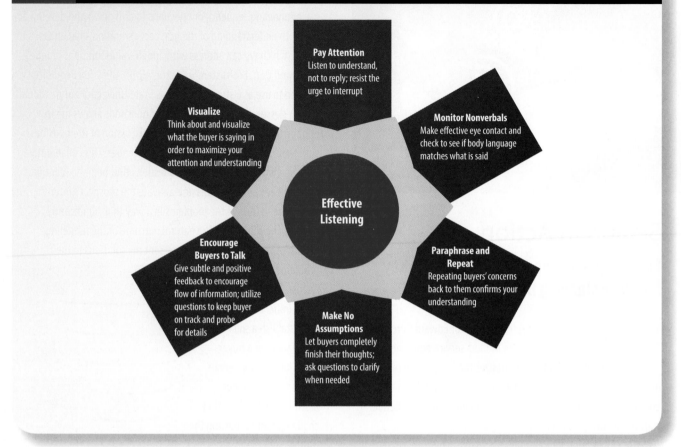

The six facets of effective listening enable salespeople to better pick up, sort out, and interpret buyers' verbal and nonverbal messages.

and is typically used in conversation with a friend or a store clerk or listening to music, a concert, a television program, or even a play. The received messages are taken at face value and do not require a high degree of concentration or thinking to sort through, interpret, and understand. However, **serious listening** is associated with events or topics in which it is important to sort through, interpret, understand, and respond to received messages. The serious form of listening is often referred to as *active listening*, as it requires high levels of concentration and cognition about the messages being received.

serious listening A form of listening that is associated with events or topics in which it is important to sort through, interpret, understand, and respond to received messages.

active listening The cognitive process of actively sensing, interpreting, evaluating, and responding to the verbal and nonverbal messages of current or potential customers.

SIER A model that depicts active listening as a hierarchical, four-step sequence of sensing, interpreting, evaluating, and responding.

Concentration is required to break through the distractions and other interference to facilitate receiving and remembering specific messages. *Cognition* is used to sort through and select the meaningful relevant messages and interpret them for meaning, information, and response.

4-5   ACTIVE LISTENING

In a selling context, **active listening** is defined as "the cognitive process of actively sensing, interpreting, evaluating, and responding to the verbal and nonverbal messages of current or potential customers."[8] This definition is very useful to those wishing to master active listening skills. First, it underscores the importance of receiving and interpreting both verbal and nonverbal cues and messages to better determine the full and correct meaning of the message. Second, it incorporates a well-accepted model of listening. As illustrated in Figure 4.3,[9] the **SIER** model depicts

An Ethical Dilemma

Royce Ramey, a new salesperson for AEG Financial, has just completed the company's two-month training program. Discussing the training with a friend, Royce described it as primarily focused on (a) legal and industry issues required for licensing and (b) product knowledge detailing the financial products he was hired to sell. However, coverage of basic sales skills was minimal. With training completed, Royce has returned to his agency office, where he was given a three-ring binder of selling tips and daily activity goal charts. The first page contained the CEO's motivational message followed by what was titled "The 4 Keys to Successful Selling:"

Key #1: Everybody needs a financial planner! Make your daily calls and ask for the appointment.

Key #2: Prospects do not know what products they need! At the appointment, present the standard sales presentation, show each product, and ask for the order until they buy.

Key #3: Always be closing! If you do not ask for the order, nobody will buy!

Key #4: Success in selling is simply a numbers game! Contact enough prospects and you will make your quota. Want to sell more? Make more contacts!

What should Royce do?

a) Play it safe and follow his company's selling tips.
b) Customize the standard sales presentation to match prospects' needs.
c) Always be closing.

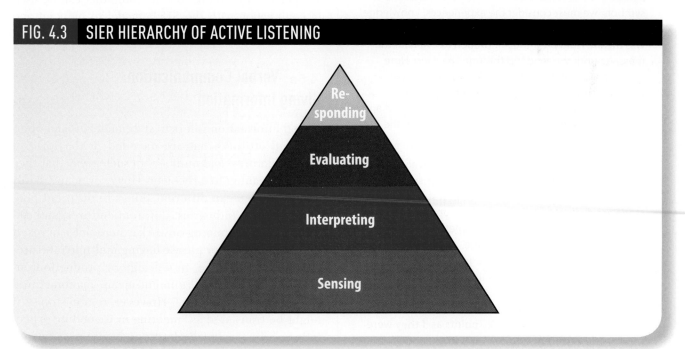

FIG. 4.3 SIER HIERARCHY OF ACTIVE LISTENING

Responding
Evaluating
Interpreting
Sensing

Active listening is a cognitive process of actively sensing, interpreting, evaluating, and responding to verbal and nonverbal messages from buyers and prospects.

active listening as a hierarchical, four-step sequence of sensing, interpreting, evaluating, and responding.[10] Effective active listening requires each of these four hierarchical process activities to be carried out successfully and in proper succession.

- *Sensing.* Listening is much more than simply hearing. Nevertheless, the first activities in active listening are sensing (i.e., hearing and seeing) and receiving (i.e., paying attention to) the verbal and nonverbal components of the message being sent. Sensing does not occur without practice and should not be taken for granted. In fact, research indicates that most of us listen at only 25 percent of our capacity. Think about yourself. How often have you had to ask someone to repeat what he or she said or perhaps assumed you knew what the sender was going to say before he or she could say it? Increased concentration and attention can improve sensing effectiveness. Taking notes, making eye contact with the sender, and not interrupting can improve sensing skills. Let the sender finish and provide the full content of the message. This not only improves the concentration of the receiver, but also encourages the sender to provide more information and detail.

- *Interpreting.* After the message is received, it must be correctly interpreted. Interpreting addresses the question of "What meaning does the sender intend?" Both content and context are important. That is, in addition to the semantic meaning of the words and symbols, we must consider the experiences, knowledge, and attitudes of the sender to understand fully what was meant. Hold back the temptation to evaluate the message until the sender is through speaking. Note the nonverbal and verbal cues along with possible consistencies and inconsistencies between them. Incorporate knowledge of the sender's background and previous relevant statements and positions into the message interpretation.

- *Evaluating.* Active listening requires the receiver to decide whether he or she agrees with the sender's message. The results from the interpretation stage are evaluated to sort fact from opinion and emotion. Too often, receivers complete this activity prior to receiving the full message, and on hearing something with which they disagree, the sender is effectively tuned out. As a result, communication is stifled. Evaluating can be improved through better concentration and thoughtful consideration of the full message. Summarizing the key points as if they were going to be reported to others can further enhance evaluation skills. Searching for areas of interest rather than prejudging the message can also facilitate the evaluation process.

- *Responding.* Responding is both an expectation and a requirement for active listening to be effective. Collaborative, two-way communication requires that the listener respond to the sender. Responses provide feedback to the other party, emphasize understanding, encourage further elaboration, and can serve as a beginning point for the receiver to transition into the role of sender for the next message sent. Responses can take many forms. Nonverbal cues such as nodding and smiling can indicate that the sender's message was received. Responses in the form of restating and paraphrasing the sender's message can provide strong signals of interest and understanding. Asking questions can elicit additional details and clarification.

The SIER model provides a useful framework for evaluating communication accuracy and pinpointing the sources of problems. Similarly, it can be effectively used for planning activities and behaviors designed to improve communication effectiveness. As the SIER model depicts, active listening is a hierarchical and sequential process. One must sense the message before it can be interpreted. In turn, the message must be interpreted before it can be evaluated. Finally, it must be effectively evaluated prior to generating a proper response. When diagnosing a listening breakdown, one should look for the lowest level in the hierarchy where the breakdown could have originated and take proper action to remedy the problem. Exhibit 4.7[11] describes 10 specific keys to effective listening that can be used in conjunction with the SIER model to pinpoint and improve listening problems.

4-5a Verbal Communication: Giving Information

Verbal information refers to statements of fact, opinion, and attitude that are encoded in the form of words, pictures, and numbers in such a way that they convey meaning to a receiver. However, many words and symbols mean different things to different people. Different industries, different cultures, and different types of training or work experience can result in the same word or phrase having multiple interpretations. For instance, to a design or production engineer, the word *quality* might mean "manufactured within design tolerance." However, to a customer it might be translated as "meeting or exceeding expectations." To maximize clarity and minimize misunderstandings, understand and use the vocabulary and terminology that corresponds with the perspective of the customer.

Exhibit 4.7

Ten Keys to Effective Listening

The Key Practice	The Weak Listener	The Strong Listener
1. Find areas of interest	Tunes out dry subjects	Actively looks for opportunities of common interest
2. Judge content, not delivery	Tunes out if the delivery is poor	Skips over delivery errors and focuses on content
3. Hold your fire until full consideration	Evaluates and enters argument prior to completion of message	Does not judge or evaluate until message is complete
4. Listen for ideas	Listens for facts	Listens for central themes
5. Be flexible	Takes intensive and detailed notes	Takes fewer notes and limits theme to central theme and key ideas presented
6. Work at listening	Shows no energy output; attention is faked	Works hard at attending the message and exhibits active body state
7. Resist distractions	Is distracted easily	Resists distractions and knows how to concentrate
8. Exercise your mind	Resists difficult expository material in favor of light recreational materials	Uses complex and heavy material as exercise for the mind
9. Keep an open mind	Reacts to emotional words	Interprets color words but does not get hung up on them
10. Capitalize on the fact that thought is faster than speech	Tends to daydream with slow speakers	Challenges, anticipates, mentally summarizes, weighs evidence, and listens between the lines

4-6 UNDERSTANDING THE SUPERIORITY OF PICTURES OVER WORDS

Studies in cognitive psychology have found that pictures tend to be more memorable than their verbal counterparts.[12] The fact that pictures enhance understanding and are more easily recalled than abstract words and symbols has several implications for effective selling.

- The verbal message should be constructed in a manner that generates a mental picture in the receiver's mind. For example, the phrase "Tropicana juices are bursting with flavor" is more visual than the more abstract version "Tropicana juices have more flavor." This can also be accomplished by providing a short and illustrative analogy or illustrative story to emphasize a key point and bring it alive in the buyer's mind.

- Rather than using abstract words that convey only a broad general understanding, use words and phrases that convey concrete and detailed meaning. Concrete expressions provide the receiver with greater information and are less likely to be misunderstood than their abstract counterparts. For example, "This Web transfer system will increase weekly production by 2,100 units" provides more detail than "This Web transfer system will increase production by 10 percent." Similarly, "This conveyor is faster than your existing system" does not deliver the same impact as "This conveyor system will move your product from production to shipping

Sales aids such as samples, brochures, and charts reinforce the verbal message and enhance the receivers' understanding and recall.

at 50 feet per second as compared with your current system's 20 feet per second."

- Integrate relevant visual sales aids into verbal communication. Sales support materials that explain and reinforce the verbal message will aid the receiver's understanding and enhance recall of the message. As an additional benefit, sales aids such as samples, brochures, graphs, and comparative charts can be left with the buyer to continue selling until the salesperson's next call on the buyer.

4-6a Impact of Grammar and Logical Sequencing

Grammar and logical sequencing are also important in the process of giving information to others. The use of proper grammar is a given in business and social communication. In its absence, the receiver of the message tends to exhibit three closely related behaviors. First, the meaning and credibility of the message are significantly downgraded. Second, the receiver begins to focus on the sender rather than the message, which materially reduces the probability of effective communication. Last, the receiver dismisses the sender and the sender's organization as being unqualified to perform the role of an effective supplier and partner. The importance of proper grammar should not be overlooked.

Similarly, whether one is engaged in simply explaining details or making a formal proposal,

nonverbal communication
The conscious and unconscious reactions, movements, and utterances that people use in addition to the words and symbols associated with language.

logical sequencing of the material is critical. The facts and details must be organized and connected in a logical order. This is essential to clarity and assists the receiver in following the facts. A discussion or presentation that jumps around runs the risk of being inefficient and ineffective. At best, the receiver will have to ask many clarification questions. At worst, the receiver will dismiss the salesperson as incompetent and close off the sales negotiation. Advance planning and preparation can improve organization. Outline what needs to be covered and organize it into a logical flow. The outline becomes the agenda to be covered and can serve as an aid for staying on track.

4-7 NONVERBAL COMMUNICATION

Nonverbal behaviors have been recognized as an important dimension of communication since medieval times. As early as 1605, Francis Bacon focused on the messages conveyed by *manual language*. Verbal communication deals with the semantic meaning of the message itself, whereas the nonverbal dimension consists of the more abstract message conveyed by how the message is delivered. **Nonverbal communication** is the conscious and unconscious reactions, movements, and utterances that people use in addition to the words and symbols associated with language. This dimension of communication includes eye movements and facial expressions; placement and movements of hands, arms, head, and legs as well as body orientation; the amount of space maintained between individuals; and variations in vocal characteristics. Collectively, the various forms of nonverbal communication carry subtle as well as explicit meanings and feelings along with the linguistic message and are frequently more informative than the verbal content of a message.[13]

Research indicates that highly successful salespeople are capable of picking out and comprehending a higher number of behavioral cues from buyers than less successful salespeople are able to sense and interpret. In addition, research indicates that 50 percent or more of the meaning conveyed within the communication process stems from nonverbal behavior.[14] As the nonverbal components of a message carry as much or more meaning than the language portions, it is critical for salespeople to sense effectively, interpret accurately, and evaluate fully the nonverbal elements of a message as well as the verbal components. In addition

Fifty percent or more of the meaning conveyed in interpersonal communication comes through nonverbal bevaviors.

to sensing verbal messages, learn to sense between the words for the thoughts and feelings not being conveyed verbally.

4-7a Facial Expressions

Possibly reflecting its central point of focus in interpersonal communication, the various elements of the face play a key role in giving off nonverbal messages. Frowning, pursed lips, and squinted eyes are common in moments of uncertainty, disagreement, and even outright skepticism. Suspicion and anger are typically accompanied by tightness along the jaw line. Smiles are indicative of agreement and interest, whereas biting of one's lip can signal uncertainty. Raised eyebrows can signify surprise and are often found in moments of consideration and evaluation.

4-7b Eye Movements

In North America and Western Europe, avoiding eye contact results in a negative message and is often associated with deceit and dishonesty. However, a sender's increased eye contact infers honesty and self-confidence. Increased eye contact by the receiver of the message signals increasing levels of interest and concentration. However, when eye contact becomes a stare and continues unbroken, either by glances away or blinking, it is typically interpreted as a threat or inference of power. A blank stare or eye contact directed away from the conversation can show disinterest and boredom. Repeated glances made toward one's watch or possibly an exit door often indicate that the conversation is about to end.

4-7c Placement and Movements of Hands, Arms, Head, and Legs

Smooth and gradual movements denote calm and confidence, whereas jerky and hurried movements are associated with nervousness and stress. Uncrossed arms and legs signal openness, confidence, and cooperation. However, crossed arms and legs psychologically close out the other party and express disagreement and defensiveness. Increased movement of the head and limbs hints at increasing tension, as does the tight clasping of hands or fists. The placement of a hand on the chin or a tilted head suggests increased levels of evaluation, whereas nodding of the head expresses agreement. Growing impatience is associated with drumming of the fingers or tapping of a foot. The fingering of one's hair and rubbing the back of the neck signifies increasing nervousness and apprehension.

4-7d Body Posture and Orientation

Fidgeting and shifting from side to side is generally considered to be a negative message associated with nervousness and apprehension. Leaning forward or sitting forward on the edge of a chair is a general sign of increasing interest and a positive disposition in regard to what is being discussed. Similarly, leaning away can indicate disinterest, boredom, or even distrust. Leaning back with both hands placed behind one's head signifies a perceived sense of smugness and superiority. A rigid erect posture can convey inflexibility or even defensiveness, whereas sloppy posture suggests disinterest in the topic. Similar to sitting backward in a chair, sitting on the edge of the table or the arm of a chair is an expression of power and superiority.

4-7e Proxemics

Proxemics refers to the personal distance that individuals prefer to keep between themselves and other individuals and is an important element of nonverbal communication. The distance that one places between oneself and others implies a meaningful message and affects the outcome of the selling process. If a salesperson pushes too close to a prospect who requires more distance, the prospect may perceive the salesperson to be manipulative, intimidating, and possibly threatening. However, salespeople who put too much distance between themselves and the customer risk being perceived as rigidly formal, aloof, or even apprehensive.

Proxemics differs across cultures and regions of the world. For

> **proxemics** The personal distance that individuals prefer to keep between themselves and other individuals; an important element of nonverbal communication.

FIG. 4.4 PERSONAL SPACE AND INTERPERSONAL COMMUNICATION

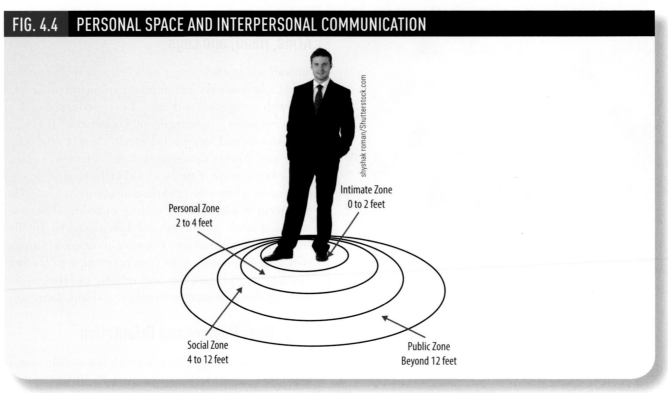

Individuals utilize four preferred spatial zones for interaction in different social and business situations.

example, in North Africa and Latin America business is conducted at a much closer distance than in North America. As depicted in Figure 4.4, North Americans generally recognize four distinct proxemic zones. The *intimate zone* is reserved for intimate relationships with immediate family and loved ones. The *personal zone* is for personal relationships with close friends and associates. The *social zone* is for business client relationships and is the zone in which most business is conducted. The *public zone* is for the general public and group settings such as classrooms and presentations.

It is critical that salespeople understand proxemics and monitor the progression of their buyer-seller relationships so as to position themselves with different customers properly. Typically, salespeople begin working with a prospect at the far end of the *social zone*. As the salesperson-buyer relationship develops, the salesperson is in a position to move closer without violating the customer's space and causing him or her to become defensive.

4-7f Variations in Vocal Characteristics

Nonverbal vocal characteristics such as speaking rates, pause duration, pitch or frequency, and intensity have been linked to communication effectiveness and selling performance. These voice characteristics convey direct as well as subtle and implied meanings and feelings that can complement or accent the corresponding verbal message.

4-7g Speaking Rates and Pause Duration

Within normal speaking rates, faster speakers are generally evaluated more favorably than slower speakers. Contrary to the often-cited fast-talking salesperson being perceived as high pressure, faster rates of speech and shorter pause duration are actually associated with higher levels of intelligence, credibility, and knowledge. Slower speakers are perceived as being less competent as well as less benevolent. However, speech rates that are jerky and beyond normal rates of speech can present problems in sensing and interpreting the complete message. Varying the rate of speech has also been found to be conducive to maintaining interest.

4-7h Pitch or Frequency

Vocal pitch carries a great deal of information to the receiver. Varying pitch and frequency during the course of a message encourages attentiveness of the listener and accents certain forms of statements. A rising pitch during the message is associated with questions and can often be perceived as reflecting uncertainty. Just the opposite, a falling pitch is associated with declarative statements and completion of the message. Overall, high-pitched voices are judged as less truthful, less emphatic, less potent, and more nervous. Lower-pitched voices are considered more persuasive and truthful and have a positive impact on selling performance.

4-7i Intensity and Loudness

Dominance, superiority, intensity, and aggression are commonly associated with loud voices, whereas soft voices characterize submission and uncertainty. However, it is the variability of intensity that has been found to be most effective in communication. Varying levels of loudness allow the sender to adapt to different situations and environments. Variation also increases the receiver's attention and can provide additional information inputs by accenting key points of a message.

4-7j Using Nonverbal Clusters

Nonverbal clusters are groups of related expressions, gestures, and movements. Similar to a one-word expression, a single isolated gesture or movement should not be taken as a reliable indication of the true intent or meaning of a message. Sensing and interpreting groups or clusters of nonverbal cues provides a more reliable indicator of the message and intent. When the individual behaviors and gestures begin to fit together, they form a common and unified message that the salesperson should consider. Common nonverbal clusters applicable to selling communication are described in Exhibit 4.8.[15]

nonverbal clusters Groups of related nonverbal expressions, gestures, and movements that can be interpreted to better understand the true message being communicated.

Exhibit 4.8

Common Nonverbal Clusters

Cluster Name	Cluster Meaning	Body Posture and Orientation	Movement of Hands, Arms, and Legs	Eyes and Facial Expressions
Openness	Openness, flexibility, and sincerity	• Moving closer • Leaning forward	• Open hands • Removing coat • Unbutton collar • Uncrossed arms and legs	• Slight smile • Good eye contact
Defensiveness	Defensiveness, skepticism, and apprehension	• Rigid body	• Crossed arms and legs • Clenched fists	• Minimal eye contact • Glancing sideways • Pursed lips
Evaluation	Evaluation and consideration of message	• Leaning forward	• Hand on cheek • Stroking chin • Chin in palm of hand	• Tilted head • Dropping glasses to tip of nose
Deception	Dishonesty and secretiveness	• Patterns of rocking	• Fidgeting with objects • Increased leg movements	• Increased eye movement • Frequent gazes elsewhere • Forced smile
Readiness	Dedication or commitment	• Sitting forward	• Hands on hips • Legs uncrossed • Feet flat on floor	• Increased eye contact
Boredom	Lack of interest and impatience	• Head in palm of hands • Slouching	• Drumming fingers • Swinging a foot • Brushing and picking at items • Tapping feet	• Poor eye contact • Glancing at watch • Blank stares

Just as salespeople can interpret nonverbal messages to better interpret and understand communication with prospects and buyers, those same prospects and buyers can also sense and interpret the nonverbal messages the salesperson is sending. Consequently, it is important that salespeople monitor the nonverbal cues they are sending to ensure consistency with and reinforcement of the intended message.

STUDY TOOLS 4

LOCATED IN TEXTBOOK

☐ Rip-out and review chapter review card

LOCATED AT WWW.CENGAGEBRAIN.COM

☐ Review key term flashcards and create your own from StudyBits

☐ Organize notes and StudyBits using the StudyBoard feature within Online

☐ Complete practice and graded quizzes to prepare for tests

☐ Complete interactive content within the exposition

☐ View chapter highlight box content at the beginning of each chapter

TECH SOLUTIONS AND BARTLETT & ASSOCIATES

BACKGROUND

This case involves a salesperson representing the institutional sales division of Tech Solutions, a leading reseller of technology hardware and software and Gage Waits, Director of Technology for Bartlett & Associates, a prominent, Dallas-based law firm specializing in corporate litigation. Bartlett & Associates is preparing to move to larger facilities and want to update their computer technology in the new facilities. Chicago-based Tech Solutions has established itself as a major competitor in the technology marketplace specializing in value-added systems solutions for business institutions and government entities nationwide. This past year, Tech Solutions has added sales and distribution centers in Burlington, New York, Los Angeles, California, and Dallas, Texas.

CURRENT SITUATION

As an integral part of their move to new and larger facilities, Bartlett & Associates want to replace their computers and information technology systems including laptop/desktop combinations for each of their 21 attorneys, desktop systems for their 10 staff members, along with archive and e-mail servers. Tech Solutions specializes in this type of systems selling and uses their network of hardware and software providers in combination with their own in-house engineering, programming, and systems group to consistently provide higher value solutions than the competition.

In preparation for an initial meeting with Gage Waits, the Tech Solutions sales representative is outlining his/her information needs and developing a draft set of needs discovery questions. These needs discovery questions will be the focus of the meeting with Gage Waits and enable Tech Solutions to better identify and confirm the actual needs, desires, and expectations of Bartlett & Associates in relation to new and expanded computer and information technology capabilities.

QUESTIONS

1. What information does the Tech Solutions salesperson need in order to fully understand the technology needs of Bartlett & Associates?

2. Following the ADAPT methodology for needs discovery questioning, develop a series of salesperson questions and anticipated buyer responses that might apply to this selling situation.

ROLE PLAY

Situation: Review the above Tech Solutions-Bartlett & Associates case and the ADAPT questions you developed in response to the questions associated with this case.

Characters: Yourself, salesperson for Tech Solutions; Gage Waits, Director of Technology for Bartlett & Associates

Scene:
Location—Gage Waits' office at Bartlett & Associates

Action—As a salesperson for Tech Solutions, you are making an initial sales call to Gage Waits for the purpose of identifying and detailing the specific needs and expectations Bartlett & Associates has for new and expanded computers and information technology. Role play this needs discovery sales call and demonstrate how you might utilize SPIN or ADAPT questioning sequences to identify the technology needs.

4 CHAPTER ROLE PLAY
Communication Skills

APPLAB SERVICES

BACKGROUND

AppLab Services specializes in providing wireless information technology for businesses having 10 to 500 employees and needs for wireless communication, information processing, and digital data transmittal. The company offers a full range of services ranging from the one-time design of applications for smart phones and digital devices to the design and building out of full enterprise systems. As a business development specialist for AppLab, you are making an initial sales call to Mark Crandall, technology manager for Southwest Claims & Adjusters, LLC. As a preferred provider for inspection and adjusting insurance claims across the southern U.S., Southwest serves as an outsource provider of claims and adjusting services to many of the top 25 property and casualty insurance companies and has experienced rapid growth over the last five years. The company currently employs 65 people: 50 adjusters out in the field, 10 assistants located at company headquarters in Tulsa, and 5 administrative and executive staff members.

The purpose of this initial call is to assess Southwest's current use and needs for wireless communication and data services. According to the initial information you gained from a short phone conversation with Crandall, Southwest is currently using a variety of different smart phones on Sprint's cellular and data service. However, they are exploring the combination of custom designed apps for the Microsoft Surface Pro Tablet for use by their adjusters in the field. This combination would enable adjusters to complete and submit data forms complete with pictures and eliminate the added processing required in their current use of paper-based forms and records. During the phone conversation, Crandall mentioned that some of the benefits are obvious; nevertheless they have concerns about the custom apps and transitioning to a fully digital system.

ROLE PLAY

Location—Mark Crandall's office at Southwest Claims & Adjusters.

Action—Role play this needs discovery sales call and demonstrate how you might utilize SPIN or ADAPT questioning sequences to identify the needs and concerns of the prospect.

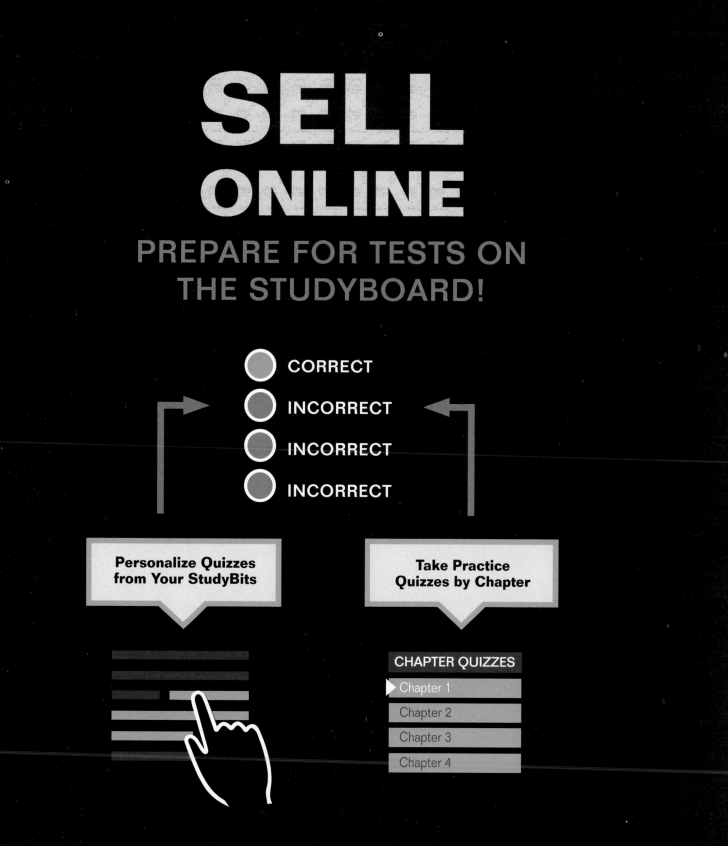

SELL
ONLINE
PREPARE FOR TESTS ON THE STUDYBOARD!

CORRECT

INCORRECT

INCORRECT

INCORRECT

Personalize Quizzes from Your StudyBits

Take Practice Quizzes by Chapter

CHAPTER QUIZZES

Chapter 1

Chapter 2

Chapter 3

Chapter 4

4LTR
PRESS

Access SELL ONLINE at www.cengagebrain.com

Part Two

5 | Strategic Prospecting and Preparing for Sales Dialogue

LEARNING OBJECTIVES

After completing this chapter, you should be able to:

5-1 Discuss why prospecting is an important and challenging task for salespeople.

5-2 Explain strategic prospecting and each stage in the strategic prospecting process.

5-3 Describe the major prospecting methods and give examples of each method.

5-4 Explain the important components of a strategic prospecting plan.

5-5 Discuss the types of information salespeople need to prepare for sales dialogue.

After finishing this chapter go to
PAGE 124 for STUDY TOOLS.

Gustavo Frazao/Shutterstock.com

Most salespeople have to spend time prospecting to generate business from new customers and to increase business with existing customers. Although some salespeople are responsible for identifying their prospects, many firms are integrating the marketing and sales function with the latest technology to generate leads, qualify and prioritize prospects, and set appointments for sales dialogue.

Consider the process developed by Ricoh in the office equipment industry. Sales in the office equipment industry were flat, budgets for advertising were tight, and buyers were moving halfway through their buying process before contacting a vendor. Ricoh needed a process that would identify potential customers and begin interactive communication with them much earlier. The basic objectives of their strategic prospecting process were to start conversations earlier, nurture prospects longer, and provide salespeople with qualified prospects ready to make a purchase.

Leads were generated from a variety of sources to include campaign emails, the company website, service technicians, and 800-number phone calls. Based on the initial contact, Ricoh provided the lead opportunities to obtain information that would help them determine how

TODAY'S PREPARATION... TOMORROW'S SUCCESS!

to solve their business problem. These could be access to white papers, articles, case studies, events, webinars, and infographics. Marketo was used to run personalized email campaigns to different market segments with automated emails tailored to how a prospect responded to an earlier email. When a prospect accesses any of this information, a score is given for the activity and recorded on their Salesforce.com CRM system, which is linked to Marketo. Once a prospect gets a high-enough score from their interactions, they become a prospect in Salesforce.com. The best prospects are those with the highest scores. Then, someone from the telephone sales team calls the prospect to see if they are ready for a face-to-face meeting. If so, the qualified sales prospect is turned over to a field salesperson to engage in the remainder of the sales process. In preparation for the initial sales dialogue, the salesperson is able to view all of the previous interactions Ricoh has had with the prospect from

information stored on Marketo and Salesforce.com. This process has been very successful in increasing the conversion of sales leads into customers.

The Ricoh example illustrates a situation where the strategic prospecting process is conducted by effective teamwork between the marketing and sales functions. However, many sales organizations give almost total responsibility for all prospecting activities to the salesperson. In between these two extremes, there are many approaches where the different strategic prospecting activities are shared between marketing and sales in various ways. The discussion in this chapter is oriented toward situations where salespeople are involved actively in all or most of the prospecting activities.

Regardless of the strategic prospecting approach used by a firm, most salespeople have to cultivate new business if they are to sustain the sales growth objectives their company establishes. However, salespeople typically achieve

The Ricoh example illustrates a situation where the strategic prospecting process is conducted by effective teamwork between the marketing and sales teams.

sales growth objectives by finding the right balance between getting new customers and generating additional business from existing customers. Various prospecting approaches are available, with each having advantages and disadvantages. New technological advances are increasing the tools salespeople can use to determine the best sales opportunities. The purpose of this chapter is to examine the importance and challenges of prospecting, introduce the strategic prospecting process, present different prospecting methods, and discuss preparation for sales dialogue.[1]

5-1 THE IMPORTANCE AND CHALLENGES OF PROSPECTING

Prospecting is extremely important to most salespeople. Salespeople who do not regularly prospect are operating under the assumption that the current business with existing customers will be sufficient to generate the desired level of future revenue. This is a shaky assumption in good times, but it is especially questionable in the tough business environment of recent years. As market conditions change, existing customers might buy less. Or, customers might go out of business. Some customers might be acquired by another firm, with the buying decisions now being made outside

the salesperson's territory. The salesperson could also simply lose customers due to competitive activity or dissatisfaction with the product, the salesperson, or the selling firm. Because there is typically a considerable time lag between the commencement of prospecting and the conversion of prospects to customer status, salespeople should spend time prospecting on a regular basis. Otherwise, lost sales volume cannot be regained quickly enough to satisfy the large majority of sales organizations—those that are growth oriented.

Despite its importance, salespeople often find it difficult to allocate enough time to prospecting. Many salespeople do not like to prospect because of their fear of rejection. Today's buyers are busy, and many are reluctant to see salespeople. An emerging trend faced by Ricoh and other sellers is that more B2B buyers are not relying on salespeople to provide information early in their buying process. These buyers are completing most of their prepurchase research online before they want to interact with a salesperson. Studies indicate that the buying process may be over 50 percent complete before a buyer contacts a salesperson and that more people are involved in the buying process than in the past. Therefore, salespeople must be more proactive in identifying prospects earlier in their buying process and in identifying all members of the buying center sooner, so they can have more of an impact on the final buying decision. This trend increases the difficulty of prospecting for many salespeople.[2]

Salespeople can overcome the challenges of prospecting and become more effective in determining the best sales opportunities by following a strategic sales prospecting process, utilizing a variety of prospecting methods, developing a strategic prospecting plan, and preparing for sales dialogue with prospects.

5-2 THE STRATEGIC PROSPECTING PROCESS

The first step in the trust-based sales process presented in Chapter 1 is strategic prospecting. **Strategic prospecting** is a process designed to identify, qualify, and prioritize sales opportunities, whether they represent potential new customers or opportunities to generate additional business from existing customers. The basic purpose of strategic prospecting is to help salespeople determine the best sales opportunities in the most efficient way. Effective strategic prospecting helps salespeople spend their valuable selling time in the most productive manner.

FIG. 5.1 SALES FUNNEL

Generating Sales Leads

Qualifying Sales Leads

Determining Sales Prospects

Prioritizing Sales Prospects

Preparing for Sales Dialogue

Remaining Stages in
the Trust-Based Sales Process

The sales funnel presents the trust-based sales process and highlights the major steps of the strategic prospecting process.

The strategic prospecting process (illustrated in Figure 5.1) is often viewed as a **sales funnel** or **sales pipeline** because it presents the entire trust-based sales process and the strategic prospecting process in the form of a funnel. The funnel is very wide at the top, as salespeople typically have a large number of potential sales

> The most productive salespeople pursue the best sales opportunities and translate a larger percentage of these opportunities into sales than less productive salespeople do.

opportunities. As salespeople move through the strategic prospecting process and the other stages in the trust-based sales process, the funnel narrows because only the best sales opportunities are pursued and not all sales opportunities result in a sale or new customer relationship. For the most productive salespeople, the sales funnel is normally much wider at the bottom than the bottom of the funnel for less productive salespeople. The most productive salespeople pursue the best sales opportunities and translate a larger percentage of these opportunities into actual sales than less productive salespeople do. We will now discuss each step in the strategic prospecting process.

5-2a Generating Sales Leads

The first step in the strategic prospecting process is to identify sales leads. **Sales leads** or **suspects** are organizations or individuals who might possibly purchase the product or service a salesperson offers. This represents the realm of sales opportunities for a salesperson. In the Ricoh example, all organizations that might need office equipment would be sales leads. USA Financial sells financial and marketing products to independent financial advisors, so sales leads would include all independent financial advisors.[3]

Although more sales leads are usually better than fewer sales leads, there are normally large differences in sales opportunities among all of the sales leads generated by salespeople. For example, larger organizations might purchase more office equipment, and larger independent financial advisor firms might buy more financial and marketing products. Thus, the larger organizations and firms would typically represent better sales opportunities than the smaller ones. If salespeople merely generate as many leads as possible and pursue most of them, they are likely to be spending a great deal of their time with sales leads that are not good sales opportunities for them.

5-2b Determining Sales Prospects

The most productive salespeople evaluate sales leads to determine which ones are true prospects for their product or service. This evaluation process is usually called **qualifying sales leads**. Salespeople search for, collect, analyze, and

sales funnel or **pipeline**
A representation of the trust-based sales process and strategic sales prospecting process in the form of a funnel.

sales leads or **suspects**
Organizations or individuals who might possibly purchase the product or service a salesperson offers.

qualifying sales leads
The salesperson's act of searching out, collecting, and analyzing information to determine the likelihood of the lead being a good candidate for making a sale.

use various types of screening procedures to determine if the sales lead is really a good sales prospect. Although specific companies define sales prospects in different ways, a **sales prospect** is typically an individual or organization that:

- Has a need for the product or service.
- Has the budget or financial resources to purchase the product or service.
- Has the authority to make the purchase decision.

Those that meet these criteria move down the sales funnel (see Figure 5.1) into the sales prospect category, while those that do not are set aside. Ricoh awards points to sales leads based on the number and types of materials accessed in responses to company emails. Once a specified number of points are accumulated, the lead becomes a prospect in Salesforce.com. USA Financial emails each lead five key questions about the situation at their firm. Those scoring above 190 on these questions are considered qualified prospects. Interestingly, only 14 percent of the independent financial advisors responding to recent emails were found to be qualified prospects. Salespeople who spend the time and effort qualifying their leads limit the time wasted on making calls with a low probability of success and focus their efforts on the more fruitful opportunities.

5-2c Prioritizing Sales Prospects

Even though the qualifying process has culled out the least promising sales leads, the remaining prospects do not all represent the same sales opportunity. The most productive salespeople prioritize their sales prospects to ensure that they spend most of their time on the best opportunities. One approach is to create an **ideal customer profile** and then analyze sales prospects by comparing them with this ideal customer profile. Those who most closely fit the profile are deemed to be the best sales prospects. Another approach is to identify one or more criteria, evaluate sales prospects against these criteria, and either rank all of the sales prospects based on this evaluation or place the sales prospects into A, B, and C categories, with A sales prospects representing the best sales opportunities. Ricoh and USA Financial both prioritize their prospects according to the points assigned to

sales prospect An individual or organization that has a need for the product or service, has the budget or financial resources to purchase the product or service, and has the authority to make the purchase decision.

ideal customer profile The characteristics of a firm's best customers or the perfect customer.

Salespeople can network for prospects electronically.

a prospect from their scoring system—the more points, the better the prospect. At Ricoh, the telephone sales team calls the best prospects to set up an appointment with a Ricoh field salesperson. At USA Financial, the salespeople contact the highest scoring prospects directly to schedule a meeting. The net result in both situations is that their salespeople are spending their valuable time with the best sales opportunities.

5-2d Preparing for Sales Dialogue

The final step in the strategic prospecting process is to prepare for the initial contact with a sales prospect by planning the sales dialogue. The information accumulated to this point in the process is helpful, but additional information is usually required to increase the chances of success in the initial sales dialogue. The types of additional information required are discussed later in this chapter. An example of the strategic prospecting process is presented in "From the Classroom to the Field: Effective Strategic Prospecting."

5-3 PROSPECTING METHODS

Many different sources and methods for effective strategic prospecting have been developed for use in different selling situations. A good selling organization and successful salespeople will have a number of ongoing prospecting methods in place at any given time. The salesperson must continually evaluate prospecting methods to determine which methods are bringing in the best results. New methods must also be evaluated and tested for their effectiveness. Many popular prospecting methods are presented in Exhibit 5.1.

From the Classroom to the Field

Effective Strategic Prospecting

Justin Price graduated from the University of Louisville in May 2013 and is an outside media representative for YP. He sells print and Internet advertising to new and existing small business customers. Justin talks about how what he learned in his sales classes has helped him become more effective at prospecting:

My sales classes emphasized the importance of qualifying sales leads and prioritizing sales prospects to identify the best sales opportunities. Acquiring new business customers is essential for success in my position, and I am responsible for the entire prospecting process. I gather sales leads from a variety of sources, such as direct mail, online directories, competing phone book directories, business card boards, etc. Qualifying sales leads includes checking our internal system to see if they are or have been YP customers. I then investigate the amount and types of advertising the prospect currently does to help prioritize my prospects. Then, I use bbb.org, manta.com, and the prospect's website and Facebook page to learn more about the company and the person to contact. The last step is to contact the appropriate person by phone, gather additional information, and set up an appointment to meet with the prospect. This process helped me lead our division in new business accounts last year.

A specific example of this process started when I received a direct mail piece from a paving company. The next day I found that the paving company had been a YP customer years ago, but was not now. I used several sources to identify the person to contact, the size of the company, services provided, and that the company did not have a website. I also found out that they were advertising on a competing online directory. This information helped, because I knew that YP had several advantages over this competitor. So, I called and asked for the person by name, discussed their current advertising, and described how YP electronic products could help grow his business at a lower cost per lead. The prospect agreed to a meeting and I was able to sell him an online advertising program.

Exhibit 5.1

Prospecting Methods

Cold Canvassing	Networking	Company Sources	Commercial Sources
• Cold Calling	• Centers of Influence	• Company Records	• Directories
• Referrals	• Noncompeting Salespeople	• Advertising Inquiries	• Lead Management Sources
• Introductions	• Social Media	• Telephone Inquiries	
		• Trade Shows	
		• Seminars	

An Ethical Dilemma

Meg Hagan is a sales representative for United Office Furniture. She sells all types of office furniture to professional firms. Meg has been especially successful in using referrals to get appointments with the decision makers at prospect firms. For example, she used a referral to set up a meeting with Max Pursell, managing partner at an accounting firm, and ended up making her largest sale. Max is very satisfied with the office furniture he purchased for a satellite office. During a recent Chamber of Commerce event, Meg was talking with Max, and Max told a story about a fishing trip with his friend, Patrick Bassett. Meg knows that Patrick is the managing partner at a small, but growing law firm. She recently saw in the business news that his law firm was going to open a new office in the suburbs and would announce the exact location in the next two weeks. Meg asked Max if he would be willing to refer her to Patrick and send an email to Patrick introducing her. Max said he normally does not like to make referrals, but he might make an exception in her case. He said he would think about it and let her know within a week, if he would send a referral email. Meg was excited and began to gather information about Patrick and his firm. After a week went by, Meg had not

heard from Max, so she called his office and found out that he was on a three-week vacation in Europe. Meg knows that it is extremely important that she talk with Patrick as soon as possible to have the best chance for the office equipment at the new office location. A sale to Patrick's firm would lead to a hefty bonus for her. But, she does not have the referral approval from Max. Without the referral email, Meg knows it will be harder to get a meeting with Patrick, and she will not have the favorable comments from Max about the satisfied experience he had working with her.

What should Meg do?

1. Contact Patrick by phone, mention the positive experience she had working with Max, and try to set up an appointment without a direct referral and email from Max.
2. Contact Patrick by phone and indicate that Max had referred her to him for his office equipment needs and try to set up a meeting.
3. Wait until Max is back at work and call to see if Max would write the referral email to Patrick. Once the email is sent, contact Patrick by phone to set up an appointment.

---

cold calling Contacting a sales lead unannounced and with little or no information about the lead.

referral A name of a company or person given to the salesperson as a lead by a customer or even a prospect who did not buy at this time.

introduction A variation of a referral where, in addition to requesting the names of prospects, the salesperson asks the prospect or customer to prepare a note or letter of introduction that can be sent to the potential customer.

5-3a Cold Canvassing

Cold canvassing occurs when salespeople contact a sales lead unannounced with little if any information about the lead. **Cold calling** is the most extreme form of cold canvassing because salespeople merely "knock on doors" or make telephone calls to organizations or individuals. This is a very inefficient prospecting method. Typically, a very

small percentage of cold calls produce, or lead to future sales dialogue with, qualified prospects. Because there is so much rejection, many salespeople do not like to cold call sales leads.

Using referrals or introductions can improve the success of cold calling. A **referral** is a sales lead a customer or some other influential person provides. Salespeople are often trained to ask customers and others for the names and contact information of potential prospects. Sometimes salespeople can also obtain sufficient information to qualify the lead as a good sales prospect. Additionally, salespeople can get permission to use the person's name when contacting the prospect. In some cases, the person might agree to provide an **introduction** by writing a letter or making a phone call to introduce the salesperson to the prospect. This referral approach can work well, but ethical issues might arise, as depicted in "An Ethical Dilemma."

5-3b Networking

Salespeople can use various types of networking as effective methods for prospecting. Many salespeople join civic and professional organizations, country clubs, or fraternal organizations, and these memberships provide the opportunity for them to build relationships with other members. Sometimes these relationships yield prospects. Some members might be influential people in the community or other organizations, making them **centers of influence** for the salesperson and potentially providing help in locating prospects. Accountants, bankers, attorneys, teachers, business owners, politicians, and government workers are often good centers of influence.

Networking with salespeople from noncompeting firms can also be a good source of prospects. Business Networking International (BNI) is a formal organization with each local group consisting of **noncompeting salespeople**. The basic purpose of this organization is for the members to generate prospects for each other. There are other sales and marketing organizations that salespeople can join to create the opportunity to identify prospects by networking with members.

It is important for salespeople to strike up conversations with other sales representatives while waiting to see buyers. Noncompeting salespeople can be found everywhere and can help in getting valuable information about prospects. An example of how noncompeting salespeople can help each other was demonstrated when a Hershey Chocolate, U.S.A., salesperson went out of his way to tell a Hormel sales representative about a new food mart going into his territory. The Hormel representative was the first

Participating in trade shows is an effective prospecting method.

of his competitors to meet with the new food mart management team and was given valuable shelf space that his competitors could not get. A few months later, the Hormel sales representative returned the favor when he found out that an independent grocer was changing hands. The Hershey salesperson was able to get into the new owner's store early and added valuable shelf space for his products. The operating principle of "you scratch my back, and I scratch yours" works when information flows in both directions.[4]

Social media are increasingly being used by salespeople to engage in **electronic networking** by identifying, gathering information about, and communicating with prospects. Studies indicate that salespeople using social media actively are more productive and perform better than salespeople not involved with social media. These salespeople use LinkedIn most often, followed by Facebook, Google Plus, and Twitter. Social media help salespeople identify more leads and better prospects earlier in the buying process, and provide them the opportunity to share valuable content that leads to conversations with prospects.[5]

Consider one suggested approach for using LinkedIn. A salesperson can identify leads from the networks of their LinkedIn connections and from the "Who's Viewed Your Profile" on their LinkedIn screen. They can then send a connection request to the lead. Once connected to the lead, the salesperson can email a message with meaningful content as a way to start a conversation with the lead and to

Noncompeting salespeople can be found everywhere and can help in getting valuable information about prospects—see the Hershey and Hormel example.

centers of influence Well-known and influential people who can help a salesperson prospect and gain leads.

noncompeting salespeople A salesperson selling noncompeting products.

electronic networking Using social media to help salespeople identify, gather information about, and communicate with prospects.

determine if the lead is a qualified prospect. If so, the salesperson can continue the conversation and try to move into the remainder of the sales process at the appropriate time. If not, the salesperson can still share relevant content, because the lead might become a qualified prospect in the future.

5-3c Company Sources

Many companies have resources or are engaged in activities that can help their own salespeople with strategic prospecting. **Company records** can be a useful source of prospects. Salespeople can review company records to identify previous customers who have not placed an order recently. Contacting previous customers to determine why they have stopped ordering could provide opportunities to win back business. Examining the purchasing behavior of existing customers can also help in identifying opportunities to sell additional products to specific customers.

Advertising inquiries are potentially a good source of prospects. For example, one manufacturer's rep in the natural gas industry speaks highly of his company's advertising plan. They only advertise in trade magazines that they believe their buyers read. The salesperson's territory includes Idaho, Utah, Montana, and Wyoming. Their advertising message is simply, "If we can help you with any of your natural gas needs (e.g., flow meters, odorizers), please give us a call." These leads are then turned over to the salesperson who calls on that territory. One salesperson cannot cover territories of this size. The advertising program qualifies the prospect (with the help of the telephone) before the salesperson is sent out on the call.[6]

The Ricoh and USA Financial examples presented earlier in this chapter represent different approaches companies

are implementing to employ Web-based and email marketing campaigns to identify sales leads, qualify and prioritize prospects, and help salespeople focus on the best sales opportunities.

Chapman Kelly is one company that has used Web-based marketing effectively. The company redesigned its Web site to include interactive features that created a dialogue with visitors. It worked on the site's search engine optimization to get into the top five listings for healthcare audit-related terms and started a company blog. These efforts increased traffic to its Web site from 10 to 15 visits per week to 1,500–2,000, generated qualified sales prospects, and increased new business by $2 million. This Web-based marketing approach has replaced cold calling as the major source of new customers.[7]

Many organizations today use both inbound (prospect calls the company) and outbound (salesperson contacts the prospect) telemarketing. **Inbound telemarketing** involves a telephone number (usually a toll-free number) that prospects or customers can call for information. Companies distribute toll-free numbers by direct mail pieces (brochures), advertising campaigns, and their **outbound telemarketing** program. United Insurance Agency uses both inbound and outbound telemarketing to serve their market niche of hotels across America.[8] They use outbound telemarketing to generate and then qualify leads for their salesforce. Qualified leads are turned over to experienced salespeople. Usually, interns do all the outbound telemarketing. Inbound telemarketing is used to resolve problems, answer questions of prospects, and take orders from existing customers.

Attending conventions and **trade shows** presents salespeople with excellent opportunities to collect leads. Generally, the company purchases booth space and sets up a stand that clearly identifies the company and its offerings. Salespeople are available at the booth to demonstrate their products or answer questions. Potential customers walk by and are asked to fill out information cards indicating an interest in the company or one of its products. The completed information card provides leads for the salesperson. Trade shows can stimulate interest in products and provide leads. For example, bank loan officers attend home improvement trade shows and can offer the homeowner immediate credit to begin a project. Those who sign immediately may be offered a reduction in their interest rate.

Firms can use **seminars** to generate leads and provide information to prospective customers. For

company records Information about customers in a company database.

advertising inquiries Sales leads generated from company advertising efforts.

inbound telemarketing A source of locating prospects whereby the prospect calls the company to get information.

outbound telemarketing A source of locating prospects whereby the salesperson contacts the prospect by telephone.

trade shows Events where companies purchase space and set up booths that clearly identify each company and its offerings and that are staffed with salespeople who demonstrate the products and answer questions.

seminars A presentation salespeople give to generate leads and provide information to prospective customers who are invited to the seminar by direct mail, word of mouth, or advertising on local television or radio.

example, a financial planner will set up a seminar at a local hotel to give a presentation on retirement planning, inviting prospects by direct mail, word of mouth, or advertising on local television and radio. The financial consultant discusses a technique or investing opportunities that will prepare the audience for retirement. Those present will be asked to fill out a card expressing their interest for follow-up discussions. The financial consultant hopes this free seminar will reward him or her with a few qualified prospects.

5-3d Commercial Sources

A variety of sources in print and electronic form can be very useful in prospecting. **Directories** offer an inexpensive, convenient means of identifying leads. Telephone books today contain a business section that lists all the community's businesses. This list is usually broken down further by business type. Manufacturers, medical facilities, pharmacies, and grocery stores, to name a few, can be easily identified by using the business pages of the phone book. Many other directories exist, such as chamber of commerce directories and trade association lists. The online versions of these directories are especially valuable, because they are updated regularly and usually have search capabilities to facilitate the identification of targeted leads.

There are a growing number of companies providing a variety of **lead management services**, such as lists of targeted businesses or individuals with detailed contact and other information, as well as email, direct mail, telephone, and Web-based marketing services to connect with the targeted leads. Examples of companies providing different types of lead management services include: InfoUSA (www.infousa.com), ZoomInfo (www.zoominfo.com), Hoovers (www.hoovers.com), and Marketo (www.marketo.com).

Companies like Hoovers, provide lead management services to other organizations.

5-4 DEVELOPING A STRATEGIC PROSPECTING PLAN

The most productive salespeople use a variety of prospecting methods and follow the strategic prospecting process by generating leads, qualifying them to identify true prospects, and then prioritizing these prospects so that they pursue the best sales opportunities. The use of a strategic prospecting plan can help salespeople continuously improve their prospecting effectiveness. An example of increasing prospecting effectiveness is presented in "TECHNOLOGY IN SALES: Improving the Strategic Prospecting Plan."

A **strategic prospecting plan** should fit the individual needs of the salesperson. As illustrated in Figure 5.2, the focal point of a prospecting plan should be the goal stating the number of qualified prospects to be generated. Formalized goals serve as guides to what is to be accomplished and help to keep a salesperson on track. The plan should also allocate an adequate and specific daily or weekly time period for prospecting. Having specific time periods set aside exclusively for prospecting helps to prevent other activities from creeping in and displacing prospecting activities. A good **tracking system** should also be a part of the prospecting plan. A tracking system can be as low-tech as a set of 3 × 5-inch note cards or employ one of the many computerized and online contact management or customer relationship management software applications. Exhibit 5.2 shows an example of a simple, but effective, paper-and-pencil tracking form. The tracking system should record comprehensive information about the prospect, trace the prospecting methods used, and chronologically archive outcomes from any contacts with the prospect. A fourth element of the prospecting plan is

directories Electronic or print sources that provide contact and other information about many different companies or individuals.

lead management services Lists of targeted businesses or individuals with detailed contact and other information, as well as email, direct mail, telephone, and Web-based marketing services to connect with targeted leads.

strategic prospecting plan A salesperson's plan for gathering qualified prospects.

tracking system Part of the strategic prospecting plan that records comprehensive information about the prospect, traces the prospecting methods used, and chronologically archives outcomes from any contacts with the prospect.

Technology in Sales

Improving the Strategic Prospecting Plan

Tom Raisor is former managing director and development officer at Northwestern Mutual (NM). He has been with NM for 35 years and is involved in sales as well as training all salespeople in his region. Tom talks about how the introduction of technology has improved the strategic prospecting plan at NM:

> Developing and implementing a strategic prospecting plan is extremely important to the success of salespeople at NM. We recommend that salespeople have a goal of at least 15 qualified prospects each week. They also need to spend time prospecting at the end of each fact-finding appointment and at the conclusion of presenting the comprehensive financial plan. Finally, it is critically important to keep prospecting records, evaluate results, and make improvements over time as indicated in the following example.

We have used a referred lead prospecting approach for many years. After a meeting with a satisfied client, the salesperson asks the client for anyone he/she knows that might benefit from our services and to contact the prospect and let them know that someone from NM will be contacting them soon. This approach worked well, but sometimes the client could not provide many prospect names, sometimes they would not contact the prospect, and if they did contact the prospect, it was not known when or what the client said. So, we have integrated technology into our referred lead prospecting approach to address these issues. First, prior to a client meeting, the salesperson uses LinkedIn Groups, Facebook, and other sources to identify 5–6 people that the client knows who are likely to be good prospects. This feeder list is presented to the client, who then selects the best prospects from it and explains why each should be a good prospect. Then, the salesperson asks the client to email or text each prospect with a short note introducing the salesperson, providing some favorable comments, and copying the salesperson. The new approach has been very successful, because clients provide more good prospects, are more likely to text or email the prospect with a more favorable introduction, and the salesperson knows when the client contacted the prospect and what was said. The salesperson can then call the prospect to set up an initial meeting. Employing widely used social media, texting, and email technology has produced a better strategic prospecting plan, generated more favorable introductions to qualified prospects, and led to a much higher success rate in securing effective appointments with these prospects.

a system for analyzing and evaluating the results of prospecting activities. Continuous evaluation should be employed to ensure that the salesperson is meeting prospecting goals and using the most effective prospecting methods. The fifth and final element of a prospecting plan should be a program to review and stay up-to-date on product knowledge and competitor information to emphasize and underscore that the salesperson's products and services offer the best solutions to customer needs and problems. Self-confidence is critical to success in selling, and a base of comprehensive knowledge and understanding is the key to believing in one's self.

As with all phases of the sales process, salespeople must exercise judgment and set priorities in prospecting. There is a limited amount of time for prospecting, and a better understanding of the concepts and practices illustrated in this chapter can help a salesperson be more productive. An added bonus is that the sales process is more enjoyable for salespeople calling on bona fide prospects who can benefit from the salesperson's offering.

FIG. 5.2   PROSPECTING PLANS ARE THE FOUNDATION FOR EFFECTIVE PROSPECTING

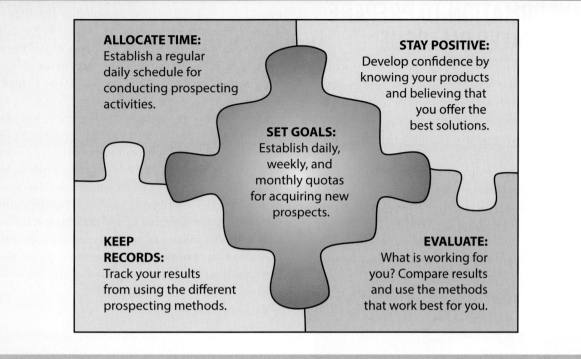

ALLOCATE TIME: Establish a regular daily schedule for conducting prospecting activities.

STAY POSITIVE: Develop confidence by knowing your products and believing that you offer the best solutions.

SET GOALS: Establish daily, weekly, and monthly quotas for acquiring new prospects.

KEEP RECORDS: Track your results from using the different prospecting methods.

EVALUATE: What is working for you? Compare results and use the methods that work best for you.

The strategic prospecting plan sets goals, allocates specific times to be used for prospecting, and continuously evaluates results in order to maximize the effectiveness of prospecting time and effort.

Exhibit 5.2

Personal Prospecting Log

PERSONAL PROSPECTING LOG

Name   Tom Jenkins

Team   Indianapolis commercial   **Date**   4/16

Organization	Contact Person	Source of Lead	Phone	Date of Appointment	Outcome of Call	Follow-up Activity
Cummins Engine	Tyler Huston	Personal contact	765-444-1234	4/11 8:30 A.M.	Need info on printer	Send in mail
Ontario Systems	Darrell Beaty	Referral	765-223-4117	4/19 4 P.M.		
Chase	Alice Arnold	Direct mail sent back 6/02	317-663-2214	4/16 Lunch	Didn't seem impressed need more work	Need more contact with Alice PACER GAME?
Thomson Consumer Electronics	Doug Lyon	Phone	317-212-4111	4/15 3 P.M.	Had bad experience with us several years ago	This one will take time

5-5 GATHERING PROSPECT INFORMATION TO PREPARE FOR SALES DIALOGUE

The basic objective of the strategic prospecting process is to provide salespeople with a list of prioritized sales prospects. Salespeople can then select the best opportunities and move into the next stage of the trust-based sales process, which is covered in Chapter 6, "Planning Sales Dialogues and Presentations." Some information about the prospect has been collected throughout the strategic prospecting process, but more is needed to be effective at each stage of the trust-based sales process. In many cases, the next step is for the salesperson to contact the prospect by telephone. Although the purpose of this call is usually to set up an appointment, salespeople are often able to collect additional useful information. All of the information collected prior to meeting with a prospect provides a foundation for completing the Sales Dialogue Template addressed in Chapter 6. An example of assembling prospecting information before meeting with current customers to generate more business is presented in "SELLING IN ACTION: Prospecting Information for Current Customers."

The more information a salesperson has about a prospect, the better chance a salesperson has to make a sale. Thus, gathering relevant information is an ongoing activity throughout the trust-based sales process, but especially important prior to the initial sales dialogue with a prospect. The information needed varies depending on the product or service being sold and the specific buyer's situation. We will examine the types of basic information about the prospect and information about the selling situation. Then, sources of this information will be discussed.

Selling in Action

Prospecting Information for Current Customers

Brittany Morriston is an account manager at Consolidated Electrical Distributors (CED). She presents her approach for gathering information to prepare for sales dialogue in order to generate more business from existing customers:

My sales job focuses on strengthening relationships and increasing our business with current customers. A major objective of a sales call is relationship-building, but it also represents a potential opportunity to generate more business from the customer. The most useful prospecting information is to access our company database to create a gap analysis. This report indicates the products the customer is currently buying and not buying from us, and I make note of all the products the customer is not buying from us. I then review my customer database to determine which of the products the customer is not buying from us and would represent the best sales opportunity to address during my sales call. My focus is one specific product during each sales call.

My approach to gathering prospecting information prior to a sales call can turn a relationship-building meeting into new business from an existing customer. For example, I was preparing for a sales call with an industrial customer. After studying the gap analysis and my customer database, my objective was to discuss automation and controls during our meeting. However, during our conversation the buyer brought up fuses. Even though I had planned to focus on automation and controls, I immediately switched to a discussion of fuses, because fuses were of interest to the customer. The customer gave us the opportunity to quote their entire fuse line, and we are now getting all of their fuse business. My gathering of prospecting information, especially studying the gap analysis, prepared me to be able to adapt my initial plan to meet the needs of the customer and generate more business from this customer.

Exhibit 5.3

Basic Information about the Prospect

About the Buyer	About the Company
• Buyer's name, title, and contact information	• Type of business
• Educational and work background	• History of business
• Community and organizational involvement	• Number of employees
• Hobbies and interests	• Target market served
• Communication style	• Products and services offered
	• Key competitors
	• Current strategy and performance

5-5a Basic Information about the Prospect

There is usually a great deal of basic information about the prospective buyer and company that can be obtained and evaluated prior to the initial sales dialogue with a prospect. Examples of the most valuable information are presented in Exhibit 5.3. It is very important for salespeople to do their homework and obtain as much of this information as possible before meeting with a prospect. The basic information about the buyer helps the salesperson understand the buyer from a personal perspective. This knowledge will be useful in establishing rapport with the buyer, which is extremely important early in the trust-based sales process. The basic information about the company provides the salesperson with an understanding of the prospect company that will help the salesperson determine the best questions to ask during sales dialogue. Some companies are employing the latest technology to provide salespeople with useful prospect information. For example, Cintas has created a virtual office of various types of prospect information. Salespeople can access this information electronically and obtain valuable information before contacting a prospect. Prospects are typically impressed with salespeople who are prepared and know a lot about them and their company before the first meeting.[9]

5-5b Information about the Selling Situation

Specific information about the selling situation is extremely valuable to salespeople. Although much of the basic information about the prospect can normally be gathered prior to meeting with a prospect, much of the information about the selling situation will be obtained from the prospect during sales dialogues. However, salespeople should try to obtain this information as soon as possible, because it is useful during each stage of the trust-based sales process.

> The more a salesperson knows about a prospect, the better chance a salesperson has to make a sale.

Specific types of selling situation information are presented in Exhibit 5.4. Most of this information helps the salesperson understand all aspects of the

Exhibit 5.4

Information about the Selling Situation

- Type of purchase
- Motivation for buying
- Current supplier
- Buying center members and roles
- Buying process
- Available budget
- Competitors involved

prospect's buying process and was discussed in Chapter 3, "Understanding Buyers" and is part of the Sales Dialogue Template prepared in Chapter 6. Several pharmaceutical firms are using smartphone apps so that salespeople can get the latest information about a physician's situation before a sales call. A few clicks on the app and the salesperson is alerted to any changes in the physician's patient population or prescribing habit, as well as any physician engagements with digital media. Selling situation information that cannot be obtained prior to meeting with a prospect becomes a key focus during the sales dialogue.[10]

5-5c Sources of Information

Salespeople have a variety of sources for the needed information. Examples of useful sources are presented in Exhibit 5.5. The use of social media as a valuable information source for salespeople has been increasing in recent years. Facebook, LinkedIn, and blogs are especially useful information sources. Many companies are also accumulating information about prospects and making it readily available to salespeople using the latest technology.

The use of new and emerging technologies will certainly improve the availability of prospect information for salespeople in the future.

Even the most thorough preparation will usually not provide salespeople with all of the desired prospect information. The additional information is typically collected through questioning the prospect during sales dialogues.

Exhibit 5.5
Sources of Information

- Online searches
- Online and print directories
- Prospect Web site
- Social media
- Annual reports
- Trade and business press
- Professional organizations
- Company databases
- Contact with prospect

Alexmillos/Shutterstock.com

LEAD GENERATION

The information salespeople collect about prospects prior to the first meeting and throughout the trust-based sales process should be accumulated and updated on a regular basis. Although some salespeople do this manually with paper files, the use of contact management, salesforce automation (SFA) and customer relationship management (CRM) systems is increasing. These technologies are being improved continuously and are valuable tools for salespeople.

STUDY TOOLS 5

LOCATED IN TEXTBOOK
- [ ] Rip-out and review chapter review card

LOCATED AT WWW.CENGAGEBRAIN.COM
- [ ] Review key term flashcards and create your own from StudyBits
- [ ] Organize notes and StudyBits using the StudyBoard feature within 4LTR Press Online

- [ ] Complete practice and graded quizzes to prepare for tests
- [ ] Complete interactive content within the narrative portion of 4LTR Press Online
- [ ] View chapter highlight box content at the beginning of each chapter

DEVELOPING A STRATEGIC PROSPECTING PLAN

BACKGROUND

Jennifer Hamman graduated from the state university and was hired as a sales representative for the Logistics Company. The Logistics Company is a transportation broker that links companies needing products shipped with trucking firms to carry the shipments. After an initial training program, Jennifer was given a couple of existing company customers and a small list of leads to get her started. She began by serving the shipment needs of the existing customers. This gave her some confidence, but she realized that for her to be successful, she must begin prospecting and try to identify the best sales opportunities. The Logistics Company provides an ongoing list of leads that can be accessed by all salespeople. Once a salesperson contacts one of these leads, no other salesperson can contact them. Jennifer started her prospecting by contacting these leads.

CURRENT SITUATION

Jennifer has been calling a number of leads each day, but has not been very successful in generating much business. She feels like she is wasting much of her time on leads that are not good sales opportunities. The leads provided by her company are not qualified in any way and the training program she attended focused on cold calling as the basic prospecting method. Jennifer took a professional selling class in college and remembered that the chapter on prospecting emphasized the need to follow the strategic prospecting process to identify the best sales opportunities. She found her professional selling textbook, went to the chapter on prospecting, and decided to create a strategic prospecting plan.

QUESTIONS

1. What methods should Jennifer use to generate sales leads beyond those provided by her company?

2. How should Jennifer qualify the leads provided by her company and those she generates herself? What is the profile of an ideal prospect?

3. How should Jennifer prioritize her qualified prospects?

4. What information should Jennifer collect to prepare for sales dialogue with a prospect?

5. Jennifer used LinkedIn during college and wanted to employ it in her strategic prospecting process. How can she best use LinkedIn?

ROLE PLAY

Situation: Read case and prepare a strategic prospecting plan.

Characters: Jennifer and her sales manager.

Scene: Jennifer has implemented her strategic prospecting plan and been very successful. She has been the top seller in her office for the past two months. Her sales manager is impressed and he asks her what she is doing to be so successful. She indicates that her success is due to spending most of her time with the best sales opportunities. He wants to talk to her about her strategic prospecting plan and sets up a meeting.

Location: Sales manager's office.

Action: Role play the meeting between Jennifer and her sales manager. The sales manager should ask many questions and Jennifer will respond to these questions. The use of LinkedIn has been valuable to Jennifer and no other salespeople at the Logistics Company are using LinkedIn, so make sure the role of LinkedIn is included in the role play.

PROSPECTING AND GAINING PROSPECT INFORMATION

BACKGROUND

Preston Adams has just completed the sales training program for the Office Copier Company (OCC). Adams has been assigned a territory in Illinois that includes the metro areas of Bloomington, Decatur, and Peoria. The company once commanded a significant market share in these markets. However, due to a problem with a previous salesperson in these markets three years ago, OCC has not been directly working this particular region of central Illinois. Although there is a large number of their machines still in use across this territory, it has been a while since a salesperson has called on any accounts. As with any geographic area, there have likely been a lot of changes with existing companies moving or even going out of business and new companies opening up.

CURRENT SITUATION

Adams's sales manager, Eric Waits, is coming in two weeks to spend three days in the field with Adams calling on prospective accounts. Adams is working to develop a list of leads that he can qualify and then contact in order to set up the sales calls he will be making with his manager.

ROLE PLAY

Situation: Read the Role Play Prospecting and Gaining Prospect Information.

Characters: Preston Adams, salesperson for OCC; Jerri Spencer, office manager with purchasing responsibilities for Peoria-based McKelvey and Walters, Attorneys-at-Law.

Scene:

Location—Preston Adams's office at OCC.

Action—In the course of Adams's prospecting activities, Spencer and the McKelvey and Walters law firm have come up as a strong prospect for OCC's new line of professional copiers. McKelvey and Walters operate a large office in Peoria that occupies most of two floors in the Planter's Bank Building and a branch office in Bloomington. They were previously a customer of OCC, but the information that Adams has obtained indicates that they are using an unspecified variety of different brands of copiers.

Role play the phone conversation between Adams and Spencer as Adams introduces himself and his company to Spencer, gathers needed information to better qualify the prospect, and asks for an appointment for an initial sales call.

6 | Planning Sales Dialogues and Presentations

LEARNING OBJECTIVES

After studying this chapter, the student should be able to:

6-1 Explain why it is essential to focus on the customer when planning sales calls.

6-2 Understand alternative ways of communicating with prospects and customers through canned sales presentations, written sales proposals, and organized sales dialogues and presentations.

6-3 Discuss the nine components in the sales dialogue template that can be used for planning an organized sales dialogue or presentation.

6-4 Explain how to write a customer value proposition statement.

6-5 Link buying motives to benefits of the seller's offering, support claims made for benefits, and reinforce verbal claims made.

6-6 Engage the customer by setting appointments.

After finishing this chapter go to
PAGE 146 for **STUDY TOOLS.**

Rawpixel/Shutterstock.com

College students and professional salespeople have a lot in common: Performance is largely determined by preparation. The best salespeople know that their success depends on their ability to properly plan for customer encounters. According to Dr. Joël LeBon of the University of Houston, best practices in preparation for sales encounters are crucial to performance in three areas: gathering competitive intelligence, striving for mindfulness, and setting high goals. Salespeople need to be knowledgeable about customers, prospects, competitors, and the overall market. Mindful salespeople are more alert to what the customer is saying and thus better prepared to focus on the customer's objectives. Goal setting is critical, as ambitious goals can drive forward-looking behaviors and make salespeople more creative and strategic.

Bill Bartlett, a sales trainer in the Chicago area, reinforces the concept of the salesperson as a student, noting that high performers continuously learn about the marketplace and its changing nuances. Through continuous learning, salespeople become valued information resources for their customers, and less reliant on guesswork and mind reading. This leads to deeper, more enduring customer relationships.

In today's fast-changing, information-rich business world, top salespeople must be inquisitive and able to assess their own efforts when it comes to pre-call preparation. For example, salespeople should ask themselves if they are fully prepared in terms of what information they will need from the buyer, what they will want to convey to the buyer, what support information they will need, and what obstacles they will need to overcome. Their pre-call preparation must be guided by a firm objective that specifies the customer action sought as a result of the upcoming call.

Sales technology is assisting pre-call planning far beyond checking out the prospect's Web site. While customer Web-site searches can yield valuable information, other sources are rapidly growing in popularity. For example, LinkedIn has become a powerful tool for researching companies and individuals within those companies. Prospective buyers often seek advice on potential vendors on LinkedIn, and sales organizations are monitoring the site as part of pre-call preparation. InsideView.com offers an online tool that monitors LinkedIn and Twitter for relevant sales opportunities and prospect information. Google (Google.com/finance and Google alerts) and Hoovers (www.hoovers.com) also offer salespeople efficient ways for preparing for sales calls.

With an abundance of information at their fingertips, salespeople have no excuse for arriving unprepared for a sales call. With most business decision makers starved for time, showing up unprepared is essentially an insult to the buyer. Top salespeople already know this, and they would not dare insult their prospects or existing customers.[1]

6-1 CUSTOMER-FOCUSED SALES DIALOGUE PLANNING

As noted in the introduction, buyers are generally well-informed and have little time to waste. This means that salespeople must invest a significant amount of time in planning sales calls on prospective and existing customers so that they can communicate in a clear, credible, and interesting fashion. A **sales call** takes place when the salesperson and buyer or buyers meet in person to discuss business. This typically takes place in the customer's place of business, but it may take place elsewhere, such as in the seller's place of business or at a trade show.

The importance of focusing on the customer when planning sales dialogues is reflected in the popular trade book *The Collaborative Sale* by Keith M. Eades and Timothy T. Sullivan.

sales call An in-person meeting between a salesperson or sales team and one or more buyers to discuss business.

sales dialogue Business conversations between buyers and sellers that occur as salespeople attempt to initiate, develop, and enhance customer relationships. Sales dialogue should be customer-focused and have a clear purpose.

sales presentations Comprehensive communications that convey multiple points designed to persuade the customer to make a purchase.

As defined in Chapter 1, **sales dialogue** is a business conversation between buyers and sellers that takes place over time as salespeople attempt to initiate, develop, and enhance customer relationships. The term *sales conversation* is used interchangeably with sales dialogue. Some sales calls involve

sales presentations as part of the dialogue. Sales presentations are comprehensive communications that convey multiple points designed to persuade the prospect or customer to make a purchase.

Ideally, sales presentations focus on customer value and only take place after the salesperson has completed the ADAPT process (introduced in Chapter 4). As a reminder, the ADAPT process means the salesperson has *assessed* the customer's situation; *discovered* his or her needs, buying processes, and strategic priorities; *activated* the buyer's interest in solving a problem or realizing an opportunity; helped the buyer *project* how value can be derived from a purchase; and then made a *transition* to the full sales presentation. Salespeople who attempt to make a sales presentation before building a foundation through sales dialogue risk being viewed as noncustomer-oriented and overly aggressive.

To focus on customer value and implement the trust-based selling process as discussed in Chapter 1 (see Figure 1.4), salespeople must have a basic understanding of the value they and their companies can deliver to customers. Further, they must recognize that what constitutes value will typically vary from one customer to the next. Finally, as the process continues and relationships are established with customers, salespeople must work continually to increase the value their customers receive. Before, during, and after the sale, selling strategy must focus on customer needs and how the customer defines value. For additional insights on sales call planning, see, "SELLING IN ACTION: Planning Sales Dialogues."

To better understand the process of planning sales dialogues and presentations, we will now discuss the three most common sales communications formats. A planning template that serves as a guide for sales dialogues and comprehensive presentations will then be presented. The chapter concludes with a discussion of how to foster better sales dialogues when attempting to initiate relationships with customers.

Selling in Action

Planning Sales Dialogues

Lisa Rose is a sales consultant and trainer with The Brooks Group, a well-respected organization with clients around the globe. She clearly understands the importance of thoughtful planning for upcoming sales calls:

> Some of life's greatest experiences come from acting on off-the-cuff, impulsive decisions. But if you are a smart salesperson, you save these impromptu endeavors for weekends and vacations. That's because in any professional venture, planning is important; in sales, it is often the difference between success and failure. The most commonly overlooked, but critically important step in the sales process is a thorough pre-call plan. The more you know about the buyer in advance, the better chance you have of being perceived as a strategic resource for your prospect, and for maximizing the time you have in the face-to-face phase of the sales process. It is good practice to set a specific objective for the sales call, including your preferred next steps at the end of the meeting. You need to address critical issues such as your competitors' strengths and weaknesses, the key people involved in the buying process, and how you can add value through problem solving or provision of an opportunity. If you are in the process of planning a sales call, you better be thinking like Sherlock Holmes if you want to stand out from your competition. Typically, you are not the only one trying to earn the prospect's business. In this competitive landscape, knowing everting there is to know about the prospect can definitely give you the edge.

Source: Lisa Rose, "Planning a Sales Call: How to Make Sure You're as Prepared as Possible," posted on The Brooks Group blog at http://www.brooksgroup.com, May 1, 2015.

6-2 SALES COMMUNICATIONS FORMATS

In planning customer encounters, salespeople must decide on a basic format, such as a canned sales presentation, a written sales proposal, or an organized sales dialogue. Exhibit 6.1 summarizes the types of communications sales professionals use. Each of these alternatives varies greatly in terms of how much customization and customer interaction is involved. A salesperson might use one or more of these formats with a particular customer. Each format has unique advantages and disadvantages. To be successful, these communications must be credible and clear. In addition, the salesperson must communicate in the right environment at an appropriate time to maximize the probability of a successful outcome.

For any of the three communications types, salespeople must plan to be as specific as possible in developing their sales message. For example, it is better to tell a prospect "This electric motor will produce 4,800 RPM and requires only one hour

Exhibit 6.1
Types of Sales Communications

Canned Presentations
- Include scripted sales calls, memorized presentations, and automated presentations
- Can be complete and logically structured
- Do not vary from buyer to buyer; should be tested for effectiveness

Written Sales Proposals
- Proposal is a complete self-contained sales presentation
- Written proposals often accompanied by sales calls before and after the proposal is submitted
- Thorough customer assessment should take place before customized proposal is written

Organized Sales Dialogues and Presentations
- Address individual customer and different selling situations
- Allow flexibility to adapt to buyer feedback
- Most frequently used format by sales professionals

of maintenance per week" than to say "This motor will really put out the work with only minimum maintenance."

6-2a Canned Sales Presentations

Canned sales presentations include scripted sales calls, memorized presentations, and automated presentations. The telemarketing industry relies heavily on scripted sales calls, and memorized presentations are common in trade show product demonstrations. Automated presentations often incorporate computer graphics, video, or slides to present the information to the prospect.

When done right, canned presentations are complete and logically structured. Objections and questions can be anticipated in advance, and appropriate responses can be formulated as part of the presentation. The sales message varies little from customer to customer, except that some sales scripts have "branches" or different salesperson responses based on how the customer responds. Canned presentations can be used by relatively inexperienced salespeople, and using this format might boost the confidence of some salespeople. Canned sales presentations should be tested for effectiveness, ideally with real customers, before they are implemented with the entire salesforce.

> Buyers expect clear, informative sales messages, and they are less tolerant of sloppy communication.

Canned sales presentations make an implicit assumption that customer needs and buying motives are essentially homogeneous. Therefore, canned presentations fail to capitalize on a key advantage of personal selling—the ability to adapt to different types of customers and various selling situations. The salesperson can only assume the buyer's needs and must hope that a lively presentation of product benefits will cause the prospect to buy. The canned presentation can be effective, but is not appropriate for many business-to-business situations—simply because customer opportunity to interact is minimized. During a memorized presentation, the salesperson talks 80 to 90 percent of the time, only occasionally allowing the prospect to express his or her feelings, concerns, or opinions. Canned presentations do not handle interruptions well, may be awkward to use with a broad product line, and may alienate buyers who want to participate in the interaction.

Despite its limitations, the canned sales presentation can be effective in some situations. If the product line is narrow and the sales force is relatively inexperienced, the canned presentation might be suitable. Also, many salespeople find it effective to use instead of a sales dialogue to introduce their company, to demonstrate the product, or for some other limited purpose.

canned sales presentations
Sales presentations that include scripted sales calls, memorized presentations, and automated presentations.

written sales proposals
A complete self-contained sales presentation on paper, often accompanied by other verbal sales presentations before or after the proposal is delivered.

6-2b Written Sales Proposals

The second basic type of sales communication is the **written sales proposal**. The proposal is a complete self-contained sales presentation, but it is often accompanied by sales dialogues before or after the proposal is delivered. In some cases, the customer may receive a proposal and then request that the salesperson make a sales call to further explain the proposal and provide answers to questions. Alternatively, preliminary sales dialogues may lead to a sales proposal. In any event, the sales proposal should be prepared after the salesperson has made a thorough assessment of the buyer's situation as it relates to the seller's offering.

The sales proposal has long been associated with important, high-dollar-volume sales transactions. It is frequently used in competitive bidding situations and in situations involving the selection of a new supplier by the prospect. One advantage of the proposal is that the written

IQoncept/Shutterstock.com

A written sales proposal should follow a strategic sales process.

word is usually viewed as being more credible than the spoken word. Written proposals are subject to careful scrutiny with few time constraints, and specialists in the buying firm often analyze various sections of the proposal.

Sales proposal content is similar to other comprehensive sales presentations, focusing on customer needs and related benefits the seller offers. In addition, technical information, pricing data, and perhaps a timetable are included. Most proposals provide a triggering mechanism such as a proposed contract to confirm the sale, and some specify follow-up action to be taken if the proposal is satisfactory.

With multimedia sales presentations becoming more routine, it is natural to think that written sales proposals would be declining in importance. Actually, the opposite is true. With the widespread use of multimedia, the standards for all sales communication continue to rise. Buyers expect clear informative sales messages, and they are less tolerant of sloppy communication. Because everyone knows that word processing programs have subroutines to check spelling and grammar, for example, mistakes are less acceptable than ever.

Because written communication provides a permanent record of claims and intentions, salespeople should be careful not to overpromise, but still maintain a positive and supportive tone. No buyer wants to read a proposal full of legal disclaimers and warnings, yet such information may be a necessary ingredient in certain written communication. As with all communication, salespeople should try to give buyers the information they need to make informed decisions.

6-2c Writing Effective Proposals

Whether the proposal is in response to a buyer's request for proposals (RFP) or generated to complement and strengthen a sales presentation, it is essential that the proposal be correctly written and convey the required information in an attractive manner. Professionals who specialize in the creation of sales proposals give these reasons why proposals might fail[2]:

1. Customer does not know the seller.

2. Proposal does not follow the customer-specified format.

3. Executive summary does not address customer needs.

4. Proposal uses the seller's (not the customer's) company jargon, which forces readers to interpret the message.

5. Writing is flat, technical, and without passion. A technical data dump is not effective.

6. Generic material does not match the targeted prospect, indicating a lack of customer-focused consultative selling.

7. Proposal is not convincing, and does not substantiate claims made.

8. Proposal has poor layout and glaring grammatical errors.

9. Proposal does not address key decision criteria. Don't assume what is important to the buyer, ask!

10. Proposal is vague, lacking specifics in key areas such as pricing and buyer/seller roles and responsibilities.

Clearly, developing an effective proposal takes time and effort. When beginning the proposal-writing process, it is important for the salesperson to adopt the right mind-set with a key thought of, "Okay, this will take some time to get the details down, but it will be worth it." To reinforce this mind-set, consider the advice given in Exhibit 6.2: Tips for Creating Effective Sales Proposals.[3]

Breaking the proposal down into its primary and distinct parts can simplify the process of writing an effective proposal. Five parts common to most proposals are an executive summary, customer needs and

Exhibit 6.2

Tips for Creating Effective Sales Proposals

- When writing a proposal, pretend you are one of the buyer's decision makers and decide what you need to know to make a decision.
- Think of the proposal as an in-depth conversation with the buyer's decision makers.
- Give the decision makers all of the information they need to make an informed decision.
- Avoid boilerplate proposals that use the same wording for all customers.
- Avoid so-what proposals that do not give customers the financial justification for buying your product.
- Realize that you must educate the buyer and provide information accordingly.
- Ensure that your proposal has a logical flow that the customer can easily follow.

proposed solution, seller profile, pricing and sales agreement, and an implementation section with a timetable.

EXECUTIVE SUMMARY This summary precedes the full proposal and serves two critical functions. First, it should succinctly and clearly demonstrate the salesperson's understanding of the customer's needs and the relevance of the proposed solution. An effective summary will spell out the customer's problems, the nature of the proposed solution, and the resulting benefits to the customer. A second function of the summary is to build a desire to read the full proposal. This is important as many key members of the organization often read little more than the information provided in the summary. A question new salespeople commonly ask refers to the length of the executive summary. A good rule of thumb is that an executive summary should be limited to two typewritten pages—especially if the main body of the report is fewer than 50 pages in length.

CUSTOMER NEEDS AND PROPOSED SOLUTION This section is typically composed of two primary parts. First, the situation analysis should concisely explain the salesperson's understanding of the customer's situation, problems, and needs. Second, the recommended solution is presented and supported with illustrations and evidence on how the proposed solution uniquely addresses the buyer's problems and needs. The emphasis in this section should be on the benefits resulting from the solution and not on the product or service being sold. It is important that these benefits be described from the perspective of the customer. Proprietary information required in the proposal can be protected in a number of ways. The most common method is to place a confidential notice on the cover. Many technology companies ask the prospect to sign a nondisclosure agreement that is part of the overall document, and in some instances, the selling organization will even copyright the proposal.

SELLER PROFILE This section contains information that the customer wants to know about the selling company. It offers a succinct overview and background of the firm, but the emphasis should be on the company's capabilities. Case histories of customers for whom the company solved similar problems with similar solutions have proved to be an effective method to document and illustrate organizational capabilities and past successes.

PRICING AND SALES AGREEMENT The previous sections are designed to build the customer value of the proposed solution. Once this value has been established, the proposal should "ask for the order" by presenting pricing information and delivery options. This information is often presented in the form of a sales agreement for the buyer to sign off on and complete.

IMPLEMENTATION AND TIMETABLE The purpose of this section is to make it as easy as possible for the buyer to make a positive purchase decision. In effect, this section should say, "If you like the proposal and want to act on it, this is what you do." There may be a contract to sign, an order form to fill out, or instructions regarding who to call to place an order or request additional information. A timetable that details a schedule of key implementation events should also be included.

6-2d Evaluating Proposals Before Submission

In the customer's eyes, the standards for written sales proposals are high. Poor spelling and grammatical mistakes send a negative message that the seller has little regard for attention to detail. The quality of a salesperson's written documents is a surrogate for that salesperson's competence and ability as well as the capabilities and overall quality of the organization. If the proposal does not properly interpret the buyer's needs or fails to make a compelling case to justify the purchase, the odds of success are low. Although a well-written proposal is no guarantee of making the sale, a poorly written proposal will certainly reduce the probability of success.

Because the stakes are usually high when written sales proposals are used, it is a best practice to evaluate proposals carefully before they are submitted to the customer. In fact, it is a good idea to build the evaluative criteria into the proposal writing process early on, then use the criteria shown in Exhibit 6.3[4] as a final check before submitting a sales proposal.

6-2e Organized Sales Dialogues

In most situations, the process of converting a prospect into a customer will take several sales conversations over multiple encounters. These conversations constitute an **organized sales dialogue**. For example, salespeople often speak by telephone with a qualified

organized sales dialogue
Also known as the organized sales presentation. Unlike a canned sales presentation, an organized sales dialogue has a high level of customer involvement.

Exhibit 6.3

Evaluating Sales Proposals

It is a best practice to evaluate sales proposals before they are submitted to the customer. Five important dimensions for evaluating proposals are reliability, assurance, tangibles, empathy, and responsiveness.

Reliability: reflects the seller's ability to identify creative and practical business solutions that will help the buyer achieve their goals and objectives.

Does the Proposal:

1. Present a solid business solution that meets the buyer's expectations?
2. Effectively describe the seller's offering and clearly define how it will work?
3. Describe all of the seller's fees, prices, and expenses the buyer will incur?
4. Present seller capabilities and convert them into buyer-specific financial and nonfinancial benefits?

Assurance: increases the buyer's trust and confidence in the seller's ability to deliver successful results.

Does the Proposal:

1. Assure the buyer that the seller has the experience and capability required to fulfill the contract?
2. Present the seller's roles, responsibilities, and business practices to fulfill the contract?
3. Provide a schedule with clear specification of major work activities?
4. Provide customer references that are easy to verify and that demonstrate a solid track record?

Tangibles: enhances and differentiates the communication of the seller's message and invites readership by its content, structure, and overall appearance.

Does the Proposal:

1. Focus on the customer, provide a logical flow, and have high standards for mechanics and readability?
2. Convert the intangibles into tangibles such as schedules, diagrams, graphics, or charts?
3. Effectively use appendices to control length and provide more detail for interested readers?
4. Contain an Executive Summary that condenses the entire proposal into no more than 2–4 pages?

Empathy: reflects the seller's thorough understanding of the buyer's unique business environment, operations, organization, improvement opportunities, needs, and objectives.

Does the Proposal:

1. Reflect a thorough understanding of the buyer's business operations?
2. Clearly define the buyer's critical business issues or improvement opportunities?
3. Clearly define the buyer's needs for addressing critical issues or improvement opportunities?
4. Propose a product or service that satisfies the buyer's time frame and unique business needs?

Responsiveness: demonstrates the seller's willingness to work closely with the buyer to understand their unique situation, present viable business solutions, and ensure achievement of promised results.

Does the Proposal:

1. Demonstrate the willingness to ask questions, gather information, and gain a thorough knowledge of the buyer's unique business issues or improvement opportunities?
2. Present a custom offering tailored to the customer's unique situation?
3. Offer a review between buyer and seller to answer questions and clarify issues?
4. Match the seller's consultative selling process?

Before making a comprehensive sales presentation, a salesperson will have several conversations with a potential customer.

salesperson (e.g., solving a problem or realizing an opportunity). Feedback from the prospect is encouraged, and therefore this format is less likely to offend a participation-prone buyer.

When the situation calls for a full sales presentation, the organized sales presentation is usually favored over both the canned presentation and the written proposal. Such an approach allows much-needed flexibility to adapt to buyer feedback and changing circumstances during the presentation. Organized presentations may also include some canned portions. For example, a salesperson for Caterpillar might show a videotape to illustrate the earth-moving capabilities of a bulldozer as one segment of an organized presentation. Due to its flexibility during the sales call and its ability to address various sales situations, the organized presentation is the most frequently used format for professional sales presentations.

prospect to get an appointment for a later meeting. The second conversation with the customer typically focuses on fact finding and parallels the ADAPT process. The next step would come after the salesperson has developed a tailored solution for the customer. The salesperson may make a comprehensive sales presentation, but in this case, it is designed for dialogue with the customer throughout. To reiterate, this is not a one-way presentation or monologue—it is a sales dialogue with a high level of customer involvement. This type of comprehensive presentation is commonly called an **organized sales presentation**.

Organized sales dialogues may precede or follow other sales communications such as a written sales proposal. Sales dialogues are much more than mere conversation—they are a chance for the salesperson to seek information and/or action from the prospect and to explore the business reasons the prospect has for continuing the dialogue with the

> By fully participating in the dialogue, both buyer and seller have an opportunity to establish a mutually beneficial relationship.

One reality of this presentation format is that it requires a knowledgeable salesperson who can react to questions and objections from the prospect. Further, this format may extend the time horizon before a purchase decision is reached, and it is vulnerable to diversionary delay tactics by the prospect. Presumably, those who make these arguments think that a canned presentation forces a purchase decision in a more expedient fashion. Overall, however, most agree that the organized presentation is ideal for most sales situations. Its flexibility allows a full exploration of customer needs and appropriate adaptive behavior by the salesperson. By fully participating in the dialogue, both buyer and seller have an opportunity to establish a mutually beneficial relationship.

The trust-based relational selling presentation, often combining elements of need-satisfaction and consultative selling, is a popular form of an organized presentation. The first stage of the process, the need development stage, is devoted to a discussion of the buyer's needs. As seen in Figure 6.1, during this phase the buyer should be talking 60 to 70 percent of the time. The salesperson accomplishes this by using the first four questioning techniques of the ADAPT process.

organized sales presentation A sales presentation that allows a salesperson to implement appropriate sales strategies and tactics based on customer research or information gathered during previous sales calls. Organized sales presentations feature a two-way dialogue with a high level of customer involvement.

The second stage of the process (need awareness) is to verify what the buyer thinks his or her needs are and to make the buyer aware of potential needs that might exist. For instance, fast-food restaurants were generally slow to recognize the need to offer more low-fat and low-carbohydrate menu items until their sales volume suffered. Others, such as Subway, gained a competitive advantage by working with their suppliers to formulate a significant number of menu alternatives for the health-conscious consumer.

A logical conclusion of the needs awareness stage is to have the prospects confirm their needs. It is a positive step when the salesperson discovers the prospect's needs, but far more effective when the prospect confirms the importance of those needs. The need-awareness stage is a good time to restate the prospect's needs and to clarify exactly what the prospect's needs are.

During the last stage of the presentations, the need-fulfillment stage, the salesperson must show how his or her product and its benefits will meet the needs of the buyer. As seen in Figure 6.1, the salesperson during the need-fulfillment stage will do more of the talking by indicating what specific product will meet the buyer's needs. The salesperson, by being a good listener early in the process, will now have a better chance to gain the buyer's interest and trust by talking about specific benefits the buyer has confirmed as being important.

To engage in effective sales dialogue, salespeople should try to think like the customer and anticipate key issues that should be addressed. To reiterate a point made earlier in this chapter, researching the prospect or customer is essential in preparing for effective dialogue during organized sales presentations. For more discussion on preparing for sales calls, see "FROM THE CLASSROOM TO THE FIELD: Preparing for Sales Calls"

FIG. 6.1 THE TRUST-BASED SELLING PROCESS: A NEED-SATISFACTION CONSULTATIVE MODEL

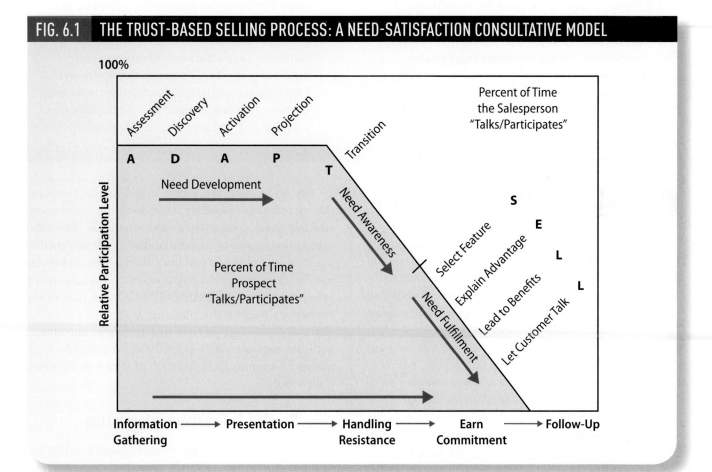

At some points in the two-way sales dialogue, the customer will do more talking; at other points, the salesperson will do more of the talking.

From the Classroom to the Field

Preparing for Sales Calls

Jordan Lynch, a 2009 graduate of Colorado State University, is a Workforce Management Consultant for ADP in Denver, Colorado. ADP is a multinational leader in the payroll and human resource services industry. He learned the importance of preparation for sales calls while he was interviewing for sales positions during his senior year in college:

> When I was a senior in college, I took a professional selling course and competed in the National Collegiate Sales Competition. The more I learned about sales, the more I wanted to pursue a career in sales and sales management. As I began interviewing, I quickly realized that I needed to apply some of the lessons I had learned about being prepared for sales calls. After all, a job interview is just like a major sales call. Both parties are trying to determine if there is a mutually beneficial fit. For every interview that I had, I researched the company so that I clearly understood what they were looking for and how I could match up with their needs. I thought of myself as a value-add product that employers needed. I knew that employers would have some tough questions and I tried to anticipate those questions and formulate my responses. I wanted to be sure the employers understood what I could for them, so I developed a written plan for each employer that laid how I would operate a sales territory. I also tried to get a commitment at the end of every interview. I wanted the offer, and I also wanted to show employers that I was enthusiastic about working with them. I apply the same principles today to build business with ADP. I prepare for a back-and-forth dialogue and try to help customers make wise business decisions. To maximize your opportunities, think like your customer and do your homework!

6-3 SALES DIALOGUE TEMPLATE

Sales dialogues are not scripted in advance as canned sales presentations are; however, salespeople should think ahead about what questions and statements to include in the conversation and be prepared to hold up their end of the conversation with an appropriate amount of detail. A **sales dialogue template** (see Exhibit 6.4) is a useful tool to ensure that all pertinent content areas are covered with each prospect. The template is flexible and can be used either to plan a comprehensive organized sales presentation or to guide sales dialogues of a more narrow scope. The template is not meant to be a script for a sales encounter, but rather an aid in planning and assembling the information required of the salesperson.

sales dialogue template
A flexible planning tool that assists the salesperson in assembling pertinent information to be covered with the prospect.

By addressing the issues noted in the template, salespeople can facilitate trust-building by demonstrating their competence and expertise, customer orientation, candor, dependability, and compatibility. It is true that trust is built through behavior, not just by planning and having good intentions; however, salespeople who are aware of what it takes to earn the customer's trust in the planning stages have a better chance of earning that trust in subsequent encounters with the customer. The sales dialogue template is organized into nine sections, each of which is discussed individually.

6-3a Section 1: Prospect Information

This section is used to record specific information on the prospect such as the company name, key decision maker's name and job title, and the type of business. In most business-to-business situations, it is critical to know who else is involved

Exhibit 6.4

Sales Dialogue Template

1. Prospect Information

A. Company and key person information

Company Name: _____	Type of Business: _____
Prospect's Name: Key Decision Maker: _____	Job Title: _____

B. Other influences on the purchase decision: For all key people involved in the buying process, provide names, job titles, departments, and roles in the purchase decision.

Name(s)/Job Title	Departments	Role in Purchase Decision
Add other people as necessary		

2. Customer Value Proposition: A brief statement of how you will add value to the prospect's business by meeting a need or providing an opportunity. Include a brief description of the product or service:

3. Sales Call Objective (must require customer action such as making a purchase, supplying critical information, etc.)

4. Linking Buying Motives, Benefits, Support Information, and Reinforcement Methods: This section should address the buying motives of all persons who will be involved in the upcoming sales call.

A. *Buying Motives:* What is most important to the prospect(s) in making a purchase decision? **Rational** motives include economic issues such as quality, cost, service capabilities, and the strategic priorities of the prospect's company. **Emotional** motives include fear, status, and ego-related feelings. List all relevant buying motives in order of importance.	B. *Specific Benefits Matched to Buying Motives:* Benefits to be stressed are arranged in priority order (sequence to be followed unless prospect feedback during the presentation indicates an alternative sequence). Each benefit should correspond to one or more buying motives.	C. *Information needed to support claims for each benefit.*	D. *Where appropriate, methods for reinforcing verbal content (AV, collateral material, illustrations, testimonials, etc.).*
1. ────────────▶	────────────▶	──────▶	
Continue listing all relevant buying motives and information in columns B, C, and D.			

5. Current Suppliers (if applicable) and Other Key Competitors.

Competitor	Strengths	Weakness
Complete for all key competitors		

(Continued)

Exhibit 6.4

Sales Dialogue Template (*Continued*)

6. Beginning the Sales Dialogue.

Plans for the first few minutes of the sales call:

Introduction, thanks, agenda agreement. Then begin ADAPT as appropriate or transition into other sales dialogue or presentation:

Assessment _____

Discovery _____

Activation _____

Projection _____

Transition to Presentation _____

Note: The ADAPT process might take place over several sales conversations during multiple sales calls. In other cases, it might be concluded in a single sales call, then immediately followed by a sales presentation.

7. Anticipated Prospect Questions and Objections, with Planned Responses.

Questions and Objections	Responses
Include a comprehensive set of questions and objections with your corresponding responses.	

8. Earn Prospect Commitment.

A preliminary plan for how the prospect will be asked for a commitment related to the sales call objective.

9. Building Value through Follow-up Action.

Statement of follow-up action needed to ensure that the buyer-seller relationship moves in a positive direction.

---

in the buying decision and what role he or she plays, such as gatekeeper, user, or influencer. (Refer to Chapter 3 if you need to review the buying center concept.) It is also important that the salesperson make sure that all of the key players are receiving the appropriate information and getting the proper attention they deserve. A mistake salespeople often make is not identifying all the buying influencers.

customer value proposition
A statement of how the sales offering will add value to the prospect's business by meeting a need or providing an opportunity.

6-4 SECTION 2: CUSTOMER VALUE PROPOSITION

In this section, the salesperson develops a preliminary **customer value proposition**, which is a statement of how the sales offering will add value to the prospect's business by meeting a need or providing an opportunity. Essentially, the customer value proposition summarizes the legitimate business reason for making the sales call by answering the prospect's question, "Why should I spend my time with you?" A good customer value proposition clearly states why the customer will be better off by doing business with the salesperson and his or her firm, but at this point does not try to list all of the reasons.[5]

At the planning stage, the customer value proposition is preliminary. The salesperson has good reason to believe that customer value can be enhanced by delivering on the contents of the proposition, but the true value of the proposition will be accepted or rejected by the customer as the sales process moves along. It is during this sales dialogue process that the actual customer value to be delivered will be refined and modified. This section of the template provides a point of departure for planning purposes and assumes that the value proposition is likely to be modified prior to the purchase decision. In writing the preliminary customer value proposition, salespeople should attempt to:

1. Determine the primary business reasons that customers would use your offering. Key reasons include revenue generation, cost savings, customer retention, building market share, productivity gains, profitability, legal and safety compliance, and return on investment.

2. Keep the statement fairly simple so that the direction for upcoming sales dialogues is clear.

3. Choose the key benefit(s) likely to be most important to the specific customer who is the audience for this particular dialogue or presentation. (At this point, it is not necessary to list all of the benefits of their offerings.)

4. Make the value proposition as specific as possible on tangible outcomes (e.g., improvements to revenues, cost containment or reduction, market share, process speed, and efficiency) and/or the enhancement of the customer's strategic priority.

5. Reflect product or service dimensions that add value, whether or not the customer pays for them. For example, some companies offer delivery, installation, and training along with the purchase of their products. Added value may also accrue from what the seller's sales team provides (e.g., work in the field with a distributor's salespeople or certification training for the buyer's technicians).

6. Promise only what can be consistently delivered. Strictly speaking, a customer value proposition in the planning stage is not a guarantee, it is a belief based on the salesperson's knowledge and best judgment. As the sales process moves along, appropriate guarantees can be made.

7. Use action verbs that show a departure from the status quo such as increase, improve, cut, save, accelerate, enhance, grow, eliminate, minimize, and maximize.

8. Be as specific as possible about key metrics, including time frame, financials, and percentage targets.

9. Practice the verbal communication of the customer value proposition with people not familiar with your business. Do they understand the proposition and can they repeat it? If not, rework the proposition until it is easily recalled.

Using these points as a guide, this is an example of a customer value proposition that could provide clear direction for planning an upcoming sales presentation or a series of sales dialogues.

"ABC Company can improve its market share by a minimum of four percentage points in a one-year period in its San Francisco and Dallas markets by implementing our customer satisfaction and retention training for its customer service personnel."

By contrast, here is an example of a poorly constructed customer value proposition.

"By adopting our customer satisfaction and retention programs, ABC Company will see a dramatic increase in its market share."

This second proposition opens the salesperson to a potential barrage of questions:

Dramatic increase in market share? What's dramatic?

"We operate in 22 markets. Are you saying that we will increase market shares in all 22 markets?"

What do you mean by programs? Are you referring to training programs?

In the planning stages, salespeople may or may not be fully aware of the prospect's needs and priorities—and, until they are aware of these needs and priorities, the sales dialogue should focus on the first two stages of the ADAPT process: assessing the prospect's situation and discovering his or her needs. Unless these stages are completed, the customer value proposition will not contain enough detail to be useful. Done correctly, a customer value proposition will portray the seller's company in a favorable light and

give the customer reasonable expectations of the selling company. As illustrated in "An Ethical Dilemma," this sometimes requires caution in communicating the customer value proposition.

6-4a Section 3: Sales Call Objective

Section 3 asks the salesperson to determine the objective for his or her sales call. Salespeople must have an objective for each sales call. Basically, sales call objectives state what salespeople want customers to do as a result of the sales call. The objectives should be specific enough to know whether or not they have been accomplished at the conclusion of the call, and they should require customer actions such as placing an order, agreeing to participate in a test market, or supplying specific information useful to the salesperson. Many salespeople think that there is only one objective: to get an order. Other legitimate sales call objectives do exist. For instance, during an introductory call the objective may be simply to introduce the salesperson and his or her company and to gather information on the buyer's needs. Eventually, the major sales presentation objective will be to earn a commitment from the customer by making a sale, but this is not always the only objective.

After the sale is made, the objective may be to follow up and determine whether or not the customer is satisfied with the salesperson's efforts. The salesperson can also look for openings to cover additional objectives. Gwen Tranguillo of Hershey's always looks for ways to introduce other products in her presentation if the buyer expresses interest. Tranguillo made a major sales presentation on a Halloween display of king-size candies and found that the buyer was very interested in adding more king sizes immediately. She shifted gears and gained a commitment on the new king-size display and later in the presentation went back to her Halloween proposal. At the very least, the heart of any presentation should be to advance the process toward an order.

6-5 SECTION 4: LINKING BUYING MOTIVES, BENEFITS, SUPPORT INFORMATION, AND OTHER REINFORCEMENT METHODS

In Section 4 of the planning template, the prospect's buying motives are linked to specific benefits offered. For each benefit identified, the salesperson will also assemble the information needed to support the claims to be made in the upcoming dialogue or presentation.

In some cases, verbal claims must be reinforced with audio-visual portrayal, illustrations, printed collateral material, or testimonials from satisfied customers, as appropriate to the situation.

Buying motives refers to the most important factors from the customer's perspective in making a purchase decision. In other words, what will motivate the buyer to make a purchase? Buying motives may be rational or emotional, or a combination of both rational and emotional. **Rational buying motives** typically relate to the economics of the situation, including cost, profitability, quality, services offered, and the total value of the seller's offering the customer perceives. **Emotional buying motives** such as fear, the need for security, the need for status, or the need to be liked, are sometimes difficult for salespeople to uncover, as prospects are generally less likely to share such motives with salespeople. In business-to-business selling, rational motives are typically the most important buying motives, but salespeople should not ignore emotional motives if they are known to exist.

In linking benefits to buying motives, benefits should be distinguished from features. **Features** are factual statements about the characteristics of a product or service, such as, "This is the lightest electrical motor in its performance category." **Benefits** describe the added value for the customer—the favorable outcome derived from a feature. For example, "The lightweight motor supports your mobile repair service strategy in that it is very portable. The ease of use allows your technicians to complete more service calls per day, thus increasing impact on your profitability." To make such a claim about increasing profitability, the salesperson would need to gather specific information to support it. For example, in this case the claim that technicians can complete more service calls per day because the motor is easy to use might call for competitive comparisons and actual usage data, and/or a demonstration.

Some situations may lead the salesperson to decide that a product demonstration and testimonials from satisfied customers will reinforce the spoken word. In other cases, third-party research studies or articles in trade publications might be used to reinforce oral claims. Another powerful option is material developed by the salesperson, such as a break-even chart showing how quickly the customer can recoup the investment in the new product or service. A note of caution: It is always a good idea to use these types of sales support materials sparingly—prospects do not react positively to information overload. Chapter 7 discusses in greater detail sales tools and how they can enhance the sales effort.

6-5a Section 5: Competitive Situation

Understanding the competitive situation is essential in planning sales dialogues and presentations. Because buyers make competitive comparisons in their decision processes, salespeople should be prepared for it. This section of the planning template asks the salesperson to identify key competitors and to specify their strengths and weaknesses. By knowing their own product's strengths and weaknesses as well as those of their competitors, salespeople are better equipped to articulate customer value relative to their competitors. This competitive positioning is important, as most major purchase decisions are made in a highly competitive business environment. If the prospect is already buying a similar product, knowledge about the current supplier can give the salesperson critical insight into which buying motives and product attributes are likely to be affecting the buyer's decisions.

6-5b Section 6: Beginning the Sales Dialogue

Section 6 addresses the critical first few minutes of the sales call. During this period, salespeople will greet the prospect and introduce themselves, if necessary. There is typically some brief polite conversation between the salesperson and the buyer as the salesperson is welcomed to the buyer's office, then both parties are usually eager to get down to business as quickly as possible. It is recommended that the salesperson propose an agenda, to which there may or may not have been previous agreement. Then, depending on the situation, the salesperson will proceed with questions designed to assess the

buying motive A need-activated drive to search for and acquire a solution to resolve a need or problem; the most important factors from the customer's perspective in making a purchase decision.

rational buying motives Typically relate to the economics of the situation, including cost, profitability, quality, services offered, and the total value of the seller's offering as perceived by the customer.

emotional buying motives Includes motives such as security, status, and need to be liked; sometimes difficult for salespeople to uncover these motives.

features A quality or characteristic of a product or service that is designed to provide value to a buyer.

benefits The added value or favorable outcome derived from features of the product or service the seller offers.

Planning the first few minutes of a sales dialogue can help the salesperson make a positive impression and build trust.

prospect's situation, discover the prospect's needs, or make a transition into a sales dialogue or presentation. A typical first few minutes might sound like this:

Buyer: Come on in, Pat. I am John Jones. Nice to meet you. (*Introduction/greeting.*)

Seller: Mr. Jones, I am Pat Devlin with XYZ Company. Nice to meet you, too. I appreciate the time that you are spending with me today. (*Thanks, acknowledges importance of the buyer's time.*)

Buyer: Glad you could make it. We have had a lot of cancellations lately due to the bad weather. Did you have any problems driving over from Orlando? (*Polite conversation may last for several minutes depending on the buyer-seller relationship and on how much the buyer wants to engage in this sort of conversation.*)

Seller: Not really, it was pretty smooth today. Say, I know you are busy, so I thought we could talk about a couple of key ways I think we can really help you build market share with your end-user market. How does that sound? (*A simple illustration of getting the buyer to agree to the agenda.*)

Buyer: Sure, let us get right to it. What do you have in mind?

Seller: Well, based on our phone call last week, I believe that our training programs for your customer service representatives can improve your customer satisfaction ratings and customer retention. I can share the details with you over the next 20 minutes or so . . . (*Transition to a*

sales dialogue or presentation based on customer needs and customer value.)

In planning the first few minutes of the sales call, salespeople should remind themselves to be friendly and positive. They should also remain flexible in terms of their proposed agenda—customers like to have an agenda but sometimes want to modify it. The salesperson should be prepared to make an adjustment on the spot. For example, in the previous dialogue, the prospect might have said, "Yes, I want to hear about your training programs for our customer service reps, but I am also interested in your thoughts on how we can build a service-based culture across our entire marketing organization." The salesperson might respond accordingly, "I would be happy to do that. In fact, let me start with an overview that shows you the big picture from a strategy and company culture perspective, then later I will show you how the customer service training piece fits into the overall strategy. How does that sound?"

These first few minutes are critical in the trust-building process. By showing sensitivity to customer needs and opinions, and by asking questions to clarify the customer's perspective, salespeople demonstrate a customer orientation. Salespeople can demonstrate their expertise and competence by being sharp and well prepared. First impressions are crucial in all human interactions, so time spent on planning the first few minutes is a good investment on the salesperson's part. But remember that the planning template is not intended as a script. It is imperative that salespeople think logically—and from the buyer's point of view—in planning what to say after greeting the customer. For more on how to initiate effective dialogue with customers, see "Professional Selling in the 21st Century: Tips for Developing Dialogue with Customers."

When companies use team selling, pre-call planning by the sales teams can be facilitated by technologies that allow real-time access from multiple locations. For more on this topic, see "TECHNOLOGY IN SALES: Facilitating Team Selling with Google Apps."

6-5c Initiating Contact

When you are planning the first few minutes of the sales dialogue or presentation, there are few ironclad rules. Instead, the situation and the prospect's preferences suggest the appropriate sequence—but a few general rules do apply:

- Following an adequate introduction of the salesperson and the salesperson's company, the salesperson should use questions, careful listening, and confirmation statements to clarify and define explicit customer needs and motives as related to his or her offering.

Technology in Sales
Facilitating Team Selling with Google Apps

Major account and global sales teams must collaborate and coordinate efficiently and quickly to be effective. Technical product experts must provide their inputs, financial analysts and researchers must analyze data and make recommendations, and team leaders must finalize the entire package together prior to in-person sales calls. Google is a market leader in providing web-enabled applications that allow communications and information sharing from mobile and stationary devices. Using these apps, sales teams can collaborate on sales proposals and presentation plans using Google Docs, which provides simultaneous content creation and real-time feedback to members of the sales team. Written content, visual designs, and videos can be stored on Google Drive. Files can be accessed and edited on any device without using email to access the files. If additional preparation, training, or strategy sessions are needed to prepare for an upcoming key account sales call, Google Hangout can be used for virtual meetings without the travel time and costs of live meetings. If the sales call involves a formal presentation, Google Slides offers a tool for crafting key content and graphics into a compelling message. In a fast-paced, competitive marketplace, sales teams must move quickly when new opportunities arise, and collaboration through technology is increasingly popular.

Source: "Top Ten Google Apps Tips for Sales and Marketing Users," available on online from Google at http://learn.googleaps.com/home/top-1--google-aps-tips-for-sales-and-marketers -users, accessed May 29, 2015.

- The salesperson should present benefits in order of importance according to the prospect's needs and motives, and these benefits may be repeated during the presentation and at the conclusion of the presentation.

- If the sales presentation is a continuation of one or more previous sales calls, the salesperson should make a quick summary of what has been agreed on in the past, moving quickly into the prospect's primary area of interest.

- As a general rule, the salesperson should not focus on pricing issues until the prospect's needs have been defined and the salesperson has shown how those needs can be addressed with the product or service being sold. After prospects fully understand how the product or service meets their needs, they can make informed judgments on price/value issues.

Obviously, the first few minutes of the sales call will be greatly influenced by previous interaction (if any) between the buyer and the salesperson. For example, if previous sales calls have established buyer needs and the buyer has agreed to a sales presentation, the first few minutes will be quite different than if this is the first sales call on this prospect. The ADAPT questioning process (refer to Chapter 4) can be used in part or whole to acquire needed information and make a transition to the sales dialogue or presentation. As a guide, the salesperson should respect the buyer's time and get to the presentation as soon as circumstances allow. The salesperson should not rush to get to the presentation, and certainly should not launch into a presentation without establishing buyer needs and interest in it.

6-5d Section 7: Anticipate Questions and Objections

For reasons to be explained fully in Chapter 8, prospects will almost always have questions and objections that salespeople must be prepared to answer. In the planning stages, salespeople can prepare by asking themselves, "If I were the buyer, what would I want to be certain about before I make a purchase?" By anticipating these issues and preparing responses, salespeople can increase their chances of ultimate success.

6-5e Section 8: Earn Prospect Commitment

As sales dialogues and presentations progress, there eventually comes a critical time to ask for a customer's purchase decision. In many cases, this is an obvious point in the sales conversation, but at other times the salesperson may feel the need to probe to see if the timing is right. Earning a commitment from a customer as discussed in Chapter 8 should be a natural step in the conversation, not a forced or high-pressure attempt by the salesperson. Although circumstances will dictate exactly when and how commitment will be sought, a preliminary action plan for seeking customer commitment should be part of the overall planning process. Most buyers expect the salesperson to seek a commitment—and, if the commitment is sought at the right time, buyers appreciate that effort from the salesperson.

6-5f Section 9: Build Value Through Follow-Up Action

Finally, the salesperson must always be looking for ways to enhance the relationship and move it in a positive direction. The salesperson should always make a note of any promises that he or she has made during the sales calls and especially during the proposal presentation. The buyer may ask for information that the salesperson is not prepared to give during the presentation. By taking notes, the salesperson ensures that the appropriate follow-up activities will happen.

This planning template for sales dialogues and presentations is an extremely useful tool for all salespeople, especially inexperienced salespeople. It guarantees that all the appropriate steps are covered and that all of the pertinent information is collected. Using this template will make the task of customizing sales dialogues and presentations easier.

6-6 ENGAGING THE CUSTOMER

Most initial sales calls on new prospects require an appointment. Requesting an appointment accomplishes several desirable outcomes. First, the salesperson is letting the prospect know that he or she thinks the prospect's time is important. Second, there is a better chance that the salesperson will receive the undivided attention of the prospect during the sales call. Third, setting appointments is a good tool to assist the salesperson in effective time and territory management. Further, prospects may not appreciate salespeople who drop in unannounced, as their visit could be an unwelcome interruption in the prospect's busy work day. Given these realities, it is a good idea to request an appointment if there is any doubt about whether one is required.

A salesperson can request an appointment by phone, mail (including e-mail), or personal contact. Combining mail and telephone communications to seek appointments is also commonplace. Regardless of the communication vehicle used, salespeople can improve their chances of getting an appointment by following three simple directives: give the prospect a reason why an appointment should be granted; request a specific amount of time; and suggest a specific time for the appointment. These tactics recognize that prospects are busy individuals who do not spend time idly.

In giving a reason why the appointment should be granted, a well-informed salesperson can appeal to the prospect's primary buying motive as related to one of the benefits of the salesperson's offering. Be specific. For example, it is better to say that "you can realize gross margins averaging 35 percent on our product line" than "our margins are really quite attractive."

Specifying the amount of time needed to make the sales presentation alleviates some of the anxiety a busy prospect feels at the idea of spending some of his or her already scarce time. It also helps the prospect if the salesperson suggests a time and date for the sales call. It is very difficult for busy individuals to respond to a question such as, "What would be a good time for you next week?" In effect, the prospect is being asked to scan his or her entire calendar for an opening. If a suggested time and date is inconvenient, the interested prospect will typically suggest another. Once a salesperson has an appointment with the prospect and all the objectives have been established, the salesperson should send the agenda to the customer. This is a highly professional way to remind the buyer of the upcoming meeting.

NIMBLEFOOT

BACKGROUND

Nimblefoot is a manufacturer of women's running shoes, which are sold through major sporting goods chain stores and specialty stores. Nimblefoot has targeted Trailrunner, a regional specialty store chain as a potential prospect for its latest product. Nimblefoot's sales representative, Bradley Jackson, hopes to replace a competitor's product in the Trailrunner stores. Bradley has begun planning his upcoming sales call on Susan Holloway, head buyer at Trailrunner. At a recent trade show, Bradley had a brief conversation with Susan and learned that Trailrunner's management is interested in improving the profitability of the chain. Further,

Susan made it clear that Trailrunner would only be interested in high-quality products.

CURRENT SITUATION

Bradley and his sales manager, Ashley Zamora, have been discussing the plans for the upcoming call on Trailrunner. Ashley asked Bradley to give her a summary of Trailrunner's key buying motives and the related benefits that Nimblefoot could offer. In addition, Ashley wanted to review the information that would be required to support any claims made for the benefits, as well as additional ideas for how to reinforce the verbal content of Nimblefoot's sales message. Bradley supplied Ashley with the requested information, as shown in Exhibit A. Ashley is now reading over Exhibit A and plans to give Bradley some feedback tomorrow morning.

Exhibit A

Trailrunner's Buying Motives and Nimblefoot's Benefits

Trailrunner's Buying Motives	Related Nimblefoot Benefits	Support Information	Reinforcement of Verbal Content
Improve profitability	1. Profit margin is 6% higher than product to be replaced.	1. Cost and retail prices	1. Example income statement with and without new Nimblefoot product
	2. Nimblefoot product has significantly higher turnover rate than replacement product, thus improving total annual profitability.	2. Use historic data for existing product, projected turnover data for Nimblefoot.	2. Spreadsheet to illustrate multiplier effect of new Nimblefoot product with lower turnover rate.
High-quality product	1. Durable synthetic material features a waterproof, breathable upper	1. Nimblefoot Website	1. Customer interviews on Nimblefoot Website
	2. Support around arch and extra width through the forefoot creates better shock absorption	2. Nimblefoot Website	2. Customer interviews on Nimblefoot Website
	3. Proprietary outsole gives best durability in high-wear areas.	3. Nimblefoot Website	3. Article from *Running World* magazine

QUESTIONS

1. In the role of Ashley Zamora, what specific comments and suggestions do you have for Bradley Jackson?

2. Should a customer value proposition be developed before completing the information in Exhibit A?

ROLE PLAY

Characters: Ashley Zamora, sales manager, and Bradley Jackson, sales representative

Scene:

Location—Ashley Zamora's office

Action—One student plays the role of Ashley Zamora, and one student plays the role of Bradley Jackson. Ashley has told Bradley that she thinks it would be good exercise to act out the presentation of the key benefits shown in section four of the template. She said to Bradley "I will act like the Trailrunner buyer, and you try to convince me that your benefits are significant. Be as specific as you can."

QUESTIONS

After completing the role play, address these questions:

1. What were the strengths of Bradley Jackson's performance?

2. How could Bradley's performance be improved?

3. How important is sales call planning in determining sales call performance?

KINDLE VERSUS NOOK

BACKGROUND

For this role play, students will assume one of three roles: (1) sales representative for Amazon's Kindle; (2) sales representative for Barnes and Noble's Nook; or (3) a buyer for a major university that is considering the purchase of e-readers for students. Prior to the role play, all students should conduct a comparison of the features and benefits of the Kindle and the Nook. To do the comparison, begin by using a search engine such as Google. Enter "Kindle vs. Nook" to find features and benefits of both products.

ROLE PLAY:

Characters: One Kindle representative, one Nook representative, and a buyer for the university

Scene 1: **Location**—The buyer's office
Action—Both sellers present their products to the buyer with a focus on explaining their product's benefits to the buyer.

QUESTIONS

After completing the role play, address these questions:

1. Did the sellers demonstrate that they knew the difference between features and benefits?

2. Did the sellers have sufficient information to be convincing?

3. Can you suggest additional ways that the sellers could improve their sales communications?

Part Three

7 | Sales Dialogue: Creating and Communicating Value

LEARNING OBJECTIVES

After completing this chapter, you should be able to:

7-1 Describe the key characteristics of effective sales dialogue.

7-2 Explain how salespeople can generate feedback from buyers.

7-3 Discuss how salespeople use confirmed benefits to create customer value.

7-4 Describe how verbal support can be used to communicate value in an interesting and understandable manner.

7-5 Discuss how sales aids can engage and involve buyers.

7-6 Explain how salespeople can support product claims.

7-7 Discuss the special considerations involved in sales dialogue with groups.

After finishing this chapter go to
PAGE 169 for **STUDY TOOLS.**

Successful salespeople focus on creating and communicating value during sales dialogue by addressing the key issues of each buyer. This is a difficult task, because buyers are more informed than in the past and more reluctant to meet with salespeople, especially in the early stages of their buying process. However, technology is having an important impact on improving sales dialogue between sellers and buyers.

John Keith/Shutterstock.com

Although many salespeople conduct most of their sales dialogue in personal meetings with buyers, more salespeople are interacting with buyers using a variety of different technologies. The use of email conversations is becoming more prevalent. Many buyers are willing to engage in email interactions, if they receive valuable buying information. More sales meetings employ the telephone and various types of Web conferencing. It is often easier for buyers to schedule telephone calls or Web conferences than personal meetings. These different technologies provide salespeople more opportunities to engage in sales dialogue with buyers, but they require salespeople to adapt to the characteristics of the different technologies.

Fortunately, emerging sales technologies are available to help salespeople be more successful in all types of sales dialogue. Most of the available products are typically called insight-based customer or sales engagement platforms. ClearSide represents one example. It is a cloud-based suite of products to assist salespeople in emailing contacts, making phone calls, conducting Web conferences, and engaging in personal sales calls more effectively and efficiently. ClearSide integrates with email and CRM systems and allows salespeople easy access to presentations, text, videos, pictures, or whatever content is most appropriate for a particular buyer. All of the interactions between the salesperson and each buyer are captured, and various analytics are provided to help the salesperson understand the specific interests of the buyer and to select the most effective materials to communicate value to the buyer.

In addition to commercial products, some companies have developed their own suite of products designed for their particular selling situation. For example, Heartland provides all of its salespeople with a customized and branded iPad that contains **Atlas**. Atlas is a Web-based, comprehensive product that allows salespeople to manage all aspects of their sales career at Heartland. It contains an internally developed sales enablement platform to help salespeople prepare for and execute sales dialogue with prospects and customers using different technological media.[1]

The Introduction highlights the critical importance and difficult challenges salespeople face in creating and communicating value during sales dialogue. Sales dialogue can be conducted using different technologies, and technology products are available to provide insight and materials to salespeople, to help them customize their interactions so that they can meet the needs of each specific buyer. The key task for salespeople is to determine how to use the available technology tools to produce effective sales dialogue. Eric Brown, Manager at Malone Solutions, provides insight on the basic challenge:[2]

Salespeople represent the voice of the company— its products, services, and promises. But, communicating our knowledge of products and services in ways that resonate with buyers is challenging. Buyers rely on us to help identify and solve problems for them. Translating the complexities of our products into stories of effective problem solving helps buyers visualize the results from using our products.

7-1 EFFECTIVE SALES DIALOGUE

Preparing and completing this phase of the sales process successfully has been compared to doing surgery in that it is complex and requires preparation, knowledge, and skill. Prior to conducting surgery, the doctor has acquired a great deal of relevant information from a variety of sources

Just like a mechanic diagnoses problems, salespeople must diagnose customer problems before prescribing solutions.

and developed a comprehensive understanding of the patient's problems and needs. Based on this understanding of the patient's needs, the surgeon utilizes his or her training and skills in combination with an assortment of tools to conduct a surgical procedure unique to the individual patient's needs. Continuing the analogy, up to the point of the presentation in the selling process, the salesperson has been developing his or her knowledge and understanding of the buyer's situation and needs. Now, in the form of an effective presentation, the salesperson presents a solution that is specific and customized to the needs of the buyer, illustrates and demonstrates the benefits of the solution, and confirms the buyer's belief in and desire to obtain the benefits.

Good salespeople are very much like good surgeons in that they are serious in what they do and leave nothing to chance. They work with the prospective buyer to identify, diagnose, and clarify unsatisfied needs or problems and then show the buyer how much better the situation would be by purchasing the proposed product or service. As discussed previously, it will normally take several sales calls to complete a sales dialogue. Many firms plan for multiple sales calls in their sales process. For example, salespeople at Northwestern Mutual Financial Network conduct an initial "fact finding" sales call to identify the financial situation and objectives of potential clients. Then, one or more subsequent sales calls are used to present strategies for achieving these financial objectives.

Professional selling classes often require students to role play a sales dialogue, have sales contests within their institution, or have students competing against other colleges in events such as the National Collegiate Sales Competition, RBI National Sales Challenge, Great

Atlas a web-based, comprehensive product that allows salespeople to manage all aspects of their sales career

From the Classroom to the Field

Effective Sales Dialogue

Sara Ames graduated from the University of Louisville in May 2011. Since graduation, she has been employed as an Account Executive for Aspect Software. She sells Microsoft business productivity software solutions to B2B customers. Sara talks about how she uses what she learned in her sales classes to be successful in her sales position:

The importance of focusing on customer value and being prepared for an engaging and interactive conversation during a sales presentation is something I learned in my sales classes that has been valuable to me in my sales position. I always create a simple agenda for each sales dialogue to provide general direction for the meeting and to communicate to the buyer that I am prepared for the meeting. My interactions are with business and technology people, so I have to adjust my perspective to address the specific needs of the buyer. I try hard to engage the buyer by listening to what they are saying and using probing questions to make sure I understand what would provide value to them. Then, I communicate how I can provide the desired value in an engaging way. This normally includes the use of sample customer stories, various sales aids (product demonstrations, simple PowerPoints), and testimonials and case studies to support my product claims.

A specific example of my approach to sales dialogue is a teleconference using Microsoft Lync with C-level executives from a healthcare firm about a phone system. In preparing for this meeting, I found out that the executives would be from IT, so I added technical consultants to our team, because they easily speak the language. I created a simple agenda which included introductions, overview of what my company does, initial questions, and next steps. I prepared a short slide deck with an agenda slide, a slide of who the meeting participants are from my company, a short company overview slide, a slide with a few broad questions, a slide with healthcare customer examples, and a slide with next steps. Our team reviewed the agenda prior to the meeting. The meeting began with the first few slides. Then, I asked the initial questions and probed responses to get more information about specific needs. Our team also responded to any questions the IT executives had, and presented case studies to illustrate how we have created value for other customers. At appropriate times during the conversation I asked about budget, timeline, and other vendors being considered. I concluded the meeting by summarizing the key points and requested the next step, which was to set up another meeting for a customized product demonstration. The IT executives agreed and we set the date and time for this meeting.

Northwoods Sales Warm-Up, Ball State Regional Sales Competition, and The International Collegiate Sales Competition. Each of these sales competitions requires students to conduct a complete sales dialogue within a 15–20-minute sales call. So, because this has been found to be an effective way for students to learn about and develop skills for a sales dialogue, we will cover a complete sales dialogue in one sales call in this chapter and Chapter 8.

The keys to effective sales dialogue are presented in Exhibit 7.1. The importance of planning and practicing were emphasized in Chapter 6 and are an area

that does not receive enough attention from some salespeople. This planning and practice should focus on an organized sales dialogue and not a canned sales presentation. Salespeople who practice asking questions, getting different responses, and adapting to these responses appropriately are better prepared to be successful in a real sales dialogue. Proper planning and practice provide an important foundation for effective sales dialogue. An example of the key elements of effective sales dialogue is presented in "FROM THE CLASSROOM TO THE FIELD: Effective Sales Dialogue."

Exhibit 7.1

Keys to Effective Sales Dialogue

The most effective sales dialogues:

1. Are planned and practiced by salespeople.
2. Encourage buyer feedback.
3. Focus on creating value for the buyer.
4. Present value in an interesting and understandable way.
5. Engage and involve the buyer.
6. Support customer value through objective claims.

7-2 ENCOURAGING BUYER FEEDBACK

In a productive sales dialogue, the salesperson continually assesses and evaluates the reactions and responses of prospective buyers. The SPIN or ADAPT questioning processes are designed to get the buyer to provide feedback to specific questions the salesperson asks. During the presentation portion of a sales dialogue, the most successful salespeople encourage buyer feedback. In contrast, less successful salespeople often rush through the entire presentation from beginning to end and never stop to invite feedback from the buyer. Feedback from the prospective buyer provides the salesperson with important information measuring the climate between the salesperson and the buyer, the buyer's level of interest in the product's features and benefits, whether the salesperson has successfully responded to the buyer's concerns, and how well the presentation is progressing toward the buyer making a purchase decision.

As detailed and discussed in Chapter 4, the observant salesperson can receive a great deal of continual feedback in the form of the buyer's nonverbal cues. In addition to observing nonverbal cues, high-performing salespeople incorporate verbal probes at key points to evaluate the buyer's interest and assess the progress of the sales dialogue. These verbal probes are typically confirmatory forms of questions in search of simple "yes" or "no" responses from the buyer.

check-backs or response checks Questions salespeople use throughout a sales dialogue to generate feedback from the buyer.

The phrases **check-backs** or **response checks** have become common names for this form of questioning—seeking feedback from the buyer. Although feedback can be sought at any point in the conversation, check-backs are commonly employed at two key points: (1) after a specific feature-benefit sequence in order to confirm the benefit and better assess the prospective buyer's level of interest and (2) following the response to an objection in order to evaluate the level to which the salesperson has handled the problem. Exhibit 7.2 provides an illustrative selection of check-back examples that salespeople indicate are typical of those they commonly use.

The effective use of check-backs offers a number of advantages. Probably the most evident is increased buyer interaction. Asking for buyer feedback helps to ensure that the dialogue remains a two-way, collaborative exchange. The effective use of response checks also helps the salesperson evaluate the level of the buyer's understanding and keeps the salesperson on the right track. If feedback indicates a lack of understanding—or even worse, a lack of interest—on the part of a prospective buyer, the salesperson must make changes to improve alignment with the needs and expectations of the buyer. In contrast, positive feedback indicating a high

Exhibit 7.2

Illustrative Examples of Check-Backs

- "How does this sound to you?"
- "Does this make sense to you so far?"
- "Would this feature be useful to you in your current operations?"
- "What do you think?"
- "So is this something that would be valuable to you?"
- "Isn't that great?"
- "Do you like this color?"
- "From your comment, it sounds like you would want the upgraded memory. Is that correct?"
- "Does that answer your concern?"
- "Would this be an improvement over what you are doing right now?"
- "Is this what you had in mind?"

level of understanding and interest on the part of the buyer would signal the salesperson to stay the course and advance the presentation toward gaining the buyer's purchase commitment. A series of positive response-checks indicates that the buyer is nearing a purchase decision. The more positive affirmations a salesperson receives in relation to his or her response checks, the easier the final purchase decision becomes and the more confident the prospective buyer is in having made the appropriate decision. Specific examples of check backs within a sales dialogue will be presented at appropriate places in the remainder of this chapter.

7-3 CREATING CUSTOMER VALUE

After the introductory part of a sales call, the salesperson must try to determine what the buyer considers to be of value. A salesperson can use the SPIN or ADAPT questioning strategies (discussed in Chapter 4 and included in the Sales Dialogue Template in Chapter 6) to understand the buyer's situation and to identify needs, problems, or opportunities important to the buyer. The salesperson must ask questions, probe for details, and listen carefully to what the prospective buyer is saying. This may take more than one sales call depending on the amount of probing and clarifying that must take place to understand the prospect's needs. The salesperson's primary goal is to uncover the prospect's specific needs or problems and then focus on what products or services will solve the problem or meet the specific needs.

As discussed in Chapter 6, features are the characteristics of a product and benefits are the favorable outcome from a feature or the value received by the buyer. Most products have many features and benefits, but the buyer generally is not interested in all of a product's features and benefits. **Confirmed benefits** are those benefits the buyer has indicated are of interest. A major purpose of the use of the SPIN or ADAPT questioning process is to help the salesperson identify the confirmed benefits for the buyer. Then, the salesperson presents a recommended solution by emphasizing product features that will produce the confirmed benefits the buyer desires. Product features and confirmed benefits are linked to the buyer's specific needs in a way that generates the buyer's desire to purchase and acquire the recommended solution.

The "Beginning the Sales Dialogue" section in Chapter 6 provides an effective introduction to a sales call.

There are several factors that go into creating value for the customer; included in that is price.

The sales dialogue would then transition into a stage where the salesperson identifies the confirmed benefits the buyer desires. An example of this interaction using the ADAPT questioning process is presented here.

Seller: What are you currently doing to improve your customer satisfaction ratings and customer retention? (*Assessment question*)

Buyer: We are trying to do a number of things, such as improving our products, providing faster deliveries, and offering better customer service.

Seller: How are these efforts working? (*Discovery question*)

Buyer: Our product and delivery improvements have been effective, but we have received a number of complaints about our customer service.

Seller: What types of customer service complaints have you received? (*Discovery question*)

Buyer: Most of the complaints are that our representatives do not act professionally and cannot resolve customer issues in a timely manner. But, when I talk to our representatives, they suggest that the customers are very demanding and difficult to deal with.

Seller: What has been the impact of these customer service problems on your business? (*Activation question*)

Buyer: The impact has been twofold. First, although we have not yet lost any customers, our customer satisfaction ratings have gone down, so we could lose customers in the future. Second, we have lost some of our best customer service reps because they got tired of dealing with irate customers. Losing these reps just added to the customer service problems we have been having.

Seller: So, if we could find a way to help your reps deal with difficult customers, would it improve your customer service and reduce the turnover of your reps? (*Projection question*)

> **confirmed benefits** The benefits the buyer indicates are important and represent value.

Buyer: That would be a big help to us. *(The seller has identified a confirmed benefit.)*

Seller: Mr. Jones, have you ever provided any training to your customer service reps? *(Assessment question)*

Buyer: Yes, we sent our reps to a public customer service training program a few months ago. But the reps said the program was very general and did not address the issues they face.

Seller: Do you think your reps would find a training program customized to their situation useful? *(Activation question)*

Buyer: A customized program would be received well by our reps and would be valuable to them. *(The seller has identified another confirmed benefit.)*

Seller: Have you ever considered online training? *(Assessment question)*

Buyer: We thought about it, but many of our reps were not receptive to the idea of online training. *(The buyer has indicated that online training is NOT a confirmed benefit.)*

Seller: It seems like a customized customer service training program that focused on dealing with difficult customers would improve your service to existing customers and help reduce turnover of your customer service reps. Do you think this type of training program would be valuable to your business? *(Transition question)*

Buyer: I would certainly be interested in this type of program.

This sales dialogue example illustrates the value of the ADAPT questioning process to help salespeople identify confirmed benefits and transition into the presentation of a solution to solve the problems the buyer expresses. This presentation should focus on a customized training program that emphasizes dealing with difficult customers (confirmed benefits), but it should not be an online training program (benefit not confirmed). This example sales dialogue will be continued later in this chapter.

Sometimes salespeople understand the confirmed benefits of a buyer and know the best product to provide the best value for the customer. However, pressure from their company or other sources can put salespeople in very difficult situations. One such situation is presented in "An Ethical Dilemma."

An Ethical Dilemma

Tracey Wise has been selling computer systems for just over nine years and has earned the position of senior account manager for one of the leading companies in the industry. For several months, Wise has been working with a major insurance company that is looking for an automated information system to solve the company's growing backlog of worker compensation claims. After reviewing the information from previous sales calls with the buyer, Wise and her tech-support team decided that the R740 system offered the greatest benefits to this particular customer. However, a special sales promotion provided company salespeople additional commissions and double points toward the annual sales incentive trip to Hawaii for each R800 system sold. The higher priced R800 had all the same features and capabilities of the R740 along with many more. However, few of these additional capabilities would ever be of value to the insurance company. During her last sales call, Wise explained and demonstrated the R740 and the R800.

What should Tracey do?
a) Recommend the R740, because it offers the most value to the customer.
b) Recommend the R800 by telling the buyer that the additional features would be needed as the company grows.
c) Present a detailed comparison of all of the features offered by the R740 and R800 and let the buyer make the decision.

Anton Gvozdikov/Shutterstock.com

Creating and communicating value is also important in maintaining relationships with existing customers, because changes can occur in a customer's situation. For example, Match Eyewear had been doing business with a large account. This customer had made some changes in its business objectives and was ready to stop doing business with Match Eyewear. The Match Eyewear sales team found out about this and met many times with the customer. These meetings identified the new value needed by the customer. Match Eyewear addressed the new value requirements by improving its service and support offerings and communicating these changes effectively. The customer was retained and Match Eyewear used this situation to develop a stronger relationship with this customer.[3]

7-4 INTERESTING AND UNDERSTANDABLE SALES DIALOGUE

Once confirmed benefits have been identified, the salesperson needs to present key selling points in a manner that is interesting and understandable to the buyer. The presentation should focus on the buyer and is intended to gain and hold the buyer's attention, and to increase the buyer's understanding and retention of the information provided by the salesperson. **Verbal support** elements include voice characteristics, examples and anecdotes, and comparisons and analogies. Using these elements appropriately can produce interesting and understandable sales dialogue.

7-4a Voice Characteristics

The key aspects of **voice characteristics** are the pitch and speed of speech. Varying and changing pitch on key words adds emphasis and increases impact. It is analogous to putting different colors and hues into your voice. The increased intensity and vividness grabs attention, holds interest, and helps the buyer remember what is said. Fluctuating the speed of speech can add emphasis and guide the buyer's attention to selected points of the presentation. Important details—especially quantitative information—should be provided at a slower, more careful pace. Less critical information can be presented at a faster pace in order to grab the buyer's attention and redirect his or her interest. Changes in volume can be used to add emphasis to an important phrase or topic, and a softer volume—almost a whisper—can build intrigue

and pull the prospect into the conversation. Altering volume from loud to soft can better grab and hold the buyer's interest while simultaneously adding clarity and emphasis to increase understanding.

A salesperson can know his or her product inside and out, but if there is no energy and passion in his or her voice, the potential for making the sale will be seriously impaired. Chris Pursell, National Account Executive with DRE Medical, talks about the importance of voice characteristics:[4]

> *Your voice is an instrument. When used wisely, varying the cadence, pitch, and speed of your voice can deliver a message that captures a buyer's attention, generates interest, and adds energy to a sales conversation. I try to speak in a very confident manner and to communicate my passion for helping buyers solve problems.*

Voice quality can be used to bring excitement and drama to the presentation by doing three things: varying the pitch, fluctuating the speed, and altering the volume.

7-4b Examples and Anecdotes

An **example** is a brief description of a specific instance used to illustrate features and benefits. Examples may be either real or hypothetical and are used to further explain and emphasize a topic of interest. A production equipment salesperson might further explain the purpose of an infrared guidance control by using the following example:

> *If the feedstock coming off the main paper roll gets out of line by as little as 1/16 of an inch, the infrared guidance control will sense it and automatically make the correct adjustments. This prevents a paper jam from shutting down your package printing line and costing lost time and wasted product.*

An **anecdote** is a type of example presented in the form of a story describing a specific incident or occurrence. Stories can be very effective in keeping a buyer interested and helping the buyer understand the solution a salesperson

verbal support The use of voice characteristics, examples and anecdotes, and comparisons and analogies to make sales dialogue interesting and understandable.

voice characteristics The pitch and speed of speech, which salespeople should vary to emphasize key points.

example A brief description of a specific instance used to illustrate features and benefits of a product.

anecdote A type of example that is provided in the form of a story describing a specific incident or occurrence.

presents. The production equipment salesperson might use an anecdote such as the following:

One of my customers was having a problem with paper jams that were shutting down the firm's package printing line. Similar to your situation, there was a lot of lost production time and wasted product. We installed the infrared guidance control, which automatically adjusts the paper roll when it gets off by as little as 1/16 of an inch. This reduced paper jams, resulting in less wasted product and more production time for the customer.

A salesperson's use of examples and anecdotes keeps the buyer interested, brings clarity into the presentation, and improves the buyer's understanding and retention of what the salesperson is presenting. The use of an example and anecdote in our sales dialogue example for customer service training follows.

Seller: Customized training programs can be very effective. For example, one of our clients increased customer satisfaction ratings by 25 percent after we implemented a customized program for their reps. (*Example*). Is this the type of improvement you are looking for? (*Check-back*)

Seller: Customers of the XYZ Company were very dissatisfied with the service the firm's reps provided. We reviewed the customers' complaints, met with the customer service reps, identified the main problems, and created a specific training program to deal with the key problems. After completion of the sales training program, customer complaints decreased by 75 percent. (*Anecdote*) What do you think about these results? (*Check-back*)

7-4c Comparisons and Analogies

A **comparison** is a statement that points out and illustrates the similarities between two points. Comparisons increase the buyer's level of interest and understanding of information. A salesperson wishing to add emphasis and meaning to his or her verbal description of the Honda S2000's performance capabilities might use a direct comparison to the performance capabilities of a competitive model that the prospective buyer might also be considering:

You have the performance specifications on both cars, and as you can see . . . the 6-second 0-to-60 performance of the S2000 outperforms the Audi TT by a good 10 percent. This is a large difference in performance.

comparison A statement that points out and illustrates the similarities between two points.

analogy A special and useful form of comparison that explains one thing in terms of another.

In no other industry are comparisons and analogies used more than possibly the auto industry.

Citybrabus/Shutterstock.com

A salesperson for Newell-Rubbermaid might illustrate the benefits of setting up an end-of-aisle display of special occasion containers by using the following comparison to the store manager's sales goals for the product category:

Sales data from stores similar to yours indicate that adding an end-of-aisle display for these seasonal containers will increase their sales by 35 to 40 percent during the fourth quarter holiday season. This would certainly help you achieve—and possibly exceed—the store's goal of a 20 percent increase for this general product category.

Medical products salespeople use comparisons in their role as consultants to doctors. The salespeople will provide a direct comparison of existing products to new products that will be introduced in the near future. Doctors find these comparisons valuable and, in some cases, find the new product valuable enough to postpone non-emergency surgery until the new product is available.[5]

An **analogy** is a special and useful form of comparison that explains one thing in terms of another. Analogies are useful for explaining something complex by allowing the buyer to better visualize it in terms of something familiar that is easier to understand. A BMW salesperson presenting to an Air Force pilot the option of an in-car global positioning system map and tracking system might use the following analogy:

Having the onboard map and tracking system is like having a friendly flight controller with you on every trip. You will always know exactly where you are and what route you should travel to reach your destination. You will never get lost or be delayed because you took the wrong turn.

The use of a comparison and analogy in our sales dialogue example is presented here.

Seller: We will incorporate your reps throughout the design and execution of our training program. This gives the reps some ownership in the program. Our competitors, in contrast, develop their programs based on what management tells them is important. (*Comparison*). Do you think your reps would respond well to being included in all aspects of the training program? (*Check-back*)

Seller: Developing a customized sales training program is like planning for a family vacation. Everyone in the family is likely to be more excited about the vacation if they are involved in all aspects of the planning process. (*Analogy*) What do you think about involving your reps in all aspects of the training program? (*Check-back*)

7-5 ENGAGING AND INVOLVING THE BUYER

Simply informing the prospect about the benefits and their value to the buyer is seldom sufficient to generate the level of interest and desire required to result in a purchase decision. To maximize the effectiveness of the sales dialogue, salespeople utilize various **sales aids** to engage and involve the buyer throughout the sales interaction. These sales aids also help to capture and hold the buyer's attention, boost the buyer's understanding, increase the believability of the claims, and build the buyer's retention of information. (See Exhibit 7.3.) Not

Printed materials are effective sales aids; often providing the customer with useful information.

all sales aids are suitable for all products, selling situations, or buyers. Nor should a salesperson feel the need to use each and every tool in any given sales call. A salesperson should use the sales aids that will engage and involve each buyer most effectively in a particular sales dialogue. Many times, the selling organization provides these sales tools. However, experienced salespeople are quick to comment that some of their most effective sales aids are those that they developed themselves for specific prospects and selling situations.

7-5a Types of Sales Aids

Sales aids allow the salesperson to involve one or more of the buyer's senses in the presentation, help to illustrate features and confirmed benefits, and add clarity and dramatization to increase the effectiveness of a sales dialogue. The types of sales aids available to a salesperson include visual materials, electronic

> **sales aids** The use of printed materials, electronic materials, and product demonstrations to engage and involve buyers.

Exhibit 7.3

Reasons for Using Sales Aids

- Capture prospective buyer's attention.
- Generate interest in the recommended solution.
- Make presentations more persuasive.
- Increase the buyer's participation and involvement.
- Provide the opportunity for collaboration and two-way communication.
- Add clarity and enhance the prospect's understanding.
- Provide supportive evidence and proof to enhance believability.
- Augment the prospect's retention of information.
- Enhance the professional image of the salesperson and selling organization.

Technology in Sales

Using Sales Aids Effectively

Nick George is a Small Business Sales Consultant at Advanced Payroll Systems (APS). He discusses how he uses sales aids effectively to sell cloud-based workforce management solutions to prospects and customers:

My sales process typically consists of a phone call to set up an appointment, a needs analysis meeting, and a meeting to present customized solutions to address the prospect's needs. I employ a variety of sales aids during this presentation meeting. A short PowerPoint presentation is used to guide the first portion of the

meeting. I start by showing a list of the prospect's needs, then present the APS value proposition, and show how the APS product, service, and value proposition can address each need and improve the prospect's current situation. The next step is a demonstration of our software on a computer. The demonstration is customized using logos, information, and settings pertinent to the prospect's needs. This makes it possible for me to show specifically how each prospect need will be addressed by the APS solution. Finally, I show the versatility and usefulness of our software by demonstrating our smartphone and tablet app. This meeting is very interactive and engaging throughout as I continuously ask check-back questions to confirm prospect understanding and the prospect typically asks me questions during the demonstration.

Although most of my presentation meetings are in person, I sometimes conduct them electronically. In fact, when I was working on a very large sale with a prospect located in another state, I conducted the presentation meeting using Go to Meeting Web conferencing. This technology enabled me to share my screen and combine this with phone call capabilities for myself and three people at the prospect company. I was able to use my normal PowerPoint and demonstration approach and interact effectively with all of the people at the prospect company. The electronic meeting was very successful. I followed up with the prospect by phone and email and ended up closing my largest sale ever!

materials, and product demonstrations. An example of employing different types of sales aids is discussed in "TECHNOLOGY IN SALES: Using Sales Aids Effectively."

7-5b Visual Materials

Visual materials represent a variety of sales aids intended to engage and involve buyers visually. The major types of visual materials are printed materials, photographs and illustrations, and charts and graphs. Exhibit 7.4 provides salespeople with a number of tips for preparing printed materials and visuals.

Printed materials include items such as brochures, pamphlets, catalogs, articles, reprints, reports, testimonial letters, and guarantees. Well-designed printed materials can help the salesperson communicate, explain, and emphasize

key points during a sales dialogue. They are designed to summarize important features and benefits and can not only be used effectively during the presentation but also left behind as reminder pieces for the buyer after the salesperson has left. When printed materials are left with a buyer, the salesperson's name and contact information should be clearly printed on the material or an attached business card.

Photographs and illustrations are easy to produce and relatively inexpensive. Using images allows the salesperson to present a realistic portrayal of the product or service. Many products cannot be taken into a prospective buyer's office because of their size. A well-detailed image can give the prospect an idea of the product's appearance and size. Line drawings and diagrams can show the most important details of a product. Images are most effective when they illustrate and simplify a more complex product or feature and make it easy to communicate information about size, shape, construction, and use.

Charts and graphs are useful in showing trends and illustrating relationships. As such, they can show the

visual materials Printed materials, photographs and illustrations, and charts and graphs used as sales aids.

Multimedia sales aids are being used more in sales dialogue.

prospect what the problem is costing them or how a solution might work. Charts and graphs often illustrate relationships in terms of bars, lines, circles, or squares. For example, a salesperson for an office equipment vendor might get the cost figures associated with the buyer's use of an outside copy center for the previous two years. The salesperson could then use this information in a comparative bar graph to better illustrate the savings possible if the buyer had a copier. Salespeople for a leading medical technology company use a chart format to compare the features and benefits of their product versus the competitors' equipment the buyer is considering. The chart format succinctly and effectively supports statements of superiority made during the presentation.

7-5c Electronic Materials

Electronic materials include all sales aids in electronic format. These span individual slides and videos to complete multimedia presentations. As technology continues to develop, more options to use electronic materials become available to salespeople.

Salespeople today can customize graphic presentations for each buyer. Customizing and enriching presentations by using electronic multimedia can be done inexpensively and in a fairly short period of time. Microsoft PowerPoint, for example, allows the salesperson to build a complete, high-impact graphic presentation customized for an individual prospect quickly. The use of video has the advantage of both sound and action. These powerful multimedia presentations might include pictures of products, as well as product demonstrations and competitive comparisons. The buyer can be taken on a virtual tour of the selling organization and see the product being produced or simultaneously see and hear a personal message from the president of the selling organization as well as testimonials from satisfied customers.

Leading pharmaceutical companies are using electronic materials in two interesting ways. First, iPad applications (apps) have been developed by some firms to facilitate interaction between sales reps and doctors. The salesperson can use the app to visually illustrate how a drug works in the body and to respond to questions a doctor might have. Second, doctors are very busy and may not have time to interact with a salesperson during an office visit. In these cases, the sales rep can give the physician a card with a URL on it and invite the doctor to view a presentation electronically, engage in an online discussion, or participate in a live electronic presentation at a more convenient time. These and other forms of "e-detailing" are being explored by many pharmaceutical firms.[6]

electronic materials Sales aids in electronic format such as slides, videos, or multimedia presentations.

7-5d Product Demonstrations

The product itself is often the most effective sales tool because it provides the prospective buyer with an opportunity for hands-on experience. When the actual product does not lend itself to being demonstrated, models can be used to represent and illustrate key features and benefits of the larger product. The value of an actual product demonstration is applicable to all types of products and services. For example, aircraft salespeople use scale models to give the buyer a detailed and realistic feel for the aircraft, which cannot be tucked into the salesperson's briefcase. Major vendors of office furniture will set up an actual model office so that the prospective client can experience its actual use. Pharmaceutical companies provide doctors with actual samples of the product for trial use with selected patients.

As detailed in Exhibit 7.5, the salesperson should make sure the product being demonstrated is typical of what is being recommended. Furthermore, it should be checked to ensure that it is in good working order prior to the demonstration and that setup and removal do not detract from the presentation. The last thing the salesperson wants is to have to apologize for poor appearance or inadequate performance.

> Salespeople can increase the success of a sales dialogue by using appropriate sales aids effectively.

Whenever possible, it is important to have the buyer use the product instead of the salesperson demonstrating its use. For example, buyers often realize that many new software products have features that could be valuable to their firm. However, they may be reluctant to make a purchase because they think it will be too hard for their employees to learn to use the software. A salesperson could demonstrate the software to show how easy it is to use, but it would be more effective to have the buyer use the software to experience firsthand its ease of use.

Sometimes it is more effective to bring the buyer to another site for a product demonstration. Toshiba Medical Systems uses this approach very successfully for buyers of CT scanners and MRI systems. It conducts 20 to 40 site visits a week with potential buyers. The buyers have the opportunity to see the products in action in a clinical-like environment, and get to know the Toshiba executives. This demonstration approach has led to significant sales growth and better customer relationships for Toshiba Medical Systems.[7]

7-5e Using Sales Aids in the Presentation

Practice! Practice! Practice! Rehearsal of the presentation is the final key to conducting effective sales dialogue. Understand what features are relevant and what benefits are meaningful to the prospective buyer in terms of value to be realized. Be confident in developing and using multiple sales aids to add impact to the presentation itself. Using the SPES Sequence can facilitate the effectiveness of presentation tools and sales aids: S = *State selling point and introduce the sales aid;* P = *Present the sales aid;* E = *Explain the sales aid;* S = *Summarize.*[8]

7-5f State the Selling Point and Introduce the Sales Aid

This means stating the full selling point including the feature and potential benefit and then introducing the sales aid. For instance, "To demonstrate this benefit, I would like you to take a look at this video" or "This graph summarizes the increased performance you will experience with the Honda S2000." This prepares the buyer for the visual aid and informs him or her that attention is required.

Exhibit 7.5

Guidelines for Product Demonstrations

- Ensure that the appearance of the product is neat and clean.
- Check for problem-free operation.
- Be confident and able to demonstrate the product skillfully.
- Practice using the product prior to the demonstration.
- Anticipate problems and have back-up or replacement parts on hand.
- Make sure that setup and knockdown are easy and quick.

7-5g Present the Sales Aid

This involves presenting the sales aid to the customer and allowing a few moments for examination and familiarization before saying anything. For example, when using printed materials, place the material directly in front of the customer and allow it to be reviewed momentarily in silence. Allow the customer to review the sales aid and satisfy his or her natural curiosity before using it.

7-5h Explain the Sales Aid

No matter how carefully a sales aid is prepared, it will not be completely obvious. The customer will not necessarily understand the significance unless the salesperson provides a brief explanation. Do not rely on a chart or graph to illustrate fully the points being supported. Similarly, a prospect might enjoy a product demonstration yet totally miss the information or experience supporting the presentation. The salesperson should point out the material information and explain how it supports his or her points.

7-5i Summarize

When finished explaining the significance of the sales aid, summarize its contribution and support and remove the sales aid. If not removed, its presence can distract the prospective buyer's attention from subsequent feature and benefit points.

The use of the SPES Sequence to use a sales aid in our customer service training program sales dialogue is presented here.

Seller: You mentioned earlier that your reps are not well prepared to deal with irate customers. I would like to show you a short video from a training program we developed for another firm. The video illustrates how we use role plays to help reps develop the skills to interact with irate customers effectively. (State the *selling point and introduce the sales aid*.)

(The salesperson shows the video to the buyer.)

Seller: Did you notice how everyone involved in the training program watched the role play carefully and was able to contribute comments to improve the interaction with the irate customer? *(Explain the sales aid.)*

Buyer: The role play exercise did get everyone involved and produced some good ideas for improvement.

Seller: Although this is just one type of exercise we employ in our training programs, the role play produced some guidelines that all reps could use to deal with irate customers more effectively. (*Summarize*) Do you think this type of exercise would be valuable to your reps? *(Check-back)*

7-6 SUPPORTING PRODUCT CLAIMS

As discussed earlier in this chapter, confirmed benefits answer the buyer's question, "What is in it for me?" In a similar fashion, **proof providers** such as statistics, testimonials, and case histories can be utilized to preempt the buyer from asking, "Can you prove it?" or "Who says so?" Claims of benefits and value produced and provided to the buyer need to be backed up with evidence to highlight their believability.

7-6a Statistics

Statistics are facts that lend believability to claims of value and benefit. When available, statistics from authoritative, third-party sources carry the highest credibility. Third-party sources include independent testing organizations and labs (e.g., *Consumer Reports*, Underwriters Laboratories), professional organizations (e.g., American Dental Association, Risk Management Society), research companies (e.g., Booz Allen Hamilton, The Industry Standard, PricewaterhouseCoopers), institutions (e.g., Sandia National Laboratories, MIT), and various governmental entities (e.g., Census Bureau, state licensing bureaus, Department of Commerce). Statistics prepared by the selling organization as well as the salesperson can also be useful in providing evidence for claims. Facts and statistics are most

proof providers The use of statistics, testimonials, or case histories to support product claims.

statistics Facts that lend believability to product claims and are used as proof providers.

Salespeople can use testimonials to support their product claims.

powerful when they fairly represent all sides to the story and are presented in printed form rather than simply stated orally. Not only does the printed word carry more credibility but also it is convenient and can be left as a reminder to aid the prospect's retention of information.

7-6b Testimonials

Testimonials are similar to statistics, but in the form of statements from satisfied users of the selling organization's products and services. Supportive statements from current users are excellent methods to build trust and confidence. They predispose the prospective buyer to accept what the salesperson says about the benefits and value a recommended solution offers, and they reduce the prospect's perceived risk in making a purchase decision.

Written testimonials are especially effective when they are on the recommending user's letterhead and signed. However, testimonials that list customers, trade publications, trade associations, and independent rating organizations along with one-sentence comments in a presentation can also be effective. For instance:

Kheng Guan Toh/Shutterstock.com

- "The American Dental Association has endorsed the new Laserlite drilling system as being safe and painless for the patient."

- "In January, *Fortune* magazine recognized CDW as the top-rated technology vendor on the basis of services provided to the buying customer."

- "The *RIMS Quality Scorecard* rated Arthur J. Gallagher & Co. as the highest-rated insurance broker in North America in terms of value and service provided to its clients."

Testimonials are used extensively across industry and product/service types. To maximize their effectiveness, testimonials should be matched according to relevance and recognition to the prospective buyer. It is critical that the organization or person providing the supporting testimony be known or recognized by the prospect, above reproach, and in a position of respect.

7-6c Case Histories

Case histories are basically a testimonial in story or anecdotal form. Their added length allows more detail to be presented to further clarify an issue or better itemize the proof for a given statement. Case histories can also break the monotony of a long presentation. Like their counterpart testimonials, case histories should be used only when they clearly illustrate a particular point and are appropriate for the prospective buyer. Unrelated or tangential stories not only distract the customer but also can be a source of irritation that works against credibility building. Case histories should be short and to the point, lasting no more than a minute. They should support the presentation rather than becoming the center of attention.

The effective use of a proof provider in our customer service training program sales dialogue follows.

Buyer: I like many aspects of your approach to designing and delivering training programs. So I think your firm can develop and implement a good customer service training program for us. But I am not sure the training program will produce the increases in customer satisfaction and retention that we desire. I am concerned that my reps will take the training, like it, learn some things, but then go back to work and not do much differently. If this occurs, we have spent a lot of time and money, but not received much of a return.

Seller: I certainly understand where you are coming from, as all of my customers had similar concerns. Let me show you two letters from customers. Each is from a different industry than yours, but both are about your size and both had similar customer service problems and objectives. (*Salesperson shows each letter and points to key points in each.*) Notice how this customer indicates a 25 percent increase in customer satisfaction from the training program, and this customer has calculated a 20 percent return from its investment in our training program. I think these letters provide strong evidence that our training programs can produce real business results. Do you see how our training program can help you achieve your objectives? (*Check-back*)

7-7 **GROUP SALES DIALOGUE**

Sales dialogue with groups is fairly commonplace in business-to-business selling. For example, retail chains often employ buying committees when considering the addition of new products for their stores. Hospitals use cross-functional teams comprising medical and administrative personnel to choose vendors such as food service providers. A group of marketing and upper-management people usually makes the decision of which advertising agency will be chosen. Corporations often depend on representatives from several departments to make purchase decisions that affect all employees, such as the choice of insurance providers.

Interacting with groups presents special challenges and opportunities. In addition to the basic fundamentals of planning and delivering sales dialogue to individual buyers, there are additional strategies and tactics that can enhance sales dialogue with groups.

When selling to groups, salespeople can expect tough questions and should prepare accordingly. Although buyer questions are part of most sales dialogue whether to individuals or groups, they are particularly crucial when there are multiple buyers. Most buying groups are assembled to tap the individual expertise and interests of the group members. For example, a buying committee for a company's computer information system could include technical specialists; finance and accounting personnel; and representatives from production operations, logistics, management, and marketing. All of these individuals are experts and demand in-depth information in order to make a decision. In some situations, this calls for a sales team to address all questions adequately, while in some cases, an individual salesperson has the cross-functional expertise required to make the sale.

When selling to a group, salespeople should take every opportunity of **preselling** to individual group members prior to the group presentation. Preselling to individual buyers or subgroups of buyers takes place before a major sales presentation to the entire group. Buying procedures in a given company may or may not allow preselling. If it is an option, the salesperson should work with the individuals comprising the buying group prior to presenting to the group as a whole. By doing so, the salesperson can better determine individual and group interests and motives and possibly build a positive foundation for the group presentation. Preselling can also reveal the roles of the individuals in the buying center, as discussed in Chapter 3. Knowing who the decision maker is, along with the other roles such as users

and influencers, is crucial for success in group sales interactions. The importance of group sales dialogue and strategies for preselling are examined in "SELLING IN ACTION: Group Sales Dialogue."

7-7a Sales Tactics for Selling to Groups

Assuming that the salesperson or sales team has planned a comprehensive sales dialogue and done as much preselling as possible, there are some specific sales tactics that can enhance presentations to groups. Sales tactics for group presentations fall into three general categories: arrival tactics, eye contact, and communications tips during presentation delivery.

7-7b Arrival Tactics

Try to arrive at the location for the meeting before the buying group arrives. This provides an opportunity to set up and check audio-visual equipment, prepare collateral material for distribution to the group, and become familiar and comfortable with the surroundings. It also sets the stage for the salesperson to greet individuals from the buying team personally as they enter the room. In a symbolic way, it also signals territorial command, or that the salesperson is in charge of the meeting. Although the control of the meeting is typically shared with the buying group, arriving first sends a message that the salesperson is prepared to start promptly at the appointed time, thus showing respect for the buyer's time.

From the very beginning, the salesperson is hoping to connect with each individual in the group, rather than connecting only at the group level. By arriving first, the salesperson may have the opportunity to talk briefly with each individual. If nothing more, a friendly greeting, handshake, and introduction can help establish a rapport with individuals in the group. When not allowed to arrive first, salespeople should attempt individual introductions when joining the group. If that is not practical, salespeople must try to engage each individual through eye contact and, if appropriate, introductory remarks early in the presentation that recognize the individual interests of those present. For example, a salesperson for a food service company might begin a presentation to a hospital with the following:

Thank you for the opportunity to discuss our food service programs with you today. In planning for our meeting, I recognize that the dietary group is most concerned about the impact of

preselling Salespeople present their product/service to individual buyers before a major sales dialogue with a group of buyers.

any proposed change on the quality of patient care. Linda (the head dietician), I believe we have a program that will actually enhance the quality of care that your patients receive. John (the head of finance), we will also propose an efficient, cost-effective alternative . . .

Opening remarks such as these, when kept brief, can be most effective in building involvement with all individuals in a small group.

7-7c Eye Contact

For both small and large groups, establishing periodic eye contact with individuals is important. With small groups, this is easily accomplished. With larger groups, especially formal presentations where the salesperson is standing and the group is sitting, there may be a tendency to use the so-called overhead approach. This method calls for looking just over the heads of the group, with the idea that those seated farthest from the presenter will feel included as part of the group. This method should be avoided. It might be fine for a formal speech to a large audience in a convention hall, but it is far too impersonal for groups of 10 to 25 individuals. Also avoid a rapid scanning from side to side. This gives the appearance of nervousness and is ineffective in connecting with individual group members. The most effective eye contact is to try to connect with each individual or small subgroups for only a few seconds, moving through the entire group over the course of the presentation. Professional

Selling in Action
Group Sales Dialogue

Todd Harrett is Senior Account Executive for Northern Continental Logistics. He helps manufacturing customers improve processes throughout their supply chain. Todd talks about the importance of and strategies for selling to a group:

The supply chain services I provide impact many different business functions within a firm, such as warehousing, logistics, accounting, finance, and information technology. It is extremely important for me to interact with the appropriate people in the relevant functional areas for each prospect. I must identify the confirmed benefits for each functional area and show how I can create the desired value. But, I also need to get "buy-in" from everyone involved. My basic strategy is to communicate with each functional area initially, but then to engage in a sales dialogue with the entire

group. However, I must adapt this general strategy to fit the unique situation of each prospect. The following examples illustrate some approaches I have taken with different firms:

During a routine annual review with the transportation management team for a corporation we serve, the transportation manager asked, "What more can you do for us?" This open-ended question led to dialogue regarding a new payment solution that would personally save him time on the job and provide his department better visibility and reports. In order to advance the business, we first set a meeting with the accounting department to determine if our proposed strategy was feasible from their perspective. After addressing the accounting team's specific questions and concerns, we all convened (14 of us in the board room) to hash out the plan. All support personnel in addition to the decision makers were in the room, ensuring we received "buy-in" from all parties. Without the smaller separate functional meetings leading up to the final, we would have never received the universal buy-in required to win organizational approval of the new business.

After a couple of meetings with the finance manager of a large household goods manufacturer, I needed the buy-in of the operations manager and warehouse manager in order to implement our services. I was not able to meet with each individual prior to the group meeting so a survey of possible concerns related to my proposed services was submitted to each person. This allowed me to receive their input prior to the final group meeting, which was required to approve implementation. Understanding the perspective of the stakeholders not involved in the initial meetings prior to the final sit-down allowed me to layout my presentation in a manner that addressed all needs and concerns. Needless to say, I closed the sale.

entertainers often use this method to connect with audience members, and salespeople can do the same.

7-7d Communications Tips

When selling to groups, it is essential to make all members of the group feel that their opinions are valuable. It is also important to avoid being caught in the middle of disagreements between members of the buying group. For example, if one member likes the salesperson's proposal and another thinks it is too expensive, any resolution of this disagreement must be handled carefully. Although the salesperson may present information that resolves the issue, in some cases, disagreements among group buying members may be resolved outside the meetings. It is to the salesperson's advantage if disagreements can be handled during the presentation, as it keeps the sales process moving; unresolved issues can stall the sales process. As an example of how salespeople can play a peacemaker role, consider this exchange:

Buyer A: "I really like this system and think we should install it as soon as possible."

Buyer B: "I like it too, but it is way too expensive. Is there a less expensive alternative?"

Buyer A: "Sure, but it will not do the job."

Salesperson: (Directed to Buyer B) "Could I add something here? I believe we have a cost-effective system and that our lease-to-purchase plan reduces the capital expenditure and allows a favorable payback period. Could we take another look at the numbers?"

The point is that salespeople must be diplomatic as a participant in discussions that might develop between members of the buying group. This sometimes means remaining silent while the discussion comes to a resolution, and sometimes it means playing an active role. There are no hard and fast rules in this area, and salespeople must simply use their best judgment to guide their actions.

In delivering group presentations, it is important to maintain contact with group members. Thus, reading or overreliance on densely worded slides should be avoided.

Pokomeda/Shutterstock.com

Salespeople need to repeat or restate questions from individuals in a group presentation.

Think of slides and other audio-visual aids as support tools, not as a "roll-and-scroll" presentation to be read to the group. Natural movement can also enhance contact with the group. Too much pacing about can be detrimental to holding the group's attention, just as remaining tethered to a laptop can detract from group communication. When possible, salespeople should stand to the left of visual aids, as people read right to left. When standing to the left, it is easier to direct attention to the visual aids while momentarily deflecting attention away from the speaker. In this way, the salesperson becomes an unobtrusive narrator and the visual aid has maximum impact.

Body language can add or detract to sales effectiveness in the group setting. In general, posture should reflect an energetic, relaxed person. Conventional wisdom dictates that presenters should avoid contact with their own bodies while presenting. Salespeople who stuff their hands in their pockets, scratch their heads, or cross their arms are creating distractions to their own messages.

7-7e Handling Questions in Group Dialogue

Just as is the case with sales dialogue to individuals, questions from buyers in a group are an important part of the buyer-seller interaction that leads to a purchase decision. Salespeople should recognize that questions fill information gaps, thus allowing buyers to make better decisions. In a group setting, questions can also add a dramatic element, making the presentation more interesting for those in attendance. To the extent that it is possible, salespeople should anticipate group questions, and then decide whether to address the question before it arises or wait and address the question should it arise during the presentation.

To handle questions that arise during the meeting effectively, salespeople should listen carefully and maintain eye contact with the person asking the question. Generally, it is a good idea to repeat or restate the question. Questions should be answered as succinctly and convincingly as possible.

By listening carefully to the question, salespeople should show proper respect to the person asking the question. At the same time, they are helping direct the attention of the group to the question. As the question is posed, it is important for the salesperson to maintain eye contact with the person asking the question. Again, this demonstrates respect for the person and for his or her right to ask questions. This may require some practice, as salespeople might be tempted to glance at sales materials or perhaps their watches when the attention is shifted to the person asking the question. To do so could insult the questioner, who might feel slighted by the lack of attention.

In many cases, it is a good idea to repeat or even restate the question. This will ensure that everyone understands the question. It also signals a shift from the individual back to the group. Additionally, it allows the salesperson to state the key issue in the question succinctly. This is often important because not all questions are well formulated and they are sometimes accompanied by superfluous information. Consider this dialogue:

> In answering questions during a group dialogue, salespeople should listen carefully, answer directly, and address the individual asking the question as well as the others in the group.

Buyer: "You know, I have been thinking about the feasibility of matching our Brand X computers with Brand Y printers. Not too long ago, matching multiple brands would have been a disaster. Are you telling me now that Brand X computers are totally compatible with Brand Y printers?"

Seller: "The question is: Are your computers compatible with our printers? Yes they are—with no special installation requirements."

When restating questions, salespeople must be careful to capture the essence of the buyer's concern accurately. Otherwise, they could be perceived as avoiding the question or trying to manipulate the buyer by putting words in his or her mouth. Therefore, when in doubt, it is a good practice when restating a question to seek buyer confirmation that the restated question is an accurate representation of the original question. For example, salespeople might say, "Ms. Jackson, as I understand the question, you are concerned about the effectiveness of our seasonal sales promotion programs. Is that correct?"

When you are answering questions, there are three guidelines to follow. First, salespeople should not attempt to answer a question until he or she and the group members clearly understand the question. Second, salespeople should not attempt to answer questions that

they are not prepared to answer. It is far better to make a note and tell the group you will get back to them with the answer than to speculate or give a weak answer. Third, try to answer questions as directly as possible. Politicians are often accused of not answering the questions posed during press conferences, but rather steering the answer toward what they wish to talk about. Salespeople will quickly lose credibility if they take a long time to get to the point in their answer. To answer convincingly, start with a "yes" or "no," and then explain the exceptions to the general case. For example, say, "Yes, that is generally the case. There are some exceptions, including . . ." is preferred to answering, "Well that depends . . . ," and then explaining all of the special circumstances only to conclude with "but, generally, yes, that is the case."

When answering questions, it is important to address the entire group rather than just the individual who asked the question. Otherwise, salespeople may lose the attention of other group members. When salespeople conclude their answers, they have the option of going back to the person who asked the question, continuing their presentation, or taking a question from another group member. Salespeople can rely on their common sense and experience to decide what is appropriate in a given situation.

In larger groups, it is particularly important to avoid getting locked into a question-and-answer dialogue with one person if other people are showing an interest in asking questions. Indeed, it is important to take all questions, but it is also important to spread the opportunity to ask questions around the room, coming back to those who have multiple questions until all questions are answered. If one person is a dominant force within the buying group, other group members will typically defer their questions until that person has asked all of their questions at different points in the presentation.

When selling to a group, salespeople should have a clear objective for their presentation. To get the group to take the desired action, salespeople must make a convincing case, motivate the group to take action, and make it easy for the group to take the desired action. Some of the methods for handling buyer objections and earning a commitment, as will be discussed in Chapter 8, will prove useful for accomplishing these tasks.

In some cases, the group will wish to deliberate and let the salesperson know of their decision at a later time. This is not uncommon, because the group may need a frank discussion without outsiders to reach a final decision. Should this occur, salespeople should be certain that the group has all the information they need or offer to provide the needed information promptly and offer to follow up within a specified time period.

The process for planning and delivering a group sales dialogue is much the same as it is for sales dialogue with individuals. By paying attention to the special considerations in this section, salespeople can build on their experience with sales interaction with individuals and engage in effective sales dialogue with groups.

STUDY TOOLS 7

LOCATED IN TEXTBOOK

☐ Rip-out and review chapter review card

LOCATED AT WWW.CENGAGEBRAIN.COM

☐ Review key term flashcards and create your own from StudyBits

☐ Organize notes and StudyBits using the StudyBoard feature within 4LTR Press Online

☐ Complete practice and graded quizzes to prepare for tests

☐ Complete interactive content within the narrative portion of 4LTR Press Online

☐ View chapter highlight box content at the beginning of each chapter

OFFICE FURNITURE COMPANY

BACKGROUND

The Office Furniture Company specializes in providing customers with office furniture solutions that are customized and designed to address productivity and aesthetic needs. It sells office furniture from the leading manufacturers, but creates value by analyzing the specific needs of each customer and then developing a customized design to meet these needs. There are several competitors in the office furniture industry, but most of them focus on low prices. Customers usually pay more for an Office Furniture Company solution, but receive more value in terms of increased productivity and business effectiveness.

CURRENT SITUATION

Naiser & Associates is a small, but growing, accounting firm. The company plans to add more office staff and to increase the number of its accountants. This planned growth means that the firm will have to find new office space, because it will have outgrown its current location. Because it plans continued growth in the future, it is looking for a new office that will accommodate current and future growth objectives. Naiser & Associates also wants to purchase new and better furniture for its new office.

You are a sales representative for the Office Furniture Company and have been meeting with partner, Frank Naiser, as well as accountants and staff at Naiser & Associates. Based on these meetings, you have identified the following office furniture needs:

1. Naiser & Associates has typically met with clients at their offices. It would like to have most client meetings in the future at its new office. This means they desire furniture for these meetings that facilitates these meetings and communicates a professional and customer-friendly image.

2. Their current office furniture did not provide much storage for accountants or staff. Thus, important documents were stored at the end of a long hallway. Employees wasted a lot of time trying to retrieve important documents. Thus, they desire furniture that provides more storage for each employee.

3. Technology is changing at a rapid pace, so furniture that can be easily adapted to new technologies is very important.

4. As Naiser & Associates continues to grow, it will probably have to reorganize itself and is likely to need to adapt the physical office to different organizational arrangements. Office furniture that is adaptable to different configurations is important.

You have created an office equipment design for Naiser &Associates that addresses each of the issues presented above and are preparing for a meeting with the partner, Frank Naiser, the office manager, and a representative for the firm's accountants. You know that a competitor has already made a presentation to the same group and their offer will cost less than what you will be able to charge.

QUESTIONS

1. How will you try overcoming the lower price offer by a competitor?

2. What specific value can you offer Naiser & Associates?

3. How can you most effectively communicate the value of your proposed office equipment design?

4. What sales aids could you use to make your presentation more engaging and effective?

ROLE PLAY

Situation: Read the Office Equipment Company case.

Characters: Frank Naiser, partner; Jennifer Hamman, office manager; Jessica Attaway, accountant representative

Scene:
Location—Current Naiser & Associates office.

Action—Role play this meeting. Be sure to address the specific needs identified earlier, to communicate effectively with each person in the meeting, and to incorporate sales aids appropriately.

After completing the role plays, address the following questions:

1. How would you evaluate the role play in terms of interesting, understandable, and engaging sales dialogue? What improvements would you recommend?

2. How well did you involve each person in the meeting? What improvements would you recommend?

3. Evaluate the effectiveness of each sales aid used? What improvements in the use of sales aids would you recommend?

Sales Dialogue: Creating and Communicating Value

ALL RISK INSURANCE AND NATIONAL NETWORKS

BACKGROUND

The All Risk Insurance Company has 3,200 sales agents spread across five regions that cover the United States. They are moving toward the development of a national network that would tie each of the agent offices together with the regional offices and corporate headquarters. The improved communication capability will allow all company personnel to have full access to customer records and form the core of a comprehensive customer relationship management system that is to be rolled out in 18 months.

CURRENT SITUATION

Jim Roberts is a network account specialist for National Networks, a specialist in large corporate network solutions, and has been working with the technology-buying group at All Risk Insurance for several months now. Roberts has worked through several meetings with the buying group members and has a meeting scheduled for next Wednesday to present his recommendations and demonstrate why they should select National Networks as the supplier for this sizable project. Joyce Fields (director of information systems), John Harris (comptroller and CFO), Mike Davis (director of agent services), and Dianne Sheffield (director for customer services) will make the final decision. Roberts also knows that there is one other competitor who will be making a presentation in hopes of landing

the project. The equipment both vendors are proposing is virtually identical due to the detailed specifications that All Risk Insurance had included in the RFP. Prices are also likely to be pretty similar. The decision will most likely come down to the services each competitor includes in their proposals. Based on the information that Roberts has collected from different sources, he has come up with a comparison of customer services of National Networks and the competitor (see the table on the following page) offer.

ROLE PLAY

Situation: Read "All Risk Insurance and National Networks" background and Current Situation.

Characters: Jim Roberts—salesperson for National Networks; Joyce Fields—director of information systems for All Risk Insurance; John Harris—comptroller and CFO for All Risk Insurance; Mike Davis—director of agent services for All Risk Insurance; Dianne Sheffield—director for customer services for All Risk Insurance

Scene: *Location*—A conference room at All Risk Insurance.

Action—As described, Jim Roberts is presenting the National Networks proposal for a corporate computer network linking All Risk Insurance's corporate offices with each of its five regional offices and 3,200 sales agents out in the field.

Role play Roberts's presentation of each of the feature-benefit sets incorporating sales aids suitable for use in the group presentation.

Features	Capability of National Networks	Capability of Competitor	Benefits
Service and repair centers	175 affiliated service and repair centers across the United States	21 affiliated service and repair centers across the United States	Ensures fast and reliable repairs for hardware and software
Installation and testing	Installation and testing done by National Networks employees	Installation and testing outsourced to several different companies	Knowledge that all installations will be done the right way
Customer call center	24 hours, 7 days per week, and staffed by National Networks employees	24 hours, 7 days per week, and staffed by an outsource commercial provider	Knowledgeable staff always available to assist All Risk Insurance employees with problems

8 | Addressing Concerns and Earning Commitment

LEARNING OBJECTIVES

After studying this chapter, the student should be able to:

 8-1 Explain why it is important to anticipate and overcome buyer concerns and resistance.

 8-2 Understand why prospects raise objections.

8-3 Describe the five major types of sales resistance.

8-4 Explain how the LAARC method can be used to overcome buyer resistance.

 8-5 Describe the recommended approaches for responding to buyer objections.

 8-6 List and explain the earning commitment techniques that secure commitment and closing.

After finishing this chapter go to
PAGE 190 for **STUDY TOOLS.**

Schatzy/Shutterstock.com

EARN MORE REFERRALS AND REPEAT BUSINESS

Many salespeople become addicted to chasing opportunities and the high that comes with closing a deal. But beware of becoming the closing addict. Often, such reps sacrifice lasting success by pursuing short-term gains. A great and lasting relationship with a customer isn't something that's just handed to you; you have to earn it. Selling Power Editors offer these tips to help customers see you as a partner rather than just another business interaction where the salesperson is always trying to close the order.

Make sure your buyer-education process goes beyond your product and services. After you earn commitment, tell your new customers everything they need to know to make their post-sale interactions with your company as smooth as possible. Ideally, your company will have taken steps to do this, but unfortunately, that's not always the case. If you can't get upper management to make improvements, keep track of some of the most common

requests and frustrations your customers express, then be proactive about giving key advice and helpful tips. For example, customers might find it useful to know any of the following:

- How your products will come packaged;

- How to read the invoice;

- When they can and can't expect a rush order;

- How to follow up on back orders or make special shipping or delivery arrangements;

- How to get in touch with you or someone who can help them quickly and easily, even during off hours.

Make clear to customers that your success is based on their success. Sales resistance after the sale can be avoided by forming a collaborative partnership, which means the difference between helping your customers and simply selling them on a product or service. Show them your willingness to be available and helpful. Send emails that are concise and intelligent, take time to walk them through procedures, and know when and how to put them in touch with people on your team who will be responsive and knowledgeable.

Remember that good experiences add up. A good overall experience with your company after the sale can often mean repeat business and glowing referrals for you. Internally, be an advocate for thorough training of customer service teams and any other departments or support people who will be interacting or working with your customer.

The best salespeople quickly learn how to see a signed contract, not as an ending, but as the start of a long-term and mutually beneficial relationship for years to come. If you're truly customer focused, then you should have no problem getting plenty of repeat business and referrals.

ADDRESSING CONCERNS

An objection or sales resistance is anything the buyer says or does that slows down or stops the buying process. The salesperson's job is to uncover these objections and answer them to the prospect's or client's satisfaction. It is very difficult for a salesperson to earn commitment if there is doubt or concern on the buyer's part. Thus, the salesperson must uncover and overcome any and all objections. In doing so, the salesperson strengthens the long-term relationship and moves the sales process closer to commitment. At the very least, these concerns open dialogue between the salesperson and the prospect.

A brief discussion follows on why it is important for salespeople to anticipate and negotiate buyer concern. Following a discussion of why prospects raise objections, this chapter covers the five major types of objections. Next, different approaches to handling sales resistance are explained. Finally, techniques to earn commitment are reviewed.

> Good salespeople will anticipate their buyers' concerns.

"And that is what happens when we resist change."

Many salespeople fear sales resistance from their prospects or customers.

8-1 ANTICIPATE AND NEGOTIATE CONCERNS AND RESISTANCE

Over the years, many sales forces were taught that **sales resistance** was bad and would likely slow down or stop the selling process. Salespeople were also told that if they received resistance, then they had not done a good job explaining their product or service.

These notions have changed over the years to where objections are now viewed as opportunities to sell. Salespeople should be grateful for objections and always treat them as questions. The buyer is just asking for more information. It is the salesperson's job to produce the correct information to help buyers understand their concerns. Inexperienced salespeople need to learn that sales resistance is a normal, natural part of any sales conversation. The prospect that does not question price, service, warranty, and delivery concerns is probably not interested.

Although many salespeople fear sales resistance from their prospects

sales resistance Buyer's objections to a product or service during a sales presentation.

or customers, it should be viewed as a normal part of the sales process. At a minimum, the salesperson has the prospect involved. The salesperson can now start to determine customer interest and measure the buyer's understanding of the problem. In some situations, a salesperson cannot overcome resistance (e.g., delivery dates do not match; technology does not fit). Under these circumstances, the successful salesperson gracefully ends the sales call while leaving open the option for further business.[1] Finally, if the sales resistance is handled correctly, the outcome can lead to customer acceptance.

8-2 REASONS WHY PROSPECTS RAISE OBJECTIONS

There are many reasons why prospects will raise objections.

1. The prospect wants to avoid the sales interview. Some prospects do not want to create any more work for themselves than they already have. A sales interview takes time, and buyers already have a busy schedule handling normal day-to-day tasks. Buyers may want to avoid the salesperson because they view his or her call as an interruption in their day. Most buyers do not have the time to see every salesperson that knocks on their door.

2. The salesperson has failed to prospect and qualify properly. Sometimes, poor prospects slip through the screening process. The prospect may have misunderstood the salesperson's intentions when asked for the interview. The salesperson should attempt to qualify the prospect during the sales call. For example, a computer software company used telemarketing to qualify prospects. Leads were turned over to the salesforce for in-person visits. The major product line was an inventory control package that cost $20,000. The salesperson asked the owner of the company if she had a budget for this project. The owner responded that her budget was $5,000. The salesperson gave the owner the names of a couple of inexpensive software companies, thanked the owner for her time, and moved on. The owner was not about to spend $20,000 and said so early in the sales conversation. That resistance actually helped the salesperson. What if this condition had stayed hidden for four to six weeks while the salesperson continued to call on the owner? Both the salesperson's and owner's time would have been wasted.

3. Objecting is a matter of custom. Many purchasing agents have a motto never to buy on the first call with a salesperson. Trust has not yet been developed and a thorough understanding of the salesperson, his or her company, and the products has not been developed. The buyer will need most of this information to make a decision. Many buyers may say no during the first few calls to test the salesperson's persistence.

4. The prospect resists change. Many buyers like the way that they are currently doing business. Thus, buyers will tell the salesperson that they are satisfied with what they have now. Many prospects simply resist change because they dislike making decisions. Prospects may fear the consequences of deciding and dread disturbing the status quo. A purchase usually involves dismissing the current

supplier and handling all of the arrangements (price, terms, delivery, and product specifications) to move the new supplier in smoothly. Once a buyer is comfortable with his or her suppliers, he or she will generally avoid new salespeople until a major need arises.

5. The prospect fails to recognize a need. The prospect may be unaware of a need, uninformed about the product or service, or content with the situation as it is. In any case, the lack of need creates no motivation to change suppliers. Many purchasing agents were content with their overnight mail service and were slow to recognize the fax machine as a viable solution to getting information to their customers quickly. The poor quality of the reproduced document also turned away many buyers. Only when the need for the information outweighed the aesthetics of the document did the buyers readily embrace the fax machine.

6. The prospect lacks information. Ultimately, all sales resistance comes back to the fact that the prospect simply lacks the information he or she needs to make a decision comfortably. The salesperson must view this as an opportunity to put the right information in front of the buyer. Exhibit 8.1 summarizes why prospects raise objections and lists strategies for dealing with them.

Exhibit 8.1

Why Prospects Raise Objections and Strategies for Dealing with Them

- Buyer wants to avoid the sales interview.
  Strategy: Set appointments to become part of the buyer's daily routine.

- Salesperson has failed to prospect and qualify properly.
  Strategy: Ask questions to verify prospect's interest.

- Buyer will not buy on the first sales call.
  Strategy: A regular call on the prospect lets the prospect know the salesperson is serious about the relationship.

- Prospect does not want to change the current way of doing business.
  Strategy: Salesperson must help the prospect understand there is a better solution than the one the prospect is currently using.

- Prospect has failed to recognize a need.
  Strategy: Salesperson must show evidence that sparks the prospect's interest.

- Prospect lacks information on a new product or on the salesperson's company.
  Strategy: Salesperson must continually work to add value by providing useful information.

8-3 TYPES OF SALES RESISTANCE

Although there appears to be an infinite number of objections, most fall into five or six categories. Buyers use delay techniques to avoid taking immediate action. Comments such as "Give me a couple of weeks to think it over," can save the buyer the discomfort of saying no at the end of a presentation. "Your price is too high," or "I have no money," are easy ways for purchasing agents not to buy a salesperson's offering. Price is probably the most often cited objection and usually is not the most important issue. It is obvious that buyers do not buy merely based on price; if this were true, then the lowest price supplier would get all of the business and eventually be the only supplier left selling the product. "No need at this time," is another typical objection. The buyer may not be in the market to purchase at this time.

It is not unusual for salespeople to encounter product objections. Most buyers have fears associated with buying a product. The buyer might be afraid that the product will not be as reliable as the salesperson claimed. Not only do the salespeople have to demonstrate that their product will perform at the level they say it will, but they must also show how it stacks up to the competition. A competitor introducing a new technology (e.g., e-commerce) may change the way a salesperson competes on a particular product line (e.g., office products).

Many buyers are constantly assessing their supplier on service (e.g., delivery, follow-up, warranties, guarantees, repairs, installation, and training). If the service is good and department heads are not complaining, the buyer is likely to stay with the status quo. Service is one variable that companies and salespeople can use to differentiate their product. Enterprise Rent-a-Car will deliver cars to the home of the renter and has made this a difference factor in its advertising. A salesperson for a wholesale distributor may make the point to a prospect that his or her fresh fruit, fish, and meat can be delivered daily when competitors deliver only three times per week.

Many buyers will feel intense loyalty to their suppliers and use this as a reason not to change. Buyers may be equally committed to the salesperson from whom they are currently buying. As a nonsupplier to the company, the salesperson must continue to call on the buyer and look for opportunities to build trust with the prospect. The salesperson may want to investigate whether the buyer has had any previous bad experience with his or her company that is causing the buyer not to do business with the company. Some salespeople and their buyers will not hit it off. The salesperson has to recognize these feelings and move on if several calls do not result in an eventual sale.

At first glance, an inexperienced salesperson may be overwhelmed with the thought of how he or she will handle all of the different types of objections buyers will raise. Salespeople need to develop skills in evaluating objections.[2] It does not take long, however, for a salesperson to learn that most objections fall into just a few categories. When preparing to buy a product or service, a prospect generally obtains information in five areas: need, product or service features, company or source, price, and timing of the buy. Objections could come from any of these areas, as shown in Exhibit 8.2.

Exhibit 8.2
Types of Objections

No Need	Buyer has recently purchased or does not see a need for the product category. "I am not interested at this time."
Product or Service Objection	Buyer might be afraid of product reliability. "I am not sure the quality of your product meets our needs." Buyer might be afraid of late deliveries, slow repairs, etc. "I am happy with my current supplier's service."
Company Objection	Buyer is intensely loyal to the current supplier. "I am happy with my present supplier."
Price Is Too High	Buyer has a limited budget. "We have been buying from another supplier that meets our budget constraints."
Time/Delaying	Buyer needs time to think it over. "Get back with me in a couple of weeks."

8-3a Need Objections

Without a need, prospects have little or no reason to talk to a salesperson. If the prospect has been qualified properly, the salesperson believes the prospect has a need for the product. Many buyers have been conditioned to say automatically, "I do not need your product" (i.e., **need objection**). This may be the result of the buyer being out of budget or not having the time to look at your product or proposal. Other buyers may respond, "We are getting along just fine without your product. No one in my company is asking for your product. Call back in a few months and maybe something will change."

The salesperson has a tough challenge ahead if the buyer sincerely believes they have no need. It is the salesperson's job to establish a need in the buyer's mind; if the salesperson cannot do this, then logically, an objection can be expected.

Many prospects do not know they have a specific need for a product until a situation occurs that makes them aware of it (i.e., engineering calls and needs a special software package). Therefore, objections to the need require the salesperson to stimulate the need awareness of the prospect with relevant information—features and benefits that pique the prospect's interest. Exhibit 8.3 summarizes a number of the no-need objections.

8-3b Product or Service Objections

Often the product or service lacks something that the buyer wants and the salesperson cannot deliver. A competitive advantage for a large software firm (Ontario) is that they have a 24-hour/800 service available to all of their customers. Their number-one competitor offers only an 8:00 A.M. to 8:00 P.M. call-in phone service. For those clients who run three shifts and need 24-hour service, their choice is easy: They buy from Ontario.

> ### Exhibit 8.3
> # Possible Need Objections
>
> "I have all I can use (all stocked up)."
>
> "I do not need any."
>
> "The equipment I have is still good."
>
> "I am satisfied with the company we use now."
>
> "We have no room for your line."

> ### Exhibit 8.4
> # Possible Product or Service Objections
>
> "I do not like the design, color, or style."
>
> "A maintenance agreement should be included."
>
> "Performance of the product is unsatisfactory (e.g., the copier is too slow)."
>
> "Packaging is too bulky".
>
> "The product is incompatible with the current system (i.e., we prefer Apple over IBM)."
>
> "The specifications do not match what we have now."
>
> "How do I know if you will meet our delivery requirements?"
>
> "The product is poor quality."

Other prospect objections could be simply emotional—the prospect does not like the way the product looks or feels (i.e., **product or service objection**). Still others have a problem with the product's performance characteristics (i.e., "I need a copier that has color and staples in the bin"). The salesperson must also do an adequate job of fact-finding and qualifying. Many of these issues can be resolved by knowing what the prospect is looking for.

Objections toward the product center on understanding the fit between the product and the customer's needs. The salesperson's job is to learn what product features are important to the buyer and sell those features. Products are bundles of benefits that customers seek to fit their needs. Tying the benefits to the customer's needs helps the prospect bridge the gap from no-need to need. Exhibit 8.4 summarizes a number of product or service objections.

8-3c Company or Source Objections

Marty Reist is a manufacturer's representative for a small company in the sporting goods industry. He has to sell against many large competitors. Sales representatives from

need objection Resistance to a product/service in which a buyer says that he or she does not need the product/service.

product or service objection Resistance to a product/service in which a buyer does not like the way the product/service looks or feels.

Nike, Titleist, and Reebok probably do not have to work as hard to get past the gatekeepers. Reist, in contrast, must justify his existence every day. "I have never heard of your company" (i.e., **company or source objection**) is something Reist must continually overcome.

Other buyers may be happy with their current supplier. It is not unusual for buyer/seller relationships to last 10 to 15 years and even longer. Robert Carroll, a former sales representative from Monsanto Agricultural Division, heard the following quote from many of his farmers and farm co-ops, "I'm perfectly happy with Monsanto, my crops look good. I've been buying from them for years, and they have always treated me right." This is one of the hardest objections to overcome, especially if the prospect feels genuine loyalty to his or her current supplier.

Professional salespeople never criticize their competitors. The salesperson can point out any superior features they might have. They can also ask for a single order and ask for an evaluation against their present supplier.

Another form of source objection is a negative attitude a buyer might have about the salesperson's company or the poor presentation of a previous salesperson. A buyer might remember a late or damaged order the company did not properly handle. A former salesperson may have made promises to the buyer and did not follow through on them. The salesperson must investigate any and all source objections. The salesperson may uncover source problems that can be overcome with time. Exhibit 8.5 outlines typical company or source objections.

8-3d Price Objections

Most sales experts agree that price is the most common form of buyer resistance.[3] This objection has prospects saying that they cannot afford the product, the price is too high, or the product is not in their budget at this time (i.e., **price objection**). This objection may be a request for the salesperson to justify to the prospect how they can afford the product or how they can work it into their budget. Most salespeople feel the price objection is an attempt by the buyer to get the salesperson to lower his or her price. The salesperson must address the price objection by citing how the benefits (value) outweigh the cost. To do this, the product's value must be established before the salesperson

Exhibit 8.5
Company or Source Objections

"Your company is too small to meet my needs."

"I have never heard of your company."

"Your company is too big. I will get lost in the shuffle."

"Your company is pretty new. How do I know you will be around to take care of me in the future?"

"Your company was recently in the newspaper. Are you having problems?"

spends time discussing price.[4] Many companies never sell at the low-cost option. Stryker Medical sells hospital beds and stretchers to hospitals and emergency rooms. Stryker never offers the lowest cost. Stryker's salespeople almost always hear the price objection. First, they have to educate their prospects and customers that their products last 25 to 50 percent longer than their competitor's products. They can demonstrate with evidence, their product will still be around 5 to 10 years after their competitor's has been discarded. If one of their stretchers is $1,500 more than their competitor's, they must break down the price over the entire life of the stretcher. They can actually show a savings over time. By providing the right information, Stryker can show value over the competitor's offering.

Price objections probably occur more frequently than any other type. Price objections may be used to cover the real reason for a reluctance to buy. Probing and asking questions are the salesperson's tools to get to the real reasons for a buyer's objection. Exhibit 8.6 summarizes a number of price objections.

8-3e Time Objections

Buyers use the **time objection**, or as some salespeople call it, the stalling objection, to put off the decision to buy until a later date. Many inexperienced salespeople hear this technique and believe the prospect is going to buy in the future, but not today. Some buyers use this technique to get rid of salespeople so that the buyer does not have to reject the salesperson and his or her sales proposal formally. Sometimes proposals are very complex and the buyer does need time to think them over. The salesperson must be sensitive to this and not push too hard to get an answer until the buyer has had adequate time to make a decision. It is acceptable for the salesperson to review

Exhibit 8.6

Price Objections

"We cannot afford it."

"I cannot afford to spend that much right now."

"That is 30 percent higher than your competitor's comparable model."

"We have a better offer from your competitor."

"I need something a lot cheaper."

"Your price is not different enough to change suppliers."

Exhibit 8.7

Time Objections

"I need time to think it over."

"Ask me again next month when you stop by."

"I am not ready to buy yet."

"I have not made up my mind."

"I do not want to commit myself until I have had a chance to talk to engineering (or any other department)."

the reasons to act now or soon. Waiting can have consequences (e.g., prices rise, new tax begins the first of the year, etc.) and the buyer should be made aware of these. Exhibit 8.7 illustrates possible time objections.

8-4 USING LAARC: A PROCESS FOR NEGOTIATING BUYER RESISTANCE

The term **LAARC** is an acronym for listen, acknowledge, assess, respond, and confirm and describes an effective process for salespeople to follow to overcome sales resistance. The LAARC method is a customer-oriented way to keep the sales dialogue positive. In the early days of sales, buyers and sellers were not always truthful with each other, and manipulation was the norm. Although being persuasive is necessary to be an effective sales representative, having such a singular focus can have a detrimental effect on customer rapport and relationships.[5]

Salespeople who said whatever it took to get an order—who over-promised and under-delivered and misrepresented their offerings—were sometimes looked on favorably by their selling organization. Professional sellers today want to keep the dialogue open and build goodwill by adding value to their proposition. By listening to buyers' concerns and negotiating through open dialogue, the seller increases the likelihood of purchase decisions being made on a favorable basis, and this leads to long-term relationships. Thus, it is the salesperson's job to communicate and demonstrate value when sales resistance arises.

Here is a description of LAARC:

- *Listen:* Salespeople should listen to what their buyers are saying. The ever-present temptation to anticipate what buyers are going to say and cut them off with a premature response should be avoided. Learning to listen is important—it is more than just being polite or professional. Buyers are trying to tell the salesperson something that they consider important.

- *Acknowledge:* As buyers complete their statements, salespeople should acknowledge that they received the message and that they appreciate and can understand the concern. Salespeople should not jump in with an instantaneous defensive response. Before responding, salespeople need a better understanding about what their buyers are saying. By politely pausing and then simply acknowledging their statement, a salesperson establishes that he or she is a reasonable person—a professional who appreciates other people's opinions. It also buys a salesperson precious moments for composing his or her thoughts and thinking of questions for the next step.

- *Assess:* This step is similar to assessment in the ADAPT process of questioning. This step in dealing with buyer resistance calls for salespeople to ask assessment questions to gain a better understanding of exactly what their buyers are saying and why they are saying it. Equipped with this information and understanding, salespeople are better able to make a meaningful response to the buyer's resistance.

- *Respond:* Based on his or her understanding of what and why the buyer is resisting, the salesperson can respond to the buyer's resistance. Structuring a response typically follows the method that is most appropriate for the situation. The more traditional methods of response (see Exhibit 8.8) include forestalling, direct denial, indirect denial, translation (or boomerang), compensation, question, third-party reinforcement (or feel-felt-found), and "coming to that." Kelsey Grindle, in "From the Classroom to the Field," discusses why it is important to be persistent when calling on the gatekeeper.

> **LAARC** An acronym for listen, acknowledge, assess, respond, and confirm that describes an effective process for salespeople to follow to overcome sales resistance.

Exhibit 8.8

Techniques to Answer Sales Resistance

Technique	How It Works	Example
Forestalling	Take care of the objection before the prospect brings it up.	Many of my customers have had a concern going into my presentation that we do not have a warranty program. Let me put this to rest that we have one-, three-, and five-year warranty programs that match our competitors. I hope this answers your concern.
Direct denial	Give a rather harsh response that the prospect is wrong.	You have heard incorrectly. We are not raising prices.
Indirect denial	Soften the blow when correcting a prospect's information.	We have heard that rumor, too—even some of our best customers asked us about it. Our senior management team has guaranteed us our prices will hold firm through the rest of the year.
Translation or boomerang	Turn a reason not to buy into a reason *to* buy.	Buyer: Your company is too small to meet our needs. Salesperson: That is just the reason you want to do business with us. Because we are smaller, you will get the individual attention you said you wanted.
Compensation	Counterbalance the objection with an offsetting benefit.	Yes, our price is higher, but you are going to get the quality you said that you needed to keep your customers happy.
Questioning or assessing	Ask the buyer assessment questions to gain a better understanding of what they are objecting to.	Your concern is price. Can you please tell me who you are comparing us with, and does their quote include any service agreement?
Third-party reinforcement	Use the opinion or data from a third-party source to help overcome the objection.	Bill Middleton from Dial Electronics had the same concern going in. Let me tell you why he is comfortable with our proposal . . .
Feel-felt-found	Salesperson relates that others actually found their initial opinions to be unfounded.	Buyer: I do not think my customers will want to buy a product with all those features. We generally sell scaled-down models. Salesperson: I can certainly see how you *feel*. Lisa Richardson down the road in Louisville *felt* the same way when I first proposed that she go with these models. However, after she agreed to display them in the front of her store, she *found* that her customers started buying the models with more features—and that, in turn, provided her with larger margins. In fact, she called me less than a week later to order more!
Coming-to-That	The salesperson tells the buyer that he or she will be covering the objection later in his or her presentation.	Buyer: I have some concerns about your delivery dates. Salesperson: I am glad you brought that up. Before fully discussing our delivery, I want to go over the features that you said were important to you that will help you better understand our product. Is that okay?

From the Classroom to the Field

Kelsey Grindle (Ball State 2013 graduate), sales representative for Henry Schein Dental, talks about the challenges of getting past the gatekeepers in each office he calls on. "I've been in my territory for a little over a year now and I've put over 30,000 miles on my car. I see each one of my customers and prospects every two weeks. Many of my customers are happy to see me and it is fairly easy to see the decision maker in each of these offices. On the other hand, I have prospects who actually laugh when I walk in the door for my persistence. They have been a long-time user of one of my competitors and they are surprised to see me again and again. I tell them this is my job and I want to be ready when they need me. I treat every gatekeeper with respect and I follow each office's rules to do business with them. I'm starting to see some success in my persistence!"

Urra/Shutterstock.com

These techniques have been used both positively and negatively. Professional salespeople use these techniques to add value to their proposal. For instance, the translation or boomerang technique can be used quite effectively if the salesperson has gathered the appropriate information to support his or her response. The buyer might state, "Your company is too big, and we might slip through the cracks as a small customer." The salesperson might respond, "That is exactly why you want to do business with us. We are larger, and we are going to be able to offer you all of the levels of expertise you said you needed. Smaller companies will not be able to do this, and you will eventually have to search for another supplier. We are one-stop shopping, and we will make sure you will not fall through the cracks." Here, the salesperson took a reason not to buy and translated it into a reason to buy. Much dialogue had to go on before this for the salesperson to be able to provide the proper information to overcome the concern. Exhibit 8.8 includes examples of how a salesperson might respond to buyer concerns in a professional manner.

- *Confirm:* After responding, the salesperson should ask confirmatory questions—response checks to make sure that the buyer's concerns have been adequately met. Once this is confirmed, the presentation can proceed. In fact, experience indicates that this form of buyer confirmation is often a sufficient buying signal to warrant the salesperson's attempt to gain a commitment.

8-5 RECOMMENDED APPROACHES FOR RESPONDING TO OBJECTIONS

A brief summary of traditional methods for responding to objections follows. Exhibit 8.8 summarizes how each technique works.

8-5a Forestalling

When salespeople hear an objection arising repeatedly, they may decide to include an answer to the objection within their sales presentation before it is voiced by the prospect (i.e., **forestalling**). Marty Reist of MPRS Sales, Inc., often tells his prospects he realizes he is not Nike, Titleist, or Reebok, but his size has not kept him from providing outstanding service to his customers. Reist can add a third-party testimonial to back up his statements and put his prospect's mind at ease. This technique should be used only when there is a high probability that the prospect will indeed raise the objection.[6]

8-5b Direct Denial

When using the **direct denial** technique to handle sales resistance, the salesperson is directly telling the customer that he or she is mistaken. Prospects may have incorrect facts or may not understand the information they have.

The prospect might say the following:

Prospect: I hear you do not offer service agreements on any of your products.

The salesperson knowing this is not true cannot soft pedal his or her answer. In this situation, the prospect is clearly incorrect and the direct denial is the best solution.

Salesperson: I am sorry, that is not correct. We offer three- and five-year service contracts, and our warranty is also five years.

The important part of using the direct denial is not to humiliate or anger the prospect. The direct denial technique should be used sparingly, but it might be easier to use when the salesperson has a good feel for the relationship that he or she has with the buyer.

8-5c Indirect Denial

Sometimes it is best not to take an objection head on. The indirect approach takes on the objection, but with a softer, more tactful approach. With **indirect denial**, the salesperson never tells the prospect directly that he or she is wrong. The best way to utilize this method is to think of it as offering sympathy with the prospect's view and still managing to correct the invalid objection of the buyer. An example follows:

Prospect: I heard that your emergency room beds are $4,000 higher than your competitor's.

Salesperson: Many of our customers had a similar notion that our beds are much more expensive. The actual cost is only $1,200 higher. I have testimonials from other hospitals stating that our beds last up to five years longer. You actually save money.

The salesperson here tries to soften the blow with the opening sentence. Then the salesperson must correct the misconception. Techniques can be combined as the salesperson adds information from a third party to lend credibility to his or her statement.

8-5d Translation or Boomerang

The **translation** or **boomerang** method converts the objection into a reason that the prospect should buy. What the salesperson is trying to do is to take a reason not to buy and turn it into a reason to buy. Marty Reist of MPRS Sales, Inc., offers the following advice:

Whenever I hear the objection, "I don't think your company is large enough to meet our service needs," I immediately come back with, "That is exactly the reason you should do business with us. We are big enough to meet your service needs. In fact, you will be calling an 800 number with a larger company and you won't know who you'll get to help you. With our company, any time you have a problem, question, or concern, you'll call me and talk to a familiar voice."

Another example using the price objection might go like this:

Buyer: Your price appears to be high.

Salesperson: Our high price is an advantage for you; the premium sector of the market not only gives you the highest margin, but also it is the most stable sector of the market.

---

forestalling A response to buyer objections in which the salesperson answers the objection during the presentation before the buyer has a chance to ask it.

direct denial A response to buyer objections in which the salesperson tells the customer that he or she is wrong.

indirect denial A response to buyer objections in which the salesperson takes a softer more tactful approach when correcting a prospect or customer's information.

translation or **boomerang** A response to buyer objections in which the salesperson converts the objection into a reason the prospect should buy.

Zsolt Biczo/Shutterstock.com

The goal of the translation or boomerang method is to turn an apparent deficiency into an asset or reason to buy.

8-5e Compensation

There may be a time when a salesperson has to admit that his or her product does have the disadvantage that the prospect has noticed. The **compensation** technique is an attempt to show the prospect that a benefit or advantage compensates for an objection. For example, a higher product price is justified by benefits such as better service, faster delivery, or higher performance.

A buyer may use the objection that your company's lead time is 14 days compared with 10 days for your leading competitor. The salesperson's response could be: "Yes, our required lead time is 14 days, but we ship our orders completely assembled. This practically eliminates extra handling in your warehouse. My competitor's product will require assembly by your warehouse workers." With the compensation method, the objection is not denied at all—it is acknowledged, and then balanced by compensating features, advantages, and benefits.

8-5f Questioning or Assessing

Another potentially effective way to handle buyer resistance is to convert the objection into a question. This technique calls for the salesperson to ask **questions** or **assess** to gain a better understanding of the exact nature of the buyer's objections. Sometimes it is difficult for the salesperson to know the exact problem. This technique is good for clarifying the real objection. It can also be effective in resolving the objection if the prospect is shooting from the hip and does not have a strong reason for the objection. Effective questioning and listening will lead to less sales resistance and more closes. Exhibit 8.9 illustrates the questioning method as a tool to overcome sales resistance.

8-5g Third-Party Reinforcement Feel-Felt-Found

The **third-party reinforcement** technique uses the opinion or research of a third person or company to help overcome and reinforce the salesperson's sales points. Salespeople today can use a wide range of proof statements. Consumer reports, government

> ### *Exhibit 8.9*
> ## Questioning (Assessing) to Overcome Sales Resistance
>
> **Example 1**
> Buyer: I am not sure I am ready to act at this time.
> Salesperson: Can you tell me what is causing your hesitation?
>
> **Example 2**
> Buyer: Your price seems to be a little high.
> Salesperson: Can you tell me what price you had in mind? Have other suppliers quoted you a lower price?
>
> **Example 3**
> Buyer: Your delivery schedule does not work for us.
> Salesperson: To whom are you comparing me? Can you please tell me what delivery schedule will work for your company?

reports, and independent testing agencies can all be used to back up a salesperson's statement. Secondary data such as this or experience data from a reliable third party could be all that is needed to turn around a skeptical prospect. A salesperson must remember that this technique will work only if the buyer believes in the third-party source that the salesperson is using.

A version of using third-party reinforcement is the feel-felt-found method. Here, the salesperson goes on to relate that others found their initial thoughts to be unfounded after they tried the product. Salespeople need to practice this method—when used in the correct sequence, it can be very effective. Again, the strength of the person and company being used as an example is critical to how much influence the reference will have on the prospect.

8-5h Coming-to-That or Postpone

Salespeople need to understand that objections may and will be made to almost everything concerning them,

compensation A response to buyer objections in which the salesperson counterbalances the objection with an offsetting benefit.

questions or **assess** A response to buyer objections in which the salesperson asks the buyer assessment questions to gain a better understanding of what they are objecting to.

third-party reinforcement A response to buyer objections in which the salesperson uses the opinion or data from a third-party source to help overcome the objection and reinforce the salesperson's points.

their products, and their company. Good salespeople anticipate these objections and develop effective answers, but sometimes it may make sense to cover an objection later in the presentation, after additional questioning and information is provided. The salesperson should evaluate how important the concern is to the prospect—and, if the objection seems to be critical to the sale, the salesperson should address it immediately.

Once the salesperson has answered all the buyer's questions and has resolved resistance issues that have come up during the presentation, the salesperson should summarize all the pertinent buying signals (i.e., fair price, acceptable delivery dates, and a good service agreement).

SUMMARIZING SOLUTIONS TO CONFIRM BENEFITS The mark of a good salesperson is the ability to listen and determine the customer's exact needs. It is not unusual for salespeople to incorporate the outstanding benefits of their product into the sales presentation. A salesperson can identify many potential benefits for each product and feature. However, it does not make sense for a salesperson to talk about potential benefits that the buyer may not need. The salesperson must determine the confirmed benefits and make these the focal point of the sales summary before asking for the business. A salesperson must be alert to the one, two, or three benefits that generate the most excitement to the buyer. The confirmed benefits of greatest interest to the buyer deserve the greatest emphasis. These benefits should be summarized in such a way that the buyer sees a direct connection in what he or she has been telling the salesperson over the course of the selling cycle and the proposal is being offered to meet his or her needs. Once this is done, it is time to ask for the business.

8-6 SECURING COMMITMENT AND CLOSING

Ultimately, a large part of most salespeople's performance evaluation is based on their ability to gain customer commitment, often called closing sales. Because of this close relationship between compensation and getting orders, traditional selling has tended to overemphasize the importance of gaining a commitment.[7] In fact, there are those who think that just about any salesperson can find a new prospect, open a sale, or take an order. These same people infer it takes a

trained, motivated, and skilled professional to close a sale. They go on to say that the close is the keystone to a salesperson's success, and a good salesperson will have mastered many new ways to close the sale. This outmoded emphasis on closing skills is typical of transaction selling techniques that stress making the sales call at all costs.

Another popular but outdated suggestion to salespeople is to "close early and often." This is particularly bad advice if the prospect is not prepared to make a decision, responds negatively to a premature attempt to consummate the sale, and then (following the principles of cognitive consistency) proceeds to reinforce the prior negative position as the salesperson plugs away, firing one closing salvo after another at the beleaguered prospect. Research tells us that it will take several sales calls to make an initial sale, so it is somewhat bewildering to still encounter such tired old battle cries as "the ABCs of selling, which stand for Always Be Closing." Research based on more than 35,000 sales calls over a 12-year period suggests that an overreliance on closing techniques actually reduces the chance of making a sale.[8] Futhermore, as the Selling Power Editors suggest in the opening vignette, "spending too much time on closing and pursuing short term gains, takes away from the more important effort of pursuing long term partnerships."

Manipulative closing gimmicks are less likely to be effective as professional buyers grow weary with the cat-and-mouse approach to selling that a surprising number of salespeople still practice. It is also surprising to find many salespeople who view their customers as combatants over whom victory is sought. Once salespeople who have adversarial, me-against-you attitudes make the sale, the customer is likely to be neglected as the salesperson rides off into the sunset in search of yet another battle with yet another lowly customer.

One time-honored thought that does retain contemporary relevance is that "nobody likes to be sold, but everybody likes to buy." In other words, salespeople should facilitate decision making by pointing out a suggested course of action but should allow the prospect plenty of mental space within which a rational decision can be reached.[9] Taken to its logical conclusion, this means that it may be acceptable to make a sales call without asking for the order. Salespeople must be cognizant, however, of their responsibility to advance the relationship toward a profitable sale, lest they become the most dreaded of all types of salespeople—the paid conversationalist. Technology in Selling points out that the key to closing is not necessarily

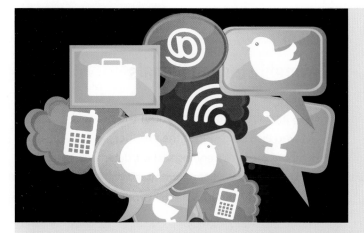

Technology in Selling

Build Sales Pipeline the Social Way and Earn More

—Selling Power Editors

As sales professionals know, the key to closing more deals is not necessarily generating more leads but generating the right leads. These days, the best way to build a robust sales pipeline is to generate those leads using LinkedIn.

Although many people think LinkedIn is just a place to post

your resume or hunt for a job, it actually represents a way to strategically build pipeline and nurture relationships. Koka Sexton, senior social marketing manager at LinkedIn, says there are two basic steps to leveraging either LinkedIn's free platform or LinkedIn's Sales navigator (http://business .linkedin.com/sales-solutions/prospecting-tool.html) for better pipeline results.

Step 1: Search LinkedIn's 300 million members and see what information is available about prospects on their profile pages. This alone can tell you a lot, and when your network is big enough, you can often request that one of your first-degree connections introduce you to a third-degree connection.

Step 2: Use LinkedIn as an engagement platform, via Status updates or comments in groups, and by sharing content or responding to content posted by others. As Sexton says, these interactions add up to stronger relationships, which can help build pipeline and reduce church.

"The more engaged you are with [buyers], the harder it is for them to break you," Sexton says. "If you engage through social media throughout the year, at year-end they know you."

Sexton predicts social selling with the norm in five years. "We are about a year away from the tipping point, when we get to critical mass."

Yakobchuk Vasyl/Shutterstock.com

---

generating more leads but generating and closing the right leads.

It has already been mentioned that the salesperson has taken on the expanded roles of business consultant and relationship manager, which is not consistent with pressuring customers until they give in and say yes. Fortunately, things have changed to the point that today's professional salesperson attempts to gain commitment when the buyer is ready to buy. The salesperson should evaluate each presentation and attempt to determine the causes of its success or failure with the customer. The difference between closing and earning commitment is that commitment is more than just securing an order. Commitment insinuates the beginning of a long-term relationship.

8-6a Guidelines for Earning Commitment

Earning commitment or gaining commitment is the culmination of the selling process. However, it should not be viewed as a formal stage that comes only at the end of the presentation. Many salespeople fail to recognize early buyer commitment by focusing on their presentation and not the comments the buyer is making. **Commitment signals** are favorable statements that may be made by the buyer, such as:

- "I like that size."
- "That will get the job done."

> **commitment signals**
> Favorable statements a buyer makes during a sales presentation that signal buyer commitment.

- "The price is lower than I thought it would be."
- "I did not realize you delivered every day."

These statements should be considered green lights that allow the salesperson to move the process forward. Positive statements by the buyer should start the process of determining the best time to close. Ultimately the salesperson should ask for the order when the buyer has enough information to make an informed decision. Making sure the buyer has the right information to make an intelligent decision is the main goal of a salesperson's sales presentation. Normally the earning commitment question is asked when the sales presentation is completed and all the questions and sales resistances have been successfully addressed.

Commitment may also be determined through the use of **trial commitments**. Throughout the presentation, it is appropriate to determine a prospect's reaction to a particular feature or product. At this time, a trial commitment is a question designed to determine a prospect's reaction without forcing the prospect to make a final yes or no buying decision. The trial commitment is an effort to identify how far along the prospect is in his or her decision making. Confirmation on the prospect's part on key features helps the salesperson determine how ready the prospect is to buy. A trial commitment can be used many times throughout a salesperson's presentation to test the buyer's level of commitment and for the salesperson to gain confirmed benefits. Exhibit 8.10 summarizes both verbal and non-verbal buying signals.

Open-ended questions are a good way to test a prospect's readiness to buy. A salesperson might ask during his or her presentation, "What do you think of our computer's larger memory capacity?" The answer to this will help direct the salesperson to his or her next sales points. However, many statements buyers make should be considered red lights, or a formal objection. The salesperson must consider each of these objections and work to overcome them. Red light statements might include:

- "I am not sure that will work."
- "The price is higher than I thought it would be."
- "Your delivery schedule does not work for us."
- "I do not see the advantage of going with your proposal."

Red light statements are commitment caution signals and must be resolved to the buyer's satisfaction before asking

trial commitment An earning commitment technique that determines the attitude of your buyer toward a particular feature or benefit.

Exhibit 8.10

Favorable Buying Signals

When the prospect:
- Makes a positive statement about the product
- Asks who else has bought the product
- Asks about price, delivery, installation, dates, or service
- Asks about methods of payment
- Begins to study and handle the product
- Appears more relaxed
- Begins to interact more intently with the salesperson

for a commitment. Closing early and often and having a closing quota for each sales call are traditional methods that buyers do not like. Nathan Schmidt in "Professional Selling in the 21st Century: Listening Leads to Earning Commitment," states that it is better to replace numerous closing efforts with better listening skills. The salesperson should put himself or herself in the buyer's shoes and think about how he or she would like to be hammered with many closes throughout a sales presentation, particularly if a few red lights are introduced. Many times, the best method for earning commitment is simply to ask for the business. If the prospect has been qualified properly and a number of confirmed benefits have been uncovered, then naturally the next step is to ask for the business.

8-6b Techniques to Earn Commitment

Some sales trainers will try to teach their salesforces literally hundreds of commitment techniques. One trainer recommended to his salesforce that the salespeople learn two new commitment techniques per week. Then at the end of the year, they would have more than 100 commitment techniques ready to use. Relationship managers today do not need many commitment techniques. A few good ones will suffice. Five techniques that are conducive to relationship building are:

1. Ask for the order/direct commitment. It is not unusual for inexperienced salespeople to lose an order simply by not asking the customer to buy. Professional buyers report that an amazing number of salespeople fear rejection. When the buyer is ready to buy, the salesperson must be prepared to

Professional Selling in the 21st Century

Listening Leads to Earning Commitment

Nathan Schmidt, Senior Sales Representative for PCE Insurance Group, has learned over the years that listening skills are critical for success in earning commitment. Nathan states,

It takes time to develop trust with a client. I try to ask several early questions of the buyer that gets them to talk about their present situation and any problems they may have at this time when dealing with their insurance issues. When it is time to present, I can use the information I gathered to make sure during my presentation that I am providing the right information that will reduce the risk in their decision-making process. I close when the buyer has enough information to make an intelligent decision. That comes from good listening and by providing my prospect (client) the right information. Once the information has been thoroughly reviewed by my buyer, then I attempt to earn their commitment.

ask for the buyer's commitment. The **direct commitment** technique is a straightforward request for an order. A salesperson should be confident if he or she has covered all the necessary features and benefits of the product and matched these with the buyer's needs. At this time, the salesperson cannot be afraid to ask, "Tom, can we set up an office visit for next week?" or, "Mary, I would like to have your business; if we can get the order signed today, delivery can take place early next week." Many buyers appreciate the direct approach. There is no confusion as to what the salesperson wants the buyer to do.

2. Ask for a legitimate choice/alternative choice. The **alternative/legitimate choice** technique asks the prospect to select from two or more choices. For example, "Will the HP 400 or the HP 600 work best for you?" An investment broker might ask his or her prospect, "Do you feel your budget would allow you to invest $1,000 a month or would $500 a month be better?" The theory behind this technique suggests buyers do not like to be told what to do but do like making a decision over limited choices.

3. Provide a summary commitment. A very effective way to gain agreement is to summarize all the major benefits the buyer has confirmed over the course of the sales calls. Salespeople should keep track of all of the important points covered in previous calls so they can emphasize them again in summary form.

In using the summary commitment technique, a computer salesperson might say:

"Of course, Tom, this is an important decision, so to make the best possible choice, let us go over the major concepts we have discussed. We have agreed that Thompson Computers will provide some definite advantages. First, our system will lower your computing costs; second, our system will last longer and has a better warranty, thus saving you money; and

direct commitment A selling technique in which the salesperson asks the customer directly to buy.

alternative/legitimate choice A selling technique in which the salesperson asks the prospect to select from two or more choices during a sales presentation.

Exhibit 8.11

T-Account Close

Reasons to Buy	Reasons Not to Buy
• Daily delivery schedule meets our needs.	• Because of extra services.
• Warranty agreement is longer than the one I have now (five years versus three years).	• Your price is too high; I can't afford it.
• You provide a training program.	
• Your service department is located in our city.	

finally, your data processing people will be happier because our faster system will reduce their workload. They will get to go home earlier each evening."

The **summary commitment** is a valuable technique because it reminds prospects of all the major benefits that have been mentioned in previous sales calls.

4. Use the T-account or the balance sheet commitment. The **T-account commitment** or **balance sheet commitment** is essentially a summary commitment on paper. With the T-account commitment, the sales representative takes out a sheet of paper and draws a large "T" across it. On the left-hand side, the salesperson and buyer brainstorm the reasons to buy. Here, the salesperson will list with the buyer all the positive selling points (benefits) they discussed throughout the selling process. Once this is completed, the salesperson asks the buyer for any reasons that he or she would

> Good salespeople are never in a hurry to earn commitment!

not want to purchase. Visually, the left-hand side should help the buyer make his or her decision, as seen in Exhibit 8.11. This will not work if the weight of the reasons not to buy outweighs the reasons to buy, or if the buyer wants to act but does not have the money at this time.

5. Use the success story commitment. Every company has many satisfied customers. These customers started out having problems, and the sales representative helped solve these problems by recommending the product or products that matched the customer's needs. Buyers are thankful and grateful when the salesperson helps solve problems. When the salesperson relates a story about how one of his or her customers had a similar problem and solved it by using the salesperson's product, a reluctant buyer can be reassured that the salesperson has done this before successfully. If the salesperson decides to use the customer's name and company, then the salesperson must be sure to get permission to do so. A **success story commitment** might go something like this:

Tom, thanks for sharing your copier problems with me. I had another customer you might know, Betty Brown, who had the same problem over at Thompson Electronics. We installed the CP 2000 and eliminated the problem completely. Please feel free to give Betty a call. She is very happy with our solution.

summary commitment A selling technique in which the salesperson summarizes all the major benefits the buyer has confirmed over the course of the sales calls.

T-account or **balance sheet commitment** A selling technique in which a salesperson asks the prospect to brainstorm reasons on paper of why to buy and why not to buy.

success story commitment A selling technique in which a salesperson relates how one of his or her customers had a problem similar to the prospect's and solved it by using the salesperson's product.

Some companies will use the success story commitment by actually taking the prospect to a satisfied customer. The salesperson may leave the prospect alone with the satisfied customer so the two can talk confidentially. A satisfied customer can help a salesperson earn commitment by answering questions a reluctant prospect needs answered before he or she can purchase. Exhibit 8.12 shows a summary of relationship-building earning commitment techniques.

8-6c Probe to Earn Commitment

Every attempt to earn commitment will not be successful. Successful salespeople cannot be afraid to ask a prospect why he or she is hesitating to make a decision. It is the salesperson's job to uncover the reason why the prospect is hesitating by asking a series of questions that reveal the key issues. For instance, a buyer may state that he or she is not ready to sign an order. The salesperson must ask, "Mary, there must be a reason why you are reluctant to do business with me and my company. Do you mind if I ask what it is?" The salesperson must then listen and respond accordingly. A salesperson cannot be afraid to ask why a prospect is reluctant to purchase.

Exhibit 8.12

Techniques to Earn Commitment

1. Direct commitment—Simply ask for the order.
2. Legitimate choice/alternative choice—Give the prospect a limited number of choices.
3. Summary commitment—Summarize all the confirmed benefits to which there has been agreement.
4. T-account/balance sheet commitment—Summary close on paper.
5. Success story commitment—Salesperson tells a story of a business that successfully solved a problem by buying his or her products.

8-6d Traditional Methods

Sales trainers across the nation teach hundreds of techniques to earn commitment. Exhibit 8.13 is a summary of the traditional commitment techniques. The vast majority of these are not conducive to building a strong

Exhibit 8.13

Traditional Commitment Method

Method	How to Use It
Standing-Room-Only Close	This close puts a time limit on the client in an attempt to hurry the decision to close. "These prices are good only until tomorrow."
Assumptive Close	The salesperson assumes that an agreement has been reached. The salesperson places the order form in front of the buyer and hands him or her a pen.
Fear or Emotional Close	The salesperson tells a story of something bad happening if the purchase is not made. "If you do not purchase this insurance and you die, your wife will have to sell the house and live on the street."
Continuous Yes Close	This close uses the principle that saying yes gets to be a habit. The salesperson asks a number of questions, each formulated so that the prospect answers yes.
Minor-Points Close	Seeks agreement on relatively minor (trivial) issues associated with the full order. "Do you prefer cash or charge?"

standing-room only close A sales closing technique in which the salesperson puts a time limit on the client in an attempt to hurry the decision to close.

assumptive close A sales closing technique in which the salesperson assumes that an agreement has been reached and places the order form in front of the buyer and hands him or her a pen.

fear or emotional close A sales closing technique in which the salesperson tells a story of something unfavorable if the purchase is not made.

continuous yes close A sales closing technique that uses the principle that saying yes gets to be a habit; the salesperson asks a number of questions formulated so that the prospect answers yes.

minor-points close A sales closing technique in which the salesperson seeks agreement on relatively minor issues associated with the full order.

An Ethical Dilemma

Rodney Piper has been selling in his territory for a little over a year and has been using a myriad of closing techniques during each sales call. He made all of his quotas for the previous year and thinks he knows how to sell. His old boss was on board with many closes during each sales call, the more the better. Rodney just spent a day with his new boss, she has had a different reaction to his closing style. She has asked him to tone it down and use closes sparingly. She has seen the reaction of Rodney's buyers, and several seemed a bit upset over his closing techniques. She will meet him next month for another day in the field.

How should Rodney handle this situation?
a) Obey orders and close less often.
b) Tell your boss you are 100% of quota and you are not sure why she is making the request.
c) Sell the way you want when she is not with you/sell her way when she is.

buyer-seller relationship. As prospects become more sophisticated, most will be turned off by these techniques and they will be ineffective. "An Ethical Dilemma" illustrates that sometimes buyers will be put off by sales people who use too many closes.

Research has clearly shown that buyers are open to consultative techniques of handling objections (e.g., questioning and assessing, direct denial with facts, and so on) and earning commitment (e.g., asking for the order in a straightforward manner, summarizing key benefits). However, buyers have stated that standard persuasive (traditional) tactics that have been used for years are unacceptable. They now view traditional techniques of handling objections (e.g., forestalling, postponing) and earning commitment (e.g., standing-room only, fear) as overly aggressive and unprofessional.[10]

STUDY TOOLS 8

LOCATED IN TEXTBOOK
- ☐ Rip-out and review chapter review card

LOCATED AT WWW.CENGAGEBRAIN.COM
- ☐ Review key term flashcards and create your own from StudyBits
- ☐ Organize notes and StudyBits using the StudyBoard feature within 4LTR Press Online

- ☐ Complete practice and graded quizzes to prepare for tests
- ☐ Complete interactive content within the narrative portion of 4LTR Press Online
- ☐ View chapter highlight box content at the beginning of each chapter

THOMPSON ENGINEERING

Tyler Houston sells for Thompson Engineering. He has been calling on Hudson Distributors for close to two years. Over the course of 15 calls, he has sold nothing to date. During an early call, Houston had Hudson's engineers in to look over and test the quality of his products. The tests and the engineer's responses were positive. He thinks that he is extremely close to getting an order. Houston knows that Hudson is happy with its present supplier, but he is aware that they have received some late deliveries. Tom Harris, Hudson's senior buyer, has given every indication that he likes Houston's products and Houston.

CURRENT SITUATION

During Houston's most recent call, Harris told him that he'd need a couple of weeks to go over Houston's proposal. Harris really didn't have any major objections during the presentation. Houston knows his price, quality, and service are equal to or exceed Hudson's present supplier.

QUESTIONS

1. Harris told Houston that he needed a couple of weeks to think about his proposal. How should Houston handle this?

2. What should Houston have done during the sales presentation when Harris told him that he needed to think it over?

3. What techniques should Houston have used to overcome the forestalling tactic?

Situation: Read Case 8; Thompson Engineering

Characters: Tyler Houston, sales representative; Tom Harris, senior buyer

Scene 1:
Location—Harris' office

Action—Harris has just stated that he needs a couple of weeks to go over Houston's proposal.

Role play how Houston should respond to Harris' needing two weeks to think it over.

Scene 2:
Location—Harris' office

Action—Houston is summarizing his product's advantages (i.e., price, quality, service).

Role play Houston's summary and his asking for the order.

Upon completion of *the role plays, address* the following questions:

1. Why do buyers hesitate and ask for more time to think over proposals?

2. How hard should Houston press to get Harris to act now?

CHAPTER ROLE PLAY
Addressing Concerns and Earning Commitment

ALLISON ENGINEERING

Brett Johnson has been selling for Allison Engineering for six months. Most of the first four months were spent in training, learning Allison's products. He spent another two weeks learning their selling process and shadowed one of their senior reps for a couple of weeks. He has barely been in the field a month and is feeling frustrated. Brett was given a hot lead the first day in the field (Parker Distributors), and the past four weeks he has made seven calls on Parker. Johnson feels he is close to getting an order from Parker. Brett knows Parker is fairly happy with their present supplier, but he is aware that they have received several late deliveries. Mary Williams, Parker's senior buyer, has given every indication that she likes Allison's products and Johnson.

During Johnson's most recent call, Williams told him she'd have to have a couple of weeks to go over his proposal. Williams really didn't have any major objections during his presentation. Johnson knows his price, quality, and service are equal to or exceeds Williams' present supplier. Williams did say she wasn't looking forward to calling their present supplier to tell them about doing business with Allison Engineering if she decided to change.

ROLE PLAY

Location: Mary William's office

Action: Role play Mary Williams telling Brett Johnson she needs a couple of weeks to think over his proposal. Discuss the sales resistance of forestalling Williams is using and how Johnson is going to overcome the objection (use LAARC). Also, role play Williams' concern telling her present supplier they are switching suppliers.

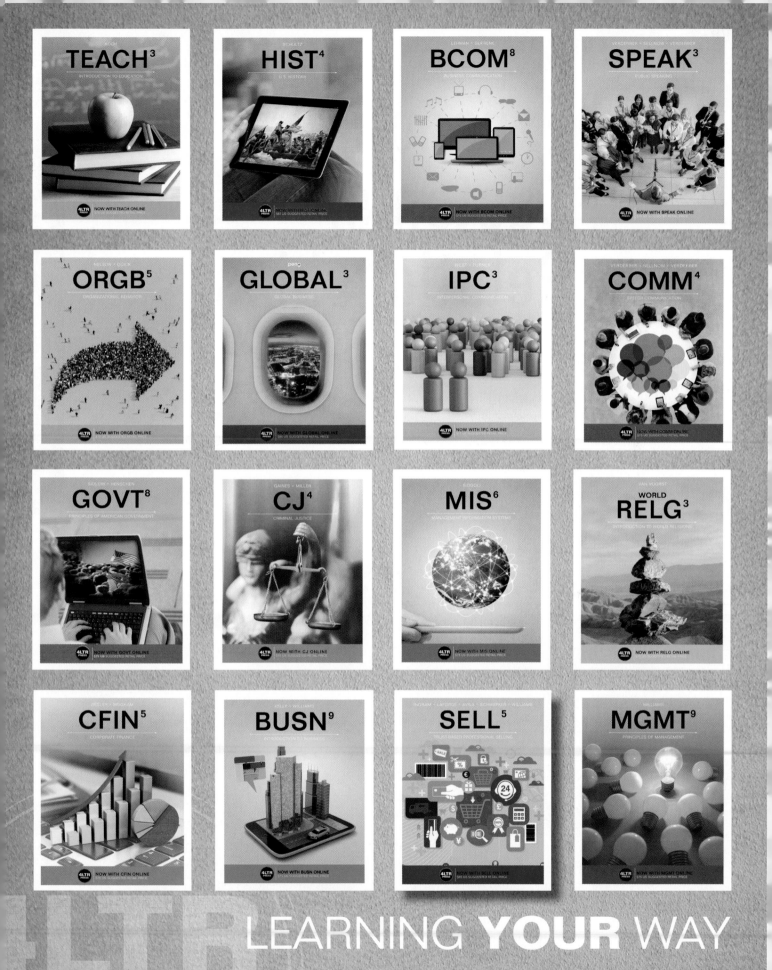

Part Four

9 | Expanding Customer Relationships

LEARNING OBJECTIVES

After completing this chapter, you should be able to:

9-1 Explain how to follow up to assess customer satisfaction.

9-2 Explain how to harness technology to enhance follow-up and buyer-seller relationships.

9-3 Discuss how to take action to ensure customer satisfaction.

9-4 Discuss how to expand collaborative involvement.

9-5 Explain how to add value and enhance mutual opportunities.

After finishing this chapter go to **PAGE 213** for **STUDY TOOLS.**

Jirsak/Shutterstock.com

"Building customer relationships requires time, effort, and sincerity." This is the philosophy espoused by Sysco and executed by its more than 8,500-member salesforce. With relationships with over 400,000 customers in the United States, Canada, and Ireland, Sysco is the world's largest food distributor. To help its salespeople build closer customer relationships, Sysco implemented a customer relationship management solution provided by Salesforce. "With Salesforce we have a level of visibility to customers that we never had before," says Wayne Shurts, CTO. "And we're able to collaborate to help them much more effectively, which is key for our continued growth."

At Sysco, salespeople spend more than 90 percent of their time on the road helping restaurants, hospitals, universities, nursing homes, schools, and companies to manage their commercial dining. Using Salesforce, Sysco reps are able to access customer information from their personal mobile devices, facilitating the discovery of cross-sell and up-sell opportunities which further strengthen customer relationships. Composed of over

70 operating companies, the ability to easily access and share relevant information across these entities is critical. "For the first time we can do team selling, and work together across geographies," says Shurts. "Salesforce is helping our entire business grow. In Houston alone, we're up 14 percent year over year."

Salespeople at Sysco also use social networks such as Facebook, LinkedIn, and Twitter to engage customers. Using Salesforce's Marketing Cloud, salespeople not only communicate one-on-one with customers, but listen to conversations to learn what customers think about its brand. "We can hear what customers say about us, and about our competitors," explains Shurts. "And if we hear about an issue, we can address it right away."

Sysco plans to develop apps what will allow its salespeople to perform more value added selling while visiting customers. A menu analysis app, for instance, will enable salespeople to utilize iPads to help customers discover new ingredients to generate improved products and margins, or learn how to optimize menu placement for high margin items. Such initiatives are undertaken to further assist salespeople in expanding customer relationships.[1]

In traditional selling, salespeople too often thought that their job was over when they closed the sale. Once the order was obtained, they moved on to the next prospect. Any follow-up or customer service was minimal. The lifeline of an organization today is repeat business. It is important to acquire new customers, but it is critical to keep your existing customer base happy. In research involving 80,000 business customers, the number-one characteristic found to define a world-class salesperson is someone who personally manages the customer's

Exhibit 9.1

Relationship Enhancers and Detractors

Enhancers	Detractors
Focus on long term	Focus on short term
Deliver more than salesperson promises	Overpromise—underdeliver
Call regularly	Call sporadically
Add value	Show up only for another order
Keep communication lines open	Be unavailable to the customer
Take responsibility for problems	Lie, exaggerate, or blame someone else

satisfaction by being accountable for the customer's desired results.[2] Not following up with a new customer is a shortsighted attitude toward selling, for it fails to consider the importance of developing and maintaining a customer for your company.

Research indicates that successfully retaining customers is critical for all companies' success. Salespeople's post-sale service behaviors are positively related to relationship quality and share of customer business.[3] Relationship marketing efforts can lead to longer term, broader, and deeper customer relationships, which results in increases in sales, profits, and positive word of mouth.[4] Companies that invest three percent or more of their revenue in customer experience have greater referral rates, superior customer satisfaction scores, and better retention rates than those who invest less in customer experience.[5] Yet it takes only a slight decline in attention from a salesperson to lead a buyer to consider alternative suppliers.[6] Given that it is generally more expensive to acquire a new customer than to sustain a current one, salespeople should take actions to develop strong customer relationships.

There are several ways that a salesperson can convert new customers into highly committed lifetime customers. Examples include (1) **building goodwill** by continually **adding value** to the product or

service through appropriate follow-up, (2) handling complaints in a timely and thoughtful manner, and (3) processing requests for rush deliveries willingly and assuring the customer that the salesperson will do everything possible to make that request happen. However, it is just as easy for a salesperson to alienate a new customer by putting the focus on the short-term order and not the long-term activities that create a partnership. This can be done by overpromising and underdelivering, using exaggeration to get an order, and blaming everyone else for problems. Exhibit 9.1 reviews relationship enhancers and detractors that can strengthen or destroy a relationship. To see what leading sales professionals believe it takes to make relationships work, see Exhibit 9.2.[7]

Relationship-oriented salespeople, such as those at Wausau Paper illustrated in the opening vignette, are creating bonds with their customers that will partially isolate them from competitive pressures or at least minimize the importance of easily altered and matched competitive variables such as price. This chapter explains the importance of follow-up to assess customer satisfaction. Next, harnessing technology to enhance follow-up and buyer-seller relationships is covered. This is followed by a discussion of why it is the salesperson's job to take action (i.e., be proactive) before problems arise and not wait for complaints (i.e., be reactive) to ensure customer satisfaction. We then discuss the importance of collaborative involvement and working to add value for the buyer. Finally, we review the value of customer service.

building goodwill
The process of converting new customers into lifetime customers by continually adding value to the product.

adding value The process of improving a product or service for the customer.

Exhibit 9.2

What Makes Customer Relationships Work?

Gerhard Gschwandtner, publisher of *Selling Power*, summarizes the thoughts shared with him by 18 leading sales contributors regarding how customer relationships are formed and nurtured, and what leads to the creation of customer value:

1. Good salespeople bring positive energy to a relationship.
2. Trust hinges on the willingness to deliver on promises. Once trust is lost, relationships cannot survive.
3. A relationship's value depends on the customer's perception of value, not on the salesperson's perception of value.
4. To the customer, the top value drivers are integrity, authenticity, and consistency.
5. Effective relationship builders are willing to listen to better understand customer challenges. They ask questions that lead to consultative conversations, which open doors to greater opportunities.
6. The salesperson's courage to resolve the difficult situations customers face enhances relationships.
7. Relationships are enhanced by the salesperson's ability to communicate in compelling and creative ways.
8. Relationships demand a long-term investment.
9. There is a difference between a transaction and a relationship. Transactions create one-time value; relationships create long-term value and a stable business foundation.
10. Relationships grow through differentiation and the willingness to contribute beyond what is expected.
11. Good salespeople use smart social-media strategies to enhance customer relationships. They make it their business to stay connected to customers through Twitter, Facebook, and LinkedIn.

9-1 ASSESS CUSTOMER SATISFACTION

Keeping customers satisfied is important, as it leads to customer trust and, ultimately, share of customer. Research shows that customer satisfaction is in part affected by salespeople's reliability and responsiveness as demonstrated by returning phone calls promptly, fulfilling commitments, satisfying customer requests, and being

Salespeople today utilize several technologies to stay in touch with customers.

readily available. Furthermore, salespeople who regularly, clearly, and concisely communicate product information to customers can enhance their satisfaction.[8] Such research points to the need to be diligent in following up and properly communicating with customers in order to build, maintain, and enhance customer relationships.

Unfortunately, many companies do a poor job understanding and satisfying their customers. Results from an annual study of customer experience and customer relationship management professionals conducted by the Strativity Group, Inc., show that most global companies (81%) are not completely dedicated to executing customer experience strategies. As a result, greater attrition rates are three times more likely for these companies, as opposed to fully committed companies, who are five times as likely to have greater referral rates.[9]

John Haack, senior vice-president of marketing and sales for Saint-Gobain Containers (a glass container manufacturer), knows the importance of enhancing customer relationships as opposed to focusing solely on current sales. With customers such as Anheuser-Busch, Quaker Oats, and Kraft, Haack says, "Making the sale is only the beginning. After that, you have to keep track of the process every step of the way. You have to make sure the product gets delivered on time and that everyone involved with the customer knows their customer's expectations." Haack continues, "Anybody can move product. I can go out and sell a ton of something, but if it is not right for that particular customer, it is just going to end up back on my doorstep as a major problem."[10]

Clearly, professional salespeople such as John Haack view their customer base as far too valuable an asset to risk losing it through neglect. In maintaining and enhancing customer relationships, salespeople are involved in performing routine post-sale follow-up activities and in enhancing the relationship as it evolves by anticipating and adapting to changes in the customer's situation, competitive forces, and other changes in the market environment. Darrell Beaty of Ontario Systems (a collections software company) states, "We spend too much time and effort learning about our prospects to not follow through and assess satisfaction." Figure 9.1[11] demonstrates the time and commitment Beaty puts in to earn an order from a prospect. Beaty states, "We cannot be afraid to ask a customer, 'How are we doing?'" This practice should go on monthly, quarterly, and yearly. Sometimes, the salesperson will not like the answers that he or she gets from the customers. New customers generally feel special because they have received a lot of attention. Long-term customers may feel neglected because the salesperson has many new customers and cannot be as attentive as he or she was previously. Routine follow-up

questions, such as "How are we doing?," can go a long way in letting a customer know that the salesperson cares and is willing to make sure that the customer is satisfied. In addition to salespeople asking their customers about their level of satisfaction, suppliers can use a number of means for gathering customer satisfaction information, such as observation, online (or written) surveys, focus groups, customer service feedback, social media, online communities and groups, email, and Web forms. "Selling in Action: Using Customer Satisfaction Surveys to Strengthen Customer Service" describes how one company uses customer satisfaction surveys to listen to customers.[12]

9-2 HARNESS TECHNOLOGY TO ENHANCE FOLLOW-UP AND BUYER-SELLER RELATIONSHIPS

Building buyer-seller relationships is easier said than done. Developing and nurturing customer relationships demands that salespeople do more than simply discover the buyer's needs and respond to them with a sales offering that resolves those needs. Relationships

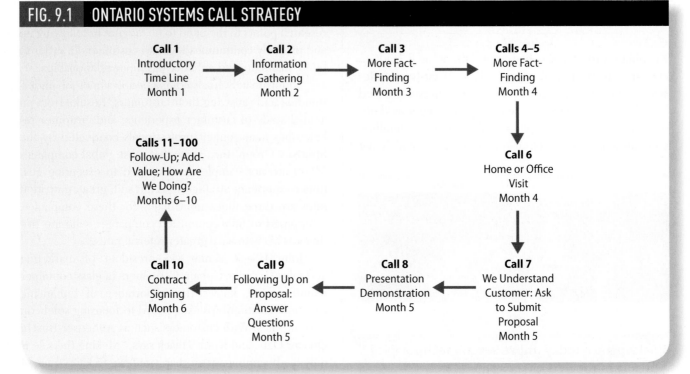

FIG. 9.1   ONTARIO SYSTEMS CALL STRATEGY

Call 1 Introductory Time Line Month 1 → **Call 2** Information Gathering Month 2 → **Call 3** More Fact-Finding Month 3 → **Calls 4–5** More Fact-Finding Month 4 ↓

Call 6 Home or Office Visit Month 4 ↓

Call 11–100 Follow-Up; Add-Value; How Are We Doing? Months 6–10 ↑ ← **Call 10** Contract Signing Month 6 ← **Call 9** Following Up on Proposal: Answer Questions Month 5 ← **Call 8** Presentation Demonstration Month 5 ← **Call 7** We Understand Customer: Ask to Submit Proposal Month 5

It takes many calls to earn commitment from a prospect. It can take months and even years to establish the trust needed to earn an order.

Selling in Action

Using Customer Satisfaction Surveys to Strengthen Customer Service

R & G Technologies, an IT support company, understands the value of customer satisfaction surveys. These are regularly utilized to determine what customers really think about their service and to identify dissatisfied customers who may be in jeopardy of terminating their contracts. Each quarter surveys assessing satisfaction with accuracy, attention to detail, partnership and helpfulness are sent to R & G's customers. Insights gleaned from the surveys help the company to improve business decisions, retain customers and grow revenue. In fact, R & G credits the surveys with helping them to increase customer satisfaction over a 12 month period, leading to greater customer retention. Using customer surveys has allowed R & G to more quickly identify areas of customer dissatisfaction and take action to alleviate customer distress. Consequently, such actions have eliminated similar problems from occurring in the future, leading to greater overall customer satisfaction and retention.

are formed over time through multiple buyer-seller interactions in which the seller wins the trust of the buyer. One survey found that one of the most important things buyers look for in sellers is accountability. They want someone they can rely on during the entire sales process and who will not abandon them after the sale is finalized.[13] According to another survey of customers, 80 percent indicated that consistent follow-up with the customer, including returning phone calls and e-mails, helps their buying process, while conversely, not focusing on after-the-sale service hindered the sale.[14] The results of these studies emphasize the importance of effective follow-up by the salesperson. As discussed in this chapter and illustrated in Figure 9.2, effective salesperson follow-up should include specific components designed to interact, connect, know, and relate with customers.

- **Interact**—The salesperson acts to maximize the number of critical encounters with buyers in order to encourage effective dialogue and involvement between the salesperson and the buyer.
- **Connect**—The salesperson maintains contact with the multiple individuals in the buying organization influencing purchase decisions and manages the various touch points the customer has in the selling organization to ensure consistency in communication.
- **Know**—The salesperson coordinates and interprets the information gathered through buyer-seller contact and collaboration to develop insight regarding the buyer's changing situation, needs, and expectations.
- **Relate**—The salesperson applies relevant understanding and insight to create value-added interactions and generate relationships between the salesperson and buyer.

Salespeople have employed a variety of technology-based salesforce automation tools in order

interact The salesperson acts to maximize the number of critical encounters with buyers in order to encourage effective dialogue and involvement between the salesperson and the buyer.

connect The salesperson maintains contact with the multiple individuals in the buying organization influencing purchase decisions and manages the various touch points the customer has in the selling organization to ensure consistency in communication.

know The salesperson coordinates and interprets the information gathered through buyer-seller contact and collaboration to develop insight regarding the buyer's changing situation, needs, and expectations.

relate The salesperson applies relevant understanding and insight to create value-added interactions and generate relationships between the salesperson and buyer.

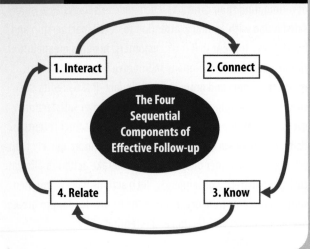

FIG. 9.2 THE FOUR SEQUENTIAL COMPONENTS OF EFFECTIVE FOLLOW-UP

The Four Sequential Components of Effective Follow-up

1. Interact
2. Connect
3. Know
4. Relate

Effective salesperson follow-up should include specific components designed to interact, connect, know, and relate with his or her customers.

to better track the increasingly complex combination of buyer-seller interactions and to manage the exchange, interpretation, and storage of diverse types of information. Among the more popular salesforce automation tools are the many competing versions of PC and Internet-based customer relationship management software applications designed to record and manage customer contact information. PC-based software applications such as Maximizer, Goldmine, and ACT! and Internet-based applications such as Netsuite and Salesforce enable salespeople to collect, file, and access comprehensive databases detailing information about individual buyers and buying organizations.

In addition to providing explicit details about customers and the multiple individuals influencing purchasing decisions within any given account, these databases also provide an archive of the interactions and purchasing decisions taking place over time. Salespeople using these systems have found them to be invaluable in helping them track and improve service to their accounts, ensuring and enhancing customer satisfaction. By understanding every transaction and buyer-seller interaction, salespeople can be more effective in communicating with each customer throughout the lifetime of the account.

The advent of the Internet has allowed these customer contact management tools to be used in multi-organization intranets and extranets. An **intranet** is an organization's dedicated and proprietary computer network offering password-controlled access to people within and outside the organization (e.g., customers and suppliers). **Extranets** are proprietary computer networks created by an organization for use by the organization's customers or suppliers and linked to the organization's internal systems, informational databases, and intranet.

> Relationships are formed over time through multiple buyer-seller interactions in which the seller wins the trust of the buyer.

Internet-activated and integrated with an organization's intranet and extranets, customer contact systems are transposed to full **customer relationship management (CRM) systems**. These systems dynamically link buyers and sellers into a rich communication network. Salespeople and buyers have immediate, 24/7 access to one another and one another's organizations. Problems can be resolved online, routine ordering procedures can be automated, and information such as product brochures and spec sheets, inventory availability, price lists, and order status can be exchanged. Salespeople can use the Web to view everything that is relevant to any account. This can include information in the organization's databases (e.g., purchasing history, credit rating) as well as pertinent information such as news stories, stock prices, and research reports from sources outside the organization (e.g., Hoovers, Standard & Poor's, etc.).

CRM systems enable salespeople to build and integrate multiple forms of customer information and create highly influential customer interactions that establish and reinforce long-term, profitable relationships. The benefits to salespeople learning to use these advanced, integrated systems effectively are self-evident. Every time a salesperson and buyer interact in a positive manner, the corresponding relationship is enriched. This enrichment translates to improved service levels, increased customer satisfaction, and enhanced revenues from loyal customers. For example, after a series of mergers and acquisitions, Honeywell Aerospace found customers telling them that it was difficult to do business with them. Two different Honeywell sales reps, for instance, might call on the same customer in the same day. After implementing a CRM system, customer satisfaction with Honeywell improved 38 percent, its on-time service request closure rate improved from 45 to 83 percent, and its sales opportunity rate improved. Moreover, Honeywell credits the CRM system with a 100 percent annual revenue improvement from $45 to $100 million in the sales of its after-market spare parts.[15] CRM professionals have begun syncing CRM systems with social media such as Facebook, LinkedIn, and Twitter through applications such as Faceconnector, which allow users to pull personal information into their CRM account so that they can keep up-to-date with customers' needs and concerns. CRM provider Salesforce, for instance, offers salespeople a means for listening and responding to customers across a range of social platforms, including Facebook, Twitter and other social networks. Business outsourcing solutions provider ADP, for example, credits Salesforce for helping it to gain customer intelligence and maintain customer connections though its ability to monitor and participate in brand conversations, as well as identify pressing customer service issues.[16]

9-3 ENSURE CUSTOMER SATISFACTION

Exhibit 9.3 illustrates the partnership-enhancement activities and the salesperson's responsibility that goes along with them. Specific relationship-enhancement activities vary substantially from company to company but are critical to the success of building long-term relationships. Key activities include:

- Remembering the customer after the sale
- Expediting orders and monitoring installation
- Training customer personnel
- Correcting billing errors
- Resolving complaints

Traditional selling focuses on getting the order. In a sense, the sales process was over once the order was signed. The salesperson's job was to focus on getting the next order, and it was left to others in the organization to deliver and install the product. However, the relational sales process shown in Figure 9.3 indicates that many activities must take place after the sale, and it is the salesperson's responsibility to oversee and participate in

Exhibit 9.3
Relationship-Enhancement Activities

Partnership-Enhancement Activities	Salesperson Responsibility
Provide useful information	• Relevant • Timely • High quality
Expedite orders/monitor installation	• Track orders • Inform on delays • Help with installation
Train customer personnel	• Train even when contract does not call for it
Correct billing errors	• Go over all orders • Correct problem before customer recognizes it
Remember the customer after the sale	• Set up a regular call schedule • Let customer know you will be back
Resolve complaints	• Preferably prevent the need to complain • Ask customer how he or she wants complaint resolved

FIG. 9.3　TRADITIONAL VERSUS RELATIONAL SALES PROCESS

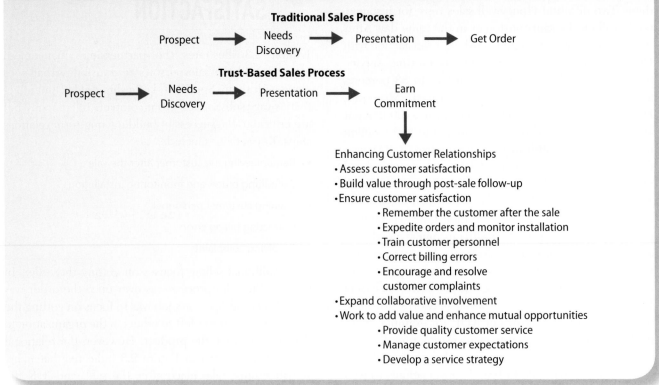

Traditional Sales Process

Prospect → Needs Discovery → Presentation → Get Order

Trust-Based Sales Process

Prospect → Needs Discovery → Presentation → Earn Commitment ↓

Enhancing Customer Relationships
- Assess customer satisfaction
- Build value through post-sale follow-up
- Ensure customer satisfaction
  - Remember the customer after the sale
  - Expedite orders and monitor installation
  - Train customer personnel
  - Correct billing errors
  - Encourage and resolve customer complaints
- Expand collaborative involvement
- Work to add value and enhance mutual opportunities
  - Provide quality customer service
  - Manage customer expectations
  - Develop a service strategy

Traditional selling focuses on getting the order. The relational sales process indicates that many activities must take place after the sale.

all of the follow-up activities. By being actively involved during this stage, the salesperson increases the odds that a long-term relationship will develop. Exhibit 9.4 discusses how salespeople can provide follow-up activities to increase customer satisfaction and build long-term customer relationships.

9-3a Remember the Customer After the Sale

Customer follow-up methods should be used to develop the relationship after the sale and to express appreciation for the purchase. Many buyers feel neglected once they place an order with a company. They were given a lot of attention before they placed the order, but after the order had been placed, the salesperson disappeared. Customers consistently cite poor service, neglect, and lack of follow-up as the primary reasons they stopped buying. At one branch office of Wallace Computer Services, there is a saying that hangs above the door that states "Remember the Customer between Calls." This is certainly a meaningful slogan given research showing that greater interaction between the salesperson and the customer after the sale, particularly in-person or via telephone, results in a more satisfied

and loyal customer who awards a larger percentage of their business to the seller.[17]

Once an economic relationship is established, the salesperson must continue to maintain open, two-way communication with the buyer and continually provide timely, relevant, high-quality information to his or her customers and be available to satisfy any additional needs or problems. The job of educating and satisfying the buyer never stops, and salespeople are responsible for updating customers and pointing out additional opportunities that will benefit them. Collaborative discussion becomes the most effective tool when dealing with customers and their problems.

Providing information that will help customers solve their problems is a must. By providing useful information, the salesperson demonstrates a commitment to the buyer. The salesperson is expressing the notion that he or she is in the relationship for the long term and that he or she values the partnership. The salesperson should remember to provide information not only to the buyer but also to the secretaries, receptionists, administrative assistants, department heads, and other influential members of the buyer's organization. If the customer believes the salesperson is

Exhibit 9.4

Building Relationships Through Follow-Up

Joseph (Joe) Sparacino, senior vice-president and national sales manager for Omega Performance, who is responsible for leading his teams in sales, consulting, and service activities for client relationships across the United States, discusses activities involved in providing exquisite customer service after the sale. According to Joe, long-term relationship building can be enhanced after the sale by:

- Foreseeing and planning post-sale customer needs prior to completing a sale.
- Developing a post-sale long-term vision and strategy for ensuring customer satisfaction.
- Making certain that customers are delighted with their purchase decision and think in terms of "Look what I bought" rather than "Look what they sold me."
- Planning and executing periodic post-sale follow-up contacts with customers to assess their level of satisfaction.
- Touching base with customers on issues or concerns discussed at the point of the initial sale.
- Recalling and recognizing customer milestones.
- Regularly evaluating the products and/or services customers use, and recommending new or upgraded products and/or services that better meet their needs.

Source: http://blog.omega-performance.com/sites/default/files/BeyondSelling.eBook_.1110.pdf accessed on 5/9/12.

sincere, listens carefully, and responds accordingly to his or her concerns, then an already-trusting relationship will become stronger.

Several post-sale follow-up methods can be used to provide helpful information. First, however, salespeople should try to determine the customer's preferred method of receiving this information and provide it in that manner if possible. Perhaps one of the best ways to provide useful information is by a personal visit. After the sale is made, it is critical to follow up personally and make sure that the customer is completely satisfied with all the promises that have been made (e.g., delivery, installation done properly, courteous installers). This is the only strategy that provides face-to-face communication and thus affords the salesperson the opportunity to read the customer's body language. When a salesperson takes the time to make a well-planned personal follow-up visit, he or she indicates to the prospect that he or she really cares. A good salesperson will use the follow-up call to keep the customer informed of new developments in the industry, new products, or new applications. Providing this information may bring about future sales. When a salesperson makes a follow-up call, he or she should always have an objective for the sales call. The salesperson should avoid long gossip sessions or chitchat. It is the salesperson's job to add value, not waste the customer's time. While the personal visit can be a very engaging method, perhaps its biggest weakness is that it can be time consuming.

A quick and efficient option for providing useful information after a sale is by using the telephone. The cell phone has provided salespeople with an opportunity to stay in touch with customers while on the road. A salesperson can easily make 7 to 10 phone calls per hour, and the cost is minimal. The telephone has the advantage of a two-way exchange of information and provides a mechanism for immediate feedback, although it, as well as other non–face-to-face methods of communication, does not provide the opportunity to read the customer's body language. The phone can be used to verify delivery, inform the customer of any changes (e.g., price, delivery schedule), check for problems in general, and provide new product, service, and industry insight.

E-mail and social media provide an efficient and cost-effective way to continuously keep in touch with customers. When getting pertinent company and buyer information, the salesperson should also get e-mail addresses. Salespeople are able to include not only text, but also sound and video to e-mail messages they send to customers. Social networking sites such as LinkedIn and Facebook allow salespeople to keep in touch with customers by posting updates, information, and feature reviews. These tools, along with Twitter, allow salespeople to have brief interactions with customers between calls to provide information, address customer concerns, and simply get to know customers on a more personal basis. Moreover, information gleaned from using social media's search features can provide salespeople with insights on industry trends, or the preferences of prospects or customers.

Finally, a handwritten thank-you card to a customer is an inexpensive and convenient form of customer follow-up. It should always be used in conjunction with the other follow-up methods. The mail can also be used to send out new promotional material, information about new products, and trade publication articles that may be of interest to customers. Periodically, a salesperson could send his or her customers a short survey that asks "How are we doing?" Checking the customer's level of satisfaction might highlight an area of concern that the salesperson can take care of before it becomes a major problem. To learn how Julie Ohlms, a manufacturer's representative at Meglio & Associates, earns customer trust to build lasting relationships through important selling skills, including follow-through, see "From the Classroom to the Field: Earning Customer Trust Through Listening, Flexibility and Follow-Through."

From the Classroom to the Field

Earning Customer Trust Through Listening, Flexibility and Follow-Through

Julie Ohlms graduated from the University of Central Missouri in May 2009 and is an Outside Sales Representative for Meglio & Associates, a manufacturer's rep firm for the electrical industry. Julie discusses how what she learned in her sales classes helps her earn customer trust and build lasting relationships.

The foundation of the selling techniques I learned in the classroom is based on the extension of the Golden Rule, the adage to treat others as you want to be treated. It is paramount to remember to treat customers as people. More importantly, customers want to trust that their salesperson will provide solutions that will improve their business. Often, experienced salespeople believe that they have already mastered the fundamentals of selling. In truth, however, the skills they take for granted need to be constantly honed to keep customers engaged and to build trusting relationships.

As I learned in the classroom, good listening skills are critical in personal selling. Salespeople are often excited with the opportunity to show new products or talk about ways we can save our customer money. However, it is equally important to take the time to listen to the customer and understand their needs. Every sales call should focus on a dialogue between both parties. Just think about how you enjoy a good conversation with a friend, rather than a lecture from a parent!

Another fundamental skill of selling is flexibility. It is not uncommon for a customer to be responsible for more than one aspect of their business. The salesperson should appreciate the opportunity to meet with the customer and must respect the time allotted by the customer. Having participated in sales competitions in college, I learned to adapt to time constraints and to present information in a clear and concise manner. Using these skills allows customers to grasp and retain the main benefits of your product before they need to move on to their next task.

But I believe one of the most important skills of today's salesperson is following through, another important facet of personal selling I learned in college. People are busier than ever, and it is the salesperson's job to reach out to the customer for feedback after the call. For me, taking the extra step to send a "thank you" e-mail or making a quick follow-up phone call has proven to be successful in setting me apart from my competitors. If I neglect to reach out to my customer, I am just like any other salesperson who walks through the door. But by making a concerted effort to follow through, I have gained the trust and respect of my customers.

9-3b Expedite Orders and Monitor Installation

Generally, salespeople will set estimates on product delivery times. The salesperson must work to prevent a delay in delivery. The salesperson's job is to track the order status and inform the customers when there are delays. It is unpleasant to inform a buyer of a delay, but the information enables buyers to work around the inconvenience and plan accordingly. Waiting until the delivery date to announce a delay is inconsiderate and hurts the trust built between the salesperson and the buyer.

Many problems with shipping and the delivery of an order are out of the salesperson's control. However, today's sophisticated tracking systems allow salespeople to track orders and find out what is causing the delay. The salesperson must keep the customer up-to-date on the delivery status and any possible delays.

Monitoring order processing and after-sale activities is critical to enhancing the relationship with a customer. Customers often have done a poor job of forecasting, run short of product, and may expect their salesperson to bring their emergency to a happy conclusion. Although it is not always possible to speed up orders, the salesperson should investigate and attempt to do everything possible to help the customers. If the buyer sees concern on the salesperson's part and knows that the salesperson is attempting to help the buyer, then the relationship will be strengthened, even if the order cannot be pushed through as quickly as the buyer had hoped.

Depending on the industry, salespeople generally do not help with installation. Nevertheless, some salespeople believe that it is in their best interest to supervise the installation process and to be available when customers have questions. Typically, installers do not have the same relationship with the customer and may not have the type of personality to deal with difficult situations. The salesperson can act as a buffer between the installation team and the customers.

9-3c Training Customer Personnel

Companies are always looking for ways to gain a competitive advantage. Once the order is placed, traditional salespeople are happy to get their commission or bonus and move on to their next conquest. Relationship managers understand the real work begins once the order is signed. Training customer personnel may or may not be included in the price terms of the agreement. Salespeople may use this to gain the competitive edge they need. For example, instead of only training one person as stated in the sales terms, the salesperson gladly trains three people for the same price. Or, perhaps there is no

Successfully training customers is a vital part in the selling process.

mention of training in the price terms, but the salesperson takes it upon him/herself to provide the necessary training. Adding value should always be a priority with any salesperson.

When the product is technical, customer training might require the assistance of the company trainer or engineer. The salesperson still has a key role, as he or she knows the customer best, and should serve as the facilitator to ensure that all of the parties have been properly introduced and start off in a positive manner. The salesperson should schedule the training sessions as conveniently as possible for the customer. Customer education is an integral part of the marketing strategy of Ontario Systems Corporation, a collections software company. What separates Ontario from its competitors is its ability to provide timely training and education for all its customers. Ontario knows service after the sale is crucial, which is why it provides a toll-free telephone number for 24-hour service. Each year, Ontario strengthens its relationship with customers by providing one week of training, seminars, and goodwill at its home office. Ontario understands the importance of the team approach to providing outstanding customer service.

9-3d Correct Billing Errors

Billing errors could turn into customer complaints if not found and corrected quickly. A salesperson should go over all orders and billing records to ensure proper billing has been sent to the customer. A customer will know the salesperson has his or her best interests in mind if the salesperson corrects problems without being prompted by the customer. As seen in "An Ethical Dilemma," a billing error can result in an ethical dilemma.

An Ethical Dilemma

Evan Celler is a sales representative for a manufacturer of windshield wipers that calls on automotive supply shops and various retail outlets. In reviewing an invoice scheduled to be submitted to one of his newest customers, he noticed a pricing error. The price should have included a quantity discount. Evan recalls mentioning the opportunity for earning quantity discounts to this customer when taking the customer's first order several months ago, but recalls not much was made of it since at that time this customer had no intent to place a large order. If Evan were to obtain this higher price, he would realize a significantly larger commission on this order. Given that this customer was relatively new, there was some question as to whether the customer would even realize he was not receiving a quantity discount. If you were Evan, what would you do?

a) Contact my billing department and have them correct the invoice prior to sending it.

b) Keep quiet, but if the customer questions the price, then inform the customer that billing made an error and that I will have them send out an invoice that includes the quantity discount.

c) Take my increased commission and treat myself to a nice dinner out since I deserve it; if the customer questions the price, tell the customer that quantity discounts only take effect after a customer has been buying from our company for at least nine months, so they will be eligible for a quantity discount very soon.

Nattika/Shutterstock.com

9-3e Resolve Complaints and Encourage Critical Encounters

Complaints will never be completely eliminated by any company. Nevertheless, it is every company's hope that it can reduce the frequency of complaints. Complaints typically arise because the product did not live up to the buyer's expectations. Research shows that companies that systematically monitor, track, and address service failures, instances in which buyer expectations are not met, are rewarded with more satisfied customers and greater customer retention.[18]

> Complaints will never be completely eliminated by any company, but they must be addressed and resolved.

Buyers complain for any number of reasons: (1) late delivery, (2) wrong order sent (e.g., too many, too few), (3) product performs poorly, or (4) nobody at the salesperson's company takes the buyer's problems seriously. (See Exhibit 9.5 for a more comprehensive list of complaints.) Many times, the complaint is not the fault of the salesperson (e.g., late delivery, wrong order, product performs poorly). However, this is not a concern to buyers, as they expect the salesperson to resolve it. Traditional salespeople have been known to pass the blame when complaints arise. A salesperson would be better off tackling the complaint by accepting responsibility and promptly fixing the problem. Salespeople get into trouble by overpromising what their product can do, being overly optimistic about delivery dates, and not being attentive to their customers when they do complain. Many complaints can be avoided by giving customers a reasonable expectation of what a company's product or service can do for them.

If periodic meetings take place between the buyer and the seller after the sale, then in all probability, most of the important issues are being discussed. Salespeople

Exhibit 9.5

Typical Customer Complaints

1. Late delivery
2. Damaged merchandise
3. Invoice errors
4. Out of stock—back orders
5. Shipped incorrect product
6. Shipped incorrect order size
7. Service department unresponsive
8. Product does not live up to expectations
9. Customer not informed of new developments
10. Customer's problems not taken seriously
11. Improper installation
12. Need more training
13. Price increase—no notice
14. Cannot find the salesperson when needed
15. Unreturned phone calls

must ask their buyers to be candid with them and encourage the buyer to discuss tough issues (i.e., late deliveries, damaged products), especially in areas where the salesperson's organization is providing less-than-satisfactory performance. Some buyers will not complain because they feel it will not do any good. Others will not complain because they feel that the salesperson should be in tune with their problems or concerns and recognize these problems on his or her own. If a salesperson encourages **critical encounters** and acts accordingly to diffuse a situation in which the buyer's expectations have not been met, then this will help with subsequent critical encounters. If the salesperson does not act on these issues, then future meetings with the buyer will not uncover problem areas because the buyer is convinced nothing will be done to solve them.

Some salespeople tell the customer what he or she wants to hear to get the order and cannot deliver on promises made. For instance, salespeople promising a delivery date they know has little chance of being met. Complaints can be avoided, in part, by being truthful when presenting a product's capabilities. Providing sales support can eliminate problems with late deliveries, order errors, and the feeling that the salesperson does not care about the customer's complaints. The following section outlines how to handle customer complaints.

9-3f A Procedure to Handle Complaints

Salespeople must have an open communication line with customers and encourage feedback, either positive or negative. Some research indicates that as many as 25 percent of business customers who encounter a problem will not complain.[19] Thus, salespeople must build relationships to the point where buyers will not hesitate to speak their minds if they are unhappy with the service. If the customer does not complain, then the salesperson does not know what needs to be fixed.

When a customer does complain, the complaint should be handled quickly and with great sensitivity. One study indicates that if a company fails to deal with customers and prospects who complain, those customers will tell on average up to 10 people about their bad experience and, with e-mail and the Internet, this may turn into thousands.[20] Another study showed that when customer complaints are addressed, these customers are 30 percent more loyal than those who do not complain and 50 percent more loyal than a dissatisfied complainant—which indicates that the effort to make amends is worth it.[21] Research in consumer services suggests that satisfactory handling of customer complaints is key to customer recommendations of a firm to others.[22] A general procedure for handling customer complaints follows.

9-3g Build the Relationship to the Point That Your Customers Are Comfortable Complaining

Salespeople have been overheard saying to their customers, "Had I known that you were unhappy with our service, I could have fixed it." The buyer typically responds, "Well, I gave you plenty of signals. Why weren't you aware of the problems?" The buyer and salesperson must work together to develop a trust so that whenever an issue arises, either person feels comfortable speaking up. Open communication channels are a must for good customer service. Salespeople cannot be afraid to ask their customers, "How are we doing?" Some companies conduct 30-, 60-, and 90-day customer satisfaction follow-up visits after the sale. Beyond that, salespeople maintain quarterly follow-ups, even if only by phone. This at least tells customers that the salesperson is interested in them and wants to service their account well.

> **critical encounters** Meetings in which the salesperson encourages the buyer to discuss tough issues, especially in areas where the salesperson's organization is providing less-than-satisfactory performance.

9-3h Listen Carefully and Get the Whole Story

The salesperson must listen carefully to what is being said and what is not being said. Good salespeople let the customer know that they are happy the complaint has been brought to their attention. Chances are that the customer will not complain again if he or she is made to feel uncomfortable with the initial complaint. The salesperson must be careful not to interrupt early in the discussion. The customer must be allowed to vent his or her frustration. Once the customer stops complaining, the salesperson may have to probe and ask follow-up questions to get the whole story. For instance, the buyer may not have told the salesperson to whom he or she talked to at the salesperson's company about the problem, and this information can be helpful to the salesperson in solving the complaint. This is a good time to show empathy. The salesperson must consider how he or she would feel if placed in the customer's position. The salesperson should apologize for any inconvenience and make the buyer aware that he or she is anxious to resolve the problem and keep the buyer as a satisfied customer.

9-3i Ask Customers How They Would Like Their Complaint Resolved

Many salespeople attempt to solve the complaint without understanding what the customer wants them to do. For example, a salesperson may reason that the last customer wanted a 20 percent discount to make things better. "Thus, I will offer this unhappy buyer the same thing." The salesperson may be surprised to find out the buyer wanted something totally different to resolve the problem. The salesperson cannot be afraid to ask the customer what it will take to make him or her happy. A salesperson could say something like, "Theresa, we value you and your company's business. I am sorry for the inconvenience we caused you. Can you please tell me what we can do to solve this problem and keep you as a satisfied customer?" Then, the salesperson must listen carefully. Perhaps the buyer simply wants an apology, a discount, or a substitute until the regular shipment arrives. Salespeople typically find that the customer is not demanding as much as they anticipated, considering the circumstances of the complaint. The solution should center on what the customer wants and not what the salesperson thinks is appropriate. When salespeople provide customers choice in the complaint resolution process, they are likely to increase customers' perceived control over the process and ultimately enhance customer satisfaction.[23]

9-3j Gain Agreement on a Solution

Once the salesperson hears what the customer wants, they must agree on a solution. Sometimes the salesperson can do exactly what the customer asks. Other times, the customer might ask for an unrealistic solution. The salesperson's focus should always be on trying to do exactly what the customer wants, if possible. When that is not possible, the salesperson's message should concentrate on what he or she can do for the customer and then do it quickly.[24] The conversation might sound like, "Jim, I'm sorry for the inconvenience we caused you. Thanks for your suggestions on what we need to do to resolve the problem. Here are a couple of things we can do—which of these will work better for you?" The salesperson is telling the buyer that he or she cannot do exactly what the buyer asked, but is providing options for what can be done. Good salespeople always focus on the positive.

9-3k Take Action—Educate the Customer

Once an agreement is reached, the salesperson must take action and solve the customer complaint immediately. The communication lines must be kept open to the customer (e.g., letting him or her know when the repair people will be arriving). Monitor complaint resolution and keep the customer up-to-date on progress. This is also a good time to convey that steps have been taken to ensure that the problem will not occur again.

If customers have unrealistic expectations of the services provided, then this would be a good time to educate them so that they will have realistic expectations. Some salespeople promise the moon to secure an order, and then let the customer down when the product or service does not meet expectations. This is not the way to develop a trusting relationship.

9-3l Follow-Through on All Promises—Add Value

Whatever promises are made, good salespeople must make sure that they are kept, and this is a good time to go beyond what has been promised. Those salespeople who over-deliver what is promised will truly impress their customers and build stronger relationships faster than their competitors. By exceeding expectations and adding value, the salesperson helps ensure repeat business. Exhibit 9.6 summarizes the procedures to handle complaints.

Exhibit 9.6

General Procedures for Handling Complaints

1. Build relationship to the point that the customer is comfortable complaining.
2. Listen carefully and get the whole story.
3. Ask the customer what he or she would like you to do.
4. Gain agreement on a solution. Tell the customer what you can do; do not focus on what you cannot do.
5. Take action; educate the customer so he or she has realistic expectations.
6. Follow through on all promises. Add value.

9-4 EXPAND COLLABORATIVE INVOLVEMENT

A salesperson's goal is to work with customers who have entered into a strategic alliance with the salesperson's firm. This is done by building trust over a long period of time. The salesperson should always look for ways to improve the relationship and create a stronger bond. One way to accomplish this goal is to expand the **collaborative involvement** between the buyer's and salesperson's organizations. The salesperson may take a group of engineers along on a sales call and introduce them to the buyer's engineers. It may be possible for the engineers to work together to enhance the product offering or perhaps provide a more customized solution. Customers often know the strengths and weaknesses of the product they use and can provide some insight into how improvements can be made.

Another example of a company's attempt to expand collaborative involvement is to host a week-long series of seminars, training sessions, and social engagements with its customers to expand the relationship. Brainstorming sessions with customers demonstrate a willingness to listen, show that the company cares, and often result in better ways to serve customers. Any time the salesperson can involve additional personnel from the buyer's company in relationship building, the relationship should become stronger.

9-5 WORK TO ADD VALUE AND ENHANCE MUTUAL OPPORTUNITIES

To build mutually satisfying relationships between buyers and sellers, professional salespeople must work toward adding value and enhancing mutual opportunities for the customer. This can be done by reducing risk through repeated displays of the seller's ability to serve the customer. By demonstrating willingness to serve the customer, the seller reduces the buyer's risk—both real and perceived. A good relationship is one that has few, if any, unpleasant surprises.

Salespeople must also establish high standards and expectations. Many relationships fail due to unmet expectations. The higher the customer's expectations, the better, provided the seller can meet or exceed those expectations. Salespeople should ensure that the customer's expectations are reasonable by soliciting customer expectations, clearly and honestly conveying the firm's offering, and continually working to improve performance.

Finally, salespeople must monitor and take action to improve customer satisfaction. Salespeople must never let up on this. Doing so only invites competitor challenges. A good salesperson must always look for cracks in the relationship and patch them before insurmountable problems occur. All relationships require work, and taking a good customer for granted is foolish. Julie Ohlms, a manufacturer's rep for Meglio & Associates, realizes the importance of maintaining strong customer relationships and uses technology to assist in this endeavor. To learn how she does it, see "Technology in Selling: Using LinkedIn to Maintain Strong Customer Relationships." Remember that the salesperson must continually add value to the relationship or he or she will run the risk of losing the customer. Exhibit 9.7[25] provides some suggestions for adding value by demonstrating to customers that the salesperson cares about them and appreciates their business.

9-5a Provide Quality Customer Service

All salespeople are looking for a competitive edge to help them differentiate their products in the eyes of customers. Many of the products that a salesperson sells have essentially the same features and benefits as those of competitors. Chris Crabtree of Lanier once said, "A

> **collaborative involvement** A way to build on buyer-salesperson relationships in which the buyer's organization and the salesperson's organization join together to improve an offering.

Technology in Selling

Using LinkedIn to Maintain Strong Customer Relationships

Julie Ohlms graduated from the University of Central Missouri in May 2009 and is an Outside Sales Representative for Meglio & Associates, a manufacturer's rep firm for the electrical industry. Julie discusses how she uses LinkedIn to maintain customer relationships.

To be a successful salesperson, it is imperative to discover the needs of one's customers and determine an effective solution. But that is only part of the process. In today's world, it is equally important to follow through after the sale and to develop a relationship with the customer. Using social media is a beneficial way to create and nurture customer relationships. It provides a platform that enables the salesperson and customer to easily share information and allows the opportunity for both parties to stay engaged on a regular basis without being intrusive.

Personally, I take advantage of using LinkedIn and find it to be a great tool for maintaining customer relationships. The site is user friendly and the 'connections' feature allows me to stay in touch with my customers between personal visits. Another feature of LinkedIn is the opportunity to 'follow' companies. This is useful as it allows one to keep up-to-date on specific companies with regard to special announcements, awards received and other valuable information posted on the company's feed. Staying in touch with the company allows me to speak intelligently about them and demonstrates my interest in my customer's organization. Also, there is an option on the site which provides users an opportunity to 'endorse' a connection. Endorsing a connection takes little effort but carries its weight. When a customer takes the time to give me an endorsement for customer service, it shows that I am more than just a salesperson. I am a person who gives them the attention and support they desire. I am someone in whom they have placed their trust and confidence.

copier is a copier, is a copier. There is just no difference between what I have to offer and my competitors. We all charge about the same price. In fact, I can match any price my competitor puts on the table. That leaves only one attribute for me to differentiate on—service."

More and more companies are turning to **service quality**, which means meeting and or exceeding customer service expectations, as a strategy to acquire and maintain customers. A salesperson must be able to convince a customer that service is important, demonstrate service quality, and then maintain a high level of service over an extended period of time.

The problem is that every salesperson claims to provide outstanding service. The goal today is not to meet customer expectations but to exceed them. Salespeople will rarely be given a second chance to prove that they provide

outstanding service if they do not get it right the first time. A sign in a small-town business reads,

> *Service is advertised . . .*
> *Service is talked about . . .*
> *But the only time service really counts . . .*
> *Is when it is delivered . . .*
> *And we promise your experience with us will be outstanding.*

Customers do not care about slogans and service claims until something happens to them. This is called a moment of truth. Each salesperson experiences daily moments of truth—brief moments that occur whenever a customer comes into contact with a salesperson, the training staff, installers, field engineers, or service personnel and has an opportunity to form an impression. These moments of truth are when the customer will determine if promises are being kept by the sales organization, and whether the salesperson truly cares about the customer or is simply an order getter.

Exhibit 9.7

Enhancing Customer Value

1. Keep in touch with customers to pass along information and solicit customer feedback.
2. Let customers know in writing that you enjoy working with them.
3. Ask customers what can be done to make it easier on them to work with you.
4. When appropriate, refer customers to others.
5. Provide customers with leads.
6. Thank customers during the relationship, not only after the sale has been made.
7. Offer advice for improving customers' operations.
8. Pass along useful articles or ideas.
9. If possible, lend a helping hand (e.g., one sales manager has been known to assist customers in their booths at trade shows).
10. Recommend customers for awards or news stories.
11. Be candid in providing opinions.
12. Come to the defense of customers who are criticized.
13. Quickly address customer problems.
14. Demonstrate reliability by promptly (the day it is received) responding to customer communication.
15. Provide customers with reports, survey results, and articles free of charge.
16. Be proactive, rather than reactive when dealing with customers. Take the initiative to do what is right or necessary before being asked.
17. Keep your word. If circumstances dictate otherwise, then quickly explain yourself.
18. Show respect by not getting "too friendly" with customers.

There are four benefits of service enthusiasm that allow the sales organization to gain an advantage over its competitors. First, reputation is an important part of any organization's ability to attract and keep new customers. Reputation allows a salesperson to distinguish him- or herself from the competition. A solid reputation indicates that the salesperson cares and will help him or her establish loyal relationships with customers. Reputations take a long time to establish and only one negative event to destroy.

Second, by providing good customer service the first time, an organization makes the profit that it needs to stay in business. Whenever mistakes are made (e.g., wrong order, short order delivered), service personnel have to sort out the problem and fix it. The result could lead to a lost customer. In any event, it does not take long to go into the red when people have to be added to fix problems. Efficient operations, cost savings, and doing things right the first time increase the chances for increased profits.

The third benefit of service enthusiasm is convenience. It is critically important to put the customer's convenience first. For example, as mentioned earlier,

most customers are uncomfortable complaining. Thus, a salesperson must make it easy for his or her customers to discuss problems or complaints. Since customers can be reluctant to complain, the salesperson must be vigilant in asking customers to express their problems or concerns. Building a strong, trusting relationship with open communication will make it easier for customers to voice their concerns. Furthermore, to be convenient, salespeople must be readily accessible to customers. This involves using technology (e.g., cell phone, e-mail) to stay accessible, quickly acknowledging customer requests, and then responding in an appropriate and expedient manner. When it comes to servicing customers, salespeople often must accommodate customers' schedules rather than their own. Naturally, this may pose some inconvenience to the salesperson, but customer needs must be considered first.

Salespeople must design user-friendly feedback systems. Periodically inquiring about customer satisfaction can greatly enhance a customer's feelings toward a salesperson and his or her organization. Ontario Systems (http://www.ontariosystems.com) provides a Client

Resource Center link on its Web site. Clients can easily get up-to-date information on product support, training, industry links, and discussion lists. Ontario Systems is always looking for ways to provide more services to its clients.

Finally, service enthusiasm goes hand in hand with spirit. A customer can be turned onto an organization by meeting many caring "can-do" people. The spirit must start with an enthusiastic, service-minded corporate culture. The salesperson, sales manager, field engineer, installer, and customer service representative must all have the same service enthusiasm to generate the benefits of service enthusiasm. That is why the salesperson must monitor and coordinate all the people who have access to the account to ensure that good customer service is taking place.

The most difficult aspect of customer service is the potential for inconsistency. For instance, field engineer A, who has a great understanding of service enthusiasm, may be called into an account early in the week. The customer is very impressed. Three weeks later, the customer calls for help again. Field engineer A is out on another account, and field engineer B, who has little or no service skills, is sent out on the next call. Field engineer B is good at fixing the problem but has a hard time relating to customers; in fact, he is downright cold! As a result of this unevenness, the customer's level of satisfaction decreases.

The inconsistency of customer service is a problem for every sales organization. By understanding the benefits of service enthusiasm and the rewards of proper spirit, the sales organization can ensure consistency and exceed customer expectations.

9-5b Customer Expectations

A salesperson must meet the needs of his or her customers. At a minimum, customers expect a warm and friendly salesperson. Buyers have enough things going on during their day that it would not be a plus to have to deal with a surly salesperson. Warmth and friendliness are the building blocks of a successful relationship.

Reliability is another attribute that buyers look for in choosing a salesperson with whom to do business. Customers must have the confidence that the expected service will be delivered accurately, consistently, and dependably. Helpfulness and assistance are two more variables that buyers expect when working with a salesperson. Will the customer be able to find his or her salesperson when he or she needs to do so? Can the salesperson provide the speed and promptness needed

service strategy A plan in which a salesperson identifies his or her business and customers, what the customers want, and what is important to them.

> ### Exhibit 9.8
> ## Customer Expectations of Salespeople
> 1. Warmth and friendliness
> 2. Reliability
> 3. Helpfulness/assistance
> 4. Speed or promptness
> 5. Assurance
> 6. Accuracy
> 7. Follow-through (as promised)
> 8. Empathy
> 9. Resolution of complaints, mistakes, or defects
> 10. Tangibles

by the customer? The salesperson can solve this issue by developing a regular call routine so that the customer knows when to expect the salesperson. Customers also want to deal with salespeople in whom they have confidence and trust will always do what is right for them (i.e., assurance). As such, salespeople must be trustworthy. Furthermore, salespeople must pay attention to detail as customers expect accuracy from them, particularly as it pertains to product or service orders. Other customer expectations include follow-through as promised, empathy, and resolution of complaints, mistakes, or defects. The customer must know that if anything goes wrong, the salesperson will move in quickly and solve the problem. Ultimately, the customer is looking for someone who is personally accountable for their desired results.[26] Exhibit 9.8 summarizes what customers expect from their salesperson.

9-5c Develop a Service Strategy

Salespeople can calculate the lifetime value of their customers. For example, Hershey Foods Corporation knows exactly how much candy it has sold at the Wal-Mart in Muncie, Indiana. It is easy for Hershey to calculate the loss if any customer decides to replace it. It is imperative for Hershey to provide the service level that each of its customers demands. Lower-quality service can lead to the loss of a customer.

Developing a **service strategy** allows salespeople to plan their actions for each customer. A service strategy asks salespeople to identify their business

Exhibit 9.9

Checklist for Developing a Service Strategy

Questions a salesperson must ask when developing a service strategy:

- What is our business?
- Who are our customers?
- What do our customers want, and what is important to them?
- How are our customers' needs and perceptions changing?
- How are social, economic, and political factors affecting current and future customer needs and our ability to respond to them? How are competitors responding to these factors?
- How do customers rate us in terms of their expectations?
- For what are we best known?
- What do we do best?
- What can we do better?
- How can we position ourselves in the market to differentiate our services?

and customers and what the customers want and what is important to them. Salespeople also have to determine how their customers' needs and perceptions are changing. Salespeople cannot be afraid to ask how the customers rate them in terms of their expectations. What does the salesperson's company do best, and what can the organization do better? Salespeople, ultimately, must determine how to position their company in the market to differentiate its products and services. All this must be done while directing efforts against the competitors. Exhibit 9.9 is an example of a check list for developing a service strategy.

9-5d Customer Service Dimensions

There are three dimensions of customer service, with **communication** being the most important. Most problems arise because the customer was not informed of a change in plans (e.g., late delivery, price increase). Salespeople are extremely busy and many times do not have the time to communicate with all their customers. Communication tools such as e-mail

or twitter can be used to quickly do mass communication to inform customers of these changes. Over time, the telephone and personal visits can be used to confirm that customers are aware of the changes.

Another customer service dimension is **resilience**. Resilience is the ability of a salesperson to get knocked down several times a day by a customer's verbal assault (i.e., complaint) and get right back up with a smile and ask for more. A salesperson cannot lose his or her cool just because a customer does. A tired salesperson must treat late-afternoon, difficult customers the same way that he or she would treat a dilemma at the day's beginning. They must both be treated well.

Finally, **service motivation** is another important customer service dimension. Salespeople must be motivated to find time each day to deal with difficult customers and problems that exist. Ignoring these activities will not make them go away. Working diligently on behalf of the customer indicates to him or her that the salesperson truly cares about the partnership. If a salesperson has a complaint from a customer and gladly fixes it, the customer becomes a more committed customer.

communication A two-way flow of information between salesperson and customer.

resilience The ability of a salesperson to get knocked down several times a day by a customer's verbal assault (i.e., complaint) and get right back up with a smile and ask for more.

service motivation The desire of a salesperson to serve customers each day.

STUDY TOOLS 9

LOCATED IN TEXTBOOK

☐ Rip-out and review chapter review card

LOCATED AT WWW.CENGAGEBRAIN.COM

☐ Review key term flashcards and create your own from StudyBits

☐ Organize notes and StudyBits using the StudyBoard feature within 4LTR Press Online

☐ Complete practice and graded quizzes to prepare for tests

☐ Complete interactive content within the narrative portion of 4LTR Press Online

☐ View chapter highlight box content at the beginning of each chapter

NATURALLY BEAUTIFUL, INC.

BACKGROUND

Naturally Beautiful, Inc. is a maker and marketer of organic cosmetics. Its cosmetics are formulated from all-natural organic ingredients. Although the company currently serves primarily the higher-end market, distributing through upscale department stores and boutiques, it would like to expand its distribution channels. It is currently developing an organic line to sell through outlets such as Walgreens, CVC, and Wal-Mart. Long-term plans include expanding internationally, first to Canada and Mexico, and eventually to Western Europe and beyond. Sales are strong and continue to rise. The company gives much of the credit for its success to its salesforce, which has done a great job expanding into new outlets while establishing and maintaining strong customer relationships.

Jill Aunaturale, a nontraditional student, was hired as a sales representative by Naturally Beautiful out of college approximately ten months ago. Since being hired she has had a good deal of success, landing several new accounts. In fact, if she can land a few more accounts by the end of the rapidly approaching fiscal year, she will exceed her quota and achieve a hefty bonus. Jill is counting on this bonus because she has planned a big family trip and does not want to let her family down.

CURRENT SITUATION

Lately, Jill has heard various concerns from several of her customers. For instance, the other day she received a voice mail from Rick at Beauty Boutique, a recently acquired customer whose order was incorrect. A few items were missing from the order. Jill figured that shipping must have inadvertently omitted the items and that Rick could give them a call to get it fixed. She figured that it was not her fault,

Rick still had product to sell and she certainly did not have time to mess with this. Similarly, she received a text from Kim at Devine's department store indicating that an expected delivery was late. Again, Jill figured she could not do anything about the delivery. She texted Kim to tell her to contact the shipping department at Naturally Beautiful about the matter. Jill also received a second e-mail from Sarah at Cosmetics Unlimited:

Dear Jill,

A few weeks ago you promised you would return to train our beauty consultants on your newest product line. Our consultants need to fully understand the benefits of this new product and how it is to be applied so that they can best serve our customers. As you know, we take great pride in providing the highest quality products and services to our customer base. We discussed this when you offered me your line. Although we like your line, if we are unable to offer our customers top-shelf service with your brand then we may have to look elsewhere.

Sincerely,

Sarah

Jill recalls telling Sarah that she would conduct training for her sales consultants but has been so busy working to get new accounts that she put it on the back burner. Jill was not sure that she could put Sarah off much longer, but felt it would be in her best interest to write her back and stall her for at least a couple more weeks. By then, she thought, she might have exceeded her quota.

To Jill, these were but minor customer issues, not even problems. In her opinion, these were nothing more than "needy" customers. As far as she was concerned, she was delivering a great product at a great price. Besides, she had more sales to make and nobody was going to help her if she came up short on providing that great family vacation she promised.

QUESTIONS

1. For each of the concerns expressed by Jill's customers in the case, explain an alternative means for handling the concern.

2. What are the potential long-run implications of how Jill is handling her current customers?

3. What types of activities can Jill do after acquiring an account to enhance customer value and ensure long-term customer relationships?

ROLE PLAY

Situation: Read the Naturally Beautiful, Inc. case

Characters: Jill Aunaturale, sales representative for Naturally Beautiful; Rick, customer at Beauty Boutique; Kim, customer at Devine's department store; Sarah, customer at Cosmetics Unlimited

Scene: Employing a more personal touch, Jill contacts each customer and takes appropriate action to ensure customer satisfaction. Role play these conversations.

CHAPTER ROLE PLAY
Expanding Customer Relationships

MIDWEST LIVE BAIT & TACKLE, LLC

BACKGROUND

Midwest Live Bait & Tackle, LLC, located in St. Louis, Missouri, is a regional wholesaler of live bait and tackle to bait shops and service stations in Missouri, Illinois, Arkansas, Kentucky, and Tennessee. Known for its high-quality live bait, reasonably priced tackle, and good customer service, the company has been able to maintain a steady market share over the years. Its five salespeople have been primarily responsible for selling and servicing the company's current accounts. This involves making sure that customers have bait and tackle when needed, assisting them with merchandising and pricing, and ensuring their complete satisfaction.

Wanting to retire, the owner recently sold the business. The new owner was very ambitious and had big plans for expanding the company's market share. He felt that the quickest and most efficient way to move in that direction was to have his current salespeople actively pursue new accounts. Thus, he mandated new customer quotas, compensated salespeople for achieving targeted growth goals and threatened their jobs if minimal new account requirements were not met.

CURRENT SITUATION

Dan Chub has been a sales representative for Midwest for over five years. Until the new ownership, he enjoyed his job very much and made a good living doing it. With his fourth child on the way, a poor economy, and a tight job market, Dan did not want to jeopardize his position with the company and reluctantly went along with the new changes. However, he was very concerned with how much time prospecting for new business was taking. He felt it may be endangering his current customer relationships. What follows are excerpts from a recent conversation with Earl Carp, a very significant customer, especially considering he sold bait and tackle out of his service station convenience store:

Earl: Dan, I've been having some problems recently with the minnows you've supplied for me. Some loss is typical, but lately the loss percentage has increased. What's going on here?

Dan: I don't know Earl. None of my other customers are having problems with their minnows. You're making sure that you don't add chlorinated water when replenishing your minnow holding tanks, aren't you?

Earl: Of course! I recently refurbished my tanks and added a new oxygen system. Maybe that has something to do with the increasing loss. Could you check it out and see what you think?

Dan: Just let me know how many minnows you think you lost and I'll see what I can do.

Earl: Okay, but since this has been going on for the last couple of weeks I was just hoping you might be able to give me your thoughts on my new system. By the way, that new line of fishing poles doesn't seem to be moving very well. How are they moving for your other customers?

Dan: I haven't heard much about those, so I guess they are moving okay.

Earl: Do you have any ideas on how I might improve my merchandising so I can move more of them? Perhaps my price point is too high. What do you think?

Dan: I'm really busy today Earl. I have several stops yet to make and I need to call on a couple of new prospects in the area.

Earl: You're not planning to supply my competition down the street, are you?

Dan: I don't know Earl. I've got to make a living, too, you know.

Earl: Last week you promised to bring by some of those new plastic cricket containers you were telling me about. Did you bring any of those for me to examine?

Dan: Oh no, those completely slipped my mind.

Earl: Hmm. Well, certainly you brought me the crayfish you promised me last week. I've had customers coming in every day asking for them. Also, how about those waterdogs we talked about? I've been getting some requests for those.

Dan: I should have told you sooner, but our usual crayfish supplier is having difficulty getting us as many crayfish as we need. I know you wanted 500 but I think I can give you 100. I thought we'd have the waterdogs by now, at least that is what I was told. We're still waiting.

Earl: Dan, I'm beginning to wonder how much you value my business. If you can't take care of me any longer, maybe I need to look for someone who can.

Dan: I've been under a lot of pressure lately to get more done in the same amount of time. My new boss is driving me nuts! I definitely want your business.

Dan needed to hurry off to meet with a new prospect. He didn't have time to preview some of the new spinner baits his company was now carrying.

ROLE PLAY ACTIVITY

Characters: Dan, sales rep; Earl, service station owner

Action: Role play the meeting between Dan and Earl. This time have Dan handle the situation (i.e., respond) as a sales rep that takes customer complaints seriously and cares about providing great customer service.

10 | Adding Value: Self-leadership and Teamwork

LEARNING OBJECTIVES

After completing this chapter, you should be able to explain, identify and, describe:

10-1 The five sequential stages of self-leadership.

10-2 The four levels of sales goals and explain their interrelationships.

10-3 Techniques for account classification.

10-4 The application of different territory routing techniques.

10-5 The usefulness of different types of selling technology and automation.

10-6 Increasing customer value through teamwork.

10-7 The six skills for building internal relationships and teams.

After finishing this chapter go to
PAGE 240 for **STUDY TOOLS.**

Vincent Laforet/Getty Images

Prepare, prepare, prepare! Todd Lenhart, president of SNI, emphasizes that the importance of preparation can't be overrated. Even Abraham Lincoln once said, "give me six hours to chop down a tree, and I will spend the first four sharpening the axe." He emphasizes that preparation is more than just research or simply Googling the prospect. While research is certainly important, it is how you apply the research to the preparation process that really makes the difference in selling. It's how you use the information gained from research in preparing for the sales meeting that matters.

Lenhart explains that research efforts should be structured, instead of just being a process of randomly gathering information. This approach allows you to more effectively develop a strategy and plan for the entire sale, next meeting, or next call. Structured research should discover "what's in your favor and what's against you," and "what's in it for you and what's in it for them." The process should also assist you in documenting "your highest goal for a meeting or negotiation, including what your walkaway point might look like." "Finally, the last stage of your preparation process should be drafting an outline script, even if it's simply bullet points, to keep you on target.

A major component of the preparation process is establishing your goal for the sale or meeting—"aim high but within reason." All too often, "salespeople make the mistake of negotiating with themselves before they even meet with the other side. They review the scenario in their heads and negotiate themselves down." Instead, your goal should be to maximize the sale. "The trick is to visualize the sale so that when you get to the client, you can deliver the message with confidence." Don't start in a place that does not afford you the opportunity to get a realistic outcome. Lenhart emphasizes that this is where preparation and scripting kick in. To reach your desired outcome, you must have precedents to support it, alternatives to give you leverage, and a deep sense of the buyer's interests in order

to personalize it. Effective sales conversations don't just automatically happen. They require extensive research, preparation, practice, and rehearsal.[1]

When observing the actions of a person who has truly mastered the skills of his or her profession, the person's actions seem to come naturally. However, closer consideration will most often reveal that these seemingly innate and natural abilities are actually the result of fervent and purposeful planning combined with many hours of practice over a period of years. This is true for world-class surgeons, sports stars, leading educators, top attorneys—and yes, even high-performance salespeople. As Todd Lenhart discussed in the Introduction for this chapter, good salespeople are not simply born, they are the result of conscious self-development and continuous preparation. Toward the objective of *developing* strong salespeople, this chapter builds on the process of self-leadership to

Like the skills of a professional athlete, the skills required for selling are the result of planning and many hours of practice.

generate a framework for developing and enhancing selling skills and abilities. First, setting effective selling goals and objectives is discussed and integrated with methods for territory analysis and account classification. This is followed by a discussion of how the objectives and information from the territory and account analysis become inputs for generating and implementing effective multilevel sales planning. The importance of assessing performance results and level of goal attainment is also reviewed. Wrapping up the chapter is an examination of teamwork as a vehicle for expanding the capabilities of an individual salesperson, increasing customer value, and creating sustainable competitive advantage for salespeople.

10-1 EFFECTIVE SELF-LEADERSHIP

How often have you said or thought to yourself, "I just don't have enough time to get everything done?" In reality, most people do not need more time. Rather, they need to prioritize the time they have. There are only so many hours in a day, and highly effective salespeople know that they can never have enough high-quality selling time.

self-leadership The process of guiding oneself to do the right things and do them well.

goals and objectives Something a salesperson sets out to accomplish.

To maximize their selling time, these high performers have developed strong self-leadership skills and treat time as a valuable, irreplaceable resource and invest it wisely where it will accomplish the most good.

Self-leadership—a critical requirement for success in any career—has been described as doing the right things and doing them well. It is not simply the amount of effort that determines an achievement, but rather how well that effort is honed and aligned with one's goals. In selling, this is often restated as selling smarter rather than selling harder. That is, before expending valuable time and resources, salespeople must establish priorities in the form of objectives. Then, and only then, do they implement the strategic plan that has been specifically developed to achieve their objectives in the light of the available resources and market potential that exist within the territory. Self-leadership translates to a process of first deciding what is to be accomplished and then placing into motion the proper plan designed to achieve those objectives.

The process of self-leadership is composed of five sequential stages. First, goals and objectives must be set that properly reflect what is important and what is to be accomplished. This is followed by an analysis of the territory and classification of accounts. Next, with goals in place and accounts classified, strategic plans designed to achieve the objectives through proper allocation of resources and effort are implemented. The next stage maximizes the effectiveness of allocated resources through the process of tapping technology and automation to expand resource capabilities. Finally, assessment activities are conducted to evaluate performance and goal attainment and to assess possible changes in plans and strategies. The nature of the sequential interrelationships between these five stages is illustrated in Figure 10.1.

10-1a Stage One: Setting Goals and Objectives

Establishing priorities by setting **goals and objectives** is the key to effective self-leadership. This first stage of self-leadership has been appropriately referred to as "beginning with the end in mind."[2] First of all, if a salesperson does not understand what is important, how does that salesperson know what to focus on? Further, if a salesperson does not understand what he or she is setting out to accomplish, how could that salesperson know where to begin, how to proceed, or even which plan is best for getting there? Finally, without clear goals, how could salespeople know when the objective has been achieved? Without clear goals and objectives, it is very natural to drift from task to task and typically focus on minor and

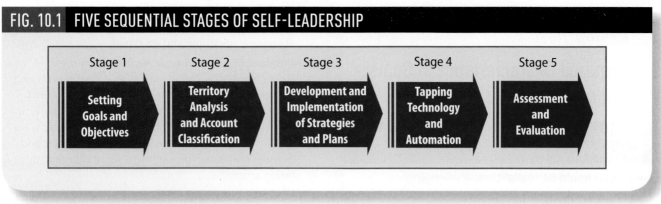

FIG. 10.1 FIVE SEQUENTIAL STAGES OF SELF-LEADERSHIP

Stage 1	Stage 2	Stage 3	Stage 4	Stage 5
Setting Goals and Objectives	Territory Analysis and Account Classification	Development and Implementation of Strategies and Plans	Tapping Technology and Automation	Assessment and Evaluation

Self-leadership is a process of first deciding what is to be accomplished, and then setting into motion the proper plan to achieve the desired objectives.

less-productive tasks, as they are the easiest to complete. The result of this natural drift is poor sales performance and frustration. The positive impact of planning ahead and preparing for each sales call is underscored by the experiences of Jaime Anderson, Senior Vice-President at SAP, in "Selling in Action: Importance of Sales Call Planning to Drive Selling Success."

10-1b What Makes a Good Goal?

Although goals and objectives might best be described as desired outcomes, these two words carry specific meaning. *Desired* implies that it is something worthy of working toward and expending resources to reach. *Outcome* connotes that it is a specific result or effect resulting from

Selling in Action

Importance of Sales Call Planning to Drive Selling Success

Jaime Anderson, Senior Vice-President of Marketing at SAP, underscores the importance of thorough planning and preparation prior to making contact with prospects and buyers.

Buyers are becoming more and more immune and even intolerant of inefficient sales

Bildagentur Zoonar GmbH/Shutterstock.com

contacts and activities. According to the What's the Future of Sales report by SAP, business buyers now receive an average of 64 to 107 approaches by salespeople over the course of a week. As a result, buyers across the globe are feeling hounded by the sales community and becoming less tolerant and less trusting of salespeople who come in too hard or without sufficient information and preparation. Aggressive salespeople (48 percent) and salespeople who lack relevant knowledge (46 percent) are the biggest frustrations with salespeople. As a result, buyers block calls and avoid initial sales advances.

Anderson emphasizes that "B2B buyers are time-challenged, they don't want the dog and pony show. They don't want the dance. They just want the salesperson to be informed and to understand where they are and what they need at that point." Today's buyers have less time and patience for meandering or scripted and inflexible sales processes. Instead, they demand relevant and focused sales interactions that can only occur as the result of significant research, planning, and preparation in advance of any sales contact.

Exhibit 10.1

Required Characteristics of Goals and Objectives

Effective Goals and Objectives Must Possess Three Fundamental Characteristics

- Goals should be realistic, yet challenging
- Goals should be specific and quantifiable
- Goals should be time specific

certain activities or behaviors—something that can be described and pointed out. As illustrated in Exhibit 10.1, properly developed goals share three key characteristics: (1) realistic, yet challenging, (2) specific and quantifiable, and (3) time specific.

- *Realistic, Yet Challenging*—Goals should be realistic and reachable. When set beyond what is possible, goals cease to motivate and often become a disincentive to performance. At the same time, goals should be challenging. If goals are continually set at a level that is too easy to reach, performance tends to regress to the lower standard. Goals that are challenging tend to be more motivating than goals that are easily achieved.

- *Specific and Quantifiable*—Without specificity, goals become ambiguous and have no clear meaning. For instance, the goal of having the top territory in the district could be interpreted in many ways. Does top territory translate to having the largest increase in sales, the fewest number of customer defections, the highest customer satisfaction scores, the smallest number of price discounts, or possibly the largest reduction in travel expenses? Without specificity, the goal becomes a moving target, and it is difficult to know where to apply one's effort. In a similar fashion, goals should be quantifiable—that is, they should be measurable. The goal of increasing sales is certainly commendable, but how might it be judged as having been accomplished? Is a 1 percent increase sufficient or is 12 percent more in line with expectations? If a 12 percent increase is the expectation, then the goal should be a 12 percent increase in sales—a quantifiable and measurable outcome that can be objectively measured and assessed.

- *Time Specific*—Stating a specific time line is the third requirement of goals and objectives. A goal of achieving a 12 percent increase in sales by December 31 is much more appealing than simply stating that one's goal is to increase sales by 12 percent. Associating time lines with goals establishes a deadline for planning purposes and provides motivation by instilling a sense of urgency for taking action.

10-2 WORKING WITH DIFFERENT LEVELS AND TYPES OF GOALS

For maximum effectiveness, salespeople establish goals at four different levels: personal goals, territory goals, account goals, and sales call goals. Although each level requires different types of effort and produces different outcomes, each of the levels is interrelated and interdependent with the others. These interrelationships and dependencies are illustrated in Exhibit 10.2. A salesperson's **personal goals** might include achieving a $70,000 annual income during the current year ending December 31. If the salesperson receives a commission of 11 percent on sales, this personal goal is directly related to and dependent on achieving the **territory goal** of selling $636,364 in products across the territory in the same time period. Assuming 19 equally sized accounts

personal goals A salesperson's individual desired accomplishments, such as achieving a desired annual income over a specific period of time.

territory goal A salesperson's desire of selling a certain amount of product within an area or territory in order to achieve personal goals.

Exhibit 10.2

Four Interdependent Levels of Salesperson Objectives

Personal Goal—Desired Annual Income	$ 70,000
Is Dependent on Annual Territory Sales Goal (11% commission on sales)	$ 636,364
Is Dependent on Annual Account Sales Goal (19 equally sized accounts)	$ 33,493
Is Dependent on Sales Call Goal (each account is called on twice a month)	$ 1,396

comprise the territory, the territory goal depends on achieving the **account goal** of an average of $33,493 in products sold to each account over the course of the year. Considering that each account is called on twice every month, a **sales call goal** of $1,396 in sales per call is required to achieve the account goal. As illustrated in this example, each higher-level goal ultimately depends on the salesperson setting and achieving lower-level, specific goals for each and every sales call.

Although illustrative of the interdependence between different levels of goals, the previous example is admittedly simplistic in its exclusive use of goals based on sales volume. In reality, there are many different types of goals that a salesperson might effectively use. Exhibit 10.3 illustrates examples of common sales goals.

10-2a Stage Two: Territory Analysis and Account Classification

Territory analysis and classification of accounts, the second stage of self-leadership, is all about finding the customers and prospects who are most likely to buy. Who are they, and where are they located? What and why do they buy? How much and how often do they purchase? Who has the authority to buy, and who can influence the purchase decision? What is the probability of selling to this account? What is the potential share of account that might be gained?

Many sources offer intelligence that will assist the salesperson in answering these questions, and the information boom on the Internet makes accessing this information easier than ever before. In addition to numerous business directories available on the Web, commercial business information suppliers such as *OneSource Information Services, Hoovers, Standard & Poor's, Dun and Bradstreet,* and *The Thomas Register* offer easy-to-use databases that are fully searchable by company, industry, and geographic location. Salespeople can also access individual company Web sites, trade directories, professional association membership listings, and commercial mailing list providers. Personal observation, discussions with other selling professionals, and company sales records are also excellent sources for gaining valuable information.

Exhibit 10.3
Common Types of Sales Goals

• Financial goals	Income, financial security
• Career advancement goals	Work in chosen field, advancement
• Personal development goals	Education, training, relationships outside work
• Sales volume goals	Dollar sales, unit sales, number of orders, aggregates or by groups
• Sales call activity goals	Calls made, calls/day, calls/account, presentations made
• Sales expense goals	Total expenses, by category, percent of sales
• Profitability goals	Gross profits, contribution margin, returns, and discounts
• Market share	Total share of potential market, peer group comparisons
• Share of account	Share of customer's purchases
• Ancillary activity goals	Required reports turned in, training conducted, service calls made
• Customer retention goals	Number of accounts lost, complaints received, lost account ratios
• New account goals	Number of new accounts
• Customer service goals	Customer goodwill generation, level of satisfaction, receivables collected
• Conversion goals	Ratio of number of sales to number of calls made

account goal A salesperson's desire of selling a certain amount of product to one customer or account in order to achieve territory and personal goals.

sales call goal A salesperson's desire of selling a certain amount of product per each sales call in order to achieve account, territory, and personal goals.

territory analysis The process of surveying an area to determine customers and prospects who are most likely to buy.

Much of this information can be plotted to develop detailed territory maps that will begin to pinpoint pockets of existing and potential business. In addition, understanding the territory at the individual account level provides the input required for account classification.

10-3 ACCOUNT CLASSIFICATION

Account classification places existing customers and prospects into categories based on their sales potential and assists salespeople in prioritizing accounts for call planning and time allocation purposes. During the process of account classification, it is common for salespeople to find that 80 to 90 percent of their sales potential is generated by 10 to 20 percent of the total accounts. Consequently, the results of account classification can guide salespeople in more efficient allocation of time, effort, and resources while simultaneously enabling them to be more effective in achieving sales goals. Two commonly used methods for classifying accounts are single-factor analysis and portfolio analysis.

10-3a Single-Factor Analysis

Single-factor analysis, also referred to as ABC analysis, is the simplest and most often used method for classifying accounts. As the name suggests, accounts are analyzed on the basis of one single factor—typically the level of sales potential. On the basis of sales potential, the accounts are placed into three or four categories denoted by letters of the alphabet, "A," "B," "C," and "D." Accounts with the highest potential are traditionally sorted into category "A," whereas those with medium potential go into "B," and so on. All accounts in the same category receive equal selling effort. For example, "A" accounts may be called on every two weeks, "B" accounts every four to six weeks, and "C" accounts might receive a personal sales call once a year and be serviced by the seller's telemarketing team during the interim. Single-factor classification schemas used by three different sales organizations are summarized in Exhibit 10.4.

> **account classification** The process of placing existing customers and prospects into categories based on their potential as a customer.
>
> **single-factor analysis** A method for analyzing accounts that is based on one single factor, typically the level of sales potential.

Exhibit 10.4

Different Single-Factor Account Analysis Schemas Used by Different Companies

Class of Account	Schema One: InquisLogic Inc.	Schema Two: Web Resource Associates, LLC	Schema Three: Federal Metal Products
"A" Accounts	Accounts with highest potential (the 20% that do or could account for 80% of sales) Annual number of calls = 24	Accounts with highest potential (the 20% that do or could account for 80% of sales) Annual number of calls = 52	High volume current customers (the 20% that currently account for 80% of sales volume) Annual number of calls = 48
"B" Accounts	Medium potential accounts (the 80% that account for 20% of sales volume) Annual number of calls = 12	Accounts with moderate sales potential, but who are regular and reliable customers Annual number of calls = 24	Accounts with high potential, but who are not current customers Annual number of calls = 12
"C" Accounts	Accounts with the least sales potential Annual number of calls = 4	Lower sales potential accounts Annual number of calls = 8	Medium potential accounts that are current customers Annual number of calls = 12
"D" Accounts	None; this schema uses only 3 classes of accounts	Accounts that cost more in time and energy than they produce in sales or profits Annual number of calls = 0	Accounts with medium potential, but who are not current customers Annual number of calls = 6

The simplicity of single-factor analysis is a prime contributor to its popularity for use by field salespeople. It is straightforward and requires no statistical analysis or data manipulation. Although this lack of complexity is appealing, its ability to use only one factor for analyzing and classifying accounts is also a significant limitation. Sales potential is certainly an important input in allocating selling effort, but other factors should also be considered. Possible other factors of interest are the selling company's competitive strength in each account, the account's need for additional attention and effort, profitability of the account, and amount of competitive pressure on the account.

10-3b Portfolio Analysis

Also referred to as two-factor analysis, the **portfolio analysis** method attempts to overcome the weakness of single-factor analysis by allowing two factors to be considered simultaneously. Each account is examined on the basis of the two specified factors and sorted into the proper segment of a matrix. This matrix is typically divided into four cells, and accounts are placed into the proper classification cell on the basis of their individual ratings ("high" and "low" or "strong" and "weak") on each factor of interest. Cell location denotes the overall attractiveness of the different accounts and serves as a guide for the salesperson's allocation of resources and effort. Typically, each account in the same cell will receive the same amount of selling effort.

Exhibit 10.5 details the account characteristics and suggested selling effort allocations for a typical portfolio analysis incorporating the factors of (1) account opportunity and (2) seller's competitive position.[3] Account opportunity takes into consideration the buyer's level of need for

portfolio analysis A method for analyzing accounts that allows two factors to be considered simultaneously.

Exhibit 10.5

Portfolio/Two-Factor Account Analysis and Selling Strategies

| | Competitive Position | |
	Strong	Weak
High (Account Opportunity)	**Segment One** **Level of Attractiveness:** Accounts are very attractive because they offer high opportunity, and the seller has a strong competitive position. **Selling Effort Strategy:** Accounts should receive a heavy investment of effort and resources in order to take advantage of high opportunity and maintain/improve competitive position. **Exemplary Sales Call Strategy = 36 calls/yr.**	**Segment Two** **Level of Attractiveness:** Accounts are potentially attractive due to high opportunity, but the seller currently has weak competitive position. **Selling Effort Strategy:** Where it is possible to strengthen seller's competitive position, a heavy investment of selling effort should be applied. **Exemplary Sales Call Strategy = 24 calls/yr.**
Low (Account Opportunity)	**Segment Three** **Level of Attractiveness:** Accounts are moderately attractive due to seller having a strong competitive position. However, future opportunity is low. **Selling Effort Strategy:** Accounts should receive a heavy moderate level of selling effort that is sufficient to maintain current competitive position. **Exemplary Sales Call Strategy = 12 calls/yr.**	**Segment Four** **Level of Attractiveness:** Accounts are minimally attractive. They offer low opportunity and the seller has weak competitive position. **Selling Effort Strategy:** Accounts should receive minimal personal selling effort. Alternatives such as telemarketing, direct mail, and the Internet should be explored. **Exemplary Sales Call Strategy = 6 calls/yr.**

and ability to purchase the seller's products, along with financial stability and growth prospects. Competitive position denotes the relationship between the account and the seller and includes variables such as seller's share of account, competitive pressure, and key decision maker's attitude toward the seller. Accounts sorted into Segment One are high on opportunity, exhibit strong competitive positions, and should receive the highest level of selling effort. Accounts falling into Segment Two are high on opportunity but weak on competitive position. These accounts should receive a high level of attention to strengthen the seller's competitive position. Segment Three contains the 80 to 90 percent of accounts doing 10 to 20 percent of the seller's volume. These accounts are loyal and regular customers (high on competitive position) but offer weak opportunity.

Strategically, these accounts should receive a lower investment of selling effort designed to maintain the seller's current competitive position. Accounts sorted into Segment Four are considered unattractive and allocated minimal selling effort as they are characterized by low opportunity and weak competitive position. Within the past several years, many sellers have been successful in servicing Segment Three and Four accounts outside the personal selling channel by using alternatives such as telemarketing, direct mail, the Internet, and proprietary extranets.

> It is common for salespeople to find 80 to 90 percent of their sales potential generated by 10 to 20 percent of their accounts.

Portfolio analysis offers the advantages of enhanced flexibility and ability to incorporate multiple variables for analyzing and sorting accounts. Reflecting these strong points, the use of portfolio analysis is gaining in popularity.

10-3c Stage Three: Development and Implementation of Strategies and Plans

Stage One provides the salesperson with the guidelines of what is important and the goals to be accomplished at the levels of individual sales calls, accounts, and the overall territory. Stage Two

sales planning The process of scheduling activities that can be used as a map for achieving objectives.

identifies and establishes the priority and potential of each account in the territory along with the relative location of each account. Top salespeople do not stop there! They use this information to develop strategies and plans that will guide them toward achieving their goals by applying their available resources in a deliberate and organized fashion that effectively cultivates and harvests the potential sales available in the territory.

10-3d Establishing and Implementing Selling Task and Activity Plans

When properly executed, **sales planning** results in a schedule of activities that can be used as a map for achieving objectives. First, start with the big picture—a long-term plan spanning the next 6 to 12 months. This big picture highlights commitments and deadlines and facilitates setting up the activities required to meet those commitments and deadlines. In turn, the longer-range plans provide the basis for shorter time frame plans and selling activities. The salesperson planning program at Federal Metal Products (FMP) offers a good overview and prototype of effective salesperson planning.

> *FMP, a middle market supplier of metal production components, trains its salespeople to prepare and submit annual territory plans and budgets by November 15 each year. With that recurring deadline marked on their schedules, FMP salespeople work backward on their calendars to establish key checkpoints for their planning activities. This establishes a time line to guide and assist salespeople in making the submission deadline.*
>
> *If salespeople project that it will take four weeks to assemble and draft their territory sales plan, they work back four weeks from the November 15 date and establish October 15 as the date to begin assembling their data and building their plans. How long will it take to collect the needed data properly? Six weeks? If so, their schedule should reflect beginning that activity by September 1.*
>
> *Sales plans should take into consideration scheduled meetings and training sessions, holidays, trade shows, and vacation time. Plans should also contain periodic checkpoints for assessing progress toward goals. A*

An effective plan works like a map showing the way from where you are to where you want to go - your objective.

salesperson's objective of $750,000 in sales for the year equates to a goal averaging $62,500 in sales every month. Accordingly, the long-term master plan should include monthly checkpoints to compare the schedule versus actual performance data. Is performance on course, ahead, or lagging behind? If not on schedule, the corresponding and more detailed weekly plans should be revised to reflect salespeople's strategies for getting back on course.

Salespeople at FMP develop weekly plans from their longer-term annual plan. These shorter-term plans detail the selling-related activities to be accomplished that week. To create a weekly plan, first identify the priorities that must be accomplished to stay on schedule. Then, for each of these priorities, detail the associated activities and schedule the time that it will take for completion. What areas of the territory will be focused on? What accounts will be called on, and what is the objective for each call? What are the best times to call for appointments? Are there account preferences as to what days and times they work with salespeople? How much time must be allowed for travel, waiting, and working with each account? What products will be featured? What information and materials will be needed?

In turn, the priorities and activities identified in the weekly plan should become the points of focus for the daily plan. Days that end on a successful note begin with a thorough and written

schedule detailing tasks and priorities for that day and the activities that must be carried out to achieve them.

The optimum schedule emphasizes tasks and activities that will make the greatest sales impact—working with customers. As illustrated by the FMP's "Daily Sales Plan Worksheet" shown in Exhibit 10.6, daily plans should detail the amount of time projected for each scheduled task and activity. To maximize the effectiveness of sales plans, general consensus indicates salespeople should adhere to two guiding principles.

- *Do them, and do them in writing.* Written plans are better developed and provide more motivation and commitment for salespeople to carry them through to completion. Furthermore, written plans help to ensure that priority items do not fall through the cracks because something was forgotten.

- *Keep it current and flexible.* Make a new daily plan every day. Try as we might, things do not always go as planned. Consequently, changes might be needed, and uncompleted priorities or activities from one day may have to be carried over to the next.

10-4 ESTABLISHING TERRITORY ROUTING PLANS

Territory routing plans incorporate information developed in the territory analysis and account classification stage to minimize the encroachment of unproductive travel time on time that could be better spent working with customers. Good routing plans minimize the backtracking and crisscrossing that would otherwise occur and allow the salesperson to use time more efficiently.

Knowing how many calls can be made each day, the required call frequency for each account classification, and the relative geographic location of and distance between accounts, a salesperson can plot different routing strategies and decide the optimal plan. Many sales professionals continue to use the traditional colored map pins and felt-tip markers on a wall map. However, a variety of easy-to-use and affordable computer applications that plot optimal routing plans are available and are growing in popularity. Optimized routing plans correspond to one of five common patterns: straight line, cloverleaf, circular, leapfrog, and major city.

Exhibit 10.6

Example of a Typical Daily Sales Plan Worksheet

Federal Metal Products
Daily Sales Plan Worksheet
Salesperson: _Earnie Cravits_____   Day: _Friday_____   Date: _8/29_____

Time	Task or Priority	Activity	People Involved	Time Needed	Goal/ Anticipated Results	Notes & Comments
8:30 AM	Set appointments	Phone calls	Jill Attaway Digital Systems	10 min	Appointment for next week	Requested that I come by
	"	"	Bart Waits EnterpriseOne	10 min	"	
	"	"	Kerri Williams Flo-Forms	10 min	"	Will be placing order in 3 weeks
9:00 AM	"	"	Marilyn Henry InQuisLogic	10 min	Clarify service problem	Send info to engineering
10:30 AM	Demonstrate new bearing line	Sales call	Mike Humphreys ICOM	60 min	Info gathering	Currently buying from Gem Rollers
12 PM	Get order commitment	Sales call— Lunch	Jack Kessler MDQG	120 min	$12,000 order	Gem submitted proposal 8/20
3:00 PM	Take sample of proposed line	Sales call	Aimee Williams MOCO, Inc.	60 min	$15,200 order	Ready to buy, wants to see prdct. sample
4:30 PM	Check on delivery	Service call	Ron Meier Web Resources	50 min	Delight the customer	First time to buy from us!!
6:00 PM	Complete paperwork	Submit call reports		45 min		
7:00 PM	Prepare daily schedule	Planning		45 min		

straight-line routing plan
A territory routing plan in which salespeople start from their offices and make calls in one direction until they reach the end of the territory.

cloverleaf routing plan
A territory routing plan in which the salesperson works a different part of the territory and travels in a circular loop back to the starting point.

10-4a Straight-Line Routing Plans

With a **straight-line routing plan**, salespeople start from their offices and make calls in one direction until they reach the end of the territory. As illustrated in Figure 10.2, at that point they change direction and continue to make calls on a straight line following the new vector. This continues until the salesperson returns to the office location. The straight-line pattern works best when accounts are located in clusters that are some distance from one another.

10-4b Cloverleaf Routing Plans

The **cloverleaf routing plan** pattern is best used when accounts are concentrated in different parts of the territory. On each trip, the salesperson works a different part of the territory and travels in a circular loop back to the starting point. An example of the cloverleaf routing plan is depicted in Figure 10.3. Each loop

FIG. 10.2 STRAIGHT-LINE ROUTE PATTERN

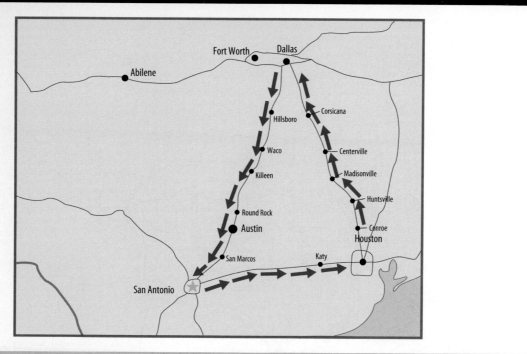

Straight-line territory routes make calls across the territory, proceed in one direction, and then change direction to work back to the starting point.

FIG. 10.3 CLOVERLEAF ROUTE PATTERN

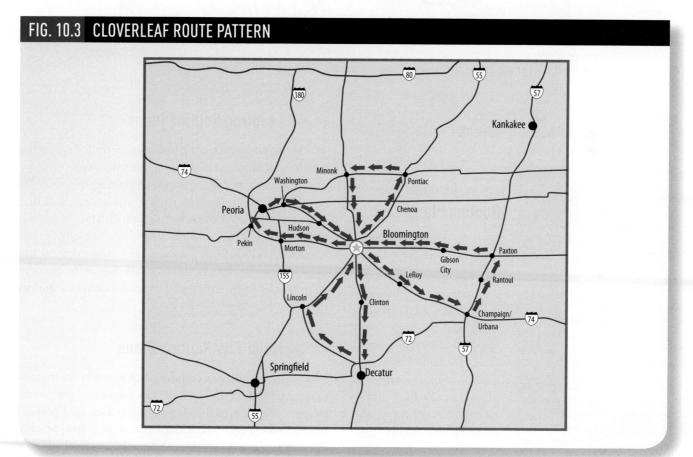

Cloverleaf territory routes work different parts of the territory in a series of circular loops.

FIG. 10.4 CIRCULAR ROUTE PATTERN

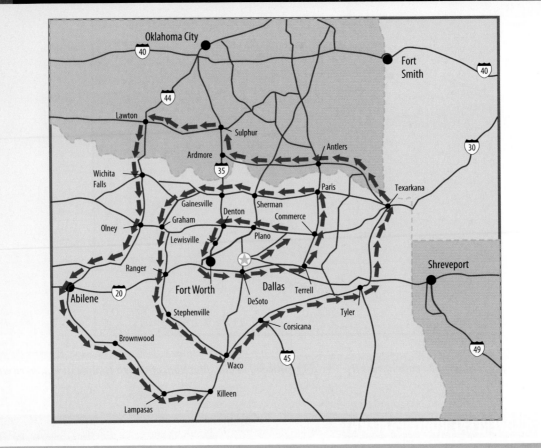

Circular territory routes cover the territory in a series of concentric circles spiraling across the territory.

could take a day, a week, or longer to complete. A new loop is covered on each trip until the entire territory has been covered.

circular routing plan
A territory routing plan in which the salesperson begins at the office and moves in an expanding pattern of concentric circles that spiral across the territory.

leapfrog routing plan
A territory routing plan in which, beginning in one cluster, the salesperson works each of the accounts at that location and then jumps to the next cluster.

major city routing plan
A territory routing plan used when the territory is composed of a major metropolitan area and the territory is split into a series of geometric shapes reflecting each one's concentration and pattern of accounts.

10-4c Circular Routing Plans

Circular routing plans begin at the office and move in an expanding pattern of concentric circles that spirals across the territory. Figure 10.4 traces an exemplary circular routing plan working from an office in Dallas. This method works best when accounts are evenly dispersed throughout the territory.

10-4d Leapfrog Routing Plans

The **leapfrog routing plan** is best applied when the territory is large and accounts are clustered into several widely dispersed groups. Beginning in one cluster, the salesperson works each of the accounts at that location and then jumps to the next cluster. As shown in Figure 10.5, this continues until the last cluster has been worked and the salesperson jumps back to the office or home. When the distance between clusters is great, the salesperson will typically make the jumps by flying.

10-4e Major City Routing Plans

When the territory is composed of a major metropolitan area, the territory is split into a series of geometric shapes reflecting each one's concentration and pattern of accounts. Figure 10.6 depicts a typical **major city routing plan**. Downtown areas are typically highly concentrated with locations controlled by a grid of city

FIG. 10.5   LEAPFROG ROUTE PATTERN

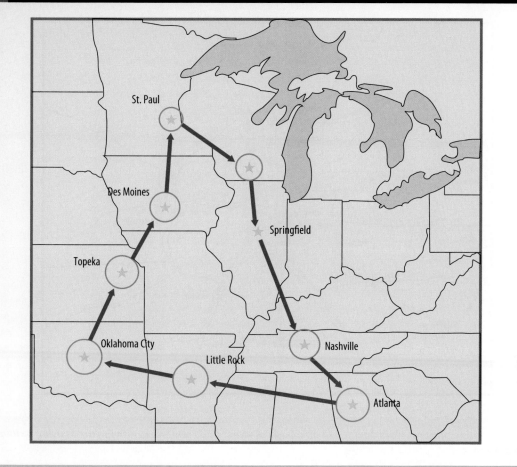

Leapfrog territory routes work accounts clustered in one location and then jump to a different cluster of accounts.

blocks and streets. Consequently, the downtown segment is typically a small square or rectangular area allowing accounts to be worked in a straight-line fashion street by street. Outlying areas are placed in evenly balanced triangles or pie-shaped quadrants, with one quadrant being covered at a time in either a straight-line or cloverleaf pattern.

10-5   STAGE FOUR: TAPPING TECHNOLOGY AND AUTOMATION

Selling technology and automation tools are here to stay and are being transformed from neat toys to necessary tools. Properly applied, selling technology spurs and creates creativity and innovation, streamlines all aspects of the selling process, generates new

and improved selling opportunities, facilitates cross-functional teaming and intraorganizational communication, and enhances multichannel communication and follow-up with customers. In summary, tapping the proper selling technologies and salesforce automation tools allow salespeople to expand their available resources for enhanced selling performance and outcomes. Tim Minahan, Chief Marketing Officer for SAP Online, discusses the importance of leveraging social media channels as interaction tools with buyers, in combination with more traditional salesforce automation technologies, in "Technology in Selling: Your Customers are Talking—Are You Listening?"

Salespeople, sales managers, and customers are unanimous in their agreement that the best salespeople are

selling technology and automation Tools that streamline the selling process, generate improved selling opportunities, facilitate cross-functional teaming and intraorganizational communication, and enhance communication and follow-up with customers.

FIG. 10.6 MAJOR CITY ROUTE PATTERN

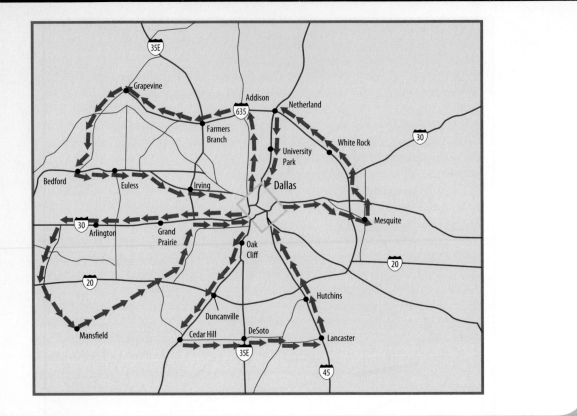

Major city territory routing patterns work downtown on a basis of street grids and work outlying areas using a cloverleaf or straight-line pattern.

those who stay up with changes in and developments of technologies with selling applications. With a multitude of rapidly changing and evolving technology choices, salespeople must not only master the technology itself, but they must also understand when and where it can be applied most effectively. Exemplary selling technologies being used by today's salespeople include the following tools.

10-5a Mobile Sales Technologies

At the center of virtually every selling technology is some form of mobile computing technology. Choices include desktops, notebooks, laptops, tablets, and smartphones. With the ever-expanding availability of broadband and wireless connectivity, today's salesperson is always in touch with customers, with sales support, and with sales data and information. For immediate immersion into the high-tech side of selling, simply walk through the waiting areas of any major airport. Salespeople can be seen entering customer orders, generating reports, and submitting proposals by using standard word-processing packages and even customized online electronic forms. Others are analyzing customer accounts by using spreadsheet applications and query-based Business Intelligence programs that access and analyze a database according to the questions the user wishes to have answered. Several will be observed reviewing and updating customer files by using one of the many mobile and highly capable contact management/CRM software applications. These user-friendly programs provide salespeople with a convenient option to catalog, search, and access comprehensive information regarding individual customers. Looking closer, numerous salespeople will be revising and polishing graphics and presentations with software such as PowerPoint, Keynote, Prezi, Flash, and Open Office Impress. Still others will be checking and responding to e-mail, submitting electronic reports, accessing online territory route maps, and using scheduling programs to set up the next day's call plans.

Technology in Selling

Your Customers Are Talking— Are You Listening?

Tim Minahan, Chief Marketing Officer for SAP Online, discusses the importance of enhancing traditional salesperson-led interactions with knowledge and insight that can be gained from engaging buyers through social media channels.

Today's buyers are more knowledgeable, informed, and digitally connected than ever before. As a result, there has been a significant shift in buyers shunning vendor-sponsored sources of information in favor of tapping their own digital networks and wisdom of crowds to make buying decisions. Social media, peer networks, and industry community sites have taken a lead role in shaping perceptions about brands, products, and companies, with 57 percent of the buying process completed, on average, before a first interaction with sales.

Savvy companies are leveraging social channels to better predict and influence buyer behavior and quickly respond to customer needs. Using tools to process billions of social media posts across millions of sites globally, these firms are extracting insights that help them to quickly identify and effectively respond to customer needs, trends, and perceptions of products. Rapid and continuing developments in digital technologies, social media, and cloud analytics tools make it possible for sales to engage buyers via multiple channels. This real-time, multichannel buyer information enables salespeople to respond immediately and in a focused manner to rapidly changing buyer needs, perceptions, and behaviors.

10-5b Salesperson Customer Relationship Management (Crm)

Effective customer relationships generate customer loyalty and the revenue increases critical for sustained performance. Toward meeting this challenge, companies of all sizes are deploying customer relationship management (CRM) applications and strategies that integrate multiple communication and customer contact channels—including the Web, e-mail, call center, and social media applications in order to maximize customer interactions. However, detailed customer information is of little use if salespeople cannot access it when they need it—such as during a sales call in a customer's office. Sales professionals often work outside the office and need up-to-date information while in the field. Being able to access and offer the right information to customers at the right point in the sales cycle enables salespeople to increase sales dramatically while simultaneously increasing customer satisfaction and loyalty. **Mobile salesperson CRM solutions**, such as Salesforce.com, Microsoft Dynamics, SAP, and SalesLogix, are the key to accessing this information from the field and provide remote access to data such as contacts, customer information, leads, reports, price lists, inventory levels, and opportunity forecasting. Mobile CRM applications utilize wireless broadband access to enable users instantly to view, create, and modify data on any Internet-capable device such as smartphones, tablets and pads, netbooks, and laptops. This handheld access to valuable account information allows a salesperson to tap into the same sales, marketing, and customer service data they have access to in the office—without having to leave the field. Mobile CRM is rapidly becoming a critical requirement for effectively competing in today's fast-paced selling environment and increasing customer expectations in terms of customized levels of service.

10-5c Deal Analytics

Deal analytics is the descriptive name given to a new set of "smart" tools in the area of salesforce automation that are proving especially useful

mobile salesperson CRM solutions Wireless broadband applications that enable users to view, create, and modify data on any Internet-capable device such as smartphones, netbooks, and laptops.

deal analytics "Smart" salesforce automation tools that analyze data on past customer behavior, cross-selling opportunities, and demographics to identify areas of opportunity and high customer interest.

for salespeople. These predictive analytical tools utilize mobile CRM systems to access and analyze data on past customer behavior, cross selling opportunities, and demographics to identify areas of opportunity and high interest to a customer. Salespeople also utilize deal analytics tools to access and compare competitive information such as pricing and bundled offers, which can result in more effective proposals and negotiations.

10-5d The Internet, Intranets, and Extranets

Company networks have been used for many years; however, the advent of the Internet has made them much more affordable and easier to maintain.

Accessing the Internet instantly networks a salesperson with the world: customers, information sources, other salespeople, sales management, and others. More importantly, the Internet puts the salesperson in contact with his or her customer community and support networks from anywhere in the world, 24 hours a day, seven days a week. Going beyond the convenience of e-mail, many sales organizations are setting up intranets and extranets—secure and proprietary organizational Web sites that are protected by passwords and security authorizations. Intranets are networks within the organization using the Internet or commercial channels to provide direct linkages between company units and individuals. Extranets are a special form of intranet that is still for proprietary and restricted use but links to specific suppliers and customers to allow them controlled and secure access to the organization's network to facilitate communication and exchange.

These secure Web sites become instant organizational intranets used for communication, training, video-conferencing, web-conferencing, and secure data interchange. Using such Web-enabled intranets, Diamond Equipment Corporation's salespeople can link to the latest product information and spec sheets, obtain updated inventory and production numbers, download company information, and print customized proposals for customer presentations from anywhere in the world. CDW provides each of its major accounts with a customized extranet that provides the customer with access to CDW on a 24-hour, seven-day-a-week basis. Buyers can track orders online, download product and technical specifications, access customer support technicians, check prices and availability of products, and even place orders for next-day delivery

throughout the United States. Rather than spending time traveling to customers' offices, Windy City Wire's salespeople deliver their sales presentations by combining teleconferences and Web presentations using WebEx. The use of Internet- and intranet-based technologies shorten the sales cycle by allowing sales meetings and presentations to be created and delivered in less time than traditional face-to-face processes would take. If a salesperson can save just 10 minutes a day by using Web-based presentation libraries and online product and pricing information, he or she will gain an additional week's worth of productivity over the course of a year. However, as illustrated by the situation described in "An Ethical Dilemma," the adoption and roll-out of advanced technologies often presents some challenges along the way.

10-5e High-Tech Sales Support Offices

Organizations having salesforces widely dispersed geographically or traveling across multiple regions of the nation or world have found it advantageous to establish **high-tech sales support offices** at multiple locations. Both resident and nonresident salespeople use these offices to access a wider range of selling technology than could be easily carried on a notebook or laptop computer. These offices also provide points of access to the various networks, intranets, and extranets the organization maintains. IBM maintains high-tech offices such as these at its installations around the world. An IBM representative in Dallas might find himself working as part of a team on a project in Chicago. While in Chicago, the representative has access to the same technology and support as was available in Dallas. Full access is available to company networks, customer accounts, communication links, and software applications. Consequently, convenience and productive time are maximized for the benefit of all parties.

10-5f Stage Five: Assessment of Performance and Goal Attainment

A critical, and often overlooked, stage in the process of self-leadership is the periodic assessment of progress. Although certainly important, this stage should involve more than a simple check at the end of the period to determine whether goals were achieved. Assessment checkpoints should be built into plans at progressive points in time to encourage and facilitate the evaluation of one's progress. These frequent comparisons of actual performance with periodic checkpoints allow time to

high-tech sales support offices Offices set up at multiple locations where salespeople can access the wider range of selling technology than could be easily carried on a notebook or laptop computer.

An Ethical Dilemma

As a salesperson for MedLab Technologies, Jack Law manages the Southwest Sales Region, selling the company's broad line of analysis equipment and software to hospitals and medical labs across the southwestern United States. MedLab is considered the leading firm in this highly competitive marketplace. Their utilization of an extensive Internet-based extranet network for customers has enabled MedLab to stay ahead of the competition. MedLab's extranet allows customers to access product and service information 24-7. Because the extranet allows customers to access proprietary information including order status, product availability, pricing, and even order entry and transactions, access is controlled through a secure password authentication process. Access is granted only to well-established customers.

Jack has just learned that one of the purchasing agents at Mercy Hospital, one of Jack's regular customers, has shared their extranet access codes with the salesperson for MedLab's main competitor. Apparently the competitor wanted access to MedLab's pricing structure so they could undercut the prices and acquire some of MedLab's customers.

What should Jack do?

a) Deactivate Mercy Hospital's codes for accessing MedLab's extranet so the competitor can no longer access the information.

b) Inform his sales manager so that MedLab can change all their pricing in reaction to the security breach.

c) Provide Mercy Hospital's purchasing department with new access codes, remind them that the codes are proprietary—not to be shared, and use the breach of trust as an opportunity to enhance the MedLab–Mercy Hospital relationship.

---

consider revisions or modifications before it is too late to make a difference. In addition to assessing progress, evaluation should also consider what is working well and what could be improved. This knowledge and understanding can be used to guide modifications in the various plans, tasks, and activities that populate the different stages of self-leadership to further enhance future success and performance.

10-6 INCREASING CUSTOMER VALUE THROUGH TEAMWORK

Excellent customer service is taking on a key role in competitive business strategy, and as customer expectations and needs continue to grow in complexity, selling organizations find that they can no longer depend solely on salespeople as the exclusive arbiter of customer satisfaction. Teamwork, both inside the organization and with customers, is being emphasized as the key to customer focus and sales performance.

10-6a Internal Partnerships and Teams

The practices and experiences of top-ranked selling organizations, as well as considerable sales research, support the emphasis on teamwork as a key to long-term selling success. The results from three studies of more than 200 companies that employ some 25,000 salespeople supported the belief that cooperating as a team player was critical for success in selling.[4] Similar results have been found in other studies that examine what business-to-business buyers expect from suppliers. In two studies incorporating 6,708 customer evaluations of vendor performance and customer satisfaction in the financial

> Salesperson effectiveness in building internal and external partnerships is a key driver of customer satisfaction.

Periodic performance assessments should be built into plans so as to encourage evaluation of progress and identify areas of improvement.

services industry, the suppliers' performance in building internal and external partnerships was found to be the key driver of customer satisfaction.[5]

Building **external relationships** is the focal point of contemporary selling techniques and reflects the ongoing paradigm shift in today's salesforces. This emphasis on building *external* customer relationships could overshadow the critical role of building *internal*, close-working relationships with other individuals in their own company. The importance of these **internal relationships** would seem to be logical, as a salesperson's success depends on the degree of support he or she receives from others in the various functional areas of the organization. Ultimately, the salesperson owns the responsibility for customer relationships, but the strength of those customer relationships depends on the joint efforts and resources contributed by multiple individuals across the selling organization.

Account managers at Contour Plastics Corporation have full responsibility for bringing together individuals from functional departments across the organization to work as a sales team dedicated to selling and providing pre- and post-sale services to a specific account. As needed, team members will incorporate research chemists, application specialists, production engineers, and logistics specialists. Coordinated by the salesperson, each team member contributes his or her special expertise toward maximizing the understanding of the customer's situation and needs, and then working

external relationships
Relationships salespeople build with customers outside the organization and working environment.

internal relationships
Relationships salespeople have with other individuals in their own company.

together to create a unique, value-added solution that few, if any, competitors can equal.

Teamwork results in a synergy that produces greater outcomes and results for all parties than would be possible with multiple individuals acting independently of one another. Consequently, it is important that salespeople also develop the ability to sell internally as they represent their customers to the selling organization and give recognition to the important role others play in winning, keeping, and growing customer accounts.

James Champy, chairman of consulting for Perot Systems, notes that customers are expecting and receiving better service and product options than ever and characterizes the role of the salesperson as having been transformed to that of a trusted advisor.[6]

In this advisor role, the salesperson works with customers to develop a mutual understanding of the customer's situation, needs, possibilities, and expectations. On the basis of this information, the salesperson assembles a team of individuals, experts from across the selling organization, who work together creating a product response that will deliver more unique customer value than the competitors' offerings. In delivering this unique and added value for customers, salespeople often find themselves working with other individuals in sales, marketing, design and manufacturing, administrative support, shipping, and customer service.

10-6b Sales Partnerships

Within the sales department, salespeople often join other salespeople to gain the strengths and expertise required for a specific selling situation or customer. Partnerships with sales managers and other sales executives are also important in winning support for developing innovative responses to customer needs. XL Capital is a global leader in alternative risk transfer products, financial risk management, and surplus lines of commercial property and casualty insurance. Selling to Fortune 500 and Fortune 1000 customers, XL Capital's salespeople (customer business unit managers) specialize along customer and industry lines. It is common for XL's salespeople to work in teams to bring together the experience and expertise required to work with customers whose businesses span a large number of different industries.

10-6c Marketing Partnerships

Teaming with individuals in the marketing department is critical for salespeople in generating integrated solutions for customers over the long term. Marketing is responsible for developing organizational marketing strategies that serve as guidelines for the salesforce. Using information gathered in the field by the salesforce, marketing also assists in the generation of new market offerings in response to changing customer needs and requests. Marketing can also be a valuable partner for salespeople in accessing information and developing sales proposals.

At Pocahontas Foods, a top-10 institutional food broker with nationwide operations, account managers regularly work with members of the marketing department to communicate changes in customer needs and activities of competitors. This collaborative partnership allows Pocahontas to continue bringing innovative product offerings to the marketplace that are designed around the inputs from their salespeople.

10-6d Design and Manufacturing Partnerships

Salespeople often find themselves selling ideas for product designs and changes in manufacturing schedules to meet the needs of customers. When individuals from design, manufacturing, and sales work as a team, performance and delivery commitments are more likely to be met and customer satisfaction further enhanced. RR Donnelly works to maintain its industry leadership in business forms and systems by aggressively nurturing a company-wide culture emphasizing customer orientation and support. As part of their training, salespeople actually work in production facilities to understand what has to be done to meet product design and delivery requirements that the salespeople might commit to in the field. By-products of this cross-training come about in the form of one-to-one personal relationships between salespeople and production staff. In the case of complex customer needs or special delivery needs, these relationships become invaluable.

10-6e Administrative Support Partnerships

Salespeople work with others from administrative support functions such as management, finance and credit, billing, and information systems. Like sales, each of these functional units has certain goals and objectives that translate to policies and procedures that govern their own activities and affect operations throughout the organization—including sales. Customer needs are served best when salespeople have worked to establish effective relationships within these units and all parties work together for the mutual good of the organization and customer. Jim Gavic, account

manager for Great Lakes Trucking, manages a territory stretching from the industrial sector of south Chicago east to Gary, Indiana, and south to Indianapolis. Gavic credits his close relationships with individuals in the company's finance and credit department for making 20 percent of his annual sales. By working together, they were able to establish special billing terms for several of his larger accounts. If finance and credit had simply enforced Great Lake's standard terms, these customers would have been lost to a competitor with more flexible credit policies.

10-6f Shipping and Transportation Partnerships

Salespeople periodically find themselves facing an urgent customer need that requires special handling of an order. Perhaps it is an expedited shipment for immediate delivery or the processing and shipping of an interim order of less-than-economical size. Whatever the need, it will affect other shipments getting out on time and could even increase the department's operating costs. Curtis James, territory manager for General Electric Appliances, found sales going better than usual at a new store opening in Oklahoma City. To keep the customer from being caught short, he hand-carried a fill-in order to the GE district office, walked it through credit approval, hand-delivered the shipping order to the warehouse, and helped load the truck. Teamwork enabled Curtis to accomplish in less than a day what normally would have taken 8 to 10 days. It takes a team effort to work through exceptions such as these, and it is common to find the salesperson actually helping to make it happen by pulling orders, packing boxes, and even helping to load the truck.

10-6g Customer Service Partnerships

Teamwork between sales and customer service can create a synergy that has a broad-based impact that can translate to higher customer satisfaction, higher rates of customer retention, and increased sales performance. On the one hand, customer service personnel, such as call center operators and service technicians, often have more extensive contact with customers than the account representatives. As such, they can serve as an early warning system for salespeople and provide valuable information regarding customer complaints, problems, developing needs, and changes that they encounter through customer contacts. As a salesperson for Southwestern School Supply, Cap Williams regularly checks in and visits with the company's customer service personnel to keep abreast of contact that they might have with any of his customers. The information he receives allows him to get ahead of any possible customer problems, provide an uncanny level of after-sale support that continues to mystify upper management, and helps to secure his consistent receipt of Top Salesperson of the Year Award year after year. When salespeople such as Williams act on the information provided by customer service to advance customer relationships and increase sales, customer service personnel will also be further inclined to work together to benefit the team. On the other hand, salespeople often assist customer service personnel by working directly with customers to address problems before they become complaints and provide instruction and training to assist customers in using the products sold.

10-7 BUILDING TEAMWORK SKILLS

Effective teams do not form by default. Nor can a team be effective in producing synergistic benefits solely because it is called a team. Like customer relationships, internal relationships are built on reciprocal trust. The salesperson that arbitrarily and repeatedly asks for special production runs, extensions to customers' lines of credit, expedited shipments, or special attention from customer service is simply asking for quick fixes. These quick fixes serve the objectives of the customer and salesperson but often work against the objectives of the functional unit and the organization as a whole.

From the Classroom to the Field

Pakou Lee graduated from Oklahoma City University in May 2014 and is a Product Manager for APMEX, the leading precious metals marketer in the United States. She sources gold, silver, and platinum bars, coins, and artifacts from national/royal mints around the world and sells them to VIP collectors and investors throughout the United States. Pakou talks about how what she learned in her sales classes has enabled her to become a top performer in the company.

My sales classes emphasized the importance of actively listening to the customer, probing with effective questions to define the customer's specific needs and to develop a sales team to positively impact sales and long-term customer satisfaction. APMEX's VIP customers spend millions of dollars on collectible bullion products, but before the sale can be completed you must spend time talking with the customer—actively listening to drill down and understand exactly what they are looking to acquire. Often, the customer's original idea of what they were looking for morphs into something very different, based on my use of probing

questions for discovery and a collaborative style of conversation. Using open-ended questions allows the customer to do most of the talking while I listen and guide the conversation in order to understand their needs in depth.

The products we sell are rare and difficult to acquire. The relationships I have developed by extending my sales team are critical to my success in acquiring the specific item my customer is seeking. My sales team includes other salespeople and product managers within APMEX, as well as key contacts at the royal mints in other countries. An example would be a recent customer seeking a specific gold bullion coin for his collection. This coin was minted by the Spanish Royal Mint and featured intricate engravings of an El Greco painting. Only 1,000 were minted, and locating one coin meeting my customer's specifications was proving most challenging. Working through my team member who works at the Royal Spanish Mint proved to be the key to locating and acquiring this coin and satisfying one of our VIP customers.

FIG. 10.7 **RELATIONSHIP OF OPTIMIZED SOLUTIONS, TRUST, AND COOPERATION**

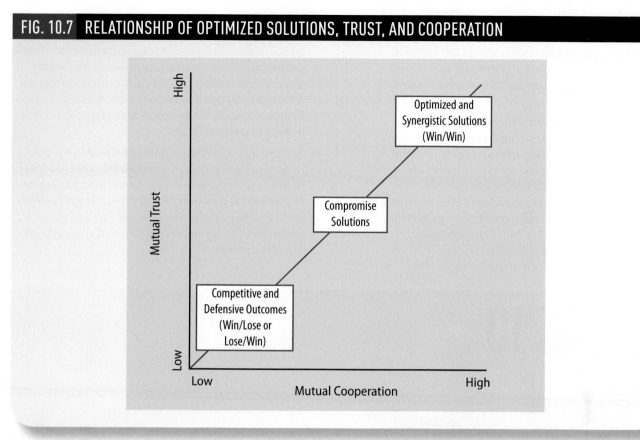

Optimum buyer-seller solutions result from a team orientation and require high levels of mutual trust and mutual cooperation. (Excerpt from **The 7 Habits of Highly Effective People** *© 2004 Stephen R. Covey. The Time Management Matrix phrase and model are trademarks of Franklin Covey Co., http://www.franklincovey.com. Used with permission. All rights reserved.)*

Synergistic teamwork requires a commitment on the part of all parties to look for and work for win/win solutions. However, in the rush to take care of a customer, it is all too easy for salespeople to fall into a win/lose orientation. It is not that they want anyone to lose, but rather that they get what they want. This win orientation is most common in everyday negotiation—in which people think and act in terms of accomplishing their own goals and leave it to others to attain theirs. As illustrated in Figure 10.7, optimum solutions develop from a team orientation based on the philosophy of win/win alternatives.[7] In turn, this can happen only when there are high levels of mutual trust and communication: "Not your way, not my way, but a better way."

In his bestselling book for personal development, Stephen Covey offers six keys to developing synergistic relationships and teams.[8] These are the six **teamwork skills** that salespeople must learn and sincerely apply in their process of building internal partnerships that translate in to increased sales and organizational performance.

- *Understanding the Other Individuals*—Fully understanding and considering the other individuals in the partnership is necessary to know what is important to them. What is important to them must also be important to the salesperson if the partnership is to grow and be effective. This means that salespeople must take time to learn the objectives of other functional areas and consider how those needs and requests might affect the salesperson's goals and objectives.

- *Attending to the Little Things*—The little kindnesses and courtesies are often small in size and great in importance. In building relationships, the little things are the big things. Properly attended to and nurtured, they enhance the interrelationships. At the same time, if they are neglected or misused, they can destroy the relationship very quickly.

- *Keeping Commitments*—We all build our hopes and plans around the promises and commitments of others. When

teamwork skills Skills salespeople must learn to build internal partnerships that translate into increased sales and organizational performance.

a commitment is not kept, disappointment and problems result. As a result, credibility and trust suffer major damage that is always difficult and often impossible to repair. However, consistency in keeping commitments builds and solidifies trust-based relationships.

- *Clarifying Expectations*—The root cause of most relational difficulties can be found in ambiguous expectations regarding roles and goals—exactly where are we going and who is responsible for what? Investing the time up front to clarify expectations regarding goals and roles can save even more time down the road when misunderstandings become compounded and turn into goal conflicts and breakdowns in communication.

- *Showing Personal Integrity*—Demonstrating personal integrity generates trust, whereas a lack of integrity can quickly undermine the best of teamwork orientations. People can seek to understand others, carry through on the little things, keep commitments, and clarify expectations but still fail to build trust by being inwardly duplicitous and pursuing a personal agenda. Be honest and open, and treat everyone by the same set of principles.

- *Apologizing Sincerely When a Mistake Is Made*—It is one thing to make a mistake. It is another thing not to admit it. People forgive mistakes. What is harder to forgive are the ill intentions and motives justifying any attempt to cover up. "If you are going to bow, bow low." The apology must be perceived as sincere and not simply as an automated lip-service response.

STUDY TOOLS 10

LOCATED IN TEXTBOOK

☐ Rip-out and review chapter review card

LOCATED AT WWW.CENGAGEBRAIN.COM

☐ Review key term flashcards and create your own from StudyBits

☐ Organize notes and StudyBits using the StudyBoard feature within Online

☐ Complete practice and graded quizzes to prepare for tests

☐ Complete interactive content within the exposition

☐ View chapter highlight box content at the beginning of each chapter

UNIVERSAL CONTROL CORP.

BACKGROUND

Universal Control Corp. is a leading supplier for process control systems and equipment used in a wide variety of production and distribution applications. You have taken a sales representative job with Universal, and having just completed training, you have been given a territory of your own. Your district manager has provided you with a list of accounts (on following page) as well as several boxes of notes and files that had been assembled and used by your predecessor. These are the accounts currently buying your products. You are expected to build these accounts and add new accounts to the list as you increase your territory's sales performance. You have summarized the account information into the summary set of account profiles, which follows.

QUESTIONS

1. Develop a portfolio classification of accounts and assess the allocation of sales calls your predecessor made over the past year.

2. What problems do you find with the previous allocation of calls on these accounts?

3. Based on your account classification analysis, suggest a new sales call allocation strategy that would make better use of your time in the territory.

ROLE PLAY

Situation: Read the provided Universal Control Corp. case material

Characters: Zack Hanna, salesperson for Universal Control Corp. Gage Waits, district sales manager and Hanna's immediate supervisor

Scene:

Location—Gage Waits' office at Universal Control Corp.

Action—Zack has just been assigned this territory and has completed an analysis of sales and customer files to profile the individual accounts and sales call allocation strategies utilized by the previous salesperson in the territory. Based

Account Name	Account Opportunity	Competitive Position	Annual Number of Sales Calls Last Year
Mueller Distribution	High	Low	30
Tri-State Specialties	Low	High	20
Birkey Paper Co.	Low	High	26
Normal Supply	Low	Low	12
Darnell Aggregate Products	Low	High	21
Reinhart Chemicals	High	High	26
ACCO Manufacturing	Low	High	23
Tri-State Manufacturing	High	Low	28
Ideal Engineering	Low	Low	11
Terracon	High	High	25
Lowry Foods	High	Low	26
SCS Industrial	High	High	27
Lowell Services	Low	High	18
Bowles and Sons	Low	High	21
American Foundry	High	Low	22
Hewitt & Associates	Low	Low	16
Bright Metals Inc.	High	High	22
Decatur Extrusions	Low	Low	14
King Chemicals	Low	High	22
Bear's Steel Corp.	Low	High	20
Hoffman Pharmaceuticals	High	Low	20
Barlow & Clark Systems	Low	High	18

on this information, Hanna has developed information responding to each of the three questions following the Universal Control Corp. case materials. This information includes a new sales call allocation strategy. Hanna is meeting with his sales manager to explain his new sales call allocation plan.

As Hanna, complete the three questions previously listed. Using this information, role play your interaction with your sales manager, Gage Waits, as you discuss and explain (1) your analysis of the previous salesperson's sales call allocation and (2) your new plans and how they will increase the effectiveness and efficiency of your selling efforts in this territory.

After completing the role play, address the following questions:

1. How might Hanna's sales allocation plan be different if he had used single-factor analysis (ABC analysis) instead of portfolio analysis?

2. Develop a sales call allocation plan using single-factor analysis. Compare the results of Hanna's portfolio analysis with the results of your single-factor analysis. Where and how are they different?

3. How might those differences translate into increased selling effectiveness and efficiency?

CHAPTER ROLE PLAY 10
Adding Value: Self-leadership and Teamwork

PAYROLL SYSTEMS, INC.

BACKGROUND

You are a business development specialist for Payroll Systems, Inc., an industry leader providing automated payroll processing and related record keeping for medium to large businesses having 15 or more employees. Your primary selling responsibility is new account development and working with existing accounts to increase share of account by selling them additional employment-related services. Account management and day-to-day servicing responsibilities are performed by a team of customer service representatives who work with customers through the phone and Internet. Due to a combination of rapid growth in the number of customers and several customer service representatives being new to the job, the resulting level of service provided by the customer service team has become inconsistent and all too often below the level you have promised to your customers. As a result, you are spending much of your time trying to patch over service shortcomings and working to win back accounts that have been lost to competitors due to the service problems. Not only are you losing business, but your own reputation—as well as Payroll Systems' reputation—is beginning to suffer.

ROLE PLAY

In discussing these problems with your sales manager, it was decided that you would meet with the team of customer service representatives in order to discuss and find a workable solution to the problems.

Role play how you would approach and initiate a positive discussion with the members of the customer service team that would generate improved experiences and outcomes for your customers and Payroll Systems, Inc. Remember to employ Covey's six teamwork skills discussed in this chapter.

ENDNOTES

1

1. Paul Nolan, "Mapping the Buyer's Journey," *Sales and Marketing Management* (March/April 2015): 33–38 and Hampus Jakobbson, "The Modern Face of Sales Shouldn't Include Selling," *Sales and Marketing Management* online at http://www.salesandmarketing.com, accessed May 4, 2015.

2. Jon M. Hawes, Anne K. Rich, and Scott Widmier, "Assessing the Development of the Sales Profession," *Journal of Personal Selling & Sales Management* 24 (Winter 2004): 27–38.

3. Synthesized from Eli Jones, Steven P. Brown, Andris A. Zoltners, and Barton A. Weitz, "The Changing Environment of Selling and Sales Management," *Journal of Personal Selling & Sales Management* 25 (Spring 2005): 105–111; Raymond W. LaForge, Thomas N. Ingram, and David W. Cravens, "Strategic Alignment for Sales Organization Transformation," *Journal of Strategic Marketing* (June–August 2009): 199–219; and Jagdish N. Sheth and Arun Sharma, "The Impact of the Product to Service Shift in Industrial Markets and the Evolution of the Sales Organization," *Industrial Marketing Management* 37 (May 2008): 260–269; For more discussion of trends in professional selling and sales management, see: Reza Sisakhti, "ATD Reveals New World-Class Sales Competency Model," posted May 8, 2015 on the Association for Talent Development website at http://www.td.org; Jonathan Farrington, "Five Magic Words and the Sales 3.0 Customer," posted May 14, 2015 at http://www.jonathanfarrington.com; and "The State of Sales Execution: 2015 Trends Report," published by consulting company Qvidian, available at http://www.qvidian.com.

4. "500 Largest Sales Forces in America: Manufacturing," *Selling Power* online at http://www.sellingpower.com/2014/selling-power-500/largest-sales-forces/manufacturing/ accessed May 5, 2015.

5. Joel Le Bon, *Competitive Intelligence and the Sales Force* (New York: Business Expert Press, 2014).

6. The basic approaches to personal selling had been in use for an undetermined amount of time before they were identified in two seminal sources: Robert F. Gwinner, "Base Theory in the Formulation of Sales Strategy," *MSU Business Topics*, (Autumn 1968): 37; and Mack Hanan, *Consultative Selling*, 1st ed. (New York, American Management Association, 1970).

7. James Buck, "Open-Ended Sales Questions: How to Get Your Prospect Talking," from the IMPACT Sales Training Blog published by The Brooks Group, May 6, 2015.

8. For more discussion of consultative selling, see Mack Hanan, *Consultative Selling*, 8th ed. (New York: American Management Association, 2011); Kevin J. Corcoran, Laura K Petersen, Daniel B. Baitch, and Mark F. Barrett, *High Performance Sales Organizations* (Chicago: Irwin, 1995): 44; and Jonathan Farrington, "Strategic Selling - All Three Roles Defined," http://www.superperformance.com/strategicsell.php (accessed August 12, 2011).

9. Terrence A. Hockenbull, "Getting the Edge in Professional Selling: Selling of Big-Ticket Items," *Business World*, April 24, 2015, p. S5/15.

10. Jon M. Hawes, Kenneth E. Mast, and John E. Swan, "Trust Earning Perceptions of Sellers and Buyers," *Journal of Personal Selling & Sales Management* 9 (Spring 1989): 1.

11. Interview by the authors with Blake Conrad, sales representative with Centurion Specialty Care.

12. Bureau of Labor Statistics, U.S. Department of Labor, *Occupational Outlook Handbook, 2010–2011 Edition,* http://www.bls.gov/oco (accessed August 16, 2011).

13. "Summary Report for: 41-4011.00 – Sales Representatives, Wholesale and Manufacturing, Technical and Scientific Products, http://www.onetonline.org/link/summary/41-4011.00 (accessed August 16, 2011); and Jennifer Salopek, "The Power of the Pyramid," *T + D* (May 2009): 70–75.

2

1. Sherry Kilgus, "Building Trust into High Level Alliances," *NAMA Journal* 34 (Winter 1998).

2. John Andy Wood, James S. Bales, Wesley Johnston, and Danny Bellinger, "Buyers' Trust of the Salesperson: An Item-Level Meta Analysis," *JPSSM* 28, no. 3 (Summer 2008): 263–283.

3. Michael Ahearne, Ron Jelinck, and Eli Jones, "Examining the Effect of Salesperson Service Behavior in a Competitive Context," *Journal of Academy of Marketing Science* 35 (2007): 603–616.

4. *Ibid.*

5. John E. Swan and Johannah Jones Nolan, "Gaining Customer Trust: A Conceptual Guide for the Salesperson," *Journal of Personal Selling & Sales Management* 5, no. 2 (November 1985): 39.

6. Robert F. Dwyer, Paul H. Schurr, and Sejo Oh, "Developing Buyer-Seller Relationships," *Journal of Marketing* 51 (April 1987): 11.

7. Lubomira Radoilska, "Trustfulness and Business," *Journal of Business Ethics* 79 (2008): 21–28.

8. This was the concluding point of the symposium on trust held by the National Account Management Association at Wake Forest University, September 24–26, 1997.

9. Kevin Bradford and Barton Weitz, "Salespersons' Management of Conflicts in Buyer-Seller Relationships," *JPSSM* 29, no. 1 (Winter 2009): 25–42.

10. Robert Petersen, "Consultative Selling: A Qualitative Look at the Salesperson Credibility Requirements," *AMA Educator Proceeding Enhancing Knowledge Development in Marketing* 8 (1997): 224.

11. *Ibid.*

12. Interview with Gary Schliessman, Gary Schliessman and Associates, January 26, 2009.

13. Interview with Darrell Beaty, Ontario Systems Corporation, February 29, 2000.

14. American Marketing Association's Code of Ethics. Reprinted by permission of American Marketing Association.

15. Gerhard Gschwandtner, "Lies and Deception in Selling: How to Tell When Customers or Prospects Are Lying to You," *Selling Power 15*, no. 9, 2010.

16. Sergio Roman and Salvador Ruiz, "Relationship Outcomes of Perceived Ethical Sales Behavior: The Customer's Perspective," *Journal of Business Research* 58 (2005): 439–445.

17. Reprinted by permission of Sales & Marketing Executives International, Inc. (http://www.smei.org). "SMEI Certified Professional Salesperson" and "SCPS" are registered trademarks of Sales & Marketing Executives International, Inc.

18. *Ibid.*

19. Thomas Ingram, Scott Inks, and Lee Mabie, *Sales and Marketing Executive Certification Study Guide* (1994).

20. Nigel F. Piercy and Nikala Lane, "Ethical and Moral Dilemmas Associated with Strategic Relationships between Business-to-Business Buyers and Sellers," *Journal of Business Ethics* 72 (2007): 87–102.

21. Interview with John Huff, Schering-Plough, November 15, 2004.

22. Nicholas McClaren,"The Personal Selling and Sales Management Ethics Research: Managerial Implications and Research Directions from a Comprehensive Literature Review of the Empirical Literature," *Journal of Business Ethics*, 112 (2013): 101–125.

3

1. http://www.salesforce.com/customers/stories/philips.jsp accessed on March 17, 2015.

2. Jakki Mohr and John R. Nevin, "Communication Strategies in Marketing Channels: A Theoretical Perspective," *Journal of Marketing* (October 1990): 36–51.

3. Alan S. Khade and Nathan Lovaas, "Improving Supply Chain Performance: A Case of Wal-Mart's Logistics," *International Journal of Business Strategy*, 9 (2009): 157–164.

4. Howard Stevens and Theodore Kinni, *Achieve Sales Excellence* (Avon, MA: Platinum Press, 2007).

5. Adapted from Jagdish N. Sheth, Bahwari Mittal, and Bruce I. Newman, *Customer Behavior: Consumer Behavior and Beyond* (Fort Worth, TX: The Dryden Press, 1999); Jagdish N. Sheth, Bruce I. Newman, and Barbara L. Gross, *Consumption Values and Market Choice: Theory and Application* (Cincinnati, OH: South-Western Publishing Co., 1991).

6. Bixby Cooper, Cornelia Drodge, and Patricia Daughtery, "How Buyers and Operations Personnel Evaluate Service," *Industrial Marketing Management* (February 1991): 81–85.

7. Adapted from Michael A. Humphreys and Michael R. Williams, "Exploring the Relative Effects of Salesperson Interpersonal Process Attributes

and Technical Product Attributes on Customer Satisfaction," *Journal of Personal Selling & Sales Management* 16 (Summer 1996): 47–58; Michael A. Humphreys, Michael R. Williams, and Ronald L. Meier, "Leveraging the Total Market Offering in the Agile Enterprise," *ASQ Quality Management Journal* 5 (1997): 60–74.

8. Howard Stevens and Theodore Kinni, *Achieve Sales Excellence* (Avon, MA: Platinum Press, 2007).

9. D. W. Merrill and R. H. Reid, *Personal Styles and Effective Performance* (Radnor, PA: Chilton Book Company, 1981).

10. Reprinted by permission of Growmark, Inc.

11. Henry Canaday, "In Transition," *Selling Power*, 31 (May/June, 2011): 38–41.

12. Wesley J. Johnston and Thomas V. Bonoma, "The Buying Center: Structure and Interaction Patterns," *Journal of Marketing* (Summer 1981): 143–156.

13. "Customers: The Future of B-to-B customer experience 2020," Walker Company, 2013.

14. *Ibid.*

15. Geoffrey James, "How to Make Technology Productive," Selling Power, June 2007, 65–68.

16. "Building Better Relationships at Dell," https://www.lattice-engines.com/wp-content /uploads/2015/03/LAT-CaseStudy_Dell-Web.pdf, accessed on April 1, 2015; Rachel King, "How Dell Predicts Which Customers Are Most Likely to Buy," *Wall Street Journal*, December 5, 2012.

17. Chris Koch, "ITSMA's Eight Big B2B Marketing Trends for 2011," ITMSA Web site, http://www .itsma.com/ezine/eight-b2b-marketing-trends-for-2011/, accessed May 11, 2011.

18. Ivana Taylor, "Business to Business Marketing Trends for 2011," DIY Marketers Web site, http:// www.diymarketers.com/2011/01/20/business-to -business-marketing-trends-for-2011/, accessed on May 11, 2011.

19. *Ibid.*

20. Robert McGarvey, "All About Us," *Selling Power*, 30 (November/December, 2010): 48–52.

21. Stevens and Kinni, *Achieve Sales Excellence*, (Avon, MA: Platinum Press, 2007).

22. Taken from Adrian Davis, "3 Secrets to Becoming Indispensable to Your Customers," (February 10, 2015), at https://www.salesforce.com /blog/2015/02/3-secrets-to-becoming-indispensable -your-customers-gp.html, accessed on April 29, 2015.

4

1. Alex Pirouz, "The Most Important Thing You Need to Know in Sales", alexpirouz.com.au, accessed on April 08, 2015.

2. Neil Rackham, *Spin Selling* (New York: McGraw Hill, 1998).

3. Thomas Ingram, Tubs Scott, and Lee Mabie, *Certification Study Guide* (New York: Sales and Marketing Executives International, 1994): 44–46.

4. Jerry Acuff and Wally Wood, *The Relationship Edge in Business* (Hoboken, NJ: John Wiley & Sons, Inc., 2004): 149–150; Geoffrey James, "How to Build Customer Relationships—An Interview with Jerry Acuff," *Selling Power* (March 2006): 43–46.

5. T. N. Ingram, C. Schwepker Jr., and D. Huston, "Why Salespeople Fail," *Industrial Marketing Management* 21 (1992): 225–230.

6. R. P. Ramsey and R. S. Sohi, "Listening to Your Customers: The Impact of Perceived Salesperson Listening Behavior on Relationship Outcomes," *Journal of the Academy of Marketing Science* 25 (Spring 1997): 127–137.

7. L. Barker, *Listening Behavior* (Englewood Cliffs, NJ: Prentice Hall, 1971): 30–32.

8. S. B. Castleberry and C. D. Shepherd, "Effective Interpersonal Listening and Personal Selling," *Journal of Marketing Theory and Practice,* 7/1 (Winter 1999): 30–39.

9. From *Effective Listening: Key to Your Success* by L. K. Steil, L. L. Barker, and K. W. Watson: 21. Reprinted by permission of The McGraw-Hill Companies.

10. *Ibid.;* Ramsey and Sohi, "Listening to Your Customers."

11. *Ibid.,* 72–73.

12. J. C. Mowen and M. Minor, *Consumer Behavior* (New York: Macmillan Publishing Co., 1997).

13. H. A. Taute, R. S. Heiser, and D. N. McArthur, "The Effect of Nonverbal Signals on Student Role-play Evaluations," *Journal of Marketing Education* 33 (April 2011): 28–40; J. S. Seiter, H. W. Weger, Jr., A. Jensen, and H. J. Kinzer, "The Role of Background Behavior in Televised Debates," *The Journal of Social Psychology* 150 (May 2010): 278–300; G. P. Thomas, "The Influence of Processing Conversational Information on Inference, Argument Elaboration, and Memory," *Journal of Consumer Research* 19 (June 1992): 83–92.

14. R. A. Avila, T. N. Ingram, R. W. LaForge, and M. R. Williams, *The Professional Selling Skills Workbook* (Fort Worth, TX: The Dryden Press, 1996): 83; H. A. Taute, R. S. Heiser, and D. N. McArthur, "The Effect of Nonverbal Signals on Student Role-play Evaluations," *Journal of Marketing Education* 33 (April 2011): 28–40; J. S. Seiter, H. W. Weger, Jr., A. Jensen, and H. J. Kinzer, "The Role of Background Behavior in Televised Debates," *The Journal of Social Psychology* 150 (May 2010): 278–300

15. Adapted from R. M. Rozelle, D. Druckman, and J. C. Baxter, "Nonverbal Communication," in *A Handbook of Communication Skills*, ed. O. Hargie (London: Croom and Helm 1986): 59–94; T. Alessandra and R. Barrera, *Collaborative Selling* (New York: John Wiley & Sons, Inc., 1993): 121–122; H. A. Taute, R. S. Heiser, and D. N. McArthur, "The Effect of Nonverbal Signals on Student Role-play Evaluations," *Journal of Marketing Education* 33 (April 2011): 28–40; J. S. Seiter, H. W. Weger, Jr., A. Jensen, and H. J. Kinzer, "The Role of Background Behavior in Televised Debates," *The Journal of Social Psychology* 150 (May 2010): 278–300.

5

1. Steven J. Meyer, "The Biggest Trend in Sales Today," http://www.forbes.com, January 1, 2015: 1–5; Suzanne Payer, "Marketing Conversations Yield Conversions at Ricoh," http://www .salesandmarketing.com (5/21/2014): 1–2.

2. Paul Nolan, "Mapping the Buyer's Journey," *salesandmarketing.com* (March 27, 2015): 1–3; Teresa Meek, "How to Build an Amazing Sales Team — For the Digital Age," www.forbes.com (April 23, 2015): 1–5.

3. Henry Canaday, "The Same Team," *Selling Power* (January/February 2011): 51–52.

4. Author interview with Gwen Tranguillo, Hershey Chocolate, U.S.A.

5. Author interview with Thomas Avila, Davis and Davis.

6. Jose Antonio Sanchez, "The Science Behind the Modern Sales Professional," socialmediatoday.com (April 16, 2015): 1–10.

7. E. A. Sullivan, "A Worthwhile Investment," *Marketing News* (December 2009): 10–11.

8. Author interview with Mark Thomas, United Insurance Agency.

9. H. Canaday, "In Transition," *Selling Power* (May/June 2011): 39–41.

10. H. Baldwin, "Big Change @ Big Pharma," *Selling Power* (May/June 2011): 29–32.

6

1. Joël LeBon, "Why the Best Salespeople Get So Lucky," *Harvard Business Review* blog, online at https://hbr.org/2015/04, accessed on April 13, 2015; Bill Bartlett, "What Will Make You a Better Salesperson in 2015?" *Daily Herald Business Ledger*, online at http://dhbusinessledger.com, accessed on November 30, 2015.

2. Edward Lowe Foundation, "How to Write a Sales Proposal," online Entrepreneur's Resource Center at http://edwardlowe.org/digital-library, accessed may 27, 2015; Geoffrey James, "How to Write A Winning Proposal," *Inc.* online at http://www.inc.com /geoffrey-james/how-to-write-a-winning-proposal. html, February 26, 2014; and Marc Wayshak, "5 Steps to Writing Better Sales Proposals," Salesforce.com blog at https://www.salesforce.com/blog/2014/08/5 -steps-to-writing-better-sales-proposals-gp.html, accessed on August 18, 2014.

3. Bob Kantin, *Sales Professionals Guide to Writing Winning Proposals* (Minneapolis, MN: Bascom Hill Publishing Company, 2007): 31–38.

4. Adapted from Bob Kantin, "Sales Proposal RATER," available from http://www.salesproposals .com, May 29, 2015.

5. For more discussion of customer value propositions, see James C. Anderson, James A. Narus, and Woutervan Rossum, "Customer Value Propositions in Business Markets," *Harvard Business Review* (March 2006): 91–99; Jill Konrath, "Value Proposition Generator," available at http://jillkonrath.com, downloaded May 25, 2015; and Norman T. Sheehan and Vince Bruni-Bossio, "Strategic Value Curve Analysis: Diagnosing and Improving Customer Value Propositions," *Business Horizons* (May 2015): 317–324.

7

1. Henry Canaday, "Engage in Sales," *Selling Power* (March 2015): 29, "http://www.clearside .com"; "Heartland," *Selling Power* (Special Edition 2014/2015): 12–14.

2. Author interview with Eric Brown, Malone Solutions.

3. Wright Wiley, "Eye-to-Eye Selling," *Selling Power* (May/June 2011): 27.

4. Author interview with Chris Pursell, DRE Medical.

5. Geoffrey James, "Lifesaving Sales," *Selling Power* (June 2009): 40–43.

6. Heather Baldwin, "Big Change @ Big Pharma," *Selling Power* (May/June 2011): 29–32.

7. Sharon Yoon, "A Site for Satisfied Eyes," *Sales & Marketing Management* (September/ October 2008): 10.

8. Adapted from Mary Ann Oberhaus, Sharon Ratliffe, and Vernon Stauble, *Professional Selling: A Relationship Approach* (Fort Worth, TX: The Dryden Press, 1995): 410–12.

8

1. Marc Deiner, "Don't Know When to Cut Your Losses and Leave the Negotiating Table? Look for These Telltale Signs," *Entrepreneur Magazine* (August 2003).

2. Brad Huisken, "Saving the Sale: Objections, Rejections and Getting to Yes," *JCK,* (January 2003): 62–63.

3. Tom Reilly, "Why Do You Cut Prices?" *Industrial Distribution* (June 2003): 72.

4. Robert Menard, "'Cost' Is About More Than the Price," *Selling* (July 2003): 9.

5. Kim Sydow Campbell and Lenita Davis, "The Sociolinguistic Basis of Managing Rapport When Overcoming Buying Objections," *Journal of Business Communication* (January 2006): 43–66.

6. Salespeople can forestall known concerns, but shouldn't bring up issues that aren't even a problem with a particular prospect. Thus, the need for good precall information gathering becomes obvious. See "Think Like a Consumer to Make Buying From a Cinch," *Selling* (November 2004): 8.

7. Mark Borkowski, "How to Succeed in Closing Deals, without Closing," *Canadian Electronics* 19 (May 2004): 6.

8. Neil Rackham, *Spin Selling* (New York: McGraw-Hill, 1988): 19–51.

9. Joan Leotta, "Effortless Closing," *Selling Power* (October 2001): 28–31.

10. Susan Del Vecchio, James Zemanek, Roger McIntyre, and Reid Claxton, "Updating the Adaptive Selling Behaviors: Tactics to Keep and Tactics to Discard," *Journal of Marketing Management* 20 (2004): 859–875.

9

1. "Salesforce Keeps Sysco on the Road to Growth," http://www.salesforce.com/customers/stories/sysco.jsp, accessed on March 27, 2015.

2. Howard Stevens and Theodore Kinni, *Achieve Sales Excellence* (Avon, MA: Platinum Press, 2007).

3. Michael Ahearne, Ronald Jelinek, and Eli Jones, "Examining the Effects of Salesperson Service Behavior in a Competitive Context," *Journal of the Academy of Marketing Science* 35 (December 2007), 603–616.

4. Robert W. Palmatier, Srinath Gopalakrishna, and Mark B. Houston, "Returns on Business-to-Business Relationship Marketing Investments: Strategies for Leveraging Profits," *Marketing Science* 25 (September–October 2006): 477–493.

5. Strativity Group, "The 2014 Customer Experience in Action Study," http://strativity.com/wp-content/uploads/2014/03/CEM-Benchmark-Study-2014-Executive-Summary.pdf, accessed on March 3, 2015.

6. John Tashek, "How to Avoid a CRM Failure," *eWeek* 18, no. 40 (October 15, 2001): 31.

7. Gerhard Gschwandtner, "What Makes Sales Relationships Work?" *Selling Power* 30 (May–June, 2010): 9.

8. Ahearne, Jelinek, and Jones, "Examining the Effect of Salesperson Service Behavior in a Competitive Context."

9. Katie Kazmierczak, "Strativity Releases Benchmark Survey Results—81% of Global Companies Are Not Committed to Customer Experience," http://strativity.com/customer-experience-benchmark-study-release-2014/, accessed on March 19, 2015.

10. Interview with John Haack, Saint-Gobain Containers, April 19, 2000.

11. Interview with Darrell Beaty, Ontario Systems Corporation, February 29, 2000.

12. Ross Beard, "11 Customer Retention Tactics with Real-World Examples," August 26, 2013, http://blog.clientheartbeat.com/customer-retention/, accessed on April 1, 2015.

13. Christine Galea, "What Customers Really Want," *Sales & Marketing Management* 158 (May 2006): 11.

14. Ken Dooley, "Why customers buy & why they don't: The latest research reveals …," http://www.customerexperienceinsight.com/why-customers-buy-why-they-dont/, accessed on October 3, 2015; Geoffrey James, "10 Things Every Customer Wants," http://www.inc.com/geoffrey-james/10-things-every-customer-wants.html, accessed on October 3, 2015.

15. "Advance CRM Solutions," *Personal Selling Power* (January/February 2007): 96–99.

16. "ADP Reps Make Every Moment a Selling Moment with Salesforce," http://www.salesforce.com/customers/stories/adp.jsp, accessed on October 3, 2015.

17. Stevens and Kinni, *Achieve Sales Excellence.*

18. Gabriel Gonzalez, Douglas Hoffman, Thomas Ingram and Raymond LaForge, "Sales Organization Recovery Management and Relationship Selling: A Conceptual Model and Empirical Test," *Journal of Personal Selling & Sales Management* 30 (Summer 2010): 223–237.

19. Eileen McDargh, "Provide Great Service," *Sales & Service Excellence* 10 (June 2010): 10.

20. John Werner, "Customer Complaints: A Gift in Disguise," *ASQ Six Sigma Forum Magazine* (May 2013): 28–30.

21. *Ibid.*

22. Sandra Rothenberger, Dhruv Grewal, and Gopalkrishnan R. Iyer, "Understanding the Role of Complaint Handling on Customer Loyalty in Service Relationships," *Journal of Relationship Marketing* 7, no. 4 (2008): 359–376.

23. Chia-Chi Chang, "When Service Fails: The Role of the Salesperson and the Customer," *Psychology & Marketing* 23 (March 2006): 203–224.

24. Robert D. Ramsey, "How to Handle Customer Complaints," *American Salesman* 55 (June 2010): 25–30.

25. John Graham, "Well, Thanks!" *Selling Power* 31 (March/April 2011): 12–15.

26. Stevens and Kinni, *Achieve Sales Excellence.*

10

1. Todd Lenhart, "Three Easy Ways to Improve Sales," salesandmarketing.com/articles, 26 December 2014. Accessed on March 12, 2015.

2. S. R. Covey, *The 7 Habits of Highly Effective People* (New York: Simon & Schuster, 2004).

3. T. Ingram, R. W. LaForge, R. Avila, C. H. Schwepker Jr., and M. Williams, *Sales Management: Analysis and Decision Making,* 7th ed. (Armonk, NY: M. E. Sharpe, 2009).

4. E. Babakus, D. W. Cravens, K. Grant, T. N. Ingram, and R W. LaForge, "Removing Salesforce Performance Hurdles," *Journal of Business and Industrial Marketing* 9, 3 (1994): 19–29.

5. J. Attaway, M. Williams, and M. Griffin, *The Rims-QIC Quality Scorecard* (Nashville, TN: The Quality Insurance Congress, 1998, 1999).

6. James Champy, "Selling to Tomorrow's Customer," *Sales & Marketing Management* (March 1999): 28.

7. Covey, *The 7 Habits of Highly Effective People.* Used with permission.

8. *Ibid.*

CHAPTER SUMMARY

1-1 Define personal selling and describe its unique characteristics as a marketing communications tool. Personal selling, an important part of marketing, relies heavily on interpersonal interactions between buyers and sellers to initiate, develop, and enhance customer relationships. The interpersonal communications dimension sets personal selling apart from other marketing communications such as advertising and sales promotion. Personal selling is also distinguished from direct marketing and electronic marketing in that salespeople are talking with buyers before, during, and after the sale. This allows a high degree of immediate customer feedback, which becomes a strong advantage of personal selling over most other forms of marketing communications.

1-2 Distinguish between transaction-focused traditional selling and trust-based relationship selling, with the latter focusing on customer value and sales dialogue. As summarized in Exhibit 1.2, trust-based selling focuses more on the customer than does transaction-focused selling. The salesperson will act as a consultant to the customer in trust-based selling, whereas transaction-based selling concentrates more on making sales calls and on closing sales. There is far more emphasis on postsales follow-up with relationship selling than with transaction selling, and salespeople must have a broader range of skills to practice relationship selling. Rather than pitching products to customers, trust-based selling focuses on establishing sales dialogue with customers, and salespeople not only communicate customer value but also help create and deliver customer value.

1-3 Understand sales professionalism as a key driver in the continued evolution of personal selling. The business environment is becoming more complex, competition is intensifying, and buyer expectations are increasing. These factors are creating more focus on sales professionalism in progressive sales organizations. Sales professionalism requires truthful, nonmanipulative tactics to satisfy the long-term needs of both the customer and the selling firm. To improve sales professionalism, salespeople can embrace high ethical standards, participate in professional organizations, and work from a continually evolving knowledge base.

1-4 Explain the contributions of personal selling to society, business firms, and customers. Salespeople contribute to society by acting as stimuli in the economic process and by assisting in the diffusion of innovation. They contribute to their employers by producing revenue, performing research and feedback activities, and comprising a pool of future managers. They contribute to customers by providing timely knowledge to assist in solving problems.

1-5 Discuss five alternative approaches to personal selling. Alternative approaches to personal selling include stimulus response, mental states, need satisfaction, problem solving, and the consultative approach. Stimulus response selling often uses the same sales presentation for all customers. The mental states approach prescribes that the salesperson leads the buyer through stages in the buying process. Need satisfaction selling focuses on relating benefits of the seller's products or services to the buyer's particular situation. Problem-solving selling extends need satisfaction by concentrating on various alternatives available to the buyer. Consultative selling focuses on helping customers achieve strategic goals, not just meeting needs or solving problems.

1-6 Understand the sales process as a series of interrelated steps. As presented in the figure below, the sales process involves initiating, developing, and enhancing customer relationships.

GLOSSARY TERMS

adaptive selling The ability of salespeople to alter their sales messages and behaviors during a sales presentation or as they encounter different sales situations and different customers.

AIDA An acronym for the various mental states the salesperson must lead customers through when using mental states selling: attention, interest, desire, and action.

business consultant A role the salesperson plays in consultative selling where he or she uses internal and external (outside the sales organization) sources to become an expert on the customer's business. This role also involves educating customers on the sales firm's products and how these products compare with competitive offerings.

combination sales job A sales job in which the salesperson performs multiple types of sales jobs within the framework of a single position.

consultative selling The process of helping customers reach their strategic goals by using the products, services, and expertise of the sales organization.

continued affirmation An example of stimulus response selling in which a series of questions or statements furnished by the salesperson is designed to condition the prospective buyer to answering "yes" time after time, until, it is hoped, he or she will be inclined to say "yes" to the entire sales proposition.

customer value The customer's perception of what they get for what they have to give up, for example, benefits from buying a product in exchange for money paid.

detailer A category of sales support personnel in the pharmaceutical industry working at the physician level to furnish information regarding the capabilities and limitations of medications in an attempt to get the physician to prescribe their product.

diffusion of innovation The process whereby new products, services, and ideas are distributed to the members of society.

economic stimuli Something that stimulates or incites activity in the economy.

inside sales Nonretail salespeople who remain in their employer's place of business while dealing with customers.

long-term ally A role the salesperson plays in consultative selling where he or she supports the customer, even when an immediate sale is not expected.

mental states selling An approach to personal selling that assumes that the buying process for most buyers is essentially identical and that buyers can be led through certain mental states, or steps, in the buying process; also called the formula approach.

missionary salespeople A category of sales support personnel who are not typically involved in

CHAPTER REVIEW 1

the direct solicitation of purchase orders. Their primary roles are disseminating information, stimulating the sales effort to convert prospects into customers, and reinforcing customer relationships.

need satisfaction selling An approach to selling based on the notion that the customer is buying to satisfy a particular need or set of needs.

order-getters Also called hunters, these salespeople actively seek orders, usually in a highly competitive environment.

order-takers Also called farmers, these salespeople specialize in maintaining current business.

personal selling An important part of marketing that relies heavily on interpersonal interactions between buyers and sellers to initiate, develop, and enhance customer relationships.

pioneers Salespeople who are constantly involved with either new products, new customers, or both. Their task requires creative selling and the ability to counter the resistance to change that will likely be present in prospective customers.

problem-solving selling An extension of need satisfaction selling that goes beyond identifying needs to developing alternative solutions for satisfying these needs.

revenue producers A role fulfilled by salespeople that brings in revenue or income to a firm or company.

sales dialogue Business conversations between buyers and sellers that occur as salespeople attempt to initiate, develop, and enhance customer relationships. Sales dialogue should be customer-focused and have a clear purpose.

sales process A series of interrelated steps beginning with locating qualified prospective customers. From there, the salesperson plans the sales presentation, makes an appointment to see the customer, completes the sale, and performs postsale activities.

sales professionalism A customer-oriented approach that uses truthful, nonmanipulative tactics to satisfy the long-term needs of both the customer and the selling firm.

stimulus response selling An approach to selling where the key idea is that various stimuli can elicit predictable responses from customers. Salespeople furnish the stimuli from a repertoire of words and actions designed to produce the desired response.

Salespeople must possess certain attributes to earn the trust of their customers and be able to adapt their selling strategies to different situations. Throughout the sales process, salespeople should focus on customer value, first by understanding what customer value is to the customer, then by working to create, communicate, and continually increase that value. Salespeople initiate customer relationships through strategic prospecting, assessing the prospect's situation, planning value-based sales dialogue, and activating the buying process. Relationships are then further developed through engaging prospects in a true dialogue to earn commitment from those prospects. Salespeople enhance customer relationships by following up after the sale, taking a leadership role, and sometimes working as part of a team to increase constantly the value received by the customer. The details of the sales process are covered in Chapters 5–10 in this book.

1-7 Describe several aspects of sales careers, types of selling jobs, and the key qualifications needed for sales success. Sales careers offer relatively good job security and reasonable opportunities for advancement. Salespeople get immediate job feedback which makes their jobs stimulating, challenging, and interesting. On a daily basis, salespeople are immersed in a dynamic environment with high levels of job variety, thus boredom is rarely an issue. Sales careers have long been associated with independence of action, although sales managers are now monitoring sales activities more closely to improve sales productivity. Sales compensation is tied closely to job performance, especially if commissions and bonuses are part of the pay package. We discuss six types of sales jobs in this chapter: sales support, new business, existing business, inside sales (nonretail), direct-to-consumer, and combination sales jobs. The skills needed for success will depend somewhat on the specific sales job. Among the most important qualifications for sales success are communications skills, a service orientation, problem solving, motivation and taking initiative, dependability, integrity, and adaptability.

TRUST-BASED SALES PROCESS

strategic orchestrator A role the salesperson plays in consultative selling where he or she arranges the use of the sales organization's resources in an effort to satisfy the customer.

technical support salespeople Technical specialists who may assist in the design and specification process, installation of

equipment, training of customer's employees, and follow-up technical service.

trust-based relationship selling A form of personal selling requiring that salespeople earn customer trust and that their selling strategy meets customer needs and contributes to the creation, communication, and delivery of customer value.

CHAPTER SUMMARY

2-1 What trust is. Trust is when an industry buyer believes that he or she can rely on what the salesperson says or promises to do in a situation where the buyer is dependent on the salesperson's honesty and reliability. One of the keys to a long-term relationship with any client is to create a basis of trust between the sales representative and the client organization.

The "trust" described here is beyond the typical transaction-oriented trust schema. Many issues—such as, Will the product arrive as promised? Will the right product actually be in stock and be shipped on time? Will the invoice contain the agreed-on price? Can the salesperson be found if something goes wrong?—are only preliminary concerns. In relationship selling, trust is based on a larger set of factors due to the expanded intimacy and longer-term nature of the relationship. The intimacy of this relationship will result in both parties sharing information that could be damaging if leaked or used against the other partner.

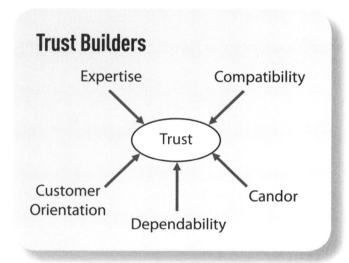

Trust Builders

Expertise → Trust
Compatibility → Trust
Customer Orientation → Trust
Dependability → Trust
Candor → Trust

2-2 Why trust is important. In today's increasingly competitive marketplace, buyers typically find themselves inundated with choices regarding both products and suppliers. Buyers are demanding unique solutions to their problems, which are customized on the basis of their specific needs. This shift toward relationship selling has altered both the roles played by salespeople and the activities and skills they exercise in carrying out these roles—the selling process itself. Today's more contemporary selling process is embedded within the relationship marketing paradigm. As such, it emphasizes the initiation and nurturing of long-term buyer-seller relationships based on mutual trust and value-added benefits. The level of problem-solving activity common to relationship selling requires deliberate and purposeful collaboration between

GLOSSARY TERMS

basis of the bargain When a buyer relies on the seller's statements in making a purchase decision.

candor Honesty of the spoken word.

compatibility/likeability A salesperson's commonalities with other individuals.

competitor knowledge Knowledge of a competitor's strengths and weaknesses in the market.

confidentiality The state of being entrusted with information from a buyer that cannot be shared.

contributions Something given to improve a situation or state for a buyer.

customer knowledge Information about customers that is gathered over time and from very different sources that helps the salesperson determine customer needs to better serve them.

customer orientation The act of salespeople placing as much emphasis on the customer's interests as their own.

dependability Predictability of a person's actions.

ethics The right and wrong conduct of individuals and institutions of which they are a part.

expertise The ability, knowledge, and resources to meet customer expectations.

express warranty A way a salesperson can create product liabilities by giving a product warranty or guarantee that obligates the selling organization even if the salesperson does not intend to give the warranty.

fairness Impartiality and honesty.

honesty Fairness and straightforwardness of conduct.

market knowledge Information salespeople must have if larger companies break their customers into

CHAPTER REVIEW 2

distinct markets; salespeople must be familiar with these markets to tailor their sales presentations.

misrepresentation False claim(s) made by a salesperson.

negligence False claim(s) made by a salesperson about the product or service he or she is trying to sell.

openness Completely free from concealment: exposed to general view or knowledge.

predictability A salesperson's behavior that can be foretold on the basis of observation or experience by a buyer.

price knowledge Knowledge tools salespeople must have about pricing policies in order to quote prices and offer discounts on products.

product knowledge Detailed information on the manufacture of a product and knowing whether the company has up-to-date production methods.

promotion knowledge Knowledge tools salespeople must possess to explain their firms' promotional programs.

reliability Consistency of a salesperson over time to do what is right.

security The quality of being free from danger.

service issues Concerns of the buyer that the salesperson should address.

technology knowledge Information salespeople must have about the latest technology.

trust The extent of the buyer's confidence that he or she can rely on the salesperson's integrity.

both parties. These joint efforts are directed at creating unique solutions based on an enhanced knowledge and understanding of the customer's needs and the supplier's capabilities so that both parties derive mutual benefits.

2-3 How to earn trust. Buyers are constantly asking themselves whether the salesperson truly cares about them. Salespeople can answer this question for the buyer by demonstrating trust-building activities. Trust can be earned by demonstrating expertise, dependability, candor, customer orientation, competence, and compatibility.

2-4 Knowledge bases help build trust and relationships. Salespeople do not have much time to make a first impression. If a salesperson can demonstrate expertise in the buyer's industry, company, marketplace, competitive knowledge, and so on, then the buyer will more likely be willing to listen to the salesperson if he or she brings valued experience to the buyer.

2-5 Sales ethics. Salespeople are constantly involved with ethical issues. A sales manager might encourage his or her salesforce to pad their expense account in lieu of a raise. A salesperson might sell a product or service to a customer that the buyer does not need. A salesperson might exaggerate the benefits of a product to get a sale. The list can go on and on. How a salesperson handles these situations will go a long way in determining the salesperson's credibility. One wrong decision can end a salesperson's career.

Three of the more popular areas of unethical behavior are deceptive practices, illegal activities, and noncustomer-oriented behavior.

- Deceptive practices: Salespeople giving answers they do not know, exaggerating product benefits, and withholding information may appear only to shade the truth, but when it causes harm to the buyer, the salesperson has jeopardized future dealings with the buyer.

- Illegal activities: Misusing company assets has been a long-standing problem for many sales organizations. Using the company car for personal use, charging expenses that did not occur, and selling samples for income are examples of misusing company assets. Some of these violations discovered by company probing also constitute violations of the Internal Revenue Service (IRS) law and are offenses that could lead to jail or heavy fines.

- Noncustomer-oriented behavior: Most buyers will not buy from salespeople who are pushy and practice the hard sell. Too much is at stake to fall for the fast-talking, high-pressure salesperson.

CHAPTER SUMMARY

3-1 Categorize primary types of buyers. Buyers are classified according to their unique buying situations that influence their needs, motivations, and buying behavior. The most common categorization splits buyers into either consumer markets or business markets. Consumers purchase goods and services for their own use or consumption whereas members of the business market acquire goods and services to use as inputs into manufacturing, for use in the course of doing business, or for resale. Business markets are further divided into firms, institutions, and governments.

3-2 Discuss the distinguishing characteristics of business markets. Among the more common distinguishing characteristics are consolidation, which has resulted in buyers being fewer in number but larger in size; demand that is derived from the sale of consumer goods; more volatile demand levels; professional buyers; multiple buying influences from a team of buyers; and increased interdependence and relationships between buyers and sellers.

3-3 List the different steps in the business-to-business buying process. This process begins with (1) recognition of the problem or need, (2) determination of the characteristics of the item and the quantity needed, (3) description of the characteristics of the item and quantity needed, (4) search for and qualification of potential sources, (5) acquisition and analysis of proposals, (6) evaluation of proposals and selection of suppliers, (7) selection of an order routine, and (8) performance feedback and evaluation.

3-4 Discuss the different types of buyer needs. Salespeople are better able to generate and demonstrate value-added solutions by understanding different types of buyer needs. The five general types of buyer needs are described as follows:

- *Situational Needs*—Needs that are related to, or possibly the result of, the buyer's specific environment, time, and place.
- *Functional Needs*—The need for a specific core task or function to be performed—the need for a sales offering to do what it is supposed to do.
- *Social Needs*—The need for acceptance from and association with others—a desire to belong to some reference group.
- *Psychological Needs*—The desire for feelings of assurance and risk reduction, as well as positive emotions and feelings such as success, joy, excitement, and stimulation.
- *Knowledge Needs*—The desire for personal development and need for information and knowledge to increase thought and understanding as to how and why things happen.

3-5 Describe how buyers evaluate suppliers and alternative sales offerings by using the multiattribute model of evaluation. Using the multiattribute model, buyers establish the attributes they perceive as important and evaluate the degree to which each of the specified attributes is present (or how well each performs) in a proposed solution. Each evaluation is then multiplied by the attribute's relative level of importance to calculate a weighted average for each attribute. These weighted averages are then totaled to derive an overall score for each supplier or product being compared. The product or supplier having the highest score is favored for purchase.

3-6 Explain the two-factor model that buyers use to evaluate the performance of sales offerings and develop satisfaction. The two-factor model is a special type of multiattribute model in

GLOSSARY TERMS

acceleration principle When demand increases (or decreases) in the consumer market, the business market reacts by accelerating the buildup (or reduction) of inventories and increasing (or decreasing) plant capacity.

actual states A buyer's actual state of being.

amiables Individuals who are high on responsiveness, low on assertiveness, prefer to belong to groups, and are interested in others.

analyticals Individuals who are low on responsiveness and assertiveness, analytical and meticulous, and disciplined in everything they do.

assertiveness The degree to which a person holds opinions about issues and attempts to dominate or control situations by directing the thoughts and actions of others.

business market A market composed of firms, institutions, and governments who acquire goods and services to use as inputs into their own manufacturing process, for use in their day-to-day operations, or for resale to their own customers.

buying teams Teams of individuals in organizations that incorporate the expertise and multiple buying influences of people from different departments throughout the organization.

competitive depositioning Providing information to evidence a more accurate picture of a competitor's attributes or qualities.

consumer market A market in which consumers purchase goods and services for their use or consumption.

deciders Individuals within an organization who have the ultimate responsibility of determining which product or service will be purchased.

delighter attributes The augmented features included in the total market offering that go beyond buyer's expectations and have a significant positive impact on customer satisfaction.

derived demand Demand in business markets that is closely associated with the demand for consumer goods.

desired states A state of being based on what the buyer desires.

drivers Individuals who are low on responsiveness, high on assertiveness and detached from relationships.

electronic data interchange (EDI) Transfer of data electronically between two computer systems.

expressives Individuals who are high on both responsiveness and assertiveness, are animated, communicative and value building close relationships with others.

functional attributes The features and characteristics that are related to what the product actually does or is expected to do.

functional needs The need for a specific core task or function to be performed.

gatekeepers Members of an organization who are in the position to control the flow of information

CHAPTER REVIEW 3

to and between vendors and other buying center members.

influencers Individuals within an organization who guide the decision process by making recommendations and expressing preferences.

initiators Individuals within an organization who identify a need.

knowledge needs The desire for personal development, information, and knowledge to increase thought and understanding as to how and why things happen.

modified rebuy decision A purchase decision that occurs when a buyer has experience in purchasing a product in the past but is interested in acquiring additional information regarding alternative products and/or suppliers.

multiattribute model A procedure for evaluating suppliers and products that incorporates weighted averages across desired characteristics.

must-have attributes Features of the core product that the customer takes for granted.

needs gap A perceived difference between a buyer's desired and actual state of being.

new task decision A purchase decision that occurs when a buyer is purchasing a product or service for the first time.

outsourcing The process of giving to a supplier certain activities that were previously performed by the buying organization.

psychological attributes A category of product characteristics that refers to how things are carried out and done between the buyer and seller.

psychological needs The desire for feelings of assurance and risk reduction, as well as positive emotions and feelings such as success, joy, excitement, and stimulation.

purchasers Organizational members who negotiate final terms of the purchase and execute the actual purchase.

requests for proposal (RFP) A form developed by firms and distributed to qualified potential suppliers that helps suppliers develop and submit proposals to provide products as specified by the firm.

responsiveness The level of feelings and sociability an individual openly displays.

situational needs The needs that are contingent on, and often a result of, conditions related to the specific environment, time, and place.

social needs The need for acceptance from and association with others.

straight rebuy decision A purchase decision resulting from an ongoing purchasing relationship with a supplier.

supply chain management The strategic coordination and integration of purchasing with other functions within the buying organization as well as external organizations.

two-factor model of evaluation A postpurchase evaluation process buyers use that evaluates a product purchase using functional and psychological attributes.

users Individuals within an organization who will actually use the product being purchased.

which further analysis of the multiple characteristics results in two primary groupings of factors: functional attributes and psychological attributes. Functional attributes are the more tangible characteristics of a market offering whereas the psychological attributes are primarily composed of the interpersonal behaviors and activities between the buyer and seller. The psychological attributes have been repeatedly found to have higher levels of influence than functional attributes on customer satisfaction and repeat purchase.

3-7 Explain the different types of purchasing decisions.

Straight Rebuy. Comparable with a routine repurchase in which nothing has changed, the straight rebuy is often the result of past experience and satisfaction with buyers purchasing the same products from the same sources. Needs have been predetermined with specifications already established. Buyers allocate little, if any, time or resources to this form of purchase decision, and the primary emphasis is on continued satisfactory performance.

Modified Rebuy. The buyer has some level of experience with the product but is interested in acquiring additional information regarding alternative products and/or suppliers. The modified rebuy typically occurs as the result of changing conditions or needs. Perhaps the buyer wishes to consider new suppliers for current purchase needs or new products offered by existing suppliers.

New Task. New task decisions occur when a buyer is purchasing a product or service for the first time. With no experience or knowledge on which to rely, buyers undertake an extensive purchase decision and search for information designed to identify and compare alternative solutions. Reflecting the extensive nature of this type of purchase decision, multiple members of the buying center or group are usually involved. As a result, the salesperson often works with several different individuals rather than a single buyer.

3-8 Describe the four communication styles and how salespeople must adapt and flex their own styles to maximize communication. Based on high and low levels of two personal traits, assertiveness and responsiveness, communication styles can be categorized into four primary types:

- Amiables are high on responsiveness and low on assertiveness.
- Expressives are defined as high on both responsiveness and assertiveness.
- Drivers are low on responsiveness but high on assertiveness.
- Analyticals are characterized as low on assertiveness as well as responsiveness.

Mismatched styles between a seller and a buyer can be dysfunctional in terms of effective collaboration and present significant barriers for information exchange and relationship building. Differences in styles manifest themselves in the form of differences in preferred priorities (relationships versus task orientation) and favored pace (fast versus slow) of information exchange, socialization, and decision making. To minimize potential communication difficulties stemming from mismatched styles, salespeople should flex their personal styles to better fit the preferred priorities and pace of the buyer.

3-9 Explain the concept of buying teams and specify the different member roles. In the more complex modified rebuy and new task purchasing situations, purchase decisions typically involve the joint decisions of multiple participants working together as a buying team. Team members bring the expertise and knowledge from different functional departments within the buying organization. Team members may also change as the purchase decision changes. Team members are described by their roles within the team: initiators, influencers, users, deciders, purchasers, and gatekeepers.

3-10 Understand means for engaging customers. To ensure that today's customers are fully engaged, selling organizations are turning to information technology, providing buyers with timely and relevant information, and adding value to buyer-seller relationships through various means.

CHAPTER SUMMARY

4-1 Explain the importance of collaborative, two-way communication in trust-based selling. The two-way exchange inherent in collaborative communication facilitates accurate and mutual understanding of the objectives, problems, needs, and capabilities of each of the parties. As a result, solutions can be generated that provide mutual benefits to all participants. This would not be possible without collaboration, and one party would benefit at the expense of the other. Although this might be good for the "winning" party, the disadvantaged party would be less inclined to continue doing business and would seek out other business partners.

4-2 Explain the primary types of questions and how they are applied in selling. Questions can be grouped into two categories according to (1) the amount of information and specificity desired and (2) the strategic purpose of the question.

- Questions typed by the amount of information and specificity desired include open-end questions, closed-end questions, and dichotomous questions. *Open-end questions* encourage the customer to respond freely and provide more expansive information. They are used to probe for descriptive information. *Closed-end questions* limit responses to one or two words and are used to confirm or clarify information. *Dichotomous questions* request the buyer to choose between specified alternatives.

- Questions typed by their strategic purpose include questions for (1) probing, (2) evaluative, (3) tactical, and (4) reactive purposes. *Probing questions* penetrate beneath surface information to provide more useful details. *Evaluative questions* uncover how the buyer feels about something. *Tactical questions* are used to shift the topic of discussion. *Reactive questions* respond to information provided by the other party and ask for additional details about that information.

4-3 Illustrate the diverse roles and uses of strategic questioning in trust-based selling. Questions are used to elicit detailed information about a buyer's situation, needs, and expectations while also providing a logical guide promoting sequential thought. Effective questioning facilitates both the buyer's and seller's understanding of a problem and proposed solutions. Questioning can also test the buyer's interest and increase his or her cognitive involvement and participation in the selling process. Questions can also be used to redirect, regain, or hold the buyer's attention subtly and strategically.

4-4 Identify and describe the five steps of the ADAPT questioning sequence for effective fact-finding and needs discovery. The five steps are assessment questions, discovery questions, activation questions, projection questions, and transition questions.

- *Assessment Questions* are broad, general, nonthreatening questions designed to spark conversation. Assessment questions elicit factual information about the customer's current situation that can provide a basis for further exploration and probing.

- *Discovery Questions* probe for details needed to identify and understand a buyer's problems and needs. The buyer's interpretations, perceptions, feelings, and opinions are sought in regard to his or her needs, wants, dissatisfactions, and expectations.

- Activation Questions help the customer evaluate the negative impact of an implied need. The objective is to "activate" interest

GLOSSARY TERMS

activation questions One of the five stages of questions in the ADAPT questioning system used to "activate" the customer's interest in solving discovered problems by helping him or her gain insight into the true ramifications of the problem and to realize that what might initially seem to be of little consequence is, in fact, of significant consequence.

active listening The cognitive process of actively sensing, interpreting, evaluating, and responding to the verbal and nonverbal messages of current or potential customers.

ADAPT A questioning system that uses a logic-based funneling sequence of questions, beginning with broad and generalized inquiries designed to identify and assess the buyer's situation.

assessment questions One of the five stages of questions in the ADAPT questioning system that do not seek conclusions but rather should address the buyer's company and operations, goals and objectives, market trends and customers, current suppliers, and even the buyer as an individual.

closed-end questions Questions designed to limit the customer's responses to one or two words.

dichotomous questions A directive form of questioning; these questions ask the customer to choose from two or more options.

discovery questions One of the five stages of questions in the ADAPT questioning system that follows up on the assessment questions; they should drill down and probe for further details needed to develop, clarify, and understand the nature of the buyer's problems fully.

evaluative questions Questions that use the open-and closed-end question formats to gain confirmation and to uncover attitudes, opinions, and preferences the prospect holds.

implication questions One of the four types of questions in the SPIN questioning system that follows and relates to the information flowing from problem questions; they are used to assist the buyer in thinking about the potential consequences of the problem and understanding the urgency of resolving the problem in a way that motivates him or her to seek a solution.

need-payoff questions One of the four types of questions in the SPIN questioning system that is based on the implications of a problem; they are used to propose a solution and develop commitment from the buyer.

nonverbal clusters Groups of related nonverbal expressions, gestures, and movements that can be interpreted to better understand the true message being communicated.

nonverbal communication The conscious and unconscious reactions, movements, and utterances that people use in addition to the words and symbols associated with language.

open-end questions Questions designed to let the customer respond freely; the customer is not limited to one- or two-word answers but is encouraged to disclose personal and/or business information.

probing questions Questions designed to penetrate below generalized or superficial information to elicit more articulate and precise details for use in needs discovery and solution identification.

problem questions One of the four types of questions in the SPIN questioning system that follows the more general situation questions to further probe for specific difficulties, developing problems, and areas of dissatisfaction that might be positively addressed by the salesperson's proposed sales offering.

projection questions One of the five stages of questions in the ADAPT questioning system used to encourage and facilitate the buyer in "projecting" what it would be like without the problems that have been previously "discovered" and "activated."

proxemics The personal distance that individuals prefer to keep between themselves and other individuals; an important element of nonverbal communication.

reactive questions Questions that refer to or directly result from information the other party previously provided.

serious listening A form of listening that is associated with events or topics in which it is important to sort through, interpret, understand, and respond to received messages.

SIER A model that depicts active listening as a hierarchical, four-step sequence of sensing, interpreting, evaluating, and responding.

situation questions One of the four types of questions in the SPIN questioning system used early in the sales call that provides salespeople with leads to develop the buyer's needs and expectations fully.

social listening An informal mode of listening that can be associated with day-to-day conversation and entertainment.

SPIN A questioning system that sequences four types of questions designed to uncover a buyer's current situation and inherent problems, enhance the buyer's understanding of the consequences and implications of those problems, and lead to the proposed solution.

tactical questions Questions used to shift or redirect the topic of discussion when the discussion gets off course or when a line of questioning proves to be of little interest or value.

transition questions One of the five stages of questions in the ADAPT questioning system used to smooth the transition from needs discovery into the presentation and demonstration of the proposed solution's features and benefits.

trust-based sales communication Talking *with* rather than *at* the customer. A collaborative and two-way form of communication that allows buyers and sellers to develop a better understanding of the need situation and work together to co-create the best response for resolving the customer's needs.

in solving discovered problems by helping the customer gain insight into the true consequences of the problem.

- *Projection Questions* encourage the buyer's decision making by "projecting" what it would be like if the problems or needs did not exist. They switch the focus from problems to benefits—the payoff for taking action and investing in a solution—and allow the buyer to establish the perceived value of solving the problem or need.

- *Transition Questions* smooth the transition to a subsequent phase in the selling process. They are typically closed end and evaluative in format and strive to confirm the buyer's desire to seek a solution and move forward with the buying/selling process.

4-5 Discuss the four sequential steps for effective active listening.

- *Sensing* is the first activity in active listening and involves receiving the message. Sensing is more than just hearing the message and requires concentration and practice.

- *Interpreting.* After sensing the message, it must be interpreted in terms of what the sender actually meant. In addition to meanings of words and symbols, the experiences, knowledge, and attitudes of the sender should also be considered.

- *Evaluating.* Effective communication requires the receiver to decide whether or not he or she agrees with the sender's message. This requires evaluating the results from the interpretation stage to sort fact from opinion and emotion.

- *Responding.* Collaborative communication requires listeners to provide feedback to the other party. Responses take the form of paraphrasing the sender's message, answering questions, or asking questions to gain additional details and clarification.

4-6 Discuss the superiority of pictures over words for explaining concepts and enhancing comprehension.

Pictures are more memorable than words. Using descriptive words to "draw" mental pictures can enhance understanding as they are more easily recalled than abstract words and symbols. Understanding and recall can be aided by providing illustrative analogies or stories to emphasize a key point and bring it alive in the buyer's mind. Rather than abstract words that convey only a broad general understanding, utilize words and phrases that convey concrete and detailed meaning. Concrete expressions provide the receiver with greater information and are less likely to be misunderstood than their abstract counterparts.

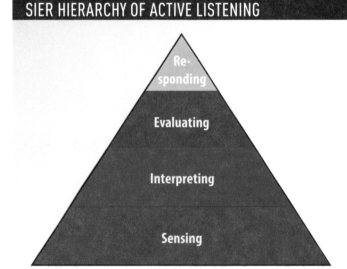

SIER HIERARCHY OF ACTIVE LISTENING

Re-sponding

Evaluating

Interpreting

Sensing

4-7 Describe the different forms of nonverbal communication.

Nonverbal behaviors are made up of the various movements and utterances that people use. These can be conscious or unconscious and include eye movement and facial expressions; placement and movements of hands, arms, head, and legs as well as body orientation; the amount of space maintained between individuals; and variations in vocal characteristics. Sensing and interpreting groups or clusters of nonverbal cues can provide a reliable indicator of the underlying message and intent. Evidence shows that nonverbal behaviors carry 50 percent or more of the meaning conveyed in the process of interpersonal communication.

CHAPTER SUMMARY

5-1 Discuss why prospecting is an important and challenging task for salespeople. Prospecting is important because market changes could cause current customers to buy less, customers could go out of business or be acquired by other firms, or business could be lost to competitors. Salespeople often fear rejection, and prospective buyers may be difficult to contact because they have never heard of a salesperson's firm, do not have the time to spend with all potential new suppliers, and are somewhat shielded by gatekeepers trained to limit access, and are not relying on salespeople to provide information early in their buying process.

5-2 Explain strategic prospecting and each stage in the strategic prospecting process. Strategic prospecting is a process to identify the best sales opportunities. The strategic prospecting process consists of generating sales leads, determining sales prospects, prioritizing sales prospects, and preparing for sales dialogue.

SALES FUNNEL

Generating Sales Leads

Qualifying Sales Leads

Determining Sales Prospects

Prioritizing Sales Prospects

Preparing for Sales Dialogue

Remaining Stages in
the Trust-Based Sales Process

GLOSSARY TERMS

advertising inquiries Sales leads generated from company advertising efforts.

centers of influence Well-known and influential people who can help a salesperson prospect and gain leads.

cold calling Contacting a sales lead unannounced and with little or no information about the lead.

company records Information about customers in a company database.

directories Electronic or print sources that provide contact and other information about many different companies or individuals.

electronic networking Using social media to help salespeople identify, gather information about, and communicate with prospects.

ideal customer profile The characteristics of a firm's best customers or the perfect customer.

inbound telemarketing A source of locating prospects whereby the prospect calls the company to get information.

introduction A variation of a referral where, in addition to requesting the names of prospects, the salesperson asks the prospect or customer to prepare a note or letter of introduction that can be sent to the potential customer.

lead management services Lists of targeted businesses with detailed contact and other information, as well as e-mail, direct mail, telephone, and Web-based marketing services, to connect with targeted leads.

noncompeting salespeople A salesperson selling noncompeting products.

outbound telemarketing A source of locating prospects whereby the

CHAPTER REVIEW 5

salesperson contacts the prospect by telephone.

qualifying sales leads The salesperson's act of searching out, collecting, and analyzing information to determine the likelihood of the lead being a good candidate for making a sale.

referral A name of a company or person given to the salesperson as a lead by a customer or even a prospect who did not buy at this time.

sales funnel or pipeline A representation of the trust-based sales process and strategic sales prospecting process in the form of a funnel.

sales leads or suspects Organizations or individuals who might possibly purchase the product or service a salesperson offers.

sales prospect An individual or organization that has a need for the product or service, has the budget or financial resources to purchase the product or service, and has the authority to make the purchase decision.

seminars A presentation salespeople give to generate leads and provide information to prospective customers who are invited to the seminar by direct mail, word of mouth, or advertising on local television or radio.

strategic prospecting A process designed to identify, qualify, and prioritize sales opportunities, whether they represent potential new customers or opportunities to generate additional business from existing customers.

strategic prospecting plan A salesperson's plan for gathering qualified prospects.

tracking system Part of the strategic prospecting plan that records comprehensive information about the prospect,

5-3 Describe the major prospecting methods and give examples of each method. Salespeople should use different prospecting methods. The major prospecting methods are cold canvassing (cold calling, referrals, and introductions), networking (centers of influence, noncompeting salespeople, and electronic networking), company sources (company records, advertising inquiries, telephone inquiries, trade shows, and seminars), and commercial sources (directories and lead management services).

5-4 Explain the important components of a strategic prospecting plan. A strategic prospecting plan consists of setting specific goals for the numbers of prospects to be identified, a regular schedule for prospecting activities, a tracking system to keep records of prospecting activities, an evaluation system to assess prospecting progress, and a positive and confident attitude.

5-5 Discuss the types of information salespeople need to prepare for sales dialogue. Salespeople must gather information about the prospect that will be used to help formulate the sales presentation. Buyer's needs, buyer's motives, and details about the buyer's situation should be determined. The more a salesperson knows about the buyer, the better chance he or she will have to meet the buyer's needs and eventually earn the commitment.

PROSPECTING PLANS ARE THE FOUNDATION FOR EFFECTIVE PROSPECTING

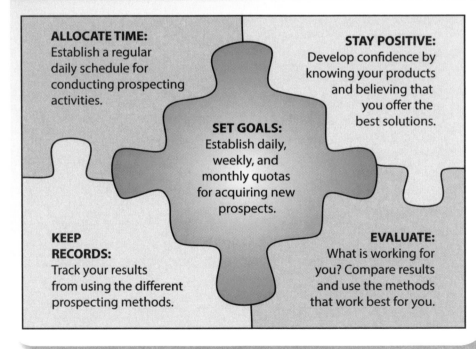

ALLOCATE TIME: Establish a regular daily schedule for conducting prospecting activities.

STAY POSITIVE: Develop confidence by knowing your products and believing that you offer the best solutions.

SET GOALS: Establish daily, weekly, and monthly quotas for acquiring new prospects.

KEEP RECORDS: Track your results from using the different prospecting methods.

EVALUATE: What is working for you? Compare results and use the methods that work best for you.

traces the prospecting methods used, and chronologically archives outcomes from any contacts with the prospect.

trade shows Events where companies purchase space and set

up booths that clearly identify each company and its offerings and that are staffed with salespeople who demonstrate the products and answer questions.

CHAPTER REVIEW 6
Planning Sales Dialogues and Presentations

CHAPTER SUMMARY

6-1 Explain why it is essential to focus on the customer when planning sales calls. Buyers are well informed and have little time to waste on unproductive conversations with salespeople. To optimize the time spent on sales calls, salespeople should focus on customer needs and how the customer defines value. Customers differ in how they define value, and salespeople must understand each customer's concept of value so that they can establish sales dialogues that are clear, credible, and interesting.

6-2 Understand alternative ways of communicating with prospects and customers through canned sales presentations, written sales proposals, and organized sales dialogues and presentations. Canned sales presentations include scripted sales calls, memorized presentations, and automated presentations. Effective canned presentations have usually been tested with real customers before an entire salesforce uses them. Canned sales presentations can be complete and logically structured. Objections are anticipated in advance, and appropriate responses can be formulated as part of the presentation. A written sales proposal is a complete, self-contained sales presentation. A sales proposal should be prepared after the salesperson has made a thorough assessment of the buyer's situation as it relates to the seller's offering. An organized sales dialogue, which could include a comprehensive sales presentation, is tailored to the prospect's particular situation and needs. It is a flexible format that allows for maximum input and feedback from the prospect. Sales dialogues and organized sales presentations (sometimes referred to as sales conversations) can take place over multiple sales calls before a purchase decision is made.

6-3 Discuss the nine components in the Sales Dialogue Template that can be used for planning an organized sales dialogue or presentation. The Sales Dialogue Template consists of nine sections: (1) prospect information; (2) customer value proposition; (3) sales call objective; (4) situation and needs analysis—linking buying motives, benefits, support information, and other reinforcement methods; (5) competitive situation; (6) beginning the sales dialogue; (7) anticipate questions and objections; (8) earn prospect commitment; and (9) building value through follow-up action. This template should not be used to develop a rigid script for a sales call. It is properly used to help the salespeople ensure that they are prepared to discuss all pertinent content with the customer.

6-4 Explain how to write a customer value proposition statement. A customer value statement should be simple so that it provides a clear direction for upcoming sales dialogues. Salespeople should not attempt to include all of their benefits in a value proposition statement—rather, they should choose the key benefit(s) that are likely to be most important to the specific customer. The value proposition should be as specific as possible on

GLOSSARY TERMS

benefits The added value or favorable outcome derived from features of the product or service the seller offers.

buying motive A need-activated drive to search for and acquire a solution to resolve a need or problem; the most important factors from the customer's perspective in making a purchase decision.

canned sales presentations Sales presentations that include scripted sales calls, memorized presentations, and automated presentations.

customer value proposition A statement of how the sales offering will add value to the prospect's business by meeting a need or providing an opportunity.

emotional buying motives Includes motives such as security, status, and need to be liked; sometimes difficult for salespeople to uncover these motives.

features A quality or characteristic of a product or service that is designed to provide value to a buyer.

organized sales dialogue Also known as the organized sales presentation. Unlike a canned sales presentation, an organized sales dialogue has a high level of customer involvement.

organized sales presentation A sales presentation that allows a salesperson to implement appropriate sales strategies and tactics based on customer research or information gathered during previous sales calls. Organized sales presentations feature a two-way dialogue with a high level of customer involvement.

rational buying motives Typically relate to the economics of the situation, including cost, profitability, quality, services offered, and the total value of the seller's offering as perceived by the customer.

CHAPTER REVIEW 6

sales call An in-person meeting between a salesperson or sales team and one or more buyers to discuss business.

sales dialogue Business conversations between buyers and sellers that occur as salespeople attempt to initiate, develop, and enhance customer relationships. Sales dialogue should be customer-focused and have a clear purpose.

sales dialogue template A flexible planning tool that assists the salesperson in assembling pertinent information to be covered with the prospect.

sales presentations Comprehensive communications that convey multiple points designed to persuade the customer to make a purchase.

written sales proposals A complete self-contained sales presentation on paper, often accompanied by other verbal sales presentations before or after the proposal is delivered.

listing tangible outcomes such as revenue improvement, cost containment or reduction gain in market share, process speed and efficiency, or the enhancement of a customer's strategic priority. Value proposition statements should promise only what can be consistently delivered. Strictly speaking, a customer value proposition in the planning stage is not a guarantee; it is a belief based on the salesperson's knowledge and best judgment. As the sales process moves along, appropriate guarantees can be made.

6-5 Link buying motives to benefits of the seller's offering, support claims made for benefits, and reinforce verbal claims made.

Organized sales dialogues and presentations should focus on the most important motives for a given buyer. Benefits must be linked to both rational and emotional motives, and supporting information must be given for each claim made of a benefit. In some cases, the claim needs support beyond the spoken word (e.g., through audio-visual content, printed collateral material, third-party research studies, or testimonials from satisfied customers).

6-6 Engage the customer by setting appointments.

Salespeople customarily set an appointment, at least for their initial sales calls on new prospects. Appointments may be arranged by telephone, e-mail, or a combination of phone and mail and should include a request for a specific time and date as well as the amount of time being requested for the sales call. Salespeople have a better chance of securing an appointment if they are prepared to give the customer a good reason for spending time with them.

CHAPTER SUMMARY

7-1 Describe the key characteristics of effective sales dialogue.

The most effective sales dialogues are planned and practiced by salespeople, encourage buyer feedback, focus on creating value for the buyer, present value in an interesting and understandable manner, engage and involve the buyer, and support customer value through objective claims.

Salespeople must diagnose customer problems before prescribing solutions.

Tetra Images/Getty Images

7-2 Explain how salespeople can generate feedback from buyers.

Salespeople can generate feedback from buyers by paying attention to nonverbal cues from the buyer and using check-backs or response-checks to get the buyer to respond to what the salesperson has said throughout the sales dialogue.

7-3 Discuss how salespeople use confirmed benefits to create customer value.

Salespeople can use the ADAPT or SPIN questioning process to interact with the buyer and determine what the buyer considers to be value. The salesperson then focuses on these confirmed benefits during the remainder of a sales dialogue.

7-4 Describe how verbal support can be used to communicate value in an interesting and understandable manner.

Salespeople need to communicate value in an interesting and understandable manner. This can be accomplished by varying the pitch and speed of speech, using examples and anecdotes, and including comparisons and analogies.

7-5 Discuss how sales aids can engage and involve buyers.

Sales aids are various tools salespeople

Salespeople need to vary the pitch and speed of their speech during sales dialogue.

Yuri Arcurs/Shutterstock.com

GLOSSARY TERMS

Atlas a web-based, comprehensive product that allows salespeople to manage all aspects of their sales career

analogy A special and useful form of comparison that explains one thing in terms of another.

anecdote A type of example that is provided in the form of a story describing a specific incident or occurrence.

case histories A testimonial in story or anecdotal form used as a proof provider.

check-backs or response checks Questions salespeople use throughout a sales dialogue to generate feedback from the buyer.

comparison A statement that points out and illustrates the similarities between two points.

confirmed benefits The benefits the buyer indicates are important and represent value.

electronic materials Sales aids in electronic format such as slides, videos, or multimedia presentations.

example A brief description of a specific instance used to illustrate features and benefits of a product.

preselling Salespeople present their product/service to individual buyers before a major sales dialogue with a group of buyers.

proof providers The use of statistics, testimonials, or case histories to support product claims.

sales aids The use of printed materials, electronic materials, and product demonstrations to engage and involve buyers.

statistics Facts that lend believability to product claims and are used as proof providers.

CHAPTER REVIEW 7

testimonials Proof providers that are in the form of statements from satisfied users of the selling organization's products and services.

verbal support The use of voice characteristics, examples and anecdotes, and comparisons and analogies to make sales dialogue interesting and understandable.

visual materials Printed materials, photographs and illustrations, and charts and graphs used as sales aids.

voice characteristics The pitch and speed of speech, which salespeople should vary to emphasize key points.

can use to engage and involve buyers, as well as generate interest and attention, and be more persuasive. Visual materials, electronic materials, and product demonstrations are the major categories of sales aids. It is important for salespeople to select the appropriate sales aids, but also to use them effectively. The SPES Sequence of stating the selling point and introducing the sales aid, presenting the sales aid, explaining the sales aid, and summarizing can help salespeople use sales aids successfully.

7-6 Explain how salespeople can support product claims. Salespeople need to be able to support the claims they make concerning their products. Proof providers, such as statistics, testimonials, and case histories, represent the major approaches for supporting product claims.

7-7 Discuss the special considerations involved in sales dialogue with groups. Sales dialogues with individual buyers and with groups have many similarities, but several important differences. Salespeople interacting with a group of buyers need to address their arrival tactics, how to handle questions, the proper use of eye contact, and how to communicate most effectively to the group and individuals within the group.

CHAPTER SUMMARY

8-1 Explain why it is important to anticipate and overcome buyer concerns and resistance. During the early years of selling, salespeople looked at sales resistance as a negative that was a likely indication that their buyer was not going to buy. This notion has changed over the years, and now objections are viewed as opportunities to sell. Salespeople should be grateful for objections and always treat them as indications that the prospect needs more information, and if the salesperson provides the correct information, they are moving closer to gaining the sale.

8-2 Understand why prospects raise objections. Some prospects are happy with their present suppliers and want to avoid the sales interview. In other instances, the salesperson has failed to qualify the prospect properly. A prospect who has recently purchased a product is probably not in the market for another. Sometimes, prospects simply lack information on the salesperson's product category, and they are uncomfortable making a decision.

Secretaries, assistants, receptionists, and even voicemail can block access to your prospect; they can be the gatekeepers.

OJO Images/Getty Images

8-3 Describe the five major types of sales resistance. Typically, objections include: "I don't need your product," "Your product is not a good fit," "I don't know your company," "Your price is too high," and "This is a bad time to buy."

8-4 Explain how the LAARC method can be used to overcome buyer resistance. LAARC allows the salesperson to listen carefully to what the buyer is saying. It allows the salesperson to better understand the buyer's

GLOSSARY TERMS

alternative/legitimate choice A selling technique in which the salesperson asks the prospect to select from two or more choices during a sales presentation.

assumptive close A sales closing technique in which the salesperson assumes that an agreement has been reached and places the order form in front of the buyer and hands him or her a pen.

commitment signals Favorable statements a buyer makes during a sales presentation that signal buyer commitment.

company or source objection Resistance to a product/service that results when a buyer has never heard of or is not familiar with the product's company.

compensation A response to buyer objections in which the salesperson counterbalances the objection with an offsetting benefit.

continuous yes close A sales closing technique that uses the principle that saying yes gets to be a habit; the salesperson asks a number of questions formulated so that the prospect answers yes.

direct commitment A selling technique in which the salesperson asks the customer directly to buy.

direct denial A response to buyer objections in which the salesperson tells the customer that he or she is wrong.

fear or emotional close A sales closing technique in which the salesperson tells a story of something unfavorable if the purchase is not made.

forestalling A response to buyer objections in which the salesperson answers the objection during the presentation before the buyer has a chance to ask it.

indirect denial A response to buyer objections in which the salesperson takes a softer more tactful approach when

CHAPTER REVIEW 8

correcting a prospect or customer's information.

LAARC An acronym for listen, acknowledge, assess, respond, and confirm that describes an effective process for salespeople to follow to overcome sales resistance.

minor-points close A sales closing technique in which the salesperson seeks agreement on relatively minor issues associated with the full order.

need objection Resistance to a product/service in which a buyer says that he or she does not need the product/service.

price objection Resistance to a product/service based on the price of the product being too high for the buyer.

product or service objection Resistance to a product/service in which a buyer does not like the way the product/service looks or feels.

questions or assess A response to buyer objections in which the salesperson asks the buyer assessment questions to gain a better understanding of what they are objecting to.

sales resistance Buyer's objections to a product or service during a sales presentation.

standing-room only close A sales closing technique in which the salesperson puts a time limit on the client in an attempt to hurry the decision to close.

success story commitment A selling technique in which a salesperson relates how one of his or her customers had a problem similar to the prospect's and solved it by using the salesperson's product.

summary commitment A selling technique in which the salesperson summarizes all the major benefits the buyer has confirmed over the course of the sales calls.

T-account or balance sheet commitment A selling technique in which a salesperson asks the prospect to brainstorm reasons on paper of why to buy and why not to buy.

Exhibit 8.2

Types of Objections

No Need	Buyer has recently purchased or does not see a need for the product category. "I am not interested at this time."
Product or Service Objection	Buyer might be afraid of product reliability. "I am not sure the quality of your product meets our needs." Buyer might be afraid of late deliveries, slow repairs, etc. "I am happy with my current supplier's service."
Company Objection	Buyer is intensely loyal to the current supplier. "I am happy with my present supplier."
Price Is Too High	Buyer has a limited budget. "We have been buying from another supplier that meets our budget constraints."
Time/Delaying	Buyer needs time to think it over. "Get back with me in a couple of weeks."

objections. After this careful analysis, the salesperson can then respond. The buyer feels the salesperson is responding to his or her specific concern rather than giving a prepared answer.

8-5 Describe the recommended approaches for responding to buyer objections. Salespeople have a number of traditional techniques at their disposal to handle resistance. Some of the more popular techniques include forestalling, or answering the objection before the prospect brings it up; direct denial; indirect denial, which softens the answer; translation or boomerang, which means to turn a reason not to buy into a reason to buy; compensation, or offsetting the objection with superior benefits; questions, which are used to uncover the buyer's concerns; and third-party reinforcements, which use the opinion or research of others to substantiate claims.

8-6 List and explain the earning commitment techniques that enhance secure commitment and closing. Many techniques can be used to earn commitment. Most are gimmicky in nature and reinforce the notion of traditional selling. Successful relationship-building techniques include the summary commitment, the success story commitment, and the direct commitment or ask for the order.

third-party reinforcement A response to buyer objections in which the salesperson uses the opinion or data from a third-party source to help overcome the objection and reinforce the salesperson's points.

time objection Resistance to a product/service in which a buyer puts off the decision to buy until a later date.

translation or boomerang A response to buyer objections in which the salesperson converts the objection into a reason the prospect should buy.

trial commitment An earning commitment technique that determines the attitude of your buyer toward a particular feature or benefit.

CHAPTER SUMMARY

9-1 Explain how to follow up to assess customer satisfaction.
Salespeople cannot be afraid to ask their customers, "How are we doing?"
Periodic follow-up is critical to long-term sales success. New customers
generally feel special because they have received a lot of attention from the
salesperson. Long-standing customers may feel neglected because the sales
rep has many new customers and cannot be as attentive as he or she was
previously. Routine follow-up to assess "How are we doing?" can go a long way
in letting a customer know that the salesperson cares and is willing to make
sure that he or she is satisfied.

**9-2 Explain how to harness technology to enhance follow-up
and buyer-seller relationships.** Effective salesperson follow-up should
include specific components designed to interact, connect, know, and relate
with their customers.

- *Interact*—The salesperson acts to maximize the number of critical encounters
  with buyers in order to encourage effective dialogue and involvement
  between the salesperson and the buyer.

- *Connect*—The salesperson maintains contact with multiple individuals in
  the buying organization influencing purchase decisions and manages the
  various touch points the customer has in the selling organization to assure
  consistency in communication.

- *Know*—The salesperson coordinates and interprets the information gathered
  through buyer-seller contact and collaboration to develop insight regarding
  the buyer's changing situation, needs, and expectations.

- *Relate*—The salesperson applies relevant understanding and insight to
  create value-added interactions and generate relationships between the
  salesperson and the buyer.

Salespeople have employed a variety of technology-based salesforce
automation tools in order to better track the increasingly complex
combination of buyer-seller interactions and to manage the exchange,
interpretation, and storage of diverse types of information. Among the
more popular salesforce automation tools are the many competing versions
of PC- and Internet-based software applications designed to record and
manage customer contact information. PC-based software applications such
as Maximizer, Goldmine, and ACT!, and Internet-based applications such as
Netsuite and Salesforce.com enable salespeople to collect, file, and access
comprehensive databases detailing information about individual buyers
and buying organizations.

GLOSSARY TERMS

adding value The process of improving
a product or service for the customer.

building goodwill The process of
converting new customers into lifetime
customers by continually adding value
to the product.

collaborative involvement A way to
build on buyer-salesperson relationships
in which the buyer's organization and the
salesperson's organization join together
to improve an offering.

communication A two-way flow of
information between salesperson and
customer.

connect The salesperson maintains
contact with the multiple individuals
in the buying organization influencing
purchase decisions and manages the
various touch points the customer has
in the selling organization to ensure
consistency in communication.

critical encounters Meetings in which
the salesperson encourages the buyer to
discuss tough issues, especially in areas
where the salesperson's organization
is providing less-than-satisfactory
performance.

**customer relationship
management (CRM) system** A
system that dynamically links buyers and
sellers into a rich communication network
to establish and reinforce long-term,
profitable relationships.

extranet Proprietary computer
networks created by an organization for
use by the organization's customers or
suppliers and linked to the organization's
internal systems, informational databases,
and intranet.

interact The salesperson acts to
maximize the number of critical
encounters with buyers in order to

CHAPTER REVIEW 9

encourage effective dialogue and involvement between the salesperson and buyer.

intranet An organization's dedicated and proprietary computer network offering password-controlled access to people within and outside the organization (e.g., customers and suppliers).

know The salesperson coordinates and interprets the information gathered through buyer-seller contact and collaboration to develop insight regarding the buyer's changing situation, needs, and expectations.

relate The salesperson applies relevant understanding and insight to create value-added interactions and generate relationships between the salesperson and buyer.

resilience The ability of a salesperson to get knocked down several times a day by a customer's verbal assault (i.e., complaint) and get right back up with a smile and ask for more.

service motivation The desire of a salesperson to serve customers each day.

service quality Meeting and or exceeding customer service expectations.

service strategy A plan in which a salesperson identifies his or her business and customers, what the customers want, and what is important to them.

9-3 Discuss how to take action to assure customer satisfaction.
Salespeople must follow up on specific relationship-enhancement activities such as:

(a) Providing useful information to their customers

(b) Expediting orders and monitoring a successful installation

(c) Training customer personnel

(d) Correcting billing errors

(e) Remembering the customer after the sale

(f) Resolving complaints in a timely manner

9-4 Discuss how to expand collaborative involvement.
The easiest way to expand collaborative involvement is to get more people involved in the relationship from both the buyer's and seller's firms.

9-5 Explain how to add value and enhance mutual opportunities.
The salesperson can enhance mutual opportunities by reducing risk for the buyer by repeated displays of outstanding customer service. The salesperson can also demonstrate a willingness to serve the customer over extended periods of time. The buyer needs to experience a willingness on the seller's part to go to bat for the buyer when things get tough.

CHAPTER SUMMARY

10-1 **The five sequential stages of self-leadership.** As a process, self-leadership is composed of five sequential stages. First, goals and objectives must be set that properly reflect what is important and what is to be accomplished. In turn, an analysis of the territory and classification of accounts is conducted to better understand the territory potential and prioritize accounts according to revenue producing possibilities. With goals in place and accounts prioritized, the third step develops corresponding strategic plans designed to achieve sales goals through proper allocation of resources and effort. The next stage maximizes the effectiveness of allocated resources by incorporating technology and sales force automation to expand salesperson resource capabilities. Finally, assessment activities are conducted to evaluate performance and goal attainment and to assess possible changes in plans and strategies.

10-2 **The four levels of sales goals and explain their relationships.** There are four different levels of goals that salespeople must establish to maximize sales effectiveness:

(a) Personal goals—what one wants to accomplish relative to oneself.

(b) Sales call goals—the priorities that are set out to be accomplished during a specific call.

(c) Account goals—the objectives relative to each individual account.

(d) Territory goals—what is to be accomplished for the overall territory.

Each level requires different types of effort and produces different outcomes, and each of the levels is interrelated and interdependent on the others. Ultimately, each higher-level goal is dependent on the salesperson setting and achieving the specific goals for each lower level.

10-3 **Techniques for account classification.** There are two basic methods of classifying accounts. In ascending order of complexity, these methods are single-factor analysis and portfolio analysis (also referred to as two-factor analysis).

- *Single-Factor Analysis*—Also referred to as ABC analysis, this is the simplest and most often used method for classifying accounts. Accounts are analyzed on the basis of one single factor—typically the level of sales potential—and placed into either three or four categories denoted by letters of the alphabet, "A," "B," "C," and "D." All accounts in the same category receive equal selling effort.

- *Portfolio Analysis (Two-Factor Analysis)*—This classification method allows two factors to be considered simultaneously. Each account is examined on the basis of the two factors selected for analysis and sorted into the proper segment of a matrix. This matrix is typically divided into four cells, with accounts placed into the proper classification cell on the basis of their individual ratings ("high" and "low" or "strong" and "weak") on each of the two factors. Accounts in the same cell share a common level of attractiveness as a customer and will receive the same amount of selling effort.

10-4 **The application of different territory routing techniques.** Territory routing plans incorporate information developed in the territory analysis and account classification to minimize unproductive travel time that could be better spent working with customers. Good routing plans minimize the backtracking and crisscrossing that would otherwise occur. Routing plans correspond to one of five common patterns.

- *Straight Line*—With a straight-line plan, salespeople start from their offices and make calls in one direction until they reach the end of the territory. At that point, they change direction and continue to make calls on a straight line on the new vector.

- *Cloverleaf*—Using the cloverleaf pattern, a salesperson works a different part of the territory and travels in a circular loop back to the starting point. Each loop could take a day, a week, or longer to complete. A new loop is covered on each trip until the entire territory has been covered.

- *Circular*—Circular patterns begin at the office and move in an expanding pattern of concentric circles that spiral across the territory. This method works best when accounts are evenly dispersed throughout the territory.

GLOSSARY TERMS

account classification The process of placing existing customers and prospects into categories based on their potential as a customer.

account goal A salesperson's desire of selling a certain amount of product to one customer or account in order to achieve territory and personal goals.

circular routing plan A territory routing plan in which the salesperson begins at the office and moves in an expanding pattern of concentric circles that spiral across the territory.

cloverleaf routing plan A territory routing plan in which the salesperson works a different part of the territory and travels in a circular loop back to the starting point.

deal analytics "Smart" sales force automation tools that analyze data on past customer behavior, cross-selling opportunities, and demographics to identify areas of opportunity and high customer interest.

external relationships Relationships salespeople build with customers outside the organization and working environment.

goals and objectives Something a salesperson sets out to accomplish.

high-tech sales support offices Offices set up at multiple locations where salespeople can access the wider range of selling technology than could be easily carried on a notebook or laptop computer.

internal relationships Relationships salespeople have with other individuals in their own company.

leapfrog routing plan A territory routing plan in which, beginning in one cluster, the salesperson works each of the accounts at that location and then jumps to the next cluster.

major city routing plan A territory routing plan used when the territory is composed of a major metropolitan area and the territory is split into a series of geometric shapes reflecting each one's concentration and pattern of accounts.

mobile salesperson CRM solutions Wireless broadband applications that enable users to view, create, and modify data on any Internet-capable device such as smartphones, netbooks, and laptops.

personal goals A salesperson's individual desired accomplishments, such as achieving a desired annual income over a specific period of time.

portfolio analysis A method for analyzing accounts that allows two factors to be considered simultaneously.

sales call goal A salesperson's desire of selling a certain amount of product per each sales call in order to achieve account, territory, and personal goals.

CHAPTER REVIEW 10

sales planning The process of scheduling activities that can be used as a map for achieving objectives.

self-leadership The process of guiding oneself to do the right things and do them well.

selling technology and automation Tools that streamline the selling process, generate improved selling opportunities, facilitate cross-functional teaming and intraorganizational communication, and enhance communication and follow-up with customers.

single-factor analysis A method for analyzing accounts that is based on one single factor, typically the level of sales potential.

straight-line routing plan A territory routing plan in which salespeople start from their offices and make calls in one direction until they reach the end of the territory.

teamwork skills Skills salespeople must learn to build internal partnerships that translate into increased sales and organizational performance.

territory analysis The process of surveying an area to determine customers and prospects who are most likely to buy.

territory goal A salesperson's desire of selling a certain amount of product within an area or territory in order to achieve personal goals.

- *Leapfrog*—When the territory is exceptionally large and accounts are clustered into several widely dispersed groups, the leapfrog routing methodology is most efficient. Beginning in one cluster, the salesperson works each of the accounts at that location and then jumps (often by flying) to the next cluster. This continues until the last cluster has been worked and the salesperson jumps back to the office or home.

- *Major City*—Downtown areas are typically highly concentrated with locations organized by a grid of city blocks and streets. Consequently, the downtown segment is typically a small square or rectangular area allowing accounts to be worked in a straight-line fashion street by street. Outlying areas are placed in evenly balanced triangles or pie-shaped quadrants, with one quadrant being covered at a time in either a straight-line or cloverleaf pattern.

10-5 The usefulness of different types of selling technology and automation.

Properly applied, selling technology spurs creativity and innovation, streamlines the selling process, generates new selling opportunities, facilitates communication, and enhances customer follow-up. Salespeople must not only master the technology itself but they must also understand when and where it can be applied most effectively. A wide selection of different-sized computers is at the center of most selling technologies. They provide the production tools for generating reports, proposals, and graphic-enhanced presentations. Spreadsheet applications and database applications facilitate the analysis of customer accounts and searching for information needed by customers. Contact management software enables the salesperson to gather and organize account information and schedule calls. Access to the Internet and World Wide Web provide salespeople access to an assortment of public and corporate networks that enable one to communicate, research, and access company information and training from anywhere in the world. Smart-phones put salespeople in touch with customers, the home office, and even the family while traveling cross-country or just walking across the parking lot to make a customer call. Voice mail and texting void the previous restrictions of time and place that accompanied the requirement to make personal contact. Messages can now be left and received 24 hours a day and seven days a week. High-tech sales support offices provide geographically dispersed salespeople with a common standard of computing technology, access to software applications, and portals to organizational networks at offices around the world. Wherever they may be working, they have the tools and capabilities identical to those available to them in their home offices.

10-6 Increasing customer value through artwork.

With increasing customer expectations and growing complexity of selling situations, teamwork has become critical for maximizing customer focus and sales performance. Teamwork results in synergies that produce greater outcomes and results for all parties than would be possible with multiple individuals acting independently of one another. Highly effective sales professionals work with customers to develop a mutual understanding of the customer's situation, needs, possibilities, and expectations. Based on that mutual understanding, the salesperson assembles a team of individuals—experts from across the selling organization—who work together in creating a product response that delivers more unique customer value than competitors' offerings. In delivering this unique and added value for customers, salespeople often find themselves working with other individuals in sales, marketing, design and manufacturing, administrative support, shipping, and customer service. Teamwork is built on reciprocal trust enhanced through six teamwork skills: (1) Understanding the other individuals; (2) Attending to the little things; (3) Keeping commitments; (4) Clarifying expectations; (5) Showing personal integrity; and (6) Apologizing sincerely when a mistake is made.

10-7 The six skills for building internal relationships and teams.

(a) *Understanding the Other Individuals*—Fully understanding and considering the other individuals in the partnership is necessary to know what is important to them. What is important to them must also be important to the salesperson if the partnership is to grow and be effective.

(b) *Attending to the Little Things*—The little kindnesses and courtesies are small in size, but great in importance. Properly attended to and nurtured, they enhance the interrelationships. However, when neglected or misused, they can destroy the relationship very quickly.

(c) *Keeping Commitments*—We build hopes and plans around the promises and commitments made to us by others. When a commitment is not kept, disappointment and problems result and credibility and trust suffer major damage that will be difficult or impossible to repair.

(d) *Clarifying Expectations*—The root cause of most relational difficulties can be found in ambiguous expectations regarding roles and goals. By clarifying goals and priorities as well as who is responsible for different activities up front, the hurt feelings, disappointments, and lost time resulting from misunderstandings and conflict can be prevented.

(e) *Showing Personal Integrity*—Demonstrating personal integrity generates trust. Be honest, open, and treat everyone by the same set of principles.

(f) *Apologizing Sincerely When a Mistake Is Made*—It is one thing to make a mistake. It is another thing to not admit it. People forgive mistakes, but ill intentions and cover-ups can destroy trust.

INTRODUCTION

The National Copier Company (NCC) sells a variety of copiers to small and medium-sized businesses. NCC has been in business for five years and has been growing at a steady pace. NCC differentiates itself from other copier companies by customizing its products to meet the specific needs of each customer and by providing excellent customer service. The company's salesforce plays a key role in creating value and managing customer relationships.

Brenda Smith has been a NCC salesperson for the past three years. She has steadily improved her sales performance during her time with NCC, and now is in the top one-fourth of all NCC sales representatives as measured by two key metrics: overall sales volume and customer satisfaction. Brenda has been especially successful with small professional firms, such as attorneys, architects, accountants, and medical professionals. She is excited to begin her fourth year with NCC and has established challenging goals to increase sales from existing customers and to generate new customers.

Brenda recently met with Pat Brady, her sales manager and was quite excited about the upcoming year. Pat had told Brenda that she was progressing toward a possible promotion into sales training if she had another good year in her sales position. In addition, Pat gave Brenda this feedback: "Brenda, I think you are doing a fine job with your customers, but I would like to see you become more of a consultative salesperson in the coming year. I would also like for you to sharpen your group communications skills, as that will be important if you are promoted into sales training. We will talk about the specifics more as the year goes along. Meanwhile, thanks for your results to date and good luck with the upcoming year."

QUESTIONS

1. Brenda had been thinking about Pat Brady's feedback that directed her to become more of a consultative salesperson. In thinking about her own selling approaches, she knew that she had been concentrating on the needs satisfaction and problem-solving approaches. What must Brenda do to become a more consultative salesperson?

2. Three months later, Brenda was having mixed results with the consultative selling approach. She was finding that some of her customers just wanted the convenience of having a copier in their offices, and did not seem eager to discuss their strategic goals. She was beginning to wonder about the consultative selling model, thinking it was not such a good idea after all. What recommendations do you have for Brenda?

3. A month before the annual meeting for all NCC sales representatives, Pat Brady told Brenda, "For the upcoming meeting, I want you to prepare a 10 minute presentation about the pros and cons of the basic selling approaches that we use at NCC compared to our competitors." NCC's sales training program

CHAPTER CONTINUING CASE 1

advocated the use of needs satisfaction, problem solving, and consultative selling. Many of NCC's key competitors used the same approaches. However some of the toughest competitors used stimulus response and mental states (AIDA) approaches. This latter category of competitors often stressed lower prices and utilized telemarketing instead of field sales representatives in selling their products. Put yourself in Brenda's role and prepare the presentation requested by Pat Brady.

4. Early in the year, Pat Brady told Brenda that her efforts were needed to gain more exposure for NCC's college recruiting program: "Brenda, I want you to be part of a two-person team to help with recruiting on two college campuses in your territory. The other team member will be an experienced recruiter who had sales experience before moving into recruiting. The two of you should seek out opportunities as guest speakers for classes and student organizations. Your role will be to talk about how sales can be a great place to start a career, and for some, a great career path. Think about the future of selling and what it takes to be successful and share your thoughts with students." Acting as Brenda, make note of ten key points you would like to make about the future of professional selling and what it takes to be successful.

NOTES

_____

_____

_____

_____

_____

_____

_____

_____

_____

_____

_____

_____

_____

_____

CHAPTER CONTINUING CASE 2
Building Trust and Sales Ethics

BUILDING TRUST

Because the National Copier Company (NCC) has only been in business for five years, Brenda Smith is concerned that most of her competitors are older than she is. The prospective customers she has been calling on state that they know they can count on her competitors, because they have a long track record. As NCC expands into new markets some of her prospects are not familiar with her company. One prospective customer, who works for one of the most prestigious and largest medical offices (30 doctors) in the area, told her he has been buying copiers from the same company for over twenty-five years. He also told her that his sales representative for the company has been calling on him for over seven years, and he knows when he calls on his copier supplier for advice he can count on him for a solid recommendation. Brenda realizes these are going to be tough accounts to crack.

Brenda does have an advantage due to the high quality of NCC products. In a recent trade publication, NCC's copiers tied for first in the industry on ratings of copier quality and dependability. NCC was also given a high rating for service. Brenda has had this information for two weeks now and has brought it up in conversations with her prospective customers without much success. To make matters worse, one of her competitors must have started rumors about NCC. In the past month, she has heard the following rumors:

"NCC is going out of business because of financial troubles."

"NCC has missed several delivery deadlines with customers."

"NCC's copiers have a software glitch that cannot be corrected."

"NCC has cut its service staff."

Brenda knows these rumors are not true, but prospects might believe the rumors. At a recent sales meeting, Brenda's manager suggested that their competitors must be getting nervous about NCC's success, causing them to start such vicious rumors.

Brenda is sitting at her desk trying to figure out what to do next and she is not exactly sure how to proceed.

QUESTIONS

1. What would you recommend Brenda do to handle the challenges she faces?

2. Brenda appears to have an advantage with her products and services. Develop a plan for Brenda to build trust in NCC with prospective customers.

3. What do you recommend Brenda do to compete effectively against competitors that have a long and successful track record?

4. How should Brenda go about handling the rumor mill?

NOTES

UNDERSTANDING TOM PENDERS

It was Monday afternoon and Brenda Smith was very excited. She just got off the phone with Tom Penders, the administrator in charge of a large medical office in her territory. After an introductory letter and several follow-up phone calls, Tom Penders finally agreed to meet with Brenda next Friday to discuss the possibility of replacing his organization's old copiers, as well as adding new copiers to keep pace with his organization's rapid growth. The primary purpose of the meeting was for Tom to learn more about the National Copier Company and its products and for Brenda to learn more about Tom's company and its specific needs.

When Brenda arrived about 10 minutes early for her meeting with Tom Penders at the medical offices on Friday, she was greeted by a receptionist who asked her to be seated. Ten minutes passed and Brenda was promptly shown to Tom's office. Brenda couldn't help but notice how organized Tom's office was. It appeared to Brenda that Tom was a man of detail. First, Tom explained that the medical offices housed over 25 doctors specializing in a variety of fields. They occupied two floors and were planning to expand to the vacant third floor in the near future. Currently, they were organized into four divisions with an office professional assigned to approximately six doctors for each division. Each division ran its own "office" with a separate copier and administrative facilities. Tom also had an assistant and a copier. Upon concluding his overview, Tom provided Brenda with an opportunity to ask questions. After this, Tom systematically went down a list of questions he had about NCC, its products, and Brenda herself. Following this, Tom had his assistant take Brenda on a tour of the facility so she could overview their processes. Before leaving, Tom agreed to meet with Brenda in two weeks.

Based on her conversation with Tom, Brenda did not find Tom to be a particularly personable individual. In fact, she found him to be somewhat cool and aloof, both deliberate in his communication and actions. Yet, Tom was willing to learn how NCC could help his medical office. While Brenda preferred communicating with someone more personable and open, such as herself, she was determined to find a way to win Tom's business.

QUESTIONS

1. What type of communication style do you believe that Tom exhibits? What are the characteristics of this communication style?

2. Based on your understanding of Tom's communication style, outline a plan for selling to Tom Penders.

3. Identify other members of Tom Penders' organization that may play a role in the buying decision and explain the role they might play. How should Brenda handle these individuals?

4. Explain the types of buyer needs that will be most important in this selling situation.

NOTES

SHARPENING THE SELLING TOOLS

Brenda Smith is working in the office this morning preparing for tomorrow's sales call with Gage Waits, managing partner, and Anna Kate Autry, operations manager, at Energy Based Funds LLC. Energy Based Funds is a major investment banking organization specializing in managing and marketing a variety of energy based mutual funds. The company operates throughout the U.S. and employs 175 people with offices occupying the top three floors of a major office building in the heart of the financial district. For the past several years, Energy Based Funds has been leasing and purchasing office equipment from Altima Systems, one of Brenda's biggest competitors. Brenda has been working her network in order to get a chance to begin a sales dialogue with Energy Based Funds and she finally has an appointment with the main players on the purchasing team – Waits and Autry.

Brenda knows that planning is a key part of success in selling and is diligently working on her strategy and plans in preparation for tomorrow's sales call with Waits and Autry at Energy Based Funds. According to the Sales Call Plan that Brenda is developing, the purpose of this initial meeting is twofold: (1) to discover more about Energy Based Funds' current operations, future plans, and the nature of their use of and needs for copiers; (2) to begin acquainting Waits and Autry with NCC and the value they can provide Energy Based Funds. At this point in her sales call plan, Brenda is considering the different pieces of information she needs to get from the dialogue and what questions she might use to elicit that information from Waits and Autry.

QUESTIONS

1. Based on the purpose of probing questions explained in your text, explain how Brenda should utilize probing types of questions in her initial sales dialogue with Waits and Autry at Energy Based Funds. Consider the types of information Brenda needs and develop several illustrative examples of probing questions Brenda might use.

2. Evaluative questions are also effective in sales conversations. Explain the purpose of evaluative questions and how Brenda might effectively utilize them in this initial sales call. Provide several illustrative examples of evaluative questions Brenda could use.

3. The ADAPT questioning system is a logic-based sequence of questions designed for effective fact-finding and gaining information about a buyer's situation. Develop a series of ADAPT questions that Brenda might use in her sales call to develop the information she needs regarding Energy Based Funds, their operations, and needs for copiers.

4. What recommendations would you provide Brenda regarding nonverbal communication and how she might use it for more effective communication in this sales call?

NOTES

FISHING FOR NEW CUSTOMERS

Brenda Smith has been very successful at getting existing customers to upgrade or purchase new copiers during the past two months. She is, however, disappointed in her efforts to get new customers. In order to add more new customers, Brenda has been spending a great deal of time prospecting. These efforts have produced a large number of leads. Once she generates a lead, she contacts the firm and tries to set up an appointment. Unfortunately, most of these leads are not interested in talking about copiers and are not willing to schedule a meeting with her. This has been so frustrating that she decided to make several cold calls this week to see if this would be a good way to get to meet with prospective customers. The cold calls were also not very successful and were extremely time consuming. Brenda did finally get a few leads to agree to meet with her, but these appointments were not very productive. The leads were typically satisfied with the copiers they were using and were not interested in learning about NCC copiers.

Pat Brady, her sales manager, accompanied her on a recent sales call to a lead. After the sales call, Pat expressed his disappointment that they had really wasted their time with this meeting. Pat then asked Brenda about her prospecting process, because it was clear that she was not identifying and spending her time with the best sales opportunities. Her approach was not working well and was taking a lot of time. If she continued doing the same things, Brenda was not likely to generate many new customers and might lose some existing customers, because she was spending too much of her time prospecting.

Brenda realizes that she must improve her prospecting process, but is not sure exactly how to proceed.

QUESTIONS

1. What is Brenda doing wrong? What would you recommend Brenda do to improve her prospecting efforts?

2. Explain the strategic prospecting process to Brenda and discuss how she can implement it.

3. What secondary lead sources would you recommend Brenda use to identify the best attorneys, architects, accountants, and medical professionals as prospects?

4. What specific types of information should Brenda obtain before contacting a qualified prospect?

CHAPTER CONTINUING CASE 5

CHAPTER CONTINUING CASE 6
Planning Sales Dialogues and Presentations

CUSTOM PRODUCT, CUSTOM PRESENTATION

During the past three months, Brenda had improved her prospecting process. She was identifying more prospects that represented better sales opportunities. Brenda knew that it is important to plan her sales calls in advance to maximize the time she spent in face-to-face selling. In this selling environment, most customers were not interested in all of the features of Brenda's products. Brenda had to determine what was important to each customer, and customize her presentations accordingly. Further, she had to clearly communicate the benefits of her products, and not overwhelm potential buyers with too much technical language. Assume that Brenda has an appointment with EFP, a non-profit organization that raises money to promote environmentally friendly practices such as recycling. The organization uses email, Web-based communications, and direct mail campaigns to reach potential donors. EFP currently uses an older-generation analog copier. Brenda hopes to sell EFP a modern digital copier that offers several advantages over the analog copier currently in use.

QUESTIONS

1. Using an Internet search engine such as Google, find the general benefits of digital copiers over analog copiers. You might enter "benefits of digital copiers" in the search engine, or examine data from copier providers such as Ricoh, Canon, or Xerox to find these benefits. List 6–8 potential benefits of a digital copier to EFP.

2. From the listing developed in # 1, select four benefits. For each benefit, write a sentence or two that Brenda might use to communicate these benefits during her sales call with EFP.

3. For the four benefits identified in # 2, describe what information Brenda should have on hand when she makes the sales call on the EFP buyer. Also describe how this information would be best communicated, i.e., what support materials will Brenda need to enhance her verbal communications?

4. Assume that the buyer acknowledged interest in at least two of benefits identified in # 2. Write a realistic buyer-seller dialogue of Brenda's interaction with the EFP buyer concerning these benefits.

NOTES

UP FOR THE CHALLENGE

Brenda has a meeting today with the office manager at the law firm Abercrombie and Wilson (A&L). A&L is a local law firm with five attorneys and one main office. During her initial telephone conversation, the office manager indicated that the firm was reasonably satisfied with their current copiers, but that he was always looking for ways to increase office productivity. He also mentioned that he was a little concerned that the firm was paying for many copier features that were not really used. The law firm needed to make a lot of legal-sized copies, and be able to collate and staple them. There was little need for other "bells and whistles." It was also important that a copier was dependable, because the law firm made many copies each day. When the copier did break down, fast service was needed to get it repaired as soon as possible.

The office manager had some familiarity with NCC products and was eager to talk to Brenda. However, he made it clear that any decision to switch to NCC copiers would require that Brenda also meet with the attorneys and office personnel to get their approval. If Brenda convinced him that NCC copiers would increase office productivity at the law firm, he would be glad to set up a meeting for her with the attorneys and office personnel.

Brenda is excited about this opportunity. She knows that NCC copiers are very dependable and that NCC provides exceptional service. She can also offer the law firm a copier with the specific features A&L desires.

QUESTIONS

1. Prepare the sales dialogue Brenda might employ to use as an example and an anecdote to communicate the dependability of NCC copiers to the office manager.

2. Brenda will not be able to demonstrate a copier during this sales call. So, describe the types of sales aids she should use to show the buyer an NCC copier with the exact features desired.

3. How can Brenda best use statistics and testimonials to support the excellent service provided by NCC?

4. Brenda did a terrific job in her sales call with the office manager. He is interested in NCC copiers and has scheduled a meeting for Brenda with the five attorneys and the office personnel. Discuss the major things Brenda should do during her sales call to this group.

CHAPTER CONTINUING CASE 7

NOTES

HANDLING SALES RESISTANCE

Brenda recently returned from a two-week training session that focused on how to handle sales resistance and how to earn commitment. Brenda has become quite familiar with the ADAPT questioning system and knows she must use assessment questions to allow the buyer to describe their present situation. She has also developed a pretty good set of discovery questions that helps her identify the buyer's pain and problems. Her challenge has been what to do with this information. Whenever Brenda attempts to use features and benefits to make her case, she encounters a myriad of objections. Brenda knows she has great products and service, but she has not been able to communicate this effectively to her prospects.

The objection she hears most often is: "I've never heard of your company, how long have you been in business?" If that is not bad enough, she heard the following objections in just one morning:

> "I'm not sure I am ready to buy at this time, I'll need to think it over."

> "Your company is pretty new; how do I know you'll be around to take care of me in the future?"

> "Your price is a little higher than I thought it would be."

> "Your company was recently in the news. Are you having problems?"

and finally,

> "I think your company is too small to meet our needs."

Brenda hears most of these objections right after she attempts to earn a commitment. She is now getting a little gun shy about asking her prospects for the order.

Brenda is sitting at her desk trying to figure out what to do next and she is not exactly sure how to proceed.

QUESTIONS

1. What would you recommend Brenda do to handle the challenges she faces?

2. Brenda appears to have an advantage with her products and services. Develop a plan for Brenda to overcome the sales resistance she is receiving.

3. Use the LAARC process to develop the suggested dialogue Brenda can use to address one of the major types of resistance she is receiving.

4. What can Brenda do in the future to encounter less sales resistance when she asks for the order?

CHAPTER CONTINUING CASE 8

NOTES

THE DISGRUNTLED CUSTOMER

It was 8:30 A.M. Friday morning when Brenda received the voice mail. It was Susan Swanson, owner of a small architecture firm, who Brenda had acquired as a customer nearly three months ago. "I'm finished with you all," she barked. "Come get my copier, I want my money back! This blasted machine you sold me keeps jamming. I was billed for extra toner that I never received. You promised me training, and I have yet to see any. And, this machine is much slower than I thought it would be. I don't see how your company stays in business. I knew I should have gone with Xerox!"

It's true, Brenda had told Susan that she would provide training on how to use some of the new advanced features of the copier. She had neglected to get back to Susan and since she had not heard from Susan she assumed Susan no longer desired the training. As for the paper jams, Brenda found this to be unusual. NCC carried high-quality copiers and she could not imagine what might be wrong. She was sure she had told Susan the specific type of paper to use for her application. However, using the wrong paper could lead to more frequent paper jams. But why hadn't Susan said anything to her about this sooner? As for the extra toner, Brenda recalls that Susan did order it and later contacted her to let her know that she did not receive it. Brenda then contacted NCC's shipping department who said they would ship Susan the product. Brenda just assumed that it was shipped. As for the speed of the machine, Brenda was certain its output was per specifications as equipment at NCC must pass strict quality-control measures. Perhaps Susan simply misunderstood the machine's capabilities. Wow, Brenda thought, now what am I going to do?

QUESTIONS

1. How should Brenda go about handling this complaint?
2. What could Brenda have done to avoid this incident?
3. What steps can Brenda take to do a better job of maintaining open, two-way communication with Susan?
4. Assuming that Brenda can retain Susan as a customer, how can she add value to her relationship with Susan's firm?

CHAPTER CONTINUING CASE 9

NOTES

MANAGING AND CLASSIFYING ACCOUNTS

Brenda's planning and extra effort in servicing and developing her accounts continue to produce increasing levels of profitable business for NCC. Her methodical approach to identifying new prospects and building repeat business within her existing accounts has been observed by her sales manager as well as the regional vice president of sales. As a result of Brenda's consistent performance, she has been given the opportunity to expand her current list of accounts by taking over part of the account list of a retiring salesperson and integrating them into an expanded territory. Brenda is working through the account information files for each of these added accounts and has summarized the information into the following table.

Account Name	Account Opportunity	Competitive Position	Annual Number of Sales Calls (Last Year)
Maggie Mae Foods	Low	High	23
C³ Industries	High	Low	28
Trinity Engineering	High	High	28
Britecon Animations	High	High	22
Lost Lake Foods	High	Low	26
Attaway Global Consulting	High	High	24
Waits and Sons	Low	High	21
Reidell Business Services	High	High	26
Ferrell & Associates	Low	Low	16
Biale Beverage Corp	High	High	18
Captain Charlie's Travel	High	Low	23
Cole Pharmaceuticals	High	Low	20
PuddleJumper Aviation	Low	High	18
Tri-Power Investment Services	Low	Low	18
Ballou Resin & Plastics	Low	Low	14
Tri-Chem Customer Products	Low	High	20
Guardian Products	High	High	25
Bartlesville Specialties	Low	High	26

QUESTIONS

1. Develop a portfolio classification of Brenda's 18 new accounts. What is your assessment of the allocation of sales calls made by Brenda's predecessor over the previous year?

2. What specific suggestions would you make in terms of sales call allocation strategy for Brenda to make better use of available selling time in calling on these new accounts?

3. Develop a classification of these 18 accounts using the single factor analysis method. How do these results differ from the results from the portfolio analysis?

4. How might the differences between the single factor analysis and the portfolio classification translate to increased selling effectiveness and efficiency for Brenda?

NOTES

_____

_____

_____

_____

_____

_____

_____

_____

_____

_____

_____

_____

_____

_____

_____

_____

_____

_____

_____

_____

_____